Radical Underworld

CW00917126

Radical Underworld

PROPHETS, REVOLUTIONARIES AND PORNOGRAPHERS
IN LONDON, 1795–1840

IAIN McCALMAN

Senior Research Fellow
in the Research School of Social Sciences,
Australian National University

CLARENDON PRESS · OXFORD

1993

Oxford University Press, Walton Street, Oxford OX2 6DP

Oxford New York Toronto
Delhi Bombay Calcutta Madras Karachi
Kuala Lumpur Singapore Hong Kong Tokyo
Nairobi Dar es Salaam Cape Town
Melbourne Auckland Madrid
and associated companies in
Berlin Ibadan

Oxford is a trade mark of Oxford University Press

Published in the United States
by Oxford University Press Inc., New York

© Cambridge University Press 1988

First published in Hardback by
Cambridge University Press 1988

This paperback edition published by
Oxford University Press 1993

British Library Cataloguing in Publication Data
McCalman, Iain.
Radical underworld: prophets,
revolutionaries and pornographers in
London, 1795–1840.
1. Radicalism–England–London–History
2. London (England)–Politics and
government
I. Title
320.9421   HN398.L7
ISBN 0–19–812286–1

Library of Congress Cataloging in Publication Data
McCalman, Iain.
Radical underworld.
Bibliography.
Includes index.
1. Radicalism–England–London–History–19th
century. 2. Spence, Thomas, 1750–1814. I. Title.
HN400.R3M34 1987   322.4'4'094212   87-11770
ISBN 0–19–812286–1

Printed in Great Britain
on acid-free paper by
Biddles Ltd.
Guildford and King's Lynn

For Heather, Lachlan, and Andrew

Preface to the Clarendon paperback edition

I am delighted that Oxford University Press has chosen to publish a paperback edition of *Radical Underworld* intended particularly to reach a new audience within the disciplines of English Literature and Cultural Studies. On its original publication in 1988 as a Cambridge University Press historical monograph, the book received generous treatment from readers and reviewers perhaps because it appeared at a fortuitous moment when traditional work-related themes of labour and working-class history were broadening under the impetus of decades of work from social historians, Marxist culturalists, Annales scholars, and others with a historical interest in cultural anthropology and socio-linguistics. The book thus benefited from a new willingness to investigate marginal and fugitive social groups outside the traditional labour constituency, whose discourses did not necessarily conform to orthodox class analysis. *Radical Underworld* was also fortunate to appear in tandem with Malcolm Chase's *The People's Farm*, a splendid study of Thomas Spence and popular radical agrarianism. Our complementarity of subject and outlook owed not a little to the common inspiration of two great historians of the British common people, John Harrison and Edward Thompson.

Perhaps more surprising was the favourable attention that *Radical Underworld* received from literary historians and critics. I had intended it as primarily a study within the genre of 'the social history of ideas' – what today might be called 'the new cultural history'. I aimed to explore the popular radical culture of late-Georgian and early-Victorian London in the manner of Robert Darnton's brilliant evocation of the literary underground of pre-revolutionary Paris, hoping at best to generate some mild interest amongst literary scholars working on popular enlightenment or on the darker sides of romanticism. Again my timing was lucky, coinciding with the beginnings of a now powerful historicist challenge to the varieties of formalism which long dominated literary studies within the 'Early Modern' and 'Romantic' periods. My slowness to grasp the full implications of this movement is, however, a matter of regret; *Radical Underworld* would have had both a wider resonance and a greater theoretical interest had I known more of the work of such scholars as Marilyn Butler and Jerome J. McGann within Romantic

studies, or Stephen Greenblatt within the Renaissance period. This ignorance helps account for the absence within the book of any specific analysis
of William Blake's cultural productions and experience; I had been deterred
in part by my respect for the magisterial historical achievements of Edward
Thompson and David Erdman, still more by formalist literary exegeses
which seemed to make Blake opaque.

Radical Underworld – or at least the work on which it was based – was also
completed too early to take cognizance of the deconstructionist-influenced
criticisms of Dominic La Capra and others, who castigate historians for
adhering to stale positivist paradigms long abandoned by modern literature,
art and science. By ignoring the constitutive and self-reflexive character of
language, claims La Capra, historians naively believe that they can continue
to locate and describe some bedrock of reality that lies beyond discourse. He
has a point. And though I would not want to sever culture from social
structure in the manner of some recent postmodernist converts, there is no
doubt that Radical Underworld could have benefited from a more rigorous
attention to the critical issue of representation that lies at the heart of the
discipline of history.

Yet the generous reception accorded the book by literary reviewers and
readers exemplifies the old surfie maxim that the strongest waves often come
from unexpected quarters. The 1990s has seen the vigorous 'new historicist'
movement spread from 'Renaissance' to 'Romantic' literary studies. Increasingly, students of romanticism are engaging in projects which con-
verge with and enrich, as well as challenge, the methods of the cultural
historian. Radical Underworld has been seen as complementing 'new historicist' efforts to throw off the chains of formalist criticism and challenge
canonical versions of 'Romanticism'. For example, Dangerous Enthusiasm,
an exciting new Oxford Clarendon Press monograph from Jon Mee of the
Australian National University's English Department, locates William Blake
firmly within the molten political culture of the 1790s and interprets his
oeuvre within the political-aesthetic tradition of 'artisan bricolage' whereby
radical texts were creatively constructed from eclectic and heterodox
combinations of discourses, idioms and cultural debris. David Worrall's new
Harvester monograph, Radical Culture, similarly explores Blake's affinities
with an underworld subculture of Spencean artisan radicals and littérateurs,
deploying semiotic theory to chart their 'verbal articulacy' and circulation
of revolutionary texts within a climate of intense state repression and
surveillance.

Radical Underworld has also profited from other recent publications out of
quite different stables – William St Clair's elegant biography of The Godwins
and the Shelleys extends their connection with the shady Regency demi-
monde of the pornographer George Cannon. Mark Philp's nuanced study of
the social and intellectual matrix of Political Justice confirms Godwin's

important link with the enigmatic banker-swindler and Jacobin, 'Jew' King. The new Edinburgh University 'Early Black Writers' series, edited by Paul Edwards and David Dabydeen, has given greater airing to the ideas of the black revolutionary prophet Robert Wedderburn and provided a context of black British culture which enables us to see him, like Blake, as a less isolated and eccentric figure within his day.

All these works share with *Radical Underworld* a concern with mapping historical contexts during the age of revolution; not necessarily – *pace* La Capra – historical context as a fixed and determining bedrock of reality independent of discursive practice, but context as a repertory of contiguous cultural representations which can provoke fresh insight. These works share also the historians' concern to track the faint spoor of vanished existences and to treat those existences as far as possible without naive celebration or condescension. Literary reviewers seem to have been genuinely astonished by the revelation that one could find such rich and variegated material traces of the fugitive political, religious and artistic culture of artisans like Blake. Properly sifted, the files of the Home Office, King's Bench, Privy Council and Treasury Solicitor's offices can yield glimpses of an underworld of alehouses, chapels, workshops, backroom cellars and brothels; echoes of toasts, boasts, debates, songs, oaths, curses, gestures, rituals and burlesques. Through them we are offered the opportunity to catch the rough idioms, explore the texts and sketch the cosmogonies of visionary plebeian prophets every bit as strange as Carlo Ginzberg's miller, Mennocchio. Yet much of this evidence is so densely embedded in the idiom, locality and topical event of its day that its decoding is as complex and exacting as the most trenchant of formalist critical exegesis. Like the deconstructionist critic, cultural historians must be alert to disguised motives, significant absences and encoded rhetorical strategies, but they must also track the protean reshaping of texts as they pass through the successive hands of author, printer, publisher, bookseller and even vendor; and they must expect diverse, aberrant and contradictory textual reception in accordance with the social and psychological attributes of reader or reading community. Above all, we cannot hope to grasp the fluid and volatile meanings of cultural texts and symbols without immersing ourselves in the idioms within which they were produced.

Our possible affinities with 'new historicism' do not stop there. The aspect of *Radical Underworld* which seems most to have attracted literary historicists is its suggestion of an alternative paradigm within which the work and experience of 'Romantic' literary rebels and revolutionaries such as Blake and – to a lesser extent – Byron and Shelley, may be interpreted. I argue that it is within the contesting but intertwined notions of respectability and unrespectability that we may recover the key shifts in meaning of early-Victorian popular culture. Implicated in turn were vital subsets of opposition and interaction – rationalist/enthusiast, self-improving/blackguard, educational/violent, feminine/masculine, familial/rough, ascetic/Rabelaisian, law-abiding/criminal and so forth. More particularly, my delineation of a persisting unrespectable subculture within early-Victorian London perhaps offers a version of what Alan Liu calls the 'most pervasive paradigm' of the new historicist method – a mirth-loving Bakhtian carnivalesque in which 'misrule tumbled rule' and 'plurality broke forth in dangerous glee'. By interpreting art and literature within the context of this saturnalian and subversive culture we implicitly dispute the canonical status and attributes of 'Romanticism' and its texts. We also challenge narrow canonical prescriptions by disinterring a range of fresh and striking cultural texts that enjoin new readings. Bricoleurs like Blake fashioned their explosive art and cosmology from the rich diversity of signs, symbols and discourses available to their milieu.

This is not to say that *Radical Underworld* would have been the same book had I written it today. Having since become familiar with the brilliant *histoire de livre* writings of Roger Chartier I would hope now to interpret cultural texts with greater self-consciousness and rigour; to use the repertoire of literary theorists and critics to sharpen my understanding of narrative tropes, rhetorical strategies, genre constraints and semiotic codes. Yet I am consoled that *Radical Underworld* should have shared, however inadvertently, some of the heterodox approaches urged by La Capra – to seek out new angles of vision, to make raids on the fugitive and inarticulate, to explore the borderlands where seemingly contradictory intellectual categories meet and mingle, to deploy unorthodox and Rabelaisian narrative perspectives, to challenge simplistic distinctions between élite and popular culture. Perhaps the cultural history wave will suddenly peter out or dump me on the rocks, but like the protagonists of this book I will have relished the ride.

Contents

Illustrations

Acknowledgements

I wish to thank the staffs and trustees of the following institutions for allowing me to use their research holdings and in some cases to quote from copyright materials in their possession: the British Library, particularly the departments of Printed Books, Maps and Drawings, Manuscripts, and the Newspaper Library at Colindale; the Public Record Office at Chancery Lane and Kew; the Bodleian Library, Oxford; the Cambridge University Library; the Corporation of London Record Office and Guildhall Library; the London County Hall Record Office; the Devon County Record Office, Exeter; the Emmanuel College Library, Cambridge; the General Register Office, London; the Huntingdon Library, California; the British Library of Political and Economic Science, London School of Economics; the University of London Library; the Manchester College Library, Oxford; the Manchester Public Library; the Prudential Assurance Company Library, London; the University of Nottingham Library; the Dr Williams Library, London; the Institute of Historical Research Library, London; the National Library of Australia, Canberra; the University of Monash Library, Melbourne; and the Baillieu Library, University of Melbourne. Dr Sarah Spilsbury generously allowed me to consult and quote from J.A. St John's journal in her private possession and she also helped me with other sources.

Grants from Monash University, Department of History, the University of Melbourne, Department of History, and the Australian Grants Research Scheme assisted me to conduct the three research trips to Britain which made possible my original doctoral thesis and this book which grew out of it. A Postdoctoral Research Fellowship in the Department of History at the University of Melbourne and a Research Fellowship in the Department of History, Research School of Social Sciences, Australian National University, enabled me to expand and rewrite my original doctoral thesis into the present book.

During the gestation of this book I have accumulated many debts. Professor John Harrison gave me the original idea for the thesis and has been a continued source of encouragement, advice and inspiration. To

Dr Ian Britain and Dr Barry Smith I owe most of all; they have been friends, advisers, patient editors and trenchant critics over many years. Professor Alan McBriar was the perfect supervisor and a great exemplar. Fellow scholars have shown extraordinary generosity in making available the fruits of their own research – especially Dr Iorwerth Prothero, Dr Malcolm Chase, Dr Anne Hone and Dr John Dinwiddy. They have immeasurably enriched this book. Many other colleagues, friends and scholars helped me with advice and sources. I would especially like to thank; Dr James Epstein; Professor Louis James; Dr Gareth Stedman Jones; Professor Anne Humpherys; Professor Joel Wiener; Dr Michael Durey; Professor Albert Goodwin; Mr Alex Tyrrell; Mr Paul Pickering; Professor Daniel McCue; Dr Ian Duffield; Professor R.K. Webb; Dr David Philips; Dr Marianne Elliott; Dr Edward Royle; Professor Marilyn Butler; Dr Lloyd Robson; Dr Stuart Piggin; Professor J.D. Walsh; Professor Randal McGowen; and particularly Dr John Ritchie. I am grateful to Professor Oliver Macdonagh and Dr Avner Offer for reading and improving portions of the text. Anne Louttit did a splendid job typing the manuscript, and Anthea Bundock and Marie Penhaligon kindly typed the bibliography for me. Finally, I would like to thank Heather McCalman for her encouragement and support without which this book would never have been written.

Abbreviations

The following abbreviations have been used in the notes and occasionally in the text.

Add. MS	British Library Additional Manuscript
BDMBR	*Biographical Dictionary of Modern British Radicals: Volume One, 1770–1830*, eds. Joseph O. Baylen and Norbert J. Gossman
BL	British Library
CLRO	Corporation of London Record Office
CPPS	M. Dorothy George, *Catalogue of Personal and Political Satires ... in the British Museum*
CPR	Cobbett's Political Register
DCRO⁻	Devon County Record Office
DM	*Deists' Magazine*
DNB	*Dictionary of National Biography*
EHR	*English Historical Review*
ELDA	East London Democratic Association
FCM	*Freethinking Christians' Magazine*
FCQR	*Freethinking Christians' Quarterly Register*
HJ	*Historical Journal*
HO	Home Office Papers
IW	*Independent Whig*
KB	King's Bench Records
LCRO	London County Record Office
LCS	London Corresponding Society
LDA	London Democratic Association
LSE	London School of Economics
LWMA	London Working Men's Association
MEPO	Records of the Metropolitan Police Office
NPU	National Political Union
NUWC	National Union of the Working Classes
PC	Privy Council Papers
PMG	*Poor Man's Guardian*

P & P	*Past and Present*
PP	Parliamentary Papers
PRO	Public Record Office
RM	*Rambler's Magazine*
S & S	'Spence and the Spenceans', London School of Economics Manuscripts
SSV	Society for the Suppression of Vice
TI	*Theological Inquirer*
TS	Treasury Solicitor's Papers
WLLA	West London Lancasterian Association

Introduction

This London political underworld began its formal existence on 18 March 1801 when Thomas Spence, pamphlet-seller and ex-state prisoner, established a society to disseminate his land-reforming ideals by means of tavern free-and-easies.[1] Its roots, however, need to be traced back to the 1790s amongst the tavern debating clubs depicted in W.H. Reid's pamphlet of 1800, *The Rise and Dissolution of the Infidel Societies in this Metropolis*.

Reid, a Jacobin and obscure littérateur, wrote his exposé and informed on his colleagues out of combined political and commercial motives. He had been compromised in a magistrate's raid of 1798 and also hoped to capitalise on popular interest in the French cleric Abbè Barruel's European conspiracy-theory, *Memoirs of Jacobinism*.[2] Borrowing both from Barruel and his own experience, Reid asserted that the London democratic movement of the 1790s comprised three separate but related elements: the mainly artisan proponents of French Jacobin-republicanism; overlapping groups of infidels, or political freethinkers, dedicated to moral and intellectual subversion; and an 'auxiliary' force of lower-class religious enthusiasts with a similar passion to overthrow the established order. All three groups converged in popular debating clubs – some of an intellectual rationalist disposition, others of a more convivial type which met in alehouses to voice a mélange of blasphemy, millenarianism and sedition, and to plot insurrection in secret. Reid wrote that incisive government action in the late 1790s had crushed this tavern political underworld, but warned that an 'incorrigible' remnant planned to regroup at the first opportunity.[3]

Spence was just this sort of incorrigible figure. His 'Spensonian' society formed the nucleus of a tiny, informal underground which gradually rallied the survivors of Jacobin revolutionary cadres smashed in the government repression of 1798–1803, then gained a fresh batch of recruits during the partial radical revival between c.1811 and Spence's death in 1814.

The foundation of the Society of Spencean Philanthropists by Thomas Evans, his successor and disciple, in October 1814, marks the advent of the underworld as a cohesive political force; it also completes the first part of this book. The second part explores the ideas and actions of the underworld during its most insurgent and influential phase, 1815–21, focussing particularly on alehouse debating clubs, blasphemous chapels and the popular press. The third and final part traces the residue of this underworld between 1821 and 1840 as it experienced defeat and dissolution, as well as adaptation, survival and revival.

Why write about a circle of radicals whom a variety of historians have dismissed as harmless cranks or destructive loonies? Certainly they were obscure, numerically few and sometimes silly. For most of our period they probably numbered around sixty dedicated activists, fanning out in post-war years to 200–300 committed followers and perhaps 2000–3000 regular attenders of meetings. Apart from some intermittent provincial links, their influence was confined to the metropolis, and – like most London radical groups – they were chronically fissiparous. Nor, in spite of their visibility and tenacity, did they succeed in imposing their language, prescriptions and practices on the London democratic movement as a whole. Yet Spencean ultra-radicals have one obvious source of interest. They were stalwarts of a small but *continuous* revolutionary-republican 'underground' which runs from the mid-1790s to early Chartism.[4] Though frequently mentioned, this underground has never been systematically traced: little is known about its membership, tactics, ideology or impact. We have not been told how such a small band of supposed oddities managed to survive this long, embattled period; how they succeeded in frightening the English state on more than one occasion, and – as our examples will show – how they gained such notoriety in their own day.

Equally importantly, this circle of London radicals serves as a case-study for exploring a range of other issues pertinent to nineteenth-century radicalism and English popular culture. One such question concerns the relationship between popular politics and ordinary crime – conventionally regarded as distinct spheres. I have used 'radical underworld' as a convenient label for a loosely-linked, semi-clandestine network of political organisations, groups, coteries and alliances, but it also has a more literal sense. 'Underworld' is defined in a modern dictionary as 'a submerged, hidden or secret region or sphere, especially one given to crime, profligacy and intrigue'.[5] It is apt because many of these ultras were also connected in various ways with London's notorious underworld of crime and profligacy. Through activities such as theft, pimping, rape, blackmail and pornography they introduce us to a region where popular politics intersected with lumpen and professional crime.

These ultras touched the edges of another supposedly apolitical sector of London's underworld – that of the labouring poor and indigent. Robert Wedderburn, a West Indian mulatto tailor and one of our central figures, is an example. Wedderburn was a migrant and an artisan of the most marginal type. We would not ordinarily expect someone with his background of dislocation, poverty, criminality and illiteracy to speak out, exercise political leadership and trouble the governments of his day, but Wedderburn – and others like him – managed to do all three. Tracing how he came to do this brings to light some of the lesser known, rougher, dimensions of popular radicalism and plebeian culture.

Such people usually escape the historian's notice because they leave few traces. That we are able to reconstruct something of Wedderburn's mentality and milieu is thanks in large part to the labours of government spies and informers. Needless to say this is partial evidence in every sense; scholars such as Edward Thompson and Richard Cobb have warned how carefully we must fumigate every fact that comes from police and intelligence records. Yet, allowing with Ben Jonson that most spies are 'of base stuff', the early nineteenth-century English variants offer a surprising diversity of testimony and perspective: they include casual observers of all classes, nosey clergymen, anonymous informers, professional shorthand writers, stolid police undercover men, self-appointed sensation seekers, needy, greedy or fearful radicals and their disgruntled relatives, and a few schizoid individuals with loyalties to both government employers and radical colleagues. Government records also contain a wealth of letters, pamphlets, prints and transcribed oral testimony from the radicals themselves, or from their (often sympathetic) neighbours, relatives and work associates. Cross checking the overlapping accounts of different spies helps to counteract some of the personal bias. And if these records provide only a murky and distorting window, they afford some tantalising glimpses into the darker corners of the history of the English common people.

Yet we are not dealing merely with fragments of a lumpen-proletariat or representatives of a disreputable radical underside. Part of the fascination of this circle lies in its fluid, ambivalent position within the popular political milieu and wider society. Tracing the lives and careers of individual members reveals a long and intricate overlap between the allegedly separate spheres of 'respectability' and 'roughness'. At the same time they show up the changing face of respectable morality during the early nineteenth century – a movement which embodied divergent ideals of masculine fraternity and feminine family life, as well as the manifold tensions of 'self-improvement'. Some elements of this ultra underworld act also as long-term carriers of 'rough' political and cultural traditions which are thought to have perished at the end of the Regency.

Most important, this political underworld sheds new light on the social and ideological diversity of English popular radicalism. Thomas Evans, Robert Wedderburn and George Cannon stand as examples. I have chosen them as focal-points of this study, first, because they were leaders who left traceable spoor, second, because they were fascinating personalities in their own right and, finally, because they can be treated as 'ideal types', each broadly representative of separate but convergent radical traditions. Evans joined the underworld as an artisan revolutionary; Wedderburn, as a plebeian social prophet; Cannon, as a marginal middle-class philosophe. Collectively they and their associates bring us into contact with a rich and febrile underworld of ideas within England and beyond. It connects with celebrated radical 'undergrounds' of other times and other places: the upside down world of Puritan sectaries; the fantasy republics of expatriate Jacobin cadres in Britain, Ireland, America and France; and the Grub Street milieux of Paris and London from prerevolutionary to mid-Victorian times. It touches prophets like Richard Brothers, utopians like Thomas Spence, poets like P.B. Shelley, libertines like Lord Byron, populists like William Cobbett, satirists like William Hone, philosophes like Baron d'Holbach and pornographers like the Marquis de Sade.

PART 1

THE UNDERWORLD IN THE
MAKING, 1795–1814

Jacobin-Spenceans: Thomas Evans and the revolutionary underground

Between seven and eight o'clock every Wednesday evening in October 1814 a gang of fisherwomen selling their wares at the door of a low alehouse called the Cock on the corner of Lumber Court and Grafton Street, Soho, would watch a group of around forty men arrive in twos and threes and make their way into the tap-room. Once inside, the men were welcomed by the publicans, Thomas and Susannah Harrison, who knew them to be members of a convivial debating club, and were sufficiently glad of their custom not to inquire too closely into their proceedings.[1] In spite of Susannah's pretended ignorance during later government interrogation, she must have known that these were followers of Thomas Spence, an eccentric pamphlet-seller and land-reformer who had been conducting political free-and-easies at the Cock for some years until his death in September 1814. Still, the government could hardly expect the Harrisons to have reported the Jacobinical views of the debating group when one of their own informers had earlier failed to do so. In an intelligence report of 1813 Arthur Kidder had thought their names not worth mentioning because they consisted mainly of 'low tradesmen' from around Grosvenor Market.[2] Had he bothered, he might have been surprised at the response; many were well known to the government from the 1790s. They would certainly have recognised Thomas Evans, a Strand braces-maker, and the man who in October 1814 was to reconstitute Spence's tavern following as the Society of Spencean Philanthropists.

Thomas Evans remains a tantalisingly obscure figure in labour historiography. There is plenty of testimony to his importance as a connecting link between the Jacobin movement of the 1790s and the mass radicalism of the post-war era. He is also acknowledged as an advocate of violent republicanism and a pioneering land nationaliser who toughened up and transmitted Spence's programme. Yet existing accounts provide us with few details of his political career up to 1816 and tell us nothing of his social background or his fate after 1820.[3] The very nature of his career, and of the fields in which he became important, was not conducive to leaving any strong traces. What little is known about Evans's character, early history and political activities still depends heavily on the testimony of that great labour archivist, Francis Place. But it is notorious that respectability and success made the Charing Cross tailor prone to exaggerate the moderation of early London Corresponding Society leaders and to denigrate those who headed the movement after his resignation in 1797.[4] His view of Thomas Evans was additionally coloured by the animosity which grew up between them after 1806. Even so, Place's bias can be turned to good effect: his rifts with Evans and other associates were themselves symptomatic of important social and ideological changes at work in London popular radicalism between 1795 and 1815.

Place's many scattered hits at Evans can be reduced to three major charges: that over the period 1797–1815 Evans showed himself to be a compulsive political fanatic, an immoral and dishonest radical, and a religious enthusiast committed to crazy biblical ideas, or, in other words, a physical force revolutionary, an unrespectable and a millenarian. Place saw himself as the antithesis: over the same period he claimed to have become a moral force reformer, a respectable, and a rationalist. In setting up such a contrast he was doing more than indict a former friend and colleague; he projected himself and Evans as embodying fundamental and divergent tendencies of the popular democratic movement after 1797. Evans's history is therefore crucial for testing the validity of Place's three broad dichotomies, of moral and physical force radicalism, respectable and unrespectable radicalism, rationalist and millenarian radicalism – dichotomies which still inform modern historiography.

Jacobin revolutionary, 1795–1802

Place claimed that most of the able and moderate reformists who led the LCS from its inception either had been arrested or had resigned by mid-1797. He and his shoemaker friend, John Ashley, represented the last of this old breed; their successors were a violent revolutionary fragment. The new president, Dr Thomas Crossfield, was a 'drunken harum scarum'; the new secretary, Evans, 'a sort of absurd fanatic continually operated upon by impulses and capable of undertaking any folly of which he could make himself one of the leaders'; and the new executive, made up of men like Benjamin Binns, an ignorant plumber's mate, and James Powell, a buffoonish baker. These and a dozen or so others, assisted by United Irish agent Rev. James O'Coigley, promptly founded a secret society called the United Englishmen which conceived a fantastical plan for a republican uprising aided by the rebellious United Irish and a French invasion. Before they could raise a single division, the leaders were arrested – providing the government with convenient evidence to fabricate an alarmist *Report from the Committee of Secrecy* which was then used to justify draconian suppression of the democratic movement between 1798 and 1803.[5]

True, the leadership and tactics of the LCS did change significantly around 1797 ('overnight', one historian asserts). Yet Evans and his associates were by no means all latecomers. It is unclear when Thomas Evans joined the LCS, but he was probably the Evans mentioned in its 'Original Journal and Minute Book' as producing a sub-delegate voucher for division eleven in April 1793. After that he seems to have served in a bewildering number of divisions – a reflection partly of the society's rapid growth before 1795 and equally swift disintegration in 1796–7. Assessment is also complicated by the failure of LCS records to distinguish between the several Evanses who were members at this time. There is no doubt, however, that Thomas quickly rose to a position of authority. Information was given to the Home Office in May 1794 that he and his wife, Janet, of Frith Street, Soho, were receiving papers and letters for the most noted of state reformers. By September 1795 he had been elected to the executive as a representative of division four. The following year, as secretary to division nine, he allowed the general committee to use his large house in Plough Court, Fetter Lane, for temporary headquarters. In summer 1797 he became general secretary.[6]

Evans was also in these early years part of a circle of LCS leaders whom Place admired and befriended. In an early draft of the history, which he later tried to alter, Place mentioned Evans as amongst the 'leading' and 'cleverest' men with whom he first associated. Others included John Bone, Richard Hodgson, Paul Lemaitre, John Binns, Colonel Despard and Alexander Galloway – all friends of Evans, all LCS office-holders before and after 1795, and all future revolutionary conspirators.[7] Evans probably owed his actual introduction to Jacobin politics to another early office-holder on the LCS executive and general committees, James Powell. They probably met through their trade; both were bakers at one time and Evans might have worked at the bakery which the Powell brothers ran in Tottenham Court Road around 1793–5. The friendship was sufficiently intimate for the Evanses to share Powell's Battle Bridge house for a time.[8] At much the same time Place also fell under Powell's spell. Although Powell was actually one of the government's best placed informers, Place thought him honest, if gullible, and helped him in 1798 to stage a temporary escape to Hamburg where he infiltrated the *emigré* revolutionary network.[9]

In the wake of the Two Acts of 1795, the LCS began to experience serious internal divisions over the most appropriate tactics for combating the mounting government repression. Yet there is no indication that Place and Evans aligned themselves in opposing moral and physical force camps. For most of the year they seem to have belonged to the same division – number four of the western district – from which Evans was elected to the executive. Once there he showed himself eager to pursue a diversity of tactics. He was elected to a constitutional committee which in September 1795 recommended that the LCS concentrate increasingly on political education. He joined John Bone in a bookselling partnership dedicated to 'diffusing knowledge' through cheap publications, then he and Bone became joint editors of the LCS magazine which shared the same educational goals.[10] Surprisingly, he did not join a militant secessionist society, the Sons of Liberty, founded by his friends Joseph Burks and John Baxter in 1795.[11] And when Place and Ashley eventually resigned in 1797, they cited a mixture of grievances against Evans: they thought he had spent too much money on the LCS magazine, and they believed that his 'constitutionalist' tactic of organising mass simultaneous meetings in defiance of government bans was dangerously confrontationist.[12]

There is no doubt that the range of tactics mooted by LCS leaders at this time included violence – both to defend civil liberties and to complete a prepared revolution. Place later conceded that some members of the society were 'for putting an end to government by any means, foreign or domestic'. John Binns went further; he claimed in his memoirs that 'the wishes and hopes of many of its influential members carried them to the overthrow of the monarchy and the establishment of a republic'.[13] A list of these members would have had to include many in salient positions before the summer of 1797 – as well as the later 'refuse' of Place's judgement. And even amongst the latter group he was forced to make individual exceptions. Galloway and Hodgson, he admitted, stayed on the committee after 1797 from 'conscientious motives'; Bone was 'an honest upright man'; John Binns 'a very well informed man … very desirous of increasing his stock of knowledge'; Despard he admired enormously, and drunken Crossfield was still 'a man of learning and talents'.[14] Republican and physical force inclinations did not dawn 'overnight'. They had been implicit within the tactical repertoire of leading London Jacobins from at least 1795 when the government began closing all other reform outlets.

The Binns brothers brought over their republican ideals from Ireland in 1794, and once in London they rapidly established links with patrician United Irish representatives. John Binns speculated retrospectively that the murder of the King and Cabinet in 1795 would have led to an instant overthrow of the government and to the establishment of a republic.[15] An espionage agent for the United Irish and the French, William Duckett, contacted several LCS members during a visit to London in 1795, including Despard and Place's supposedly moderate associate, John Ashley. Duckett, John Binns and others were later also implicated in fomenting political sedition amongst the naval mutineers of 1797.[16] It was probably fear of government prosecution rather than dislike of republican violence which led Place and Ashley to distance themselves from the LCS in 1797, for as soon as Ashley reached the safety of Paris in 1798, he joined the militant Tandyite faction of United Irish *emigrès* and began working to promote a French invasion and Irish uprising.[17] In short, the logic of events after 1795 pushed surviving elements within the LCS towards the option of violent clandestine revolution.

James O'Coigley's visit to London in the summer of 1797 presented LCS leaders with the chance to ally themselves to the wider cause of the United Irish. It also gave them an underground organisational model, a broader internationalist programme and a renewed sense of strategic purpose. The clandestine, oath-bound republican society, known variously as the United Englishmen, United Britons or True Britons, was the direct outcome. Recent detailed studies of this society disagree as sharply over its strength, coherence and impact as did the two main contemporary chroniclers, Francis Place and the government's Committee of Secrecy. The unusually complex, fragmentary and biassed evidence does not permit any definitive assessment, but we may reasonably posit that the Irish and British revolutionary conspiracy of 1797–1803 was no 'chimera'; that the United Britons developed in a number of northern towns, as well as in London; and that the leaders of the British organisation depended heavily on 'a wider United Irish programme firmly based on expectations of French military assistance'.[18]

The two chief London venues of the putative United Englishmen between summer 1797 and spring 1798 were Furnival's Inn cellar in the Strand and Evans's house at 14 Plough Court, Fetter Lane. The first was, in the words of John Binns, 'the very general resort of the most radical Jacobinical politics in London'. Here, under the cover of an uproarious free-and-easy singing and debating club, United Irish expatriates met with the visiting Irish envoy O'Coigley and with local LCS, United Englishmen and Sons of Liberty activists. They tried to forge an alliance which would lead to coordinated action between London, the provinces, Ireland and France. Intelligence reports of early summer 1797 indicate that Evans was one of the 'most inflammatory' speakers. By winter 1797–8, however, John Binns and Despard seem to have displaced him in importance because of their influence with the stand-offish cells of London Irish.[19]

If Furnival's Inn cellar was the negotiating forum for the conspiracy, Evans's house served as headquarters. It was conveniently situated near Fleet Street; it housed two important lodgers, Benjamin Binns and radical printer John Smith; and it was large enough for meetings. James O'Coigley probably stayed there on his first visit to London in summer 1797 when LCS leaders were originally persuaded to join the underground United movement. He definitely did so on a second visit in January–February 1798. Here, under the alias of Captain Green and accompanied by Lord

Edward Fitzgerald's young friend, John Allen, he talked with United Irishmen and met executive members of the newly formed United Britons, notably Evans, the Binns brothers, Crossfield and Despard. These last furnished him with a draft address to the French Directory designed to show the unity of the Irish and British movements, and to urge France to 'pour forth thy gigantic force ... united Briton burns to break her chains'.[20] And it was from Evans's house that O'Coigley, John Binns, Allen and Arthur O'Connor set off for Margate on their ill-fated mission to France in February 1798.

Evans's house was also a base for local United English planning. Spy reports of early April 1798 describe him dispatching delegates to the provinces and attempting to organise London and its surrounds into four coordinated districts. The aim was to 'form a Junction with the United Irishmen who are in London and undertake together some great Design'. It is difficult to know how seriously to take such plans. Evans was certainly discussing arming at the George alehouse in St John Street at around this time, and the United Britons' oath enjoined 'the use of arms'. Even so, Powell's reports of their state of preparedness appear to be exaggerated.[21] His description of a meeting held at Plough Court around March 1798 conveys something of the flavour:

> *Evans*: Dick [Barrow], what do you think of driving on the union again?
> *Barrow*: By all means, I have just left the Colonel [Despard], we have been talking about it. He is for going on but he has alarmed me, for we were talking about London. He said 1500 men might take it but not less than 5000 could keep [it], but that ought not to stop us.
> *Evans*: Well Jem [Powell] and I have an organized set. We shall have a Committee this week, which will meet either on Saturday night, or Sunday morning. Will you and the Colonel meet us?
> *Barrow*: Yes and we must lay on a regular plan of Insurrection which must be agreed to be acted upon, and not debated afterwards. I am going this evening to a person in the Tower (I shall never mention his name to anybody, for reasons you must see) to consult whether if we can make a Hubbub that cannot be delivered up.
> *Evans*: That would be a good thing, we could coerce the Nation immediately.[22]

Even allowing for Powell's exaggeration, there is a hollow and desperate air to all this. Yet later the same evening Evans chaired a meeting of the Battle Bridge section of the United Englishmen which appeared to have a more hard-headed concern with organisational detail. It confirmed the existence of two further sections in Spitalfields and one in Somerstown, as well as three larger 'disorganized' groups at Goodman's Fields, Queens Square and Southwark.[23] The total of around 150 men is far short of the forty divisions claimed by the government, but more substantial than the handful of Place's account.

No doubt there was a large element of bluff behind the various addresses, declarations and resolutions which emanated from Evans and his colleagues on the LCS and United Englishmen executives. Nevertheless, the bluff had some chance of working. The fraternal address and delegation which the United Britons sent to Ireland in January 1798 made a strong impression on the Dublin United Irish, and led to a marked increase in their militancy.[24] In the same way the combined addresses and delegation of United men headed by Binns, O'Connor and O'Coigley were intended to encourage the French Directory into staging a diversionary invasion of England whilst the main uprising took place in Ireland. Had the conspirators reached France, the plan might conceivably have worked. At the very least, the well-reported activities of United Britons had the effect of diverting the English government's attention and resources, even though Evans's organisation failed either to make the desired 'junction' with the London Irish or to persuade most rank-and-file LCS members to join their underground.

Whether or not Evans was deluded in attempting to found a republican-revolutionary organisation – and given the government repression he had little choice – the manner in which he went about it proved he was far from being the impulsive fanatic of Place's claim. Several outwardly puzzling facets of Evans's behaviour in 1798 arose from the habitual deviousness and caution that surrounded all his potentially treasonous activities. The United Britons' adoption of an oath and programme modelled on an early, constitutionalist phase of the United Irish movement might seem inappropriate to an underground conspiratorial organisation, but it enabled Evans to escape a high treason charge when captured with these documents in his possession.[25] The society's change of name in 1798 from United Englishmen to 'United' or 'True Britons' showed similar circumspection. Nor were the criticisms of France which Evans made in a speech to the LCS general committee on 5 April 1798 actuated by 'scruples' or a new-found moderation as some historians appear to think.[26] He denounced French foreign and domestic policy as a prelude to recommending the formation of armed Corresponding Society militia, a ploy which some speakers at the meeting immediately recognised.[27] Many must have known that he was at the same time engaged in armed republican plotting. The tactic of deploying militia corps as covers for potentially treasonable drilling had been used by some members of the LCS as early as 1794 in the guise of the Loyal Lambeth Society, and the same strategy was being urged in the mid-1790s by Evans's machiavellian associate, Jonathan 'Jew' King.[28] The government's proposed Volunteer Militia Bill of 1798 enabled Evans to use patriotic fears of a French invasion as a pretext and legal cover for arming the underground.

Whether he and his colleagues would have persuaded the LCS to adopt this policy we shall never know; the general commitee was arrested whilst

SEARCH NIGHT; or, State Watchmen, mistaking Honest Men for Conspirators.

1 *LCS plotters seized, 1798.*

further debating the issue on 19 April. A day earlier, Evans and a group of United English and LCS members had been seized at a low public house in Clerkenwell. They had apparently been engaged in negotiating a new 'junction'. Warrants were also issued against anyone visiting Evans's house – Benjamin Binns and several others were caught this way. Soon after, Evans's brother-in-law Alexander Galloway joined the prisoners, as did Spence for a short time. Further arrests produced additional incriminating documents in Evans's handwriting. A raid on the Royal Oak in Red Lion Passage in March 1799 captured a number of United Irishmen; another, on the Nags Head, St Johns Street, in April, caught most of the remaining leaders of the United movement – notably, John Baxter (former president of the Sons of Liberty), Wallis Eastburn, John Blythe and Charles Pendrill.

The serious damage inflicted on revolutionary plans and cadres in Ireland and England during the repression of 1798–9 did not prevent a resurgence of activity in London in 1801–2. During Evans's imprisonment, 1798–1801, remnants of the United Englishmen, Sons of Liberty and LCS had continued to meet wherever possible in small alehouse free-and-easies, benefit clubs and prisoners' relief committees.[29] Food riots in 1800 and an influx of refugees from the Irish Rebellion had added to popular discontent in London. On 10 March 1801 a group of newly released state prisoners and veteran activists attended a celebratory re-union at their old haunt, the Green Dragon, in Fore Street. Here, 'Evans addressed the Company upbraiding them on their supiness and inactivity during the time the prisoners were in confinement'.[30]

He was not being altogether fair; men like bookseller Joseph Burks, shoemakers William Curry, Joseph Bacon and Thomas Pemberton, tailor Robert Oliphant and gardener John Nicholls had worked hard to keep the United movement alive. They now tried to re-enlist the ex-prisoners for a renewed revolutionary attempt. Somehow Evans helped them to tack to-gether the old revolutionary alliances without getting himself captured during the following month in a new series of government raids aimed at mopping up the Green Dragon leaders. A report from Powell at the end of the year noted that Evans and others intended to conduct regular free-and-easies so as 'to keep a sett of persons united together that if occasion offered they might act with effect'.[31] By this time, too, Evans, Hodgson and Galloway were alleged to be part of a new 'National Committee' of United Irish and United Britons.

Spring and summer of 1802 saw some reason for optimism amongst London's revolutionary party – in spite of the damage done by the fresh imprisonments of 1801 and the onset of a popular peace with France. Bonaparte continued secretly to encourage the United Irish, and British hopes of a French invasion revived. United Irish emissary William McCabe and others moved industriously between underground groups in London, Ireland and the provinces. Spy reports commented on a new militancy amongst workers' combinations in places like Manchester, Derby, Wake-field, Dewsbury and Leeds. One of the delegates carrying this news was Manchester United Englishman, William Cheetham, who quickly became a force in London United Englishmen circles. The latter could also point to several promising developments: the discontent of unemployed Irish labourers in riverside and East End ghettos; the generous financial con-tributions coming in from United Irish intelligentsia; the conspicuous restlessness of soldiers faced with the threat of demobilisation; and the prospect of revitalised leadership engendered by Colonel Despard's return from Ireland.[32]

At around this time Evans's name suddenly disappears from govern-ment intelligence reports, despite earlier claims that he was deeply at-tached to the conspiracy, and despite the continued involvement of his associates Eastburn, Pendrill, Pemberton, Curry, Blythe and Despard him-self.[33] Perhaps he was simply lucky that the government raid on the Oakley Arms on 16 November 1802 was premature, trapping only Des-pard and a handful of mostly casual supporters. The Home Office was also unwilling to endanger intelligence sources by revealing too much. On the other hand, Evans might have decided to lie low when he judged a rising to be imminent. A well-placed spy reported in September 1802 that the 'wiser part' had withdrawn from the conspiracy.[34] Such timely disappearances were to become one of Evans's trademarks in later years.

Another likely reason for his disappearance at this time, and one that Place chose not to mention, was that Evans had during 1802 become an important element in Sir Francis Burdett's campaign to gain election for the seat of Middlesex. Evans had first met the brilliant young baronet and rising star of radicalism during his imprisonment in Coldbath Fields in 1798. Evans and his wife Janet bombarded government officials and parliamentarians (probably including Burdett) with letters and petitions which claimed innocence and complained of personal, family and business sufferings. At the same time he, John Bone, and Patrick William Duffin[35] – a United Irishman imprisoned for gaming and lottery offences – orchestrated an exposure of the corruption and cruelty practised by the administration of the prison governor, Thomas Aris. Through a series of prison interviews and smuggled letters they provided Burdett with detailed evidence of the ill-treatment and occasional deaths of felons, naval mutineers and the state prisoners themselves; all of which enabled him to mount a trenchant parliamentary campaign against abuses in the Coldbath Fields 'Bastille'. This forced the government to appoint a parliamentary select committee of March 1799 and, eventually, a full commission of inquiry which produced a report criticising the prison administration. The prisoners' information was also used to generate a ferocious press campaign led by Evans's old bookseller friends Joseph Burks and John Smith, and a number of others: the Paineite publisher J.S. Jordan, the radical pressmen Peter Finnerty and Henry White, the United Irish barrister James Agar, the Common Hall radical Robert Waithman and the great Horne Tooke himself. A letter from Evans, Bone and three other prisoners to Burdett in December 1798 captures the essence of the radical case: 'A specious and outward appearance has so long concealed a system of the grossest Tyranny that we feel ourselves bound to tear off the veil to trace its mysterious retreat and to expose its iniquity in a way that will place it beyond dispute.'[36]

Attempting to expose the iniquity from within prison was a risky business. Evans and Bone both received spells of solitary confinement for making repeated illicit contacts with Duffin and the naval mutineers. Janet Evans and Elizabeth Bone were also banned from visits in 1798 after they had been caught making signals to the mutineers, then instigating a small riot outside the walls by telling the mob that the prisoners were starving. This was the prelude to a larger, more dangerous riot of 14 August 1800 when a crowd of 2000 threatened to storm the prison. The riot began, the Home Office report later claimed, with 'the Prisoners in every quarter of the Gaol, by a preconcerted scheme, setting up violent and tumultuous outcries immediately after they were locked up at about half past 7'. Governor Aris was forced to run from the prison to summon help.[37]

When Burdett decided to oppose William Mainwaring – friend and apologist of Thomas Aris – at the Middlesex election of 1802, he naturally made the abuses at the Coldbath Fields 'Bastille' a central election issue. He also decided to incorporate former state prisoners like Evans in his campaign strategy. *Cobbett's Weekly Political Register* reported from the Middlesex hustings on 24 July 1802 that 'There are daily some half a dozen convicts who have served out their time in the house of correction, employed in amusing the rabble with execrations on the head of Mainwaring.' During the fifth day of the election, for example, Evans demanded an answer from Mainwaring (on the hustings) as to whether he had voted to grant new supplies to prosecute the war, and whether he had used magisterial influence to prevent voters from supporting Burdett.[38] An anti-Burdett pamphlet, *The Scum Uppermost when the Pot Boils Over*, jeered at the baronet's use of such seedy and Jacobinical election agents, and particularly mentioned Evans's friends: 'Green Finnerty', gaolbird Duffin, Nore mutineer George Welsh and surgeon-debater John Gale Jones.[39] *The Times*, 13 July 1802, also alleged that Burdett employed 500 hackney coaches to carry 'the refuse of St Giles and Wapping to Brentford'. Use of such allegedly dubious agents and tactics later rebounded on Burdett when the poll was declared invalid in 1803, but immediately it helped to ensure his election by a substantial margin. More important, it furthered his reputation as defender of the people's constitutional rights against courtiers like Aris and Mainwaring who had conspired in a system of peculation, corruption and 'concealed torture'.[40]

Evans's shift in 1802 from Despardian conspiratorial circles to Burdett's constitutionalist radical campaign demonstrates his wariness and tactical flexibility; it does not mean that he had abandoned republican revolutionary goals. Like his brother-in-law, Alexander Galloway, he probably believed 'We have only to rest on our oars for a short time, to strike with more force and intrepidity'.[41] Moreover, there are suggestions that Burdett and some of his Wimbledon circle associates were in contact at this time with pedlars of treason – including Despard himself.[42] Evans was possibly acting as an intermediary between these respectable and covert radical worlds in 1802–3: he was certainly to serve this function for Burdett on later occasions. And, typically, once the dust settled after the execution of the Despard conspirators, he reappeared amongst the remnants of the United Britons as incorrigible as ever.[43]

If the Despard conspiracy was 'the last twitch' of Jacobinism,[44] Evans and his veteran associates seemed not to notice. In the decade that followed they were to pin their revolutionary hopes on the leadership of Thomas Spence.

The Spencean-Jacobin underground, 1803–14

Francis Place offered no specific explanation for Evans's attachment to
Thomas Spence's circle after 1803, and the reasons are by no means self-
evident. True, he regarded both men as cranks and enthusiasts, but he
was emphatic that Spence's circle was small, earnest and harmless.[45]
Modern scholars tend to prefer the more menacing interpretation of the
Committee of Secrecy of 1801: they see Spence as divided from orthodox
Jacobinism by his support for agrarian socialist goals and physical force
methods. The latter in particular are regarded as the source of attraction
for revolutionary Jacobins between 1801 and 1814, but little or no evidence has been advanced to substantiate this claim, nor to identify the
membership and character of the Spencean-Jacobin underground.[46]

Admittedly, such evidence is hard to come by. Spence's free-and-easy
organisation was intended to be elusive. Government intelligence did not
take notice of his small informal tavern meetings until around 1812–13
and even then, as we have seen, the spy Arthur Kidder did not take them
seriously. A later report filed soon after Spence's death noted simply that
'small remaining Jacobin meetings' were being held by 'disciples of
Thomas Spence'.[47] It was not until the Spencean society was thoroughly
penetrated by spies in 1816–17 that a more precise idea of the membership emerged. There is no doubt that it contained numbers of former
United men. By this time, however, Evans had taken over the leadership
and a substantial radical revival was underway; the presence of veteran
Jacobins in the society during post-war years does not prove that they
were members during the earlier, quieter decade when Spence was
leader.

One important piece of retrospective evidence, however, does cast light
on the composition of the society during this earlier period. *The Polemic
Fleet of 1816* is a lengthy satirical broadsheet written in part by Evans's
Spencean colleague William Snow with the assistance of others in the
society, and published shortly before the Spa Fields uprising of December
1816.[48] Cast in the form of a fleet manifest, it lists prominent members of
the society as if they were naval captains, endowing each with an appropriately titled ship and armoury, and giving a brief description of their
fighting qualities and records. As a satire the *Polemic Fleet* is unspectacu-
lar; it guys naval bellicosity at a time of widespread popular disillusionment with the war. The real target, however, was internal; it was designed
to marshal forces, boost morale and discipline members who were showing signs of straying to a secessionist ultra-radical organisation. Most
intriguing are the retrospective references to such matters as length of
service in the fleet. The broadsheet includes the names of some radicals
who were no longer Spencean members in 1816 but who evidently be-

longed to an earlier, broader-based 'front' organisation probably known as the Polemic debating club.

The origins of this club are obscure: shoemaker Thomas Preston's auto-biography implies that he became a member around 1811–12, at much the same time as he joined Spence's following.[49] We also know from other testimonies (including that of Evans's son) that the Spenceans underwent some expansion and reorganisation at this time: the Polemic debating club was probably a result. Though primarily a 'front' for Spenceans, it also attracted some notable radical debaters like Jonathan Wooler and John Wright. These two head the fleet list, but are not otherwise known to have had Spencean affiliations.[50] In short, the Polemic debating club was a loose alliance of ultra-radicals, Jacobins and Spenceans – both new re-cruits and veterans – which met during the early Regency years and probably lost its non-Spencean attendants when Evans reorganised the society in 1814–15. Significantly, the Spenceans were to resurrect the title and format of the Polemic debating club during the winter of 1817 when they once again felt the need to disguise their Spencean affiliations and to attract a broad popular front of sympathetic radicals.

The details of the *Polemic Fleet*, combined with other retrospective evidence gleaned mainly from spy reports, enable us to reconstruct a probable list of LCS and United movement notables who associated more or less regularly with Spence from at least 1811–12 onwards. In order of fleet listings there was:

Patten (John, Joseph?), probably the United Irishman involved with Evans and Despard, 1801–2.

Constable (Thomas), a former Jacobin known to be corresponding with Spence in 1808.

Evans (Thomas), 'so well acquainted with the Navigation of the Spencean Seas he has challenged all the ships in the world to attack him there'.

Callender (Alexander?), probably the radical bookseller known to be campaigning with Evans in Westminster in 1812.

Baxter (John), probably the distinguished LCS 'apostle', Sons of Liberty president and United movement activist, awarded the title of 'Impregnable' by the Polemics.

Edwards (William?), a parish constable long friendly with Spence, who was possibly imprisoned with Evans in 1798. His brother, George, a sculptor, also attended Spence's circle briefly during this period, then later rejoined the society as a government spy.

Fair (Robert Charles), a young shoemaker-poet, formerly on the fringes of the LCS who joined the Spenceans shortly before Spence's death.

Snow (William), another erstwhile Jacobin who had been sufficiently intimate with Spence to be chosen in 1814 to deliver his funeral oration.

Maxwell (?) and Lewis (?), probably the two United Englishmen captured with Baxter at the Nag's Head in April 1799.

Clark (William, senior), an upholsterer and Corresponding Society delegate arrested in 1798, who later boasted of having worked with Spence on *Pig's Meat* (1793–5).

Blythe (John or George?), Sons of Liberty secretary and United Englishmen organiser, arrested at the Nag's Head in April 1799. According to the *Polemic Fleet* he was by 1816 only an occasional attendant at Spencean meetings.

Preston (Thomas), a shoemaker and fringe Jacobin who joined the Spenceans around 1811–12.

Pemberton (Thomas), a boot-closer implicated in the Despard conspiracy and an active Spencean until winter 1817.

Johnson (?), publican of the Mulberry Tree in Moorfields, and an old friend of Spence and Evans. His wife Mary, seems to have been interrogated at the same time as Spence and Pendrill in 1798.[51]

Missing from the *Fleet* list were the names of some other former Jacobin activists who nevertheless seem to have moved in Spencean circles during early Regency years. They included Charles Pendrill, a shoemaker and Despard conspirator; Evans's longtime friends, Robert Moggridge, a shoemaker, and William Carr, a house-painter; William Curry and Joseph Bacon, also United Englishmen and shoemakers; and John George, a paperhanger, who claimed a long Spencean lineage.[52] Place was also under the impression when collecting information in 1830 for a memoir of Spence that Moggridge, John Richter and former LCS printer Arthur Seale had been associates of the land reformer.[53]

We know, too, that between 1801 and 1812 Spence held informal free-and-easies to debate and disseminate his ideas in taverns or alehouses. They included the Swan in New Street, run by supporter and balladeer, William Tilly, and a former LCS haunt, the Fleece, in Windmill Street.[54] There is no certainty that Evans was a regular attendant at these before 1811, the date at which he and Spence issued a joint songbook (often, misdated at 1802 or 1807).[55] Nevertheless, indirect evidence points to his involvement in Spence's circle from 1803, if not before. For example, Evans had close links with Spence's two printers, John Smith and Arthur Seale. Smith, one of the revered Jacobin 'twelve apostles' and a suspected United Englishman, rented a room in Evans's house in the late 1790s. He was also implicated in the O'Coigley affair and later participated in the Coldbath Fields exposé and in Burdett's election. Seale, a one-time LCS activist, printed for Spence throughout the period 1803–14. He was convicted in 1804 for printing an anti-war pamphlet commissioned by Galloway and distributed by Evans.

Another line of connection can be made through coachmaker Jonathan Panther who was prosecuted for anti-war activity at the same time. He too, had earlier come under suspicion of involvement with the United Englishmen, and Spence had written to him for help whilst in prison in

1801. A Windmill Street bill-broker, George Cullen, completes the circumstantial chain. He furnished Spence's bail in 1801, wrote in support of Spencean ideas and worked closely with Evans in several political campaigns around 1812 and 1813.[56] Little of this evidence can be said to be conclusive, but cumulatively it supports Thompson's suggestion that Spence and his followers were essentially an underground Jacobin grouping which operated continuously throughout the war years.[57]

Why should so many former Jacobins have joined Spence's circle? Interpretations which stress Spence's role as father of a proto-socialist physical force tradition that was sharply differentiated from Paineite Jacobinism perhaps explain his ability to attract known conspirators like Evans, but do not help us much with figures like Richter, Fair, Cullen and Galloway. One suspects that the divide between Spenceanism and Jacobinism has sometimes been exaggerated, not the least by Spence himself. He had in fact been an early, active and distinguished member of the LCS. Like Evans, he hosted divisions and belonged to the general committee and committee of the constitution. He also organised meetings, drew up petitions and published and sold LCS tracts.[58] Between 1792 and December 1794 he was four times arrested by runners, three times indicted by Grand Juries and three times gaoled for varying lengths of time. Along with other prominent LCS activists he showed increasing signs of militancy in the mid-1790s, particularly after the passage of the Two Acts. In 1794 he was committed and interrogated on suspicion of high treason for allowing fellow LCS member, John Philip Franklow, to drill an armed militia in his Holborn shop. The following year he issued his well-known call for 'a few Thousands of hearty determined Fellows, well armed and appointed with Officers ... to act as a provisionary Government'. This was accompanied by a warning that 'if the Aristocracy rose to contend the matter let the people be firm and desperate, destroying them Root and Branch, and strengthening their Hands by the rich confiscation'.[59] Over the next few years he issued tracts which supported the idea of a French-assisted uprising in England and advocated the formation of an elected (and armed) national convention of parochial delegates. The government had no doubt that he was implicated in United movement plans towards these same ends, which is why he was arrested with Pendrill in 1798, and again in the dragnet of 1801.

Spence also chose in 1801 to centre his new 'Spensonian' society on a tavern free-and-easy or convivial debating club. Such clubs had been a feature of the Jacobin movement from the outset, but between 1798 and 1803 became its dominant form. The United movement met under cover of free-and-easies at alehouses like Furnival's Inn in the Strand, the Green Dragon in Moorfields and the Oakley Arms in Lambeth. Small, informal free-and-easies held in alehouse tap-rooms, parlours and club-rooms were one of the few forms of political meeting not in breach of the government's mesh of legislation, 1795–9.[60] Their ubiquity, portability and use of oblique forms of protest, such as songs and toasts, also made them difficult targets for government surveillance and prosecution. Even JP licensing proscription was localised and erratic in London, particularly when publicans were radical sympathisers and independent of brewer control as was the case with Tilly and Johnson. Spence was quick to realise that informal free-and-easies could continue to function within the interstices of the state's legislative and judicial structures: 'cannot small meetings be effected where large ones durst not be attempted', he wrote in 1811, 'Even under the modern tyrannies of China, France, Turkey, etc., what can hinder small companies from meeting in a free and easy convivial manner and singing their rights and instructing each other in their songs?'[61]

Alehouse convivial clubs had also served as screens for United movement conspiratorial activity. Spy John Tunbridge reported in 1798 that a group of United Englishmen and Sons of Liberty who drilled at night in the garden of the Seven Stars, Bethnal Green, under the leadership of Blythe, made it 'a rule to begin singing as soon as they had done business, that people might have less suspicion of them and might think it a club'. Like most Jacobins, United men also valued these clubs because they believed the diffusion of 'knowledge' or 'truth' to be an essential pre- or co-requisite of any uprising, as well as an important humanising agent.[62] John Baxter organised 'questions for the Society to debate and enlighten their minds' at the same clubs that were being used for drilling in 1798. The constitution of the United Englishmen declared national schools to be a major objective, and in an alehouse club debate of January 1799 Blythe's group of armed conspirators voted such schools as their foremost goal. United movement sections also distributed printed books and sheets containing instructive and inspirational songs like 'Erin go bragh' and 'Ça ira'.[63]

Spence's free-and-easies of 1801–14 continued this range of tactics, though the repressive climate probably encouraged him to emphasise education and propaganda. Members of the circle composed, sang and printed Spencean songs to the tune of popular folk ballads. They also debated Spence's land plan and other topics at tavern meetings of the Polemic club; they infuriated local and Home Office officials with wall chalkings; and they circulated tracts, broadsheets, posters, poems and metal tokens advertising Spence's plan. Evans and a newly acquired radical associate, 'Captain' Arthur Thistlewood, even persuaded Burdett to nominate them in June 1814 to replace Richter and Place on the committee of the West London Lancasterian Association. This was an off-shoot of Joseph Lancaster's Nonconformist monitorial school scheme for educating the poor cheaply, and had been taken up in 1813 by numbers of influential Westminster radicals. Place was forced to deploy all his considerable

manipulative skills to persuade the committee to thwart this attempt by
Evans and Thistlewood to add Spencean-Jacobin enlightenment to the
curriculum of the west London poor.[64]

During these difficult war years Spence seems to have muted but not
abandoned his simultaneous commitment to the idea of armed insurrection.
A ballad published in 1811 reiterated his belief in a militant vanguard:

> Said Spence, if a few hearty men
> Said come let us have Spence's system
> What would your behaviour be then.
> Would you hinder, or would you assist 'em.[65]

Shortly before his death in 1814 he was still looking to a revolutionary
cadre to complete the Spencean revolution (and fend off the landlords'
counter-attack?).[66] But how much Spence and his circle were implicated
in practical attempts to promote armed revolution during this period is
unclear, especially since he and Evans were by 1811 criticising France for
falling short of early revolutionary hopes. Even so, Evans was probably
one of the 'Jacobin party', headed by Thomas Hardy, who planned in
1813 to send returned Jacobin transportee Maurice Margarot and Arthur
Thistlewood 'across the pond' in a smuggling vessel: they were to persuade Bonaparte 'to attempt the immediate invasion of the country'. The
'party' also intended to found a new magazine, the *Political Censor*, 'for the
purpose of rousing the people from their torpor and enlightening them'.
Spencean involvement seems likely. Both Margarot and Thistlewood had
been keeping company with Spenceans since their arrival in the metropolis around 1810–11, and Evans was serving on the same Westminster
electoral committee as Hardy around this time. In the event, the plan
came to nothing: some of the party became disillusioned with Napoleon;
Margarot was concerned only with restoring his own solvency; and
Thistlewood failed to supply promised finance.[67]

Thistlewood did eventually make the trip to Paris in 1814. He was
accompanied by Evans's young son, Thomas John, who carried Spencean
pamphlets for distribution there, as well as letters of introduction to Jacobin *emigrés* like Richard Hodgson. The visit seems to have combined educational and conspiratorial aims. It was reported that they visited –
amongst others – former LCS president Ashley, numbers of revolutionary
Americans and the exiled United Irish agent William McCabe, alias 'Mr
Cato'. Thomas Evans also wrote from London suggesting that his son
contact former United men: Binns, Thresher, T. McGuire, Captain Perry,
the two Burgesses, Hamilton and Lee – a group whom the Paris Police
described as the worst sort of persons living in the City. News of Spence's
death added extra gravity to the instruction young Evans received to
conduct himself in France as 'an agent of mankind' propagating 'the true

Philosophy of Nature'. His return letters were to be 'put in many hands', presumably at Spencean free-and-easies. The sixteen-year-old boy seems to have discharged these responsibilities admirably. Thistlewood, by contrast, antagonised most of the *emigrés* by his compulsive gambling, but he did at least establish a connection with McCabe which led to the United Irishman's secret return to London on the eve of the Spa Fields uprising in December 1816.[68]

Though it is not hard to see why former United Englishmen found Spence's political methods congenial, their adoption of his land-reforming programme seems to imply a more drastic ideological conversion. How did they bridge that 'vast difference' which is supposed to separate Spence's ideas from those of the generality of Paineite Jacobins?[69] That there was a difference is undeniable, but it is easy to overlook how much Spence's thought drew on representative strands of the plebeian radicalism of his day. Leaving aside the important millenarian and 'Commonwealthman' strands of his ideology for discussion in later chapters, the dominant remaining element consisted of radical enlightenment theory which he had absorbed in Newcastle philosophical circles and in Jacobin London.

Spence's first prosecutions in London in 1792 were for selling Puffendorf's *Law of Nature* and – significantly – Paine's *Rights of Man*, part II, a work which contributed to his 'Spensonian' programme. His own *Rights of Man*, though silent on Paine, was steeped in natural rights language and drew specifically on Locke and Puffendorf. And his journal, *Pig's Meat*, or – under its occasional alternative title – the *Universal School of Man's Rights*, contained extracts from such Jacobin classics as Godwin's *Political Justice*, Barlow's *Advice to the Privileged Orders*, Volney's *Ruins of Empires*, and even Erskine's *Defence of Paine*.[70] Volney's *Ruins* exerted particular influence on both the form and content of several of Spence's writings, a fact of some significance since the *Ruins* was one of the formative texts of English Jacobinism and of nineteenth-century popular radicalism generally.[71]

Spence's writings knitted together many strands of enlightenment thought. There was his advocacy of a revolution of reason through popular printing and a free press; his desire for toleration of all religious opinion 'not repugnant to the Rights of Man'; his wish to throw off the 'chains of Hymen' imposed by Christian marriage and to substitute open divorce and perhaps free love; and his commitment to the abolition of slavery and to the right of all peoples to freedom of movement, association and trade.[72] The language and content of many proposals in the *Constitution of Spensonia* (1801) echoed those in the United Englishmen's *Declaration and Constitution* (1798) and in Evans's draft 'Constitution for the Republic of Ireland – Freeland' (1798). All three in turn drew heavily on the French Constitution of 1793.[73]

Even Spence's plan to transform society through the purchase and expropriation of private land as the basis for a parish-administered rent-based popular utopia can be located within an existing agrarian radical tradition. Spence – like Paine, William Ogilvie and Godwin – rested his critique of private land ownership on natural rights theory and on an historiography of exploitation. There was a pervasive nostalgia for land rights amongst nineteenth-century urban as well as rural artisans.[74] John Baxter had in 1795 declared his hostility to private landlordism and support for agrarian natural rights. 'Citizen' Lee (Evans's former bookseller-partner) and Maurice Margarot also advocated land reform schemes.[75] The United Englishmen's 'Constitution for the Republic of Ireland – Freeland' of 1798, drafted in Evans's handwriting, asserted typically that the land and seas were the gift of nature 'for the common use of all and cannot become the property of individuals'.[76] Spence's scheme represented an advance on Paine but not a fundamentally new challenge to admirers of *Agrarian Justice*. Spence assumed an essentially agrarian economy and rested his conception of labour value on natural rights (of producer to his property), differing only from Paine in his willingness to accord greater rights to the labouring class for their contribution to the improvement of cultivated land. Spence's rental plan has been aptly described as 'a utopia of small producers and cheap government'.[77] And although he differed from orthodox Paineites in viewing land reform as an essential co-requisite of democratic revolution, his analysis conformed to the prevailing artisan radical belief that economic exploitation derived from the actions of a corrupt, parasitical political elite.[78]

Former Jacobins like Thomas Evans and his United Englishmen associates did not have to cross a vast ideological divide between Paine and Spence. They had simply to make a determined stride.

2

'Old blackguard' Spenceans: Evans and unrespectable radicalism

'Refuse' was how Francis Place dismissed Thomas Evans and his radical associates – a reference not only to their predilection for extremist politics, but also to their degraded social positions and supposed low morality. From the vantage-point of the 1820s and 30s when the values of respectability had become widely diffused, Place felt able to explain and condemn the post-Jacobin political careers of men like Evans on the grounds that they adhered to the values and practices of an 'old blackguard', 'profligate' or 'dissolute' culture.

True, Place conceded that during the eighteenth century this culture had informed the lives of most of London's middling sort – lesser professionals, shopkeepers, small master tradesmen and journeymen, as well as the mass of unskilled and poor. Every facet was exemplified in his own upbringing and family background. Place's father, Simon, had been typically feckless; he squandered good prospects as a master baker on 'drinking, whoring, gaming, fishing and fighting', inflicting poverty and bitterness on his wife and children. Place claimed first-hand experience of two of the core institutions of the culture: he was born in a debtor's gaol, and he lived his early years in a low crimping alehouse during his father's interlude as a publican.

As a boy he supposedly enjoyed these rough milieux: he and a gang of 'dirty', 'vulgar' friends ('though sons of respectable tradesmen') spent their leisure time brawling, pilfering and playing rowdy games. Later, when apprenticed to a 'typical' Temple Bar breeches-maker, he grew up with his master's children who took variously to theft, drink and prostitution. He also claimed to have engaged in all the unruly work and leisure customs of Hogarth's celebrated *Idle Prentice*. He joined a gang of Fleet Street apprentices; mingled with prostitutes along St Catherine's Lane; experienced casual sex with tradesmen's daughters; drank, smoked, swore and sang bawdy songs in masculine drinking fraternities. He rubbed shoulders with thieves and highwaymen at sleazy tea-gardens such as the Dog and Duck in the company of a light-fingered Cutter Club. Theirs was, one of his associates later recalled, a complete way of life, with attendant language, customs, tricks and songs.[1]

6

2 The Radical's Arms. *A satire on rough radicalism, 1819.*

Place later excused his youthful behaviour because it was the norm amongst London's middling ranks, including the most respected and prosperous of tradesmen. Within the artisan world distinctions of status had rested more on such factors as position, custom and skill than on the later criterion of respectable behaviour. Moreover, in less censorious moments, Place understood and appreciated the old rough code of values shared by men like his father. Within his own circle, Simon Place had been well respected as 'a straight-forward, daring and honest sort of a man' – truculent when dealing with authorities, but generous to friends. He typified that eighteenth-century plebeian culture which was noted – in E.P. Thompson's words – for 'its resistance to religious homily ... its picaresque flouting of the providential virtues ... its ready recourse to disorder and ... its ironic attitude towards the law'.[2] Even in his prosperous maturity Francis Place retained a half-admiration for the freedom, independence and lack of inhibition displayed by these late eighteenth-century tradesmen and their families. He showed some appreciation of how the economic forces which structured their working lives had affected their social behaviour. He could recall how cycles of glut and scarcity caused by seasonal fluctuations and erratic trade patterns had induced chronic uncertainty and irregularity of work. Enforced idleness would be followed by frenetic, monotonous and domestically claustrophobic activity – so that even the most disciplined artisans were tempted at times to seek escape in drink or other forms of 'excitement'. On top of this, vagaries of birth, illness or death always threatened to plunge tradesmen and their families into poverty.

Nevertheless, Place believed that the majority of London's middling sort managed during the early decades of the nineteenth century to throw off this essentially brutal and degrading culture in favour of a new humane and civilising code of respectability. Writing at the end of the 1820s, it appeared to him that popular manners and morals had undergone a revolution. Only the unskilled, poor or professional criminal classes still clung to 'blackguard' norms and practices. Economic independence and possession of a skilled status had formerly been enough to define an artisan as respectable, but by the 1820s he could only expect social respect if he also *behaved* respectably and acquired sober, self-improving (though non-deferential) values. Place ascribed the change to two main causes. First, seasonal and wartime scarcities, lower prices and the activities of trade clubs had caused a marked improvement in the wages of most London tradesmen, enabling them to stabilise and improve their living conditions. Second, and most important, the dissemination of rational knowledge by democratic political societies during the 1790s had brought about a vast increase in moral and intellectual self-improvement.[3]

The change was symbolised for Place by his attendance of a Jacobin reunion at the Crown and Anchor tavern on 5 November 1822. Here he met at least twenty former LCS committee delegates who had once been journeymen or shopmen but were 'now all in business, all flourishing men'. In addition to himself, he was referring to men like Thomas Hardy, John Richter and Alexander Galloway, who had managed to build up prosperous businesses in the respective areas of shoemaking, engineering and sugar-refining. Place's own tailoring business was on its way to reaching a profit level of £3000 p.a., and Galloway was described by Samuel Bamford in 1817 as 'a cool, cautious, methodical man of business' who owned a town and country house and was courted by 'literary and scientific men of all parties and all professions'. Hand in hand with their material advances, Place noted, went a new attachment to respectable values manifested in the cultivation of family-centred rational recreation and the provision of education for their children. Many had also adopted the moderate reformist and educational goals associated with Westminster radicalism after 1807.[4]

Place pointed by contrast to a residue of former Jacobins who had failed to improve themselves – morally, intellectually or materially – remaining fixed in the feckless, dissolute and criminal patterns of the past. He cited Thomas Evans, Benjamin Binns and his own former partner, Richard Wild, another LCS veteran, as examples. These men, he implied, lacked respectability even by the old standards, since they belonged to lowly trades or to less-skilled sectors of their trade. Binns was a plumber's assistant. Evans, originally a baker like Simon Place, had by the mid-1790s become involved in an even less respectable pursuit. He and Janet Evans were allegedly making a living by colouring bawdy prints from their home. Even so, Place asserted, Evans only revealed his full blackguardism in 1806 when he borrowed £20 for 'necessaries', then used it 'for a dishonest purpose'.[5] Place immediately ended their relationship, just as he broke with his partner Wild in 1801 for marrying a supposed prostitute and thief.

After that, both Evans and Wild confirmed the overlap between their social and political roughness by involving themselves with a gang of former Jacobin blackmailers and extortionists, headed by a notorious swindling money-lender, Jonathan 'Jew' King. Their 'malignancy', Place claimed, even led them in 1813 to instigate a blackmail attempt against himself.[6] In other ways, too, their later careers followed a typical 'old blackguard' artisan course. Wild became bankrupt and a dependent of St Martins Parish. Evans joined the ragged followers of Spence, and rapidly attracted new and profligate associates of his own, such as 'Dr' James Watson, Arthur Thistlewood and Thomas Preston. The first, claimed Place, was a man of loose habits, wretchedly poor and a failure as an apothecary; the second, a ruined, reckless gambler and one-time blood-

money informer; the last, a lame, drunken, garrulous and poor shoemaker:

men whose circumstances are so desperate as to prevent them having any moral
principles, men who mistake the well being of society or are careless of the consequences of their acts upon it, who mistake themselves and believe themselves of
importance when they possess no importance, and believe also that the mischievous proceedings they resort to will answer some wild purpose and be of advantage
to themselves.[7]

Needless to say Place's analysis was self-justificatory; it probably reveals
more about the change in his own social position and outlook than about
his former Jacobin colleagues. He almost certainly exaggerated the roughness of his youth in order to accentuate his self-improvement, and he
made no mention of the crucial role that access to capital played in determining the success or failure of ex-Jacobins. Nor did he say how many of
the LCS entrepreneurs had, like himself, managed to avoid the disruptive
experience of a long prison sentence during the late 1790s. And his separation of radicals into those who became respectable, self-improving and
politically moderate, and those who remained unimproved, unrespectable
and extremist was an oversimplification. It failed, for example, to take into
account the political career of a man like John Gast, the Deptford
shipwright. Gast resembled Place in belonging to a declining handicraft
trade, and in shedding a rough past (as a publican and a convicted fortune-teller) in favour of moral and intellectual self-improvement. Yet this
in no way altered Gast's commitment to defending the shipwrights and
other artisan trades from erosions of wages and status: throughout his life
he remained an active trade unionist and ultra-radical.[8]

Place's portrait of the early nineteenth-century revolution in popular
manners and morals was equally overdrawn. He exaggerated the 'profligacy' of the old culture and the puritanism of the new, just as he exaggerated the speed and extent of the transition. Understandably his
explanation of the causes was also limited. Modern historians are more
inclined to associate early nineteenth-century changes in working-class
morality with industrial capitalism's need to generate a disciplined
labour force, and with related shifts in patterns of reproduction, family
life and gender relations.[9] The permeation of evangelical religious values
through many levels of English society at this time was also a major
influence[10] which Place overlooked.

At the same time, modern studies have vindicated some important
aspects of his analysis: namely his stress on radicalism's role in disseminating enlightenment ethics; his realisation that old assessments of respectability by social position were being rivalled by new emphases on morality
and behaviour; and his appreciation that these new values carried an

implicit challenge on behalf of the family to the masculine – fraternal character of 'old blackguard' culture.[11] Place's own social and political evolution during these years, and his analysis of it, have also been important to modern historians as symptoms of major cultural and political transformations in England. For instance, to one recent scholar Place represents the way that small masters shifted away from Jacobin-type radicalism towards Benthamite reform and ideology.[12] Place himself believed that this estrangement from former friends and political colleagues like Evans was symptomatic of wider tensions and divergences within popular radicalism. He might have been right about the divergent tendencies, but his 'unrespectable radical' typology and interpretation calls for closer scrutiny.

Unrespectable Jacobins?

At one level his charge against Evans of unrespectability seems wide of the mark. In many respects Evans's social and political career in the 1810s resembled that of Place and other ex-Jacobin exemplars. Colouring bawdy prints was – in the context of the 1790s – unexceptionable. Place elsewhere conceded that it was usual during the eighteenth century for the most respectable of booksellers to sell and display bawdy material.[13] Moreover, we have only Place's word that the prints were bawdy; Evans described himself as 'a Map, Chart and Print Colourer', and 'by profession an artist'. We also know that around this time he ran a bookselling business on Holborn Hill in partnership with John Bone. When arrested in 1798, he claimed that his print colouring business was earning a profit of £100 per year, and it certainly financed substantial premises at 14 Plough Court.[14] But Evans, unlike Place, endured a long spell of imprisonment between 1798 and 1801. He listed the results in numerous petitions: his premises accrued heavy rental debts, his furniture was seized, his family was threatened with eviction, his business was fatally disrupted and his health suffered. Prison exacerbated, if not caused, the dropsy which was to plague him for life. In a letter to Richard Hodgson in Paris in 1801 Galloway recorded the similar effects of imprisonment on the lives and businesses of other Jacobins: Nicholls the gardener was 'lost to the cause' and probably to the world through an illness contracted there; 'the Snob', shoemaker Joseph Bacon, intended to flee to France; 'pecuniary distress' had driven Bone from Fleet Street to Antwerp; Galloway's own newly founded engineering business was struggling; warehouseman Jasper Moore was in urgent need of financial help; and the plumbing business of newly married Benjamin Binns was failing.[15]

Under the circumstances Evans made a remarkable recovery. He was probably helped by a 'comfortable' legacy from Janet's father in October

1799.[16] This enabled him to establish a new business in Newcastle Street, Strand, as a manufacturer of patent braces and spiral steel springs – the last, perhaps, to service the needs of his machinemaker-engineer brother-in-law, Galloway. Evans did not prosper to the same extent as Galloway or Place, but he produced enough to cover annual rental, taxes and dues of £67 6s, and to provide his family and at least one employee with an apparently stable and adequate income for nearly twenty years. William Hone thought Evans the embodiment of a respectable independent English artisan when he visited the Strand workshop in October 1817: 'he appeared to me one of the plainest and most honest minded men I ever saw … He had … a round, good, healthy, fat looking face, the very index of a manly mind, and his speech was as bold and English as his appearance.'[17]

Place emphasised the importance of family life as much as work situation in determining respectability. Yet here especially it was difficult to fault the Evanses – though a good deal of the credit must go to Thomas's wife, Janet. She was a remarkable person. Intercepted prison correspondence shows that she had to bear the real brunt of the state repression and, like most Jacobin prisoners' wives, she showed great courage and resourcefulness in maintaining the business, feeding her children and supporting her husband. Even though she was pregnant and nursing an infant son, Janet was arrested soon after her husband in April 1798. The government took this unusual course because they knew from Powell's reports that she was deeply implicated in revolutionary conspiracy. She was locked in a prison for female felons, interrogated, and eventually released. Within a few months she gave birth to still-born twins.

Women often supported their husband's political causes in some measure, but Janet's degree of political involvement was exceptional. Whilst Evans was in prison, she helped organise a mob-riot outside Coldbath Fields prison. She smuggled information in and out of the cells. She wrote tough, articulate letters to government officials demanding support for herself and the baby, as well as a fair trial and better conditions for her husband. She probably sowed the seeds of Place's hostility by criticising the way he and his wife were distributing subscription relief funds to prisoners' families.[18] And the relationship between Janet and her husband seems to have been the opposite of the casual, promiscuous liaison which Place claimed as typical of 'old blackguard' tradesmen families. They worked together both in the print colouring business and in underground politics, and their prison correspondence shows that they felt the separation keenly. Thomas's petitions pleaded with unusual insistence for some help to be given to his struggling wife and child, and for them to be granted more liberal visiting rights. It was a close-knit family. Janet's brother, Alexander Galloway, asked to be moved into the same cell as Evans in August 1799, 'from family considerations and to gratify a friendship of longstanding'.[19] Young Thomas John was to make a similar request seventeen years later when he and his father once again became state prisoners.

Judging by her letters, Janet was at least as literate as her husband and brother – and more so than most other wives of state prisoners. These intellectual attainments were probably a family legacy; if so, it was transmitted in turn to the next generation. 'Young Tom Evans grows a fine youth, he is indeed a most excellent boy', wrote Galloway proudly to Richard Hodgson in 1811. Hodgson was able to judge for himself three years later when the sixteen-year-old youth made his visit to Paris in company with Arthur Thistlewood. Its purposes were educational, as well as conspiratorial. Thomas John was to practise French (at which he eventually became fluent), and probably to learn patrician manners from his tutor, Captain Thistlewood. The Captain probably did not take his pedagogic responsibilities too seriously during their three week stay together – much of his time was taken up with gambling at the Palais Royale. Still, when he eventually took leave of young Evans at Abbéville, he entrusted the boy with some 'crackers' to be handed over to his own son, Julian, 'in the Service of the British Republic'. And when young Evans forgot, he received – to his mortification – a reminder from Thistlewood written in 'polite and gentle style'.[20] Whether or not with Thistlewood's help, young Thomas John Evans grew into a model of moral and intellectual respectability, enough to earn him the eventual praise of his father's severest critic, Francis Place.

Thomas Evans senior also fulfilled another of Place's canons of Jacobin self-improvement – he became an active figure in the reform politics of Westminster. He was attracted to this arena by his position as an elector of the constituency, by the connections he had made with Burdett during the Coldbath Fields scandal and by his relationship with the prominent Westminster activist Galloway. Evans's earlier-noted prominence in Burdett's Middlesex election campaign of 1802 probably contributed to his appointment in September–October 1812 to a new Westminster general electoral committee in support of the candidatures of Lord Cochrane and Burdett.[21] Around this time Evans also came into direct confrontation with Place over educationalist Joseph Lancaster's West London Lancasterian Association, which since its foundation in 1813 had become a forum for leading Westminster radicals. Early in June 1814, Burdett moved a motion on the WLLA committee that Place and Richter – as suspected government spies – be expelled and replaced by Evans and three friends: Thistlewood; a brewer, Samuel Fletcher; and a shoemaker, John Hobley. For Place it was both a personal and a symbolic affront. He and Richter – archetypal self-improved radicals – were being displaced by men who were enemies and blackguards. He worked to convince the committee that they were 'persons of bad character', probably pointing out that Fletcher was a shady brewer who hoped to make money from the WLLA through the sale of a dubious corn-grinding machine, and that Thistlewood was a reckless gambler who had not long before been working as a blood-money informer. He also flatly denied that Evans and Hobley had any interest in WLLA educational ideals, claiming that they were members of a blackmailing gang responsible for instigating and attempting to exploit the spy charge against him. He might even have hinted at the possibility that they were looking for fresh prey, given that Joseph Lancaster was widely believed to have homosexual inclinations. Place's argument was convincing enough to block the nominations of Evans and company, but not to persuade Burdett to withdraw the spy charge. This, coupled with unease in the WLLA over Place's irreligious views, eventually forced the acerbic tailor to resign in June 1814.[22]

This particular contest between the respectable Mr Place and the supposedly blackguard Mr Evans thus ended in stalemate. Nevertheless, Place had been able to make a damaging countercharge in claiming that Evans and a criminal 'gang' had tried to blackmail him. This began, he claimed, after a jury of which he was foreman returned a verdict of suicide at a coroner's inquest of 1810 into the death of the Duke of Cumberland's valet, Joseph Sellis. Cumberland was widely disliked and – as the radical Whig, Colonel Wardle, told Place – 'everybody was dissatisfied'. London hummed with sensational murder rumours: that the Duke had been surprised in a 'shirt dance' (homosexual act) with Sellis, or had aroused Sellis's jealousy by taking a new manservant-lover; that Cumberland had fathered a bastard child by Sellis's wife; and, fascinatingly, that Sellis had been an ardent Jacobin who was blackmailing the Duke. (Several witnesses testified before Middlesex magistrates that Sellis had once tried to throw stones at the King.)

All these accusations resurfaced in a series of pseudonymous letters published in White's radical newspaper, the *Independent Whig*, between August 1812 and March 1813. Several displayed a close knowledge of LCS and radical affairs: they implied that Place had been part of a spy-ring with James Powell in 1798, and that he had accepted money from a Treasury official to quash the murder case against Cumberland. A freakish stroke of luck enabled Place to learn the identity of the writers when an associate of his spent some time in a Newgate prison cell with one of the instigators, Davenport Sedley. Place's informant named those responsible as Evans, Richard Wild, the Spencean George Cullen, Henry White, and four notorious blackmailer-extortionists, 'Jew' King, Patrick Duffin, Sedley and S.C. Graves (Admiral Graves's swindler son who was also in Newgate). According to Place these men helped the spy rumour become 'common conversation in Pothouses and Nightcellars', and they tried to

3 *The Duke of Cumberland haunted by Sellis's ghost.*

profit from the Sellis affair by systematic criminal extortion. Hence, when the government eventually decided to prosecute White for libels against Cumberland in the *Independent Whig*, they were helped by an anonymous letter from Place denouncing Evans and his 'gang'.[23]

Place's claim that King, Duffin and Sedley were systematic swindlers, extortionists and blackmailers, and that Evans was connected with them, is corroborated by a rich deposit of government prosecution records, as well as press and pamphlet reports. When Sedley was convicted in 1812 for conspiracy to steal bills of exchange, government law officers summed up the contents of his confiscated papers: '[they] develop a series of fraudulent and swindling transactions practised upon persons of the first distinction and character in the country in which by misrepresentations and intimidation Mr Sedley appears in some instances to have succeeded in obtaining money and in others appointments or promotion for his family and friends'. If anything, this was an understatement. Over the years 1805–11 his victims included: the Prince of Wales, the Dukes of Cumberland and York, the Prime Minister (Spencer Perceval), senior law officers, government and admiralty officials, and a variety of distinguished families.[24]

Sedley had a vulture's instinct for corruption, and the Regent's vendetta against Princess Caroline, as well as the Duke of York's indiscretions with Mary Anne Clarke, provided him with especially rich pickings. His technique was to furnish victims with a title page and extracts from a projected book containing what he typically described as 'extreamely unpleasant matter'. He would then offer to have the embarrassing material suppressed or expurgated for a price. He also hired other professionals to scent out and to market smut. Shortly after leaving Newgate in January 1811 a hopelessly profligate hack, Captain Thomas Ashe, recalled being visited with such a proposition 'by several violent characters from London amongst whom were the noted Sedley and Admiral and Colonel Graves'.[25] The Treasury Solicitor's files connect Evans to Sedley and his associates through a list of letters written between 1809 and 1810, though the letters themselves have disappeared along with most of the contents of Sedley's papers. There is also a reference – possibly savouring of Evans – to 'a supposed connection having taken place, which would, if there was any foundation for it, constitute a charge of High Treason against the person there named'. However Sedley himself seems also to have had United Irish affiliations; he had been sent in May 1799 from Dublin gaol to England on a warrant for swindling and embezzlement, and possibly became acquainted with Evans during his time in gaol.[26]

Evans's links with 'Jew' King and Patrick Duffin were more clear-cut. King, in reality a Sephardi Jew of Portuguese extraction named Jacob Rey, was a wealthy, self-made banker, merchant and money-lender, and, according to some, also a swindler, blackmailer, match-making racketeer, gamester, receiver and extortionist. There is no doubt that he was frequently before the courts: in connection with a fraudulent banking firm named Dean and Co. in 1802, for a match-making swindle in 1804 and for a perjury charge around 1810–11 (for which he was convicted). Even a lifelong friend and apologist, the writer John Taylor, admitted that King kept company with a group of shady Irish noblemen, and that his second marriage was probably bigamous. To enemies like Place he was 'an atrocious villain', and the satirical pro-Tory *Scourge* described him in 1811 as a man 'restrained by no punctilos of decorum, or principles of honour, a stranger to any emotions of shame, or any feelings of personal dignity; there is no form of manhood in which he is not ready to appear, no disguise that he is unwilling to assume, for the furtherance of his purposes'. He had ingratiated himself with leading members of the LCS in the 1790s – including Ashley, Hodgson, Galloway, Place and Evans – by purchasing their products, entertaining them at his house and offering them loans and gifts. Place later wrote that opinion had been divided as to whether King was a spy, a scavenging opportunist or a genuine revolutionary. Galloway evidently inclined to the last view; he passed on King's good wishes to Hodgson in 1801 and also expressed the hope that King could be persuaded to 'bleed' in support of impoverished Jacobins. Place himself favoured the scavenger interpretation and he further blamed King for suggesting the stratagem of enrolling Jacobins as armed militia, an idea which Evans had taken up enthusiastically.[27]

Patrick William Duffin, described by Place as King's 'retainer', was a former United Irishman who had been imprisoned in the New Compter, 1793–5, then in Coldbath Fields for a further year in 1798 for lottery fraud. It was there that he befriended Evans: they collaborated in the Coldbath Fields exposé and later in Burdett's election campaign of 1802. Place attempted to sue Duffin in 1805, probably over a lottery insurance matter – this could have been the 'dishonest' scheme on which Evans expended the £20 loan of 1806. By then Duffin was running a 'low gaming house' in Denmark Court, Strand, on behalf of King who probably also financed the *Independent Whig* co-founded by Duffin and Henry White in 1806. Duffin wrote for both the *Independent Whig* and a Sunday newspaper called the *British Guardian* founded by King around 1811. Both men contributed substantially to the radical campaign of 1808–9 against the Duke of York for allowing his mistress Mary Anne Clarke to sell military preferments. Duffin and King were also known friends of Sedley, and it is entirely plausible that all three should subsequently have been associated with White and Evans in the *Independent Whig*'s attacks on Place and Cumberland.[28]

Evans's collaboration with this gang may be likely, but its significance is more difficult to assess. It does not necessarily prove that he was a blackguard radical – we have seen that he possessed some quite opposite credentials. We need to guard also against anachronism. Definitions of acceptable and unacceptable political conduct during Regency years were not those of the 1830s when Place penned his retrospective judgement. For example, King's social and political stature was much more ambiguous than Place would have us believe. Even the implacably hostile *Scourge* conceded that King had risen unaided from shoe-black to attorney, and that he 'supported an appearance of respectability'.[29] The *Monthly Repository*'s obituary – a sign of respectability in itself – portrayed him as an exemplary self-improver who 'made his way in society by force of his talents'.[30] These last were considerable: in addition to his business achievements, King wrote treatises on politics, theology and mathematics; he belonged to literary and debating clubs frequented by luminaries like Paine, Godwin and Thomas Holcroft; and he cultivated 'men of talent' from all walks of life. His fondness for cards and pugilism was typical of the sporting gentlemen of his day, and his marriage to the dowager Lady Lanesborough, heiress to Earl Belvedere's estate, gave him entrée to fashionable circles in both England and Europe.[31] At the same time, he remained a close friend of several eminent middle-class radicals, including the barrister Henry Clifford and the Lombard Street banker Timothy Brown.

The motivation and political credibility of King and his gang might also have been less mercenary than Place claimed. He ascribed their actions entirely to greed, and depicted King as a parasite who preyed on social upheaval. Even if true, this was not the whole story. King displayed a long and consistent record of political opposition: he wrote a tract in support of the distressed populace in 1783; he supported Jacobinism throughout the 1790s; and he participated in most London radical campaigns between 1802 and 1815. The bitterness he felt towards England's established order probably derived from insecurities and hardships associated with his lowly origins, his ambiguous social position and his despised religious faith. In a lengthy introduction to a new edition of David Levi's *Dissertations on the Prophecies of the Old Testament*, published in 1817, King inveighed against the privations, injustices and persecutions which Jews had experienced at the hands of Christians:

they have been dispossessed, their titles abolished, and their dignity sullied, and have no mode of subsistence but commerce ... [having] no protection but their caution, they traffic with timidity and wariness, their fears arouse their acuteness, and their acuteness and suspicions augment the hatred; they are enjoined by their law to love their neighbours, but they have every neighbour's enmity to encounter.[32]

Sedley and Duffin, as Irishmen and probable United Irishmen, could lay claim to a similar history of persecution and discrimination. A government clerk who visited Sedley in 1810 in response to a blackmail attempt reported that the Irishman swore 'vehemently', saying 'The King, Queen and Prince might as well be d...d, us were possessed of a secret which put them in our power and which if disobeyed would compel the entire Royal Family to quit the Kingdom.'[33]

Many of King's victims and all of Sedley's were wealthy and influential members of the English ruling classes, especially ministers, government officials and members of the Royal Family and their courtiers. In this respect the interests of Sedley, King and Duffin as professional criminals intersected with their political radicalism. Sedley and Duffin resemble the alienated, opportunistic and often politicised Grub Street *canaille* of pre-revolutionary France, whom Robert Darnton has anatomised so brilliantly. King is reminiscent of the shady Bolshevik merchant-financier, Alexander Helphand-Parvus. Like Parvus, King seems to have been at some levels a genuine radical, or at least a genuine supporter of radicals. He lent them money, financed and bought their publications, and sponsored periodicals which gave them employment and political publicity. According to Mary Anne Clarke – or at least her ghost-writer, hack-journalist P.F. McCallum – King was the *eminence grise* behind Gwillam Lloyd Wardle's well-orchestrated political campaign against the Duke of York in 1809. Duffin, and possibly Sedley, dug up dirt for Wardle. King contributed money, as well as publicity through 'the force and energy of his writings' in the *British Guardian*, founded especially for muckraking purposes.[34] Duffin's and Evans's connections with Burdett, 1798–1812, suggest that King might also have had a hand in fostering the political career of the radical baronet.

The many ferocious anti-establishment exposés produced by editors, writers and patrons of the *Independent Whig* and *British Guardian* over the period 1806–15 are instructive. They fulminated against the continued cover-ups of prison governor Aris's peculations and cruelties; against the malevolent secret plot to besmirch the private life of Princess Caroline (supposedly instigated by the Prince Regent and his courtiers, Lord and Lady Douglas); against the army promotions racket run by the Duke of York's mistress, Mary Anne Clarke, with the Duke's collaboration; against the alleged use of blackmail by Perceval and his friends in order to coerce their way into office; against Cumberland for supposedly murdering Sellis, then rigging the coroner's investigation.[35] At one level such muckraking simply helped to sell newspapers. Yet there was a serious political thread throughout these apparently piecemeal and sensationalist attacks. The journalism of Duffin, King and White over this period needs to be seen in the context of a recently stifled democratic press and an emerging popular political critique of 'Old Corruption', or state parasitism, in which the personal scandals, extravagances, vices and duplicities of the Royal Family played a notable part. Dorothy George, in her meticulous analysis of late Georgian popular political prints, concluded that the Mary Anne Clarke scandal in particular saw 'corruption' displace 'popery' as the chief populist bogey.[36] 'Old Corruption' became a pervasive critique because it seemed to fit the facts – not only the financial facts, but the moral and social facts as well. Within oppositionist circles the Mary Anne Clarke scandal briefly mobilised a range of metropolitan protest comparable to the Queen Caroline affair just over a decade later. It gathered up radicals from the Common Hall, Common Council and Whig Club, artisans from Middlesex and Westminster, playhouse rioters, Newgate hacks and alehouse orators.[37]

Against such a background the actions of Evans and his 'gang' over the Sellis affair appear less disreputable. Place's anonymous letter to Henry Charles Litchfield also distinguished between the motives of Evans (and Wild) which he attributed to 'malignity', and those of the remainder of the gang which he described as 'pecuniary'. Moreover, suspicion of both Cumberland and Place was understandable in the circumstances. The *Independent Whig* cited a long list of apparent legal and medical discrepancies in

4 *Old Corruption at work: the Duke of York and Mary Anne Clarke arranging promotions.*

the coronial evidence, and medical doubts over the verdict of suicide were being expressed as late as 1850. We now know that James Powell, whom Place assisted to escape to Hamburg in 1798 and subsequently associated with in Westminster circles until at least 1811, was in fact a government spy. It was thus not unreasonable to suspect Place of collusion with the government, particularly in view of his dominance of the 1810 jury proceedings, his contingent rise to prosperity and his penchant for back-room manipulation. Burdett and Hunt never ceased to believe that he had been bribed by the government in 1810. Mary Anne Clarke's scurrilous and suppressed *Recollections* hinted that police magistrate Nathaniel Conant made himself 'useful' to the Royal Family over the Sellis affair in the same way that he had done when he helped to buy her silence over the Duke of York's misdeeds. True or false, it was echoed in popular rumour, gossip and political caricature.[38]

One gains the impression, too, that in this late Georgian and Regency period literary blackmail was, if not a respectable, then at least a tacitly accepted and widely practised political mode. Blackmailing and threatening letters were used by the 'inarticulate' eighteenth-century rural labourer to register social protest or outrage against his rulers.[39] Dorothy George has also noted 'the blackmailing virulence of personal innuendo' which informed political caricatures of the time. As often as not publishers traded in such virulence in the hope of being bought off.[40] Astute Mary Anne Clarke regarded her knowledge of the Royal Family's private life as a form of property that she, as a person without other means, was entitled to exploit to its maximum worth.[41] Where politics was still conducted on an intimate personal scale, scandal gave the powerless (as well as the powerful) a purchase with which to 'coerce' their enemies and enrich themselves. Government files often convey an impression that buying the silence of those who had acquired embarrassing knowledge was an accepted ritual, only avoided when – as in Sedley's case – the blackmailer failed to keep his side of the bargain or was thought to be insatiable.

In exchange for suppressing her printed memoirs in 1809, Mary Anne Clarke extracted from the Duke of York the colossal sum of £10,000, as well as life annuities for herself and daughter. More startling is evidence which suggests that the noted evangelical, Spencer Perceval, not only paid Newgate hack, Thomas Ashe, a salary of £400 for dredging up smut against his political opponents, but also reported to the explicit blackmailing tactics of Mrs Clarke. In winter 1806 he commissioned a discreet printer to produce 5000 copies of a secret report – the 'Delicate Investigation' into the private life of Princess Caroline ordered by the Prince of Wales earlier in the year. Given that this report – written by Lords Grenville, Ellenborough and Erskine, and Earl Spencer – substantially exoner-

5 *Plotting the 'Indelicate Investigation': Lord and Lady Douglas and the Prince Regent.*

ated Caroline, its instigation reflected badly on the Prince, who was consequently prepared to pay a high price to suppress it. Copies of 'The Book', as it was known, or at least news of its existence, reached Sedley, Mary Anne Clarke and other predatory pamphleteers, who began issuing blackmailing letters and articles claiming that Perceval had printed the work for the express purpose of 'coercing' the Prince. They insinuated that 'The Book' – not the Catholic Emancipation issue – was the lever which Perceval used to force his way into office in 1807. Whether or not this was true, he had undoubtedly ordered the printing and, once he was in office, both this action and the book itself became potential sources of embarrassment. Over the next five years he went to extraordinary lengths to prevent its publication and to quash any news of his connection with it. He paid out large sums ranging between £50 and £1500, presumably from the public purse (and promised at least one sinecure) to various printers, booksellers and blackmailing hacks in exchange for silence and the destruction of remaining copies of the report. When he could not gain compliance by these means he issued chancery injunctions prohibiting publication.[42]

Unrespectable Spenceans?

Such 'a deep political juggle' – as one participant called the affair of 'The Book' – makes Evans's smear campaign against Place in 1812–13 look far less exceptional or unrespectable. However, Place also charged Evans with unrespectability because of his association with a new group of radicals during the early Regency years, men like Thistlewood, Watson and Preston who found their way into Spence's circle at this time. Here perhaps Place was on stronger ground – judged less by his retrospective moral criteria than by an older benchmark of respectability still commonly used by Regency artisans: practice of an 'honourable' or high-status occupation based primarily on possession of a skill and membership of a trades' society, coupled with the ability to maintain a position of economic independence. Many of those known to have joined Spence's circle during these years belonged to trades that were not greatly esteemed within the artisan world because of their paucity of skill, cleverness, strength or capital, their lax apprenticeship requirements and their vulnerability to competition from unskilled or sweated workers. Admittedly, during the war years in London most artisan trades suffered from high inflation and taxation, rising food prices, cyclical unemployment, small capitalistic changes in the labour process and, above all, from the competition of cheap labour attracted by the City's enormous mercantile and commercial expansion. But old handicraft trades serving basic needs such as shoemaking, tailoring and weaving were especially hard hit by these changes,[43] and it was from these lower-status trades particularly that Spence recruited his following.

Men like Preston, Wedderburn, Fair, Evans, Allen Davenport and Wild probably also belonged to the less skilled, 'dishonourable', or casualised sectors of their trades. When Preston was accidentally lamed as a boy it was thought natural to transfer him from a silversmithing to a shoemaking apprenticeship. There was a traditional association between such handicaps and the shoemaking trade. (Two later Spencean shoemakers, Samuel Waddington and Warry, were midgets.) For similar sorts of reasons Robert Wedderburn, an illiterate mulatto seaman, apparently had no difficulty becoming a jobbing tailor in London. Such men could practice their trades without completing formal apprenticeships: Preston threw up his shoemaking apprenticeship in Somerstown to go on the tramp for three years all over England and Ireland; Davenport learnt shoemaking from two friends in Aberdeen during his spare-time as a soldier, and was working in low, non-society London shops when he first encountered Spence's writings in 1805; Wedderburn probably acquired the rudiments of tailoring at sea.[44]

Judging from their fractured work patterns and restless quests for alternative employment, these men did not feel adequately fulfilled or remunerated by their artisanal trades. Thomas Evans passed successively from baker to print colourer, bookseller, braces and steel-springs maker, coffee-house keeper and printer. During the 1790s he was also a small-scale rentier who described himself grandiloquently as 'by profession an artist'.[45] Around the same time, Preston threw up work as a shoemaker to take a job as a storekeeper on a merchant vessel bound for St Kitts. Later he returned to shoemaking but with little success: he claimed to have found the heads of the public even more resistant than his leather.[46] His writings, letters and speeches give the impression that he would rather have been an intellectual than an artisan. As Place waspishly put it:

[Preston] was one of those singular characters to whom poverty can hardly be said to be a misfortune, he was proud of his knowledge, little as it was, fond of displaying it, and cared for little beyond food and rags if when by talking nonsense he could attract the attention of two or three men as ignorant as himself.[47]

Wedderburn similarly relinquished his trade to go to sea when conditions became unendurable. Later on he also supplemented the meagre income he earned patching clothes and vending pamphlets by becoming a quasi-professional preacher and debater, and eventually by running a bawdy house. Davenport had intended to run off to sea as a young man but became a soldier instead. He then switched to shoemaking, interrupted by a period as a building overseer and gardener – all this being, in his eyes, less important than his spare-time work as a poet and writer.[48]

Some of the alternative or supplementary income resorts of these artisans were less happy. They found themselves forced on occasion to rely on charity, crime or profligacy, so crossing what Iorwerth Prothero has called 'the crucial material and psychological dividing line' of artisan respectability.[49] We have seen that Evans borrowed money in 1806 for a supposedly criminal purpose; Preston became a notorious scrounger, spending most of the receipts on drink; Wild became a charity pauper; Wedderburn was several times convicted of theft and later of brothel-keeping; and Spencean stone-cutter Thomas Porter was alleged to be a 'notorious thief' and a 'pickpocket'.[50]

Spence attracted a comparable group of marginal, degraded or failed men from middle-class occupations – law-clerks, apothecaries, surgeons, shopkeepers, military officers. Thistlewood, Watson and Preston (in one of his career phases) belong to this category. Thistlewood, an illegitimate son of a wealthy Lincolnshire farmer, was at least partially educated as a surveyor, and achieved the rank of lieutenant in the Yorkshire militia. As a result of successive marriages (his first wife died in childbirth) he became reasonably well-to-do for a time but probably lost most of his money through farming. When he arrived in London around 1810–11, he was married to a prosperous butcher's daughter, Susan Wilkinson, and possessed a young son Julian. He claimed to have attained the rank of captain whilst fighting alongside the French during the revolutionary wars, and to be expecting a substantial legacy. A spy reported to the Home Office that Thistlewood was 'quite the gentleman in manners and appearance', very much in the model of Colonel Despard. He initially also impressed both Hardy and Place. By 1813, however, the former thought him 'a mixture of a rogue and a fool' who was rapidly gambling away his inheritance. Around the same time Place claimed to have learned that the 'Captain' was earning money by the odious practice of *qui tam* or blood-money informing. True or not, Thistlewood soon became notoriously poor and shabby, though he always saw himself as a gentleman.[51]

'Dr' Watson, on the other hand, seems never to have been prosperous. Also originally from Lincolnshire, he left an ailing business as a surgeon in Cheadle, Staffordshire, around 1808 to try his luck in London. There followed a succession of surgeon-apothecary shops: at 5 Newcastle Street, Strand, near Evans; at 6 Catherine Street, in the same vicinity; and in Clarendon Place, Somers Town. All failed. One of his daughters, Eliza, died at Newcastle Street in October 1810, according to him through 'want of nourishment'. Around this time his wife moved away to Lynn taking the four youngest children with her (possibly because her husband beat them); he was left with the oldest boy and girl. According to one testimony Watson was in his early years in London a sober, serious and politically conservative man but could not make a living at his most marginal of professions.[52] Like his fellow surgeons John Thelwall and Gale Jones, Watson's social and economic incongruence apparently led him to radicalism.

Preston was neither as sober nor as serious, but he claimed at one time to have owned three shoemaking shops and to have employed forty people. This brief interlude of prosperity followed his marriage to a widow who probably provided both the capital and the spirit of enterprise (she managed one of the shops). When she fled suddenly with a lover to America leaving Preston with four daughters to support, the business collapsed.[53] Domestic crises seem to have dogged these men – a symptom as well as a cause of their relative unrespectability. Davenport began to experience economic decline after 1816 when his wife, who worked with him in the shoemaking trade, died. Watson, Preston and Thistlewood found the maintenance of their children a terrible 'clog' and burden, and had to farm them out to patients, friends or associates at various times. Perhaps their loss of what Preston called 'the sweets of domestic happiness' increased both the economic marginality of such men and their susceptibility to the attractions of 'blackguard' recreational (and political) pursuits in alehouses, bawdy houses and gaming houses.

Spence's life mirrored the experiences and predicaments of men like these: he stood at the meridian of the overlapping social categories of degraded artisan, failed shopkeeper and marginal professional. His mother had been a stockinger, his father a netmaker. As one of nineteen children, he had also experienced considerable want. According to his earliest biographer, Spence started life in his father's trade, then educated himself sufficiently to become, first, a clerk, then a grammar school teacher. As a young man he was an active participant in the debates, literary discussions and political campaigns of a lively Newcastle intelligentsia of self-taught engravers, book-binders and printers – of whom Thomas Bewick was a notable example. But migration to London brought a sharp decline in Spence's economic circumstances: for the remainder of his life he scraped a precarious living operating from a wooden barrow as a number carrier, book-binder and book, pamphlet and saloop seller. Contemporaries like Place and Hone recalled his ragged, emaciated appearance. Men of Preston's background found it easy to identify with him: 'Poor Spence, like myself, had grappled with bad fortune and like me too, stood the tug of adversity'.[54] This last included an identical domestic set-back when Spence's casually acquired wife ran off to America with 'a paramour'.

The dedication of one of his works to the 'Sons of St Crispin'[55] also suggests that Spence might have made a special effort to appeal to members of this embattled and traditionally militant trade, particularly in the wake of their disastrous London strike of 1812. Allen Davenport was one follower who believed all his life that Spence's father had been a shoe-maker.[56] Spence's 'Dream' of 1811 encapsulated many of the embittering experiences and escapist aspirations of such lowly, often migratory, artisans and failed small producers: 'destitute you fled to Cities and Towns to get employment in Trade and Manufactures. While Trade flourished Master Manufacturers could live comfortably, but Journeymen and Labourers, though they made shift to live, were always from hand to mouth. But now Trade fails what must you do? Those who could barely exist before must now starve?' However, he reminded them, 'Tillage is a trade that never fails'. Under the Spencean parochial rental plan tradesmen would never be swamped by unfair competition: 'For none will be in Trade and Manufactures, but those who can live well by them, because Tillage would then be open to all in the Case of Difficulty.'[57] His plan, he told Charles Hall in 1807, ensured that most men would be 'little farmers and little Mastermen' – few would be required to work as labourers or journeymen.[58]

No one was too poor or unrespectable to be excluded from Spence's utopia: it embraced 'every man, woman or child, whether born in wedlock or not', as well as immigrants, foreigners, blacks and even criminals – 'all those who have no Helpers'. His *Rights of Infants* (1797) depicted a plebeian woman bettering an aristocrat, and *Giant Killer* (1814) contained an admiring account of what today might be called social bandits – actually Chinese republican fraternities recruited from thieves, pirates, rebels and 'the discontented of all classes'.[59] In much of his propaganda, Spence deliberately and successfully sought to use the language and literary forms of the vulgar, poor and semi-literate (including chap-books, ballads, posters and almanacs).[60] Unlike his future chronicler Francis Place, 'Little Tommy Spence' never left the milieu of poor artisans and tradesmen, and never abandoned their idioms, ideas and practices. In opposition to those 'always preaching up temperance, labour, patience and submission', his plan catered for 'feasts of hospitality and love' with access to 'cheering beverage' and 'strong drink'.[61] Burly stonecutter-thief Thomas Porter sang of how he located Spence around 1807:

> ...To the Swan I took my flight,
> Down in the New Street Square, Sir,
> Where every Monday night,
> Friend Tommy Spence comes there, Sir.[62]

And Thomas Evans's tavern ballad of around 1811, sung to the tune of 'The Vicar and Moses', explained why Spence chose to conduct alehouse free-and-easies:

> At the sign of the Fleece,
> For a trifle a piece,
> Spence treats all the swine with a Book,
> But not for vile pelf,
> Tis all wrote by himself,
> To instruct you by Hook or by Crook,
> Tol de rol.
>
> ...Then he's wrote a Dream,
> Tis a partnership scheme,
> And it beats all the rest,
> You'll not think it long,
> It exceeds every Song,
> Oppressors it puts to the test.
>
> ...Here's Tommy so clever,
> We hail thee forever,
> And Bumpers go round in thy Name;
> While man draws his Breath,
> On the terrestial Earth
> May he witness and boast of thy Fame.[63]

On balance, then, Spence's following probably did act as something of a magnet for declining, casualised and degraded elements of the old middling sort during the Regency years. Even so, Place's unrespectability thesis still requires qualifying. In the first place, an inability to attain or maintain a position of respectability through lack of means, skill or luck did not automatically stop some from clinging tenaciously to the respectable ideal. Decline in position and status – even to the extent of outright indigence or criminality – did not necessarily eradicate respectable and self-improving aspirations. Place himself experienced several fluctuations of fortune (and probably of moral resolve) before eventually reaching a plateau of comfort and respectability. At the other extreme, Arthur Thistlewood continued to display a mixture of blackguard and genteel aspirations at the trough of his degradation in June 1818. Writing from Horsham gaol – where he had been ignominiously confined for his presumption in challenging Lord Sidmouth to a duel – he urged his son to give up the unsuitable company of a former family friend and radical associate, John Hunt.

...ask him if he has the impudence to call again whether if you should go with him if he can teach you to steal so as not to be found out for he was such a clumsy hand when ... [unintelligible] he did it in such a bungling manner that if he had not got of pritty quick he would have most likely been hanged or transported, tell him whatever you learn you are determined if possible to be taught by a man that understands his business.

He took the opportunity also to prescribe the boy a genuine, if rather pitiful, course of self-improvement:

I hope you will always speak French to Mr Faggs. You must when you go to the Kings Bench again get the address of Mr Askam junior, he lives I think in Sergants Inn Chancery Lane. You must correspond with him once or twice in the week, you must also go to Mr Lawsons and learn to play the flute. I would have you also begin and read through Gibbons Roman History ... Your mother tells me you are a good boy.[64]

Paradoxically, marginality might also in some instances have acted as an inducement to the pursuit of intellectuality or self-improvement. Jacques Rancière has recently drawn on French artisan evidence of the 1830s to argue that workers from what were seen as 'contemptible' trades such as shoemaking and tailoring frequently manifested disgust at the poor and demeaning nature of their trades by involving themselves in literary and intellectual activities, and by embracing humanistic social movements. The occupational and intellectual freedom (*disponibilité*) characteristic of shoemakers' and tailors' work-experience led them, he argues, not so much towards organisations designed to protect elite craft numbers and skills, but to utopian groups like the St Simonians, Fourierists and Icarians, which recognised them as men and intellectuals.[65] The trajectory of Place's own career in some ways resembles that of Rancière's alienated artisans and worker intellectuals. Like them, he was not above occasionally glorifying artisanal life once he had left it, though on the whole his autobiography gives off a strong sense of disgust at the monotonous, insecure and backbreaking lot of a journeyman leather-breeches-maker. Joining the LCS transfigured his life: it gave him new ideals, recognition and status, and a chance to develop an alternative and fulfilling career as an organiser and thinker. Entrepreneurial skill, capital and a measure of luck enabled him subsequently to retire at the age of forty-six and to devote the remainder of his life to organisational, literary and intellectual pursuits of a philosophical radical type. He differed from men like Evans, Preston, Wedderburn and Davenport less in his motivation than in the completeness of his escape.

Evans and his associates might have lacked the financial, educational and perhaps psychological resources to make Place's transition, but Spenceanism offered them comparable consolations. For the marginal artisan, shopkeeper or professional who felt himself slipping into degradation, pauperism or criminality, Spence's plan promised a chance to regain cherished ideals of independent self-sufficiency and a respectable living standard. Under Spence's scheme – Allen Davenport later wrote – the labouring classes 'would not then have the gloomy prospect of bringing up their children to be thieves and prostitutes'. Evans likewise believed that the actions of landlords and corrupt rulers forced many labourers into crime, from which Spence's plan would rescue them. Even Place could not have quibbled with the benefits which Davenport hoped Spenceanism would bring to pauperised and degraded tradesmen: '[they] would be able now and then to be hospitable to one another and to entertain a friend, to relax a little from the incessant toil, to appear clean and decent in their apparel and comfortable in their habitations; to educate their children; in a word, to be respectable and happy citizens'.[66]

Thomas Spence united in his person, organisation and programme the contradictory impulses and aspirations of this marginal middling sort during the early Regency years. He was a man so personally ragged, socially unexclusive, ideologically revolutionary and culturally plebeian that he attracted the insecure and declining, the casualised, pauperised and criminalised; yet he was also a man with claims to being an educator, scholar, linguist and prophet, and whose organisation offered its members an outlet to sing, debate, write and preach, and to elevate themselves as intellectuals and men. When he died in September 1814, it was natural that he should be succeeded by a man possessed of similarly diverse and ambiguous credentials. In the years 1796–1814 Thomas Evans showed himself to be a marginal, restless artisan, an incorrigible revolutionary, a tavern *bon vivant* and balladeer, a radical blackmailer and smut-pedlar; yet at the same time, an ambitious, conscientious father, an aspiring self-improver, a moderate Westminster activist, a *philosophe-manqué* and – as we shall see in the succeeding chapter – a fervent millenarian.

3

Millenarian Spenceans: Robert Wedderburn and Methodist prophecy

For Robert Wedderburn Methodism was a stepping stone to political unrespectability and extremism. However odd this may sound to some modern historians,[1] the idea would have occasioned little surprise in the early nineteenth century. Many Englishmen and women, including the ex-Jacobin commentators Reid and Place, believed that religious and political fanaticism were integrally connected and that Methodism usually lay at bottom of both. Reid's further claim that Methodism was in league with radical freethought during the 1790s seems even less likely, particularly when we remember that he was inspired by Abbé Barruel's theory that the French Revolution had been the product of a conspiracy between philosophes and mystics. English Methodism seems an unlikely counterpart of occult freemason lodges or cadres of fanatical illuminists. Historians have been more inclined to see Methodism as a conservative, or at least socially stabilising, influence in modern British history.[2] This might have been true of regular adherents of the Methodist faith (in its varying forms) but much less is known about the cosmology of transient Methodists – those for whom the religion served as a port-of-call rather than a final resting-place. Robert Wedderburn was one of these.

Wedderburn became an ardent follower of Spence in 1813 and later one of Evans's fierier colleagues, but his graduation to the Society raises some puzzles. In the first place, his oscillation between religious revivalism and radical politics was the reverse of E.P. Thompson's famous model.[3] Wedderburn became a fervent (and seemingly apolitical) Methodist during the militant 1790s, then joined the Spencean revolutionary underground twenty years later at a time of supposed radical hiatus and defeat. Furthermore, he joined the Spenceans as both a licensed dissenting minister of enthusiastic disposition and a ferocious infidel who quickly earned the nickname of 'the Devil's Engineer'. All this would seem less strange had Wedderburn been an exception, but he was not. Though in some ways a flamboyant and eccentric figure, his religious and political evolution resembled that of many Spenceans – and of other English working-class radicals as well.

Methodist prophet

Robert Wedderburn probably gained his nickname 'the Devil's Engineer' in mock recognition of his apprenticeship with a religious organisation said to comprise 'Babel's workmen'. Sidmouth used this kind of epithet when introducing a parliamentary bill in 1811 designed to check the spread of Methodist preachers. Sidmouth's real case against Methodism was summed up by one of his more forthright correspondents in the simple equation: 'to be a Methodist is to be a Jacobin in the extreme'.[4] It is not our usual image of Wesley's sober evangelists, yet a surprising number of Englishmen shared Sidmouth's belief that Methodism had inherited the mantle of Puritan sectarianism[5] and political disaffection.[6]

Reid was typical in arguing that both Methodists and 'Oliver's Preachers' were recruited from 'the lowest and most illiterate classes of society' such as apprentices, mechanics and labourers. He cited examples from the 1790s of a bird-catcher, sheeps-head seller and coal-heaver who had become Methodist preachers. Sidmouth, in a memorably nasty phrase, claimed their ministry to be open to 'any person however depraved or illiterate, whether descending from a pillory or a chimney'.[7] Behind the snobbery and condescension lay a fear that once people from such backgrounds had thrown off traditional controls and authorities they would become susceptible to 'the most dangerous doctrines'. A key clause of Sidmouth's bill restricted applicants for a dissenting minister's licence to those defined as 'respectable householders'.[8]

Robert Wedderburn was exactly the sort of 'vulgar' and disaffected person that the bill aimed to exclude. His social and religious outlook had been shaped by the tensions, ambiguities and hardships of a childhood lived on the margin of the slave and free worlds in the British West Indies of the mid-eighteenth century. His father was James Wedderburn, a Kingston doctor, male mid-wife and sugar plantation owner – a scion of the same planter family that became legally notorious in 1788 when attempting to enforce slave status on a runaway black in Scotland. Robert's mother, an African-born house slave named Rosanna, was sold by his father when she was five months pregnant. Her child thus enjoyed none of the advantages of his mulatto half-brothers who were educated as tradesmen and accepted as inferior members of the Wedderburn family. Rosanna's 'rebellious and violent temper' earned her at least one subsequent flogging from another owner, as well as a series of resales that forced a permanent separation from her son when he was still an infant.[9] The rejection by his slaver father and loss of his slave mother seems to have scarred Wedderburn for life – he returned to the subject incessantly in later years. In addition to costing him love, security and comfort, it sym-

Robert Wedderburn

Son of the late James Wedderburn Esq. *of Inveresk.*

6 *Robert Wedderburn.*

bolised his unwanted position as a free mulatto stranded between the societies of the dominant European planter and enslaved black.

Wedderburn's boyhood might have been more dislocated and deprived than that of some slave children. Although baptised into the Church of England and given a rudimentary schooling in the scriptures, his formal education ended at around the age of five when his mother's one humane owner died and Rosanna was resold. Near-illiteracy was to hamper him for life. His aunt and uncle had been transported against their will to the United States so the boy was adopted by his maternal grandmother, 'Talkee Amy', a noted Kingston magic woman and a petty agent for merchant smugglers. She was to influence the patterns of his later life in important ways. He learned how to survive on his wits without regard to the law. Amy's famous loquacity probably contributed to his later talent for popular oratory. And she undoubtedly inspired his lifelong fascination with magic and the supernatural. He also discovered that even a slave as elderly and independent as Amy could not escape the capriciousness and brutality of European slave owners. As a boy of eleven he saw her flogged for alleged witchcraft on the orders of a young master whom she had helped to rear. Such actions were a reminder, if any was needed, of how tenuous was his own hold on liberty in such a community. Like many free coloureds in late eighteenth-century Jamaica he came to believe that his legal status might be revoked at any time, and that slave owners could flout the laws with impunity.[10]

The Royal Navy's insatiable demand for able-bodied hands provided an escape-route for many blacks and mulattos from the port of Kingston; young Robert Wedderburn joined up at around the age of sixteen. The chronology of his subsequent career in the navy is unclear. He served an initial period aboard H.M.S. *Polyphemus* during which he saw action as a main gunner against the French and Spanish fleets.[11] Later in life, perhaps during the depressed mid-1790s, he seems to have re-enlisted as a top-station hand aboard a privateer – possibly he was press-ganged like his future radical associate 'Black' Davidson. Wedderburn hinted vaguely at having been present at the Nore Mutiny of 1797, but was not mentioned in any of the subsequent inquiries. Nor is there any evidence that he was influenced by Jacobin or United Irish sentiments at this time, although he later voiced the typical complaints of mutineers at the vindictiveness and brutality of naval discipline.[12] Intriguingly, a lone black is depicted amongst the otherwise Irish ringleaders in a contemporary print of the mutiny by Isaac Cruikshank.[13] At the very least 'the floating republic' of 1797 might have weakened the traditional deference of sailors like Wedderburn.

The disillusionment of servicemen after leaving the army or navy was also conducive to social discontent. Home Office files bulge with poignant and angry letters from former servicemen – both officers and other ranks – who were owed backpay, prize-money or pensions, or were disabled and helpless, or simply unable to find work after being summarily demobbed at the end of hostilities. Goaded by anger at the ingratitude of King and Country, such men were frequently attracted to popular religious or political movements which promised to restore their rightful dues. Schooling in the techniques and mores of violence and command often influenced the forms of their protest. Ex-servicemen were conspicuous in every insurrection plot in London from 1798 to 1820, as well as in most popular prophetic movements and assassination attempts by 'enthusiasts' over the same period. The West Indian mulatto or the lascar sailor featured disproportionately in protests of this kind because the experience of being demobbed bore especially heavily on him. He was, as William Davidson is supposed to have said moments before his execution in 1820, 'A stranger in a strange land', and a land that was often racially hostile as well.[14] Towards the end of the Napoleonic wars the Home Office was treated to a growing chorus of complaints about the lawless conduct of discharged blacks and lascars as they struggled to survive in their new and alien environment. One of the more sympathetic correspondents, Lieutenant-General Porter, feared that most were ending up in the 'mad-house, poor-house or Bridewell'.[15] In the years following Wedderburn's initial arrival on English soil in 1778, aged seventeen, he was to have more than a taste of the last two institutions.

Like many discharged sailors he drifted to the rookeries around St Giles where a substantial community of his countrymen, including runaway slaves, congregated alongside other immigrant minorities, Jews, lascars and Irish. Here, he likely became part of a subculture of London 'blackbirds', as they were known, who eked out a living by their wit, strength, agility and cunning – as musicians, entertainers, beggars, thieves and labourers.[16] Wedderburn later made a typical convert's claim of having associated for a lengthy period with 'an abandoned set of reprobates'. In his case this was no exaggeration. There is evidence of at least one spell in Coldbath Fields prison, as well as a near miss on a charge of theft as late as 1813.[17] He was also a witness, at least, to the Gordon riots of 1780, and claimed later to have been friendly with one of the arrested ringleaders. He might have been one of the several blacks known to have participated.[18] He was probably lucky to escape the fate of numbers of West Indian 'criminals' who were transported from London to Van Diemen's Land or Botany Bay at the turn of the century.[19]

Wedderburn was happier than many of his exiled countrymen, however, in having acquired a reasonably skilled trade. When and how he became a journeyman tailor is uncertain. He might have begun an apprenticeship in Jamaica, perhaps on the plantation of his mother's sometime owners, the Campbells, with whom he maintained an affectionate contact. Perhaps he picked up the rudiments of the trade at sea or in London itself. His claim to the title of 'flint' tailor probably indicates that he gained registration in the book of trades. He was also to display many of the typical values of a late eighteenth-century honourable artisan, including pride in his craft and status, belief in his right to economic independence and social respect, and contempt for semi-skilled 'dung' tailors who accepted sweated wages and conditions.[20]

Competition from the last contributed to Wedderburn's degradation in the early years of the nineteenth century. He became one of a considerable body of London artisans forced to supplement their incomes by unrespectable means. Distress prompted him to make several attempts to beg from his father's family who had returned to Britain. They refused him help even when he was unemployed with his wife pregnant and the quartern loaf at 1s 2½d. His involvement in petty theft during these years probably reflects the same pressures. Like other artisans at this time, he might also have suffered from the redefinition of traditional trade perquisites as crimes: an unsuccessful action against him in 1817 for stealing from a government-contracted master tailor could fit this category. By 1818 he was described in an intelligence report as 'a jobbing Taylor sitting in a kind of bulk near St Matthews Church where he patches clothes and vends cheap seditious publications'. Shortage of work from master tailors was forcing him to advertise that he would meet orders 'however small and trifling' at moderate prices.[21]

Wedderburn was primed for the levelling and restorative promises of popular radicalism, but an evangelical religious conversion provided the combustion. One day in 1786 he stopped at the rear of a crowd at Seven Dials in the heart of underworld London to hear a Wesleyan preacher 'pledge his own soul that every man conscious of the enormity of his sin, and willing to turn from the evil of his ways, and accept the Mercy offered in the Gospel, the Lord would abundantly pardon'.[22] He claimed to have been instantly converted. Modern social historians still puzzle as to why so many of England's common people were susceptible to a religion 'on the face of it so variously unattractive'.[23] In Wedderburn's case all we can do is suggest some possible predispositions to such a conversion.

To begin with there was Methodism's close identification with anti-slavery. John Wesley, Tory in so many of his social and political ideals, was nevertheless a fierce and persistent critic of slavery. And if, as has been argued, the main theological ingredients of evangelical Methodism predisposed adherents to convert to the anti-slavery cause, perhaps the process could also work in reverse? Wedderburn's first publication as a Methodist certainly displayed all the claimed theological elements – Arminianism, redemption, sanctification and some form of millennialism.[24]

More plausibly, he might have gained an early sympathy for Methodism in Jamaica, particularly as practised by more outspoken free mulatto preachers. He hinted at something of the sort in 1817: 'God bless the Methodists, they teach us [West Indian slaves] to read the Bible, and there it is written, that the slave who did not accept his liberty at the end of the seven year jubilee, must have his ears cut off, because he loved his master and mistress and despised the law of liberty.'[25]

Wedderburn claimed that his grandmother's magical practices, as well as an early exposure to Christianity, had made him 'prone' to religious feelings as a boy, though these had then lapsed until 1786. His later speeches and writings display a more than vestigial belief in sorcery and magic. He recalled, for example, having witnessed 'a judgement of God' when a woman's baby died soon after she had caused his grandmother to be flogged for witchcraft. The distraught mother made a public atonement in the market place and appointed Amy to preside over the burial rituals. This sort of experience, Wedderburn later admitted, explained his fascination with the Witch of Endor and Balaam's Ass episodes in the scriptures, and no doubt also, his belief in the power of curses and providential interventions.[26] Recent studies suggest that Methodism was frequently compatible with, and might have encouraged, popular magical beliefs (which were anyway still widespread in English plebeian culture).[27] It is possible too that Wedderburn – and Davidson, who also became a Methodist preacher for a time – found in vital Methodism echoes of the syncretic pagan-Christian beliefs so prevalent amongst West Indian blacks.[28]

Wedderburn's emphasis on prophecy and dreams, talismanic attitude to the scriptures and love of communal hymn singing were typically West Indian but they also had their counterpart in English Methodism. It was a religious movement which echoed traditional folk preoccupations at many levels: in its 'segregation by sex and age within a binding sense of congregation'; its acceptance of key aspects of folk superstition and credulity; its deployment of a theological imagery steeped in references to blood, death, fertility, rebirth and transformation; and its stress on the instructive and inspirational role of song.[29]

There is no doubting the widespread popularity and affective power of Methodist hymnody. The Wesley brothers possessed exceptional lyric talents; they also worked on well-fertilised ground. Methodist hymnody appealed to Allen Davenport because song had been the key-stone of his education. As a child in the village of Ewen he taught himself to read by memorising songs and matching them with the printed words. He also used a song as the model for his first written composition (later a Methodist sermon served a similar purpose).[30] Wedderburn's first publication, a small theological tract called *Truth Self-Supported*, was full of references from Methodist hymnody. It concluded with half-a-dozen anonymous ex-

cerpts of 'hymns of some of the most Reverend Divines' which Wedderburn left 'to the Reader's own conscience, to refer to their proper places in
the foregoing Discourse'.[31]

Both the hymns and the particular excerpts which he selected are instructive. Of the three hymns I have been able to identify, two were
written by the Calvinist Independent Isaac Watts and one by John Wesley.
All harp luridly and repetitively on the torments of the guilty sinner and
the joyful relief offered by grace. Consciously or not, Wedderburn even
substituted the word 'guilt' for 'sin' in his transcription of the fourth verse
of Wesley's hymn 340:

> Dust and Ashes
> Though we be
> Full of sin and misery
> Thine we are thou son of God
> Take the purchase of thy Blood [32]

Guilt and release were, of course, standard levers of evangelical Methodist
conversion. They feature commonly in spiritual autobiographies. Nevertheless, it is possible that Wedderburn's experiences of parental rejection,
racial and social stigmatism and criminality, when combined with an
intense early religiosity, led to unusually strong feelings of guilt and self-
disgust. He described how 'Conscience frequently smiteing him, and telling him, that the way he pursued was the road to everlasting ruin, to lull
and calm these reflections he frequently promised to reform but sin being
such a constant companion and so sweet to his taste, his efforts were all in
vain.'[33] However he claimed that the Wesleyan preacher at Seven Dials
induced a deep conviction of sinfulness followed by a sense of release and
elation at receiving the proffered gift of grace.

Hostile commentators like W.H. Reid believed that the process of Methodist conversion entailed a dangerous moral and psychological unhing-
ing. Reid distrusted the surge of theological and social self-confidence – or
'nauseating egotism' – and the hunger to proselytise which usually accompanied a new-found sense of salvation. Like 'Oliver's Preachers', converts were also prone to violent ideological instability:

neither qualified by education for the office of teachers, nor bound by the declaration of any fixed principles, nor restrained by any sense of decency or shame, and
so various their absurdities, that they seem to have no point of union except a
determination to calumniate the established Clergy, which design they execute
with unrelenting violence and malice.[34]

Wedderburn's theological tract, *Truth Self-Supported*, which appeared only
a few years after Reid penned this accusation, seemed to offer copy-book
confirmation. The tract opened with a title page quotation which evoked

the spiritual levelling of Gerrard Winstanley and other plebeian sectaries of old. It was from I Corinthians 1.27–8: 'God hath chosen the foolish things of the world to confound the wise; and God hath chosen the weak things of the world, to confound the things that are mighty, and base things of the world and things which are despised hath God chosen.' Wedderburn apologised to the reader for the tract being a 'rough diamond' in presentation and expression. Having attained a state of 'manhood in religion' and become wiser than his teachers, he felt bound to instruct.[35]

Much of what followed was – as a cryptic note in the margin of the British Library copy warned – 'unintelligible to common understandings'. By the time he wrote, Wedderburn's mind had been 'staggered' by the conflicting theological currents of Arminianism, Calvinism and Unitarianism. The pamphlet represented a crude but sincere attempt to steer an independent course between their various doctrinal snags and shoals. Modern readers must strain to find anything seditious in a work so devoid of political allusion and so informed by evangelical piety. Nevertheless it is a mistake to dismiss Methodist theology as so much irrelevant 'Custard Piety'.[36] Wedderburn's early theological speculations contain the seeds of his later growth into a Spencean prophet and ultra-radical.

What critics feared most about his sort of plebeian Methodism was its tendency to nurture socially disruptive beliefs. Among these was the Antinomianism which had erupted spectacularly amongst the sectaries of the Commonwealth. Reid implied something similar when accusing some Methodist preachers in the 1790s of behaving with 'disgusting licentiousness' and with practising religious forms 'utterly inconsistent … with morality and decency'.[37] Antinomianism tends to be associated with an extreme and irrational heretic fringe, but as doctrine it was more pervasive than many eighteenth-century religious leaders found comfortable.[38] We can imagine how the exultation of a new-found sense of grace and freedom from sin, combined with belief in God's immanence, could spill over into a conviction of personal exemption from the moral law. The biblical passage I John 3.9 pointed in the same direction: 'whosoever is born of God doth not commit sin for his seed remaineth in him: and he cannot sin because he is born of God'. During Methodism's early years Wesley had been troubled by the inclination of several of his preachers to give it an Antinomian application.[39]

Wesley himself associated Antinomianism in both its speculative and practical forms with extreme predestinarian beliefs on election and an associated rejection of good works. This had been the usual source in the seventeenth century. But his own Arminian brand of Methodism – the agent of Wedderburn's conversion – was in practice equally susceptible. Wesleyan evangelicals depended as much as their Calvinist counterparts on the emotional impact of grace as an initial detonator of conversion.[40] Once triggered, such enthusiasm could not always be contained, especially when the essence of Arminianism was the theoretical availability of grace to all – including lowly and alienated men like Wedderburn. As he put it: 'Repentence is the privilege of every man without exception ... the invitation to embrace the Gospels is also the privilege of every man for the Gospel is to be preached to every creature.'[41] The Wesleyan doctrines of Christian perfection and assurance, though carefully qualified by Wesley himself, held out the theoretical possibility of attaining sinlessness on earth, and could in the hands of plebeian preachers be interpreted in Antinomian ways.

One particularly creative Methodist preacher of this kind was an orphaned ex-ornament maker, John Church, who was known to Wedderburn and later ultra-radicals. Church was accused in 1813 of preaching the Antinomian libertinism of Commonwealth days in his Obelisk Chapel at St George's Fields, and of putting his theology into practice by seducing young men and performing mock-marriage ceremonies amongst the transvestites at the Vere Street homosexual brothel. One of his sermons of 1811 expounded the rather unfortunately termed doctrine of spiritual 'enlargements'. These came to him in sermons, bringing him a sense of 'happy release' and 'freedom from sin'.[42] He was imprisoned in 1817, though it is not clear whether for 'gammoning' or 'unnatural practices'.

Though Wedderburn was in later years to open a brothel of his own, there is no evidence that he did so under Antinomian sanction. Nevertheless he was familiar with the Antinomian religious position and could in his Methodist years have advanced there from either an Arminian or a Calvinist direction. *Truth Self-Supported* cannot be called Antinomian but there is at least one point where it put forward a doctrine tending in that direction. Wedderburn stated that from the time of his conversion he had felt

confident that God had sealed him unto the day of redemption, not only sealed, but removed him by his power from a legal state of mind, into a state of Gospel liberty, that is to say, a deliverance from the power or authority of the law, considering himself not to be under the power of the law, but under Grace.[43]

There are no signs in Wedderburn's later speeches, sermons and writings that he developed the possible implications of this statement, but it may indicate a general sympathy for the Antinomian position. If so, this would help explain why his conversion did not produce the usual transformation of moral outlook and behaviour. His conviction of sin does not seem to have been any less intense than that of other Methodists, nor his subsequent religious commitment any less sincere. He became obsessed with theology for the remainder of his life and took out a dissenting preacher's licence as soon as he was able. At the same time he apparently

made little or no attempt to become morally respectable like the Methodists of E.P. Thompson's account. In the decades after this conversion he
was to drink, steal, blaspheme, brawl, work for a pornographic publisher
and open a bawdy house. Perhaps it was his conviction of being under the
power of grace which made all this possible.

Methodism was also vulnerable to theological slippage in a different
direction, Wesleyan Arminianism 'with its liberal individualism, its view
of free contract and of natural rights' has been represented as a theological
equivalent of enlightenment theory.[44] This kind of theological liberalism was
also reflected in Wesley's strong commitment to religious toleration and
freedom for slaves, both causes dear to the heart of Robert Wedderburn.
Wesley's one-time supporter turned critic, the Calvinist A.M. Toplady,
feared Arminianism as a 'Trojan Horse' that would introduce adherents to
the temptations of religious rationalism, leading to Socianism, Unitarianism and eventually to deism. Wedderburn's case substantiates the claim.
Some time in the late 1790s he visited the Methodist stronghold of Bristol
to hear an anti-Trinitarian sermon preached. Intrigued rather than ap-
palled, he then attended a nearby Socinian Unitarian chapel and was
persuaded by their rationalist critique of the Trinity. *Truth Self-Supported*,
though orthodoxly Methodist in many of its doctrines, rejected the Trinity
as an 'error' and at one point presented a concomitantly Arian interpretation of Christ.[45] Interestingly, Reid claimed this last heresy to be a potent
doctrinal auxiliary of infidelity during the 1790s.

In Reid's eyes Methodism had only one by-product more dangerous –
the tendency of converts to take up millenarian prophecy. Here again
Wedderburn's tract was symptomatic in its menacing hint that 'there is a
day coming when his [Jesus Christ's] friends and enemies will know – the
one with pleasure, the other by woeful experience that he is possessed of
power'.[46] Another sign of prophetic inclinations was revealed in Wedderburn's conviction that he had been called by God to preach with 'boldness'
and to 'not fear the face of any man'. This included exposing the errors of
all other clergy, whom Wedderburn believed to lack the independence and
courage to speak the truth.[47]

Many contemporaries believed that would-be prophets of this kind provided a bridge between enthusiastic religion and political Jacobinism,
bringing to the latter an enhanced and potent popular appeal. Reid was
typical in asserting that self-styled prophets had greatly helped the spread
of freethought during the 1790s by undermining established religion and
representing infidels as agents of Providence. Unprecedented domestic and
foreign turmoil during the decade, especially the seemingly Providential
collapse of Catholic king and pope in Europe, had produced a spate of
prophetic speculation. By 1795 plebeian social prophecies had become so
numerous and subversive that the government, in Reid's words, 'pru-

dently transferred the prince of prophets [Richard Brothers] to a mad-house'.[48] Even though millennialist language and modes of thought were widely employed by eighteenth-century scholars, eschatological utterances had a way of becoming socially and politically seditious in the mouths of poor and alienated men like Brothers.[49] Millenarianism was, in the words of its most distinguished modern historian, 'an ideology of change. It focussed attention on the great changes which were taking place in these days and promised a vast transformation of the social order when all things would be made new.'[50] Men and women like Brothers and Joanna Southcott evoked memories of the radical prophets of the seventeenth century and of the Anabaptists before that. In the case of Brothers the government had evidence of explicit connections with the democratic movement. John Binns was only one of many Jacobins to be awed by the prophet's 'scriptural style', 'imposing manner' and terrifying predictions. He visited Brothers on several occasions and spent hours discussing his ideas (one of Binns's friends later did the same with Joanna Southcott).[51] But even in the absence of direct influence from radicals, the predictions and doctrines of such prophets threatened to turn the world upside down in a similar way to political revolutionaries.

Prophets were feared both as magnets for the disaffected and as solitary 'madmen' prone to violent actions through manipulation by treasonous elements or through their own delusions. This was not simply ruling-class paranoia: in the same year that Reid published his warnings a self-styled prophet named James Hadfield attempted to assassinate the King at a Drury Lane theatre. The government assembled evidence showing that the attempt had been at least partly instigated by another 'madman' prophet called Bannister Truelock. Intelligence – from Reid himself, amongst others – revealed that Hadfield and Truelock had frequented well-known radical public houses such as the Green Dragon in Fore Street, the Ben Jonson's Head in Red Lion Street and the Baptist's Head in St Johns Lane. Interestingly, the first two were also regular haunts of Evans and the United Englishmen. Doctors concluded that Hadfield's chronic mental instability had tipped into insanity when he received no reward after being wounded for his country (this was an almost identical background to John Bellingham, the man who later assassinated Perceval). Under Truelock's influence Hadfield had come to believe that he was next in rank to Christ and would bring peace to the world by killing the King.

The government regarded Truelock, however, as a devious character whose divine madness was feigned. His background as a sacked exciseman, longtime associate of radicals and a field preacher bore all the markings of a seditious prophet. Even his own brother thought him 'too much of a Methodist'. Other associates testified how they had often heard him prophesy that the 'little Bishop' (Jesus Christ) was soon to return to earth to take away the power of the King and invest it in himself, at which time what had cost a guinea would become a shilling.[52] The following year a further attempt was made on the King's life by another enthusiast and former LCS member named Urban Metcalfe.[53] And when in May 1812 the Prince Regent received a barrage of anonymous letters couched in chiliastic language and threatening to imitate Bellingham's assassination of Perceval, the Home Office feared a connection with the simultaneous revival of plebeian radicalism in the metropolis.[54]

Whether the millenarian hints in *Truth Self-Supported* arose out of the common currency of prophetic language, or whether Wedderburn had actually been influenced by someone like Brothers, it is hard to know. By the time he published the tract he admitted to having graduated through a number of religious teachers, some of whom might have been prophets. Brothers and Wedderburn were near-neighbours in Soho in the early 1790s, as well as being ex-naval veterans and passionate haters of slavery. Wedderburn was later to praise Brothers as 'a noted prophet of modern times ... under sincere impressions, derived ... by pondering the Scriptures', and to point out that he had only been locked away as a madman after 'he began to launch out against the government'.[55] Interestingly, also, the publisher of *Truth Self-Supported* was one George Riebau, a former Jacobin and disciple of Brothers, who issued the prophet's works under the proud title of 'Bookseller to the Prince of Hebrews'.[56]

Still, neither Wedderburn nor his future colleague, Thomas Evans, needed to have made direct contact with someone like Brothers to have become imbued with a prophetic outlook by the early 1800s. Reid's account of the 'raving' visionaries and fanatics of the 1790s was undoubtedly exaggerated; nevertheless, Methodism was inclined to nurture eschatological hopes and ideas in its early, less stable days.[57] It often also served as a ferry to independent prophetic movements. Joanna Southcott fell under the spell of Methodism in the same year as Wedderburn. Her one-time disciple, John 'Zion' Ward, also passed gradually from Methodism to infidel-radical prophecy, in a career that resembled Wedderburn's to a remarkable degree. He too immigrated to England from a foreign country (Ireland); fell into 'profligate' and criminal company; moved to London and joined a declining artisan trade (shoemaking); joined the navy and served on a man o'war; became converted to Methodism and moved restlessly through a variety of sects before becoming acquainted with Southcottianism around 1814.[58]

Behind such bald facts often lay histories of bitter hardship and social disaffection. 'To my unfortunate origins I owe all my subsequent miseries', wrote Wedderburn at the start of his brief autobiography. By early in the new century he had become one of those enthusiasts who, in Reid's words, 'naturally detest every establishment'.[59] 'Thus have I been treated by men ... at a time when I could not support my children. Yes, Sir, I have suffered hunger to that degree that you will find mentioned in Isaiah, vii, 21.'[60] Modern readers may find *Truth Self-Supported* muddled, eccentric and innocuous, but to many of Wedderburn's contemporaries it signified something very different. They would have seen it, not as a harmless quasi-Methodist tract, but as the first halting steps of a radical millenarian prophet.

Thomas Spence and millenarian-radical culture

Around 1813–14, when Zion Ward was becoming a disciple of the prophetess, Joanna Southcott, Wedderburn joined Thomas Spence's circle. For a religious enthusiast and putative prophet, Ward's choice would seem more logical. Having shown no prior interest in politics, Wedderburn had attached himself to a radical land reformer whose following contained numbers of republican revolutionaries. The decision is less surprising, however, when we consider Spence's affinities with millenarian prophets like Brothers and Southcott.

Spence shared the typical millenarian's familiarity with the ideological and institutional heritage of Puritan sectarianism. Through his Scottish netmaker father he acquired a pabulum of intense and inquiring biblicism. He might also have learned of the simple fundamentalist communitarianism of the Glassite sect through his brother, Jeremiah, who was a member. And an early mentor, Rev. James Murray – whose family had once been persecuted as covenanters – endowed Spence with a sympathy for the values of radical Presbyterianism.[61] Some of Spence's writings and songs also show traces of the older folk-magic tradition that usually touched the lives of prophets at some point. A legacy of omens, auguries, lore, dreams, riddling rhymes, ancient prophecies and divinations – often mingled with popular Puritan sentiments – persisted into the late eighteenth century through oral transmission and resilient almanack–chap-book genres. The engraver, Bewick, a friend of Spence, showed in his *Memoir* that the countryside around Newcastle was rich in this folk tradition.[62]

When as a young man Spence sought to explain the 'piercing grievance' of his family's poverty and hardship,[63] he naturally drew on this matrix of popular Puritanism and biblicism. His most recent biographer believes, however, that it was the disorienting experience of moving to London and becoming an impoverished number carrier, combined with an exposure to millenarian currents there, that pushed Spence into adopting an eschatological language and vision.[64] Either way, he became convinced that 'God was a very notorious Leveller', and that it was possible for humble men to turn the world upside down.[65] From Genesis and the Psalms came the notion that the earth belonged to all men; and from

Isaiah, the last three chapters of Revelations and, above all, Leviticus 25 came the vision of an impending communitarian 'Jubilee' – represented in Spencean verse as:

> Hark how the Trumpets Sound,
> Proclaims the Land around,
>   The Jubilee;
> Tells all the Poor oppressed
> No more shall they be cess'd,
> Nor landlords more molest,
>   Their Property.[66]

Spence has often been called a crank; but the idea of a millenarian Jubilee based on the model of Moses was not as outlandish in late eighteenth-century England as we are sometimes led to believe. The urbane and rationalist *Universalist's Miscellany*, edited by breakaway Unitarian, William Vidler, devoted a good deal of space in 1797–8 and 1801 to outlining a very Spencean vision of 'the Millenial age' which was to commence when 'the trumpet of jubilee be sounded'.[67] Spence's notion that man's fall from grace was a consequence of a greedy few appropriating private property from God's common storehouse had been anticipated in the seventeenth century by radical sectarians like Winstanley. Even the furore over the enclosure of Newcastle Town Moor which inspired the non-scriptural components of Spence's utopian blueprint was redolent of Digger agitations.

The millennial promise gave Spence a potent means of achieving his desired social and political transformation. His own envisaged role within the process differed little in substance from that of many other plebeian prophets. He saw himself in the model of Moses as a 'law-giver' and 'teacher' who had come to proclaim the news of a new land of Canaan. Like Moses, too, he had to struggle against false prophets and enemies of the true system.[68] His autobiographical ballad, 'The propagation of Spensonianism – written in Shrewsbury gaol in the year 1801', described how:

> One night as slumbering I lay on my bed,
> A notable vision came into my head.
> Methought I saw Numbers going forth to preach,
> And justice and peace among Mankind to teach,
> Saying Men mind your interest if you've Common Sense,
> And Hearken to Reason and Friend, Thomas Spence.
> ...I beheld till these Preachers were well understood
> When the People in all Places arose like a Flood.
> All ancient Oppressions were then swept away.[69]

He believed that hostility to his ideas necessitated gathering a group of believers in the form of 'a sect' who would help him in 'spreading the gospel' of the coming land of Canaan by meeting, singing, field preaching, debating, writing, chalking and all other available means – for it was written in the scriptures 'they that understand among the People shall instruct the many'.[70]

When this preparation had reached its full fruition the millennium would arrive; violence if needed at all would be confined to a defensive or concluding role. Technically, as a recent scholar has pointed out, Spence's eschatology belonged in the mould of scholarly post-millennialists who envisaged the millennium as arriving gradually through human action, but his 'tone and temper' was that of more apocalyptic pre-millennialists who believed that Christ's advent would precipitate an abrupt transformation.[71]

Then shall the whole earth, as Isaiah saith, be at rest and quiet; and shall break forth into singing; and they shall say 'Now we are free indeed. Our lands which God gave us to dwell are now our own. Our governments, now free from aristocracy, are easily supported with a small proportion and the remainder being our own, we can spend on parochial business and divide amongst ourselves.'[72]

Tommy Spence was also – as we have seen – a child of the Enlightenment. To some historians this is a puzzling anomaly. Because of the rationalist strands in his writings and his specific reference on one occasion to the millennium as 'figuratively set forth by the prophets', Spence is depicted as a secular revolutionary who exploited biblical language and imagery because of its popular appeal. This overlooks the pervasiveness of figurative interpretation as a tool of contemporary exegesis (both popular and scholarly). The scriptural key which Spence borrowed from *An Introduction to the Prophetic Records* and included in his *Giant Killer* of 1814 was typical of such prophetic exegesis: it interpreted phrases like 'the dissolution of the Heavens' to mean the ruin of the world polity, the falling of the stars and the subordination of princes and great men.[73] Moreover, the idea of Spence cynically deploying scriptural language is out of character with everything we know about the man. Where religious and secular ideas coexisted we cannot assume that one was any more real than the other, nor that new ideas inevitably supplanted older ones, even if it seems logical for them to have done so. Spence, like so many religious and political plebeians of his time, was a bricoleur who constructed his ideology from disparate elements. Evans was happy to describe Spence's plans as 'easily deducible from the light of nature, the laws of Moses, the dispensation of the Gospel, and the right use of reason applied to the rules of morality'.[74]

There is a long history of convergence between millenarian religious ideas and popular forms of scepticism or materialism. Some 'mechanic preachers' in the seventeenth century came to equate God with Reason, and Reason with the law of the universe. They evolved a form of immanent materialist pantheism which drew no clear distinction between the sacred and the secular.[75] The ground was thus prepared for eighteenth-century popular fusions of enlightenment rationalism, materialist scepticism and millenarian religion. And it was these which confirmed Reid's belief that Jacobin radicalism, infidelity and enthusiasm were related evils.

Spence similarly did not distinguish between secular and religious strands of his thought. The 'age of reason' heralded by enlightenment philosophers paralleled God's promise of the 'Millennium', and Spence was happy to lace them together.[76] This explains his particular attraction to Volney's *Ruins of Empires*: its visionary form and benedictory tone offered an enlightenment equivalent to the Levitical Jubilee.

Even Spence's contemporary critics were unsure whether he was a political revolutionary or a lunatic prophet. He was tried and imprisoned in 1793 as a Jacobin publicist. But his prosecution in 1801 for publishing the *Restorer of Society to its Natural State* followed the Committee of Secrecy's recommendation of that year that the activities of prophets like Brothers be checked. And after listening to Spence's court defence, the reporter of the *Morning Chronicle* suggested that he be placed with Brothers in Bethlem Hospital.[77] Seven years later a disenchanted follower, ex-Jacobin Thomas Constable, wrote a letter to Spence criticising him because 'you have read the Bible till you are blind as one without eyes – literally'.[78] Pitt himself is said to have thought Spence a harmless religious crank. Robert Southey, on the other hand, believed that he would have been more dangerous had he been a religious rather than political enthusiast. In truth Thomas Spence was both.

Most of those who moved in Spence's circle in the years 1801–14 seem to have shared his view that millenarianism, political radicalism and even freethought were intertwined, if not synonymous. Jonathan King's ardent wish to hasten and perhaps exploit social upheaval led him to cultivate Southcottians as well as Jacobins, and his association with Evans and Cullen around 1810–13 suggests that he regarded the Spenceans in a similar light. His lengthy introduction to Levi's *Dissertations on the Prophecies* used the prophetic idiom so menacingly that it bordered on the chiliastic. He endorsed prophetic trances, dreams and visions as a way of receiving God's communications and he used this divine intelligence to argue that present-day tyrants would perish when they had fulfilled their function as instruments of Jehovah's vengeance. The 'natural and political convulsions that alarm the world' signified 'the approaching period of God's judging the earth and redeeming his faithful people'. In the meantime he applauded the rapid spread of Unitarianism and infidelity because they undermined Christian tyranny and served as agents of Providence in preparing for the millennium.[79] Whether or not King hoped to profit from the chaos of the last days, there is no doubting his sincere belief in millen-arian modes of thought. The radical printers Arthur Seale and John Smith (Evans's one-time lodger) also combined commercial and ideal interests in the twin cultures of millenarianism and radicalism; they printed for the LCS and for Brothers, Southcott and Spence.[80] To them prophets and radicals were part of a common culture.

A number of Spencean figures usually known for their ultra-radical and republican political views have also left testimonies of their religious convictions. Ex-soldier and shoemaker William Benbow was introduced to Spenceanism by Thomas Evans at the Cock tavern in 1816 whilst visiting London as a Hampden Club delegate from Manchester. In December the same year Benbow wrote a letter from Coldbath Fields prison consoling himself and his wife with his certainty of 'the Millennium, the Millennium':

> Truth will triumph in the end – oh! what a happy people … we shall be … How stupid not to see that the vision was for an appointed time, but in the end it shall speak and not lie – How calous not to feel the energetic exhortation of the prophet – when he said 'though tarry wait for it, because it will come, it will not tarry' – O! Gratitude Heaven's best gift – take up thy abode and dwell for ever in my heart.[81]

Thomas Preston maintained that 'however much the Spencean Philan-thropists might have been scouted by the profane, the powerful and the ignorant, they still continued to rest their pretensions on holy writ, and many passages in the Books of Leviticus, Kings &c were resorted to as fitter and better guides than the casuistry of modern Bishops and Deacons'. When imprisoned in February 1817 he called for a Bible and 'read it more attentively than I had ever done before, and was fortified in my opinions by its perusal'.[82]

As a young soldier in Aberdeen in the 1790s Allen Davenport had been a regular attender at the Methodist chapel where the preacher 'so capti-vated' his feelings that he had longed for martyrdom and composed his own sermons in private. Later when working in a 'dishonourable' shoe-making workshop in Bell Street, London, a chance reading of one of Spence's pamphlets induced a response akin to conversion. Suddenly all political faiths 'were as rush-lights to the meridian sun' in comparison with Spence. Davenport preached his new-found doctrine to workmates and anyone who would listen, but admitted that many laughed at him as a 'visionary'. One of his published poems of 1819 described the Bible as:

> The greatest gift that Heaven ever gave,
> It binds the broken heart and frees the slave.

And he still thought when advocating Spencean land reform in 1836 that 'the only question to be decided is which is right, the Bible, or the land-lord's title-deeds'. He rested his authority on Leviticus 25.xxxii.[83]

We do not know whether Evans had been a Methodist but it was probably at least a port-of-call on his route to religious enthusiasm. To Place, he was someone who 'like many other half-crazy people ... found the principles of his system in the Bible', who marched into public houses 'with an old bible under his arm' and 'as other fanatics before him ... attempted to found a society which was to renovate the world and produce a millennium'.[84] Nor can we say whether Evans was attracted by Spence's politics or his millenarianism. Most likely he saw them as indivisible. His brief biography of Spence written in the early 1820s certainly cast the little bookseller in a messianic role.[85] Evans also felt bound to insert a millenarian warning in the opening manifesto of the Society of Spencean Philanthropists in 1815: 'the sacred records declare that such establishments shall not endure in peace and the awful visitations arising here from in our own days are evidence that the abomination and desolation will continue till men, perceiving their true interest, shall establish a just system of administration, for that which is the natural property of all'.[86]

If anything Evans's writings of 1815–16 went further than Spence in fusing together elements of biblicism, rationalism and artisan radicalism. The religious provenance of his pamphlet *Christian Policy* (1816) showed in his use of an epochal structure fashionable in millennial scholarship: he began with the agrarian commonwealth of Moses, moved on to Alfred's Saxon democracy and culminated in the Spencean-Christian millennium. He invoked God's sanction for man's right to hold all land in common and castigated those who opposed the reintroduction of such a system as 'enemies of God'. Man's fall from innocence was located with historical precision in the fourth or 'pagan epoch' begun by Constantine's establishment of a state-protected church and a clergy possessed of expropriated common lands. The fruits of this paganism were corrupt kings, lords, priests and landlords who maintained themselves by war, oppression, slavery, obscurantism and superstition. The solution was a 'return to the first principles of Christianity' laid down in Spence's plan and practised by similar communities of brothers and friends such as the Quakers, Moravians, Harmonites and Shakers.[87]

Also reminiscent of earlier sectarianism was the way that Evans equated the 'laws of nature' and 'laws of God'. Like Winstanley, he gave the Jubilee a materialist basis by describing it as 'a heaven on earth'. And he united the Spenceans' spiritual and secular aims in a complex blend: 'for Christianity being founded in natural Justice, is more a political than a spiritual institution: the spiritual part being introduced as an auxiliary to effect the establishment of the political. Christianity is, in fact, true philosophy, and philanthropy.'[88]

Some of Spence's followers were evidently lured solely by his religious vocabulary. John Nichols Tom, alias Sir William Courtenay, the celebrated 'madman' who ended his life in a chiliastic uprising near Bossenden Wood, is thought to have been influenced by Spenceanism in his early years.[89] Another with an obsessive religious outlook was one-time Methodist preacher, John Shegog. He became a 'furious Spencean' whilst he was preacher to a millenarian sect of 'Christian Believers' in the Borough chapel vacated through John Church's imprisonment. However, he so disliked the revolutionary and infidel strands of Spenceanism that he eventually became an informer for the government against his colleagues. He even tried to persuade the government to finance him on a foot-pilgrimage of every town in England and Ireland so he could preach obedience to the Gospel, invoke the example of the primitive church of Jesus Christ and warn against 'the delussions and crafts and subtiltys of a nest of Deistical writers (the scholars of Voltaire and Tom Pain)'.[90]

Shegog's antipathy to the radical-infidel side of Spenceanism was not typical. Wedderburn shared a similar non-political and evangelical background but responded immediately and avidly to the political, infidel and millenarian dimensions of Spenceanism. He found in Spence's ideas and idioms a perfect means to express his own peculiar sources of disaffection. Masculine fraternities had been integral to his life as sailor, tailor and criminal but Spence's sect-like following probably satisfied deeper needs. Perhaps it replaced the family and community of kinfolk that slavery had cost him in childhood. He seems also to have been kindled by Spence's enlightenment sympathies for non-white peoples. Had Wedderburn been a Jacobin he might have encountered these sorts of ideas in the 1790s through the speeches and writings of the black, Olaudah Equiano, as well as those of Thomas Hardy, Thomas Clarkson, Dr William Hodgson and others. In the years 1803–14, however, Spence was the only plebeian radical to keep intact this strand of Jacobin ideology. He used American Indian and African communities as models and settings for his plan. He expressed fierce opposition to slavery. And he also drew explicit parallels between the slave system abroad and the way that English landed monopoly created inequality, hardship and oppression.[91] Only a few months before his death in September 1814, *Giant Killer* carried a version of Cowper's poignant anti-slavery poem 'The Negro's Lament' (which Wedderburn was also to reproduce later on).

Not surprisingly, *Axe Laid to the Root* [1817] – the title redolent of Paine, Spence and the Bible – conveys a feeling of intense exhilaration as it adapts Spence's vision to the needs and circumstances of Wedderburn's troubled life. From the opening pages Wedderburn adopted a prophetic role similar to that of a seventeenth-century 'holy fool'. Knowing he would be taunted by opponents as 'possessed with the spirit of Beezlebub', he declared himself 'proud to wear the title of madman'. But, like the Leveller John Erbury, Wedderburn used his buffoonery with serious intent.

Because Spenceans shared much of the vision, manner and idiom of popular prophets, they ran the same risk of being seen through the eyes of the respectable as madmen. Wedderburn's response was to flaunt his divine frenzy to the point of burlesque.

In becoming a Spencean, he was also reliving his earlier Methodist conversion. He claimed to feel the same urge to proselytise: 'Spenceans', he declared, 'believe it their duty before God and man to preach Spenceanism at all times and in all countries.' He expressed the same confidence in his ability to confound the learned and powerful: clergymen were warned that 'a simple Spencean, who cannot write his name, will receive his opponent as David did the giant Goliah [*sic*] and with simple means destroy his gigantic impositions'.[92] Methodist preachers had eased the plight of his enslaved countrymen in the West Indies, but Spence's doctrines would liberate them altogether. Spence offered redemption not only to slaves but to London's criminal refuse as well: Spence 'knew', stated Wedderburn exultantly, 'that the earth was given to the children of men, making no difference for colour or character, just or unjust'.[93] Even Arminian Methodism could hardly hope to match such universalism. Above all, Spence's critique of private landlordism provided theoretical underpinning for Wedderburn's corrosive hatred of slave owner and planter society. Accordingly, he exhorted 'Ye Africans and relatives now in bondage' to accept 'the only tribute the offspring of a slave can give' – Spence's promise of an earthly millennium based on the redistribution of land.

Wedderburn's adaptation of Spence's plan was contained in a lengthy article extending over two issues of *Axe to the Root*. Though influenced by Spence's 'Crusoenian' utopia and Evans's 'Christian commonwealth', it was – even by their standards – an extraordinary social blueprint. Like Evans, Wedderburn drew on the idioms of biblicism, plebeian Dissent, artisan radicalism and Spencean parochial reform, but the novelty of his plan derived from its nominal setting in West Indian slave society, and from a series of detailed proposals distilled from his experience as a slave offspring, sailor, degraded artisan, Methodist prophet and petty thief.

He began by pointing out to his enslaved countrymen that English liberty was largely a myth. For all their libertarian pretensions, Englishmen were prepared to buy and sell votes for money and drink, and had allowed their original democratic constitution to be taken over by priests, kings and lords (especially landlords). These three 'states' had usurped God and gained limitless powers for themselves: they could at whim dissolve marriages, legitimise bastards and steal Africans 'like cattle'. When West Indians eventually came to throw off their oppressors, they should not, therefore, derive the model of their new society from contemporary England. Instead, they should institute universal suffrage – women were included – and elect an annual assembly of delegates, excluding whites and those worth over £500. Primogeniture should be abolished and land redistributed equally. Those who did not work should be driven off: 'the founders of Christianity have set you a pattern, Paul laboured with his hands'. All individuals over the age of eighteen – men and women alike – should be armed to defend the state, which should permit no standing army or barracks.

Some of this was standard radical stuff, but Wedderburn's plan also carried echoes of Jamaica, and of the days of 'Cromwell the Great, who humbled Kings at his feet and brought one to the scaffold'. Like Winstanley, Wedderburn wanted prisons abolished: 'they are only schools of vice and depots for victims of tyranny'. He wanted no capital punishment and no flogging of adults. Transgressions of the law were to be tried on the spot by a group of twenty-four elected elders, composed equally of men and women over the age of fifty. Punishment was to stress rehabilitation not retribution and include the ancient device of making offenders wear caps describing their crime. A similar totemic system of caps was to be used for education; children would learn by wearing dunce's caps, caps of wisdom, alphabet caps and so forth. They were also to be taught hymns to remind them of their terrible history of enslavement.

Wedderburn, like the Levellers and Fifth Monarchists before him, believed that two particular professions should be excluded from his ideal society. Lawyers were to be prohibited because they customarily practised a conspiracy against the poor 'with an invisible thread framed in language the vulgar cannot understand' – they were like 'tricking gamblers playing the game of pricking in the garter'. And established clergy were to be banned because they were 'bound by law and interest in all countries to preach agreeable to the will of the governor under whom they live'.[94]

Wedderburn was flexible or ambivalent about how the Spencean Jubilee was to arrive. His proposals took both chiliastic and meliorist forms, exactly paralleling the mixture of tactics urged by Jacobin colleagues. He believed from English experience that petitioning for reform was degrading and ineffective, but that the London artisan tactic of withdrawing labour was suitable for use by West Indian slaves. They could demonstrate their power initially by stopping work for an hour on a specified signal. He also urged the example of the rebellious St Domingo Maroons, who had employed successful guerrilla tactics by living off sugar-cane and using their bill-hooks as weapons. In this mood Wedderburn urged West Indian blacks to 'slay man, woman and child, and not spare the virgin, whose interests are connected with slavery'. When he pondered his own and his mother's hardships he sounded exactly like a prophetic madman: 'My heart glows with revenge'. Yet on other occasions he asserted that liberation and revolution could come about automatically through the diffusion of Spencean literature amongst free mulattos and by the contagious actions of enlightened landowners like his half-sister, Miss Campbell. He claimed that she had been censured by the horrified assembly in Jamaica for freeing her slaves and redistributing her land along Spencean lines, an idea which they blamed on the Methodists teaching slaves how to read the Bible.[95]

But in the final analysis, details of how the Jubilee was to be brought about did not matter. Wedderburn, like Spence and Brothers, was sustained by an intense millenarian conviction that somehow a New Jerusalem would arise both in England and the West Indies. He concluded his 'Address to the Slaves' with an ecstatic vision derived from Spence and the scriptures:

Will not priests follow their princes and sing the solemn dirge of tyranny and corruption falling into contempt, and hail the Kingdom of Christ forwarded by Spence, and experience the new birth, 'for a nation shall be borne in a day'. Then shall the worthless kings who thirst for human blood to support their tottering thrones turn their swords and spears into ploughshares and pruning hooks, then will it be said, and not before, as the apple tree amongst the trees of the wood, so is my beloved sovereign amongst the sons. I sat down under its shadow with great delight, and its fruit was pleasant to my taste.[96]

He signed himself 'R.W., a Spencean enthusiast'.

4

Infidel Spenceans: George Cannon and rationalist philosophy

Like those of Evans and Wedderburn, George Cannon's background and early life are obscure, but when he first emerged on the London scene in 1812 he appeared to be a young man of very different cast from his two future associates. He was more than twenty-five years younger, having been born in Middlesex in 1789, and his social standing was superior. At about the time Wedderburn was accused of stealing from a master tailor and Evans of swindling and blackmail, Cannon was admitted to Staple Inn to train as a solicitor.[1] His radical connections were also more respectable: in 1812, the same year that Evans befriended seedy Arthur Thistlewood, Cannon became one of the 100 founder members of Major Cartwright's Union for Parliamentary Reform. His fellow signatories included wealthy banker-brewer Timothy 'Equality' Brown, Horne Tooke's friend, Colonel William Bosville, and radical notables, Cobbett, Sir Charles Wolseley and Burdett.[2]

Cannon's religious views and associations can be established in greater detail and also seem far removed from those of Evans and Wedderburn. From early 1812, if not before, he probably began attending meetings of the Freethinking Christians and corresponding in the columns of their journal. The Freethinking Christians, or Church of God as they were alternatively known, had been founded by the drink merchant and City radical, Samuel Thompson, on Christmas day, 1798, in a meeting room at 38 Old Change, Cheapside. They comprised discontented Universalists from William Vidler's Bishopsgate congregation and some renegade Baptists and Unitarians. According to a later account by Sidney Dobell they included: 'one or two country gentlemen of property, a few merchants, many tradesmen, with a few artisans and servants'.[3] Thompson's liberal theological and political leanings – he was an ardent disciple of Paine and Godwin – did not stop him from exercising patriarchal control. He was elected 'elder' and his two future sons-in-law, John Dobell and William Coates, 'deacons'. They, along with another deacon, Henry Bradshaw Fearon, shared Thompson's links with the liquor trade and City radicalism. Thompson's daughters, Julietta and Mary Ann, were also active in the society.

After harassment from City authorities, who regarded the Freethinking Christians as a disguised infidel-radical debating club, the society had taken out a licence in February 1808 for a dissenters' meeting place to be held at John Wilkes's former haunt, the old Paul's Head Tavern, 5 Cateaton Street.[4] A few years later they moved to the Crescent in Jewin Street, Cripplegate, where Cannon probably first encountered them. For him the magnet was their periodical, the *Freethinking Christians' Magazine*, begun in February 1811. Despite warnings from Place that it would be prosecuted, the new magazine promised free and unfettered rational discussion of all religious subjects. It declared uncompromising opposition to the political and spiritual tyranny of the established and dissenting churches – including Unitarians – as well as to all forms of enthusiasm.[5] In subsequent articles and letters, members also repudiated pulpit preaching, payment of preachers, all sacraments and all ritual – including public prayer and singing. They denied the divinity of Christ, the doctrine of the fall and the immortality of the soul, and they described large portions of the New Testament as fraudulent. They also countenanced many of the anti-clerical ideas of infidel philosophes such as Godwin, Raynal, Dupuis, Volney, Voltaire, Rousseau and Boulanger (Holbach).[6] Not surprisingly, government and City authorities kept a watch on the sect.

Many rationalists were impressed by the Freethinking Christians' 'enlightened and philosophic manner' but could not accept their belief in revelation and their opposition to deism. Cannon seems to have been one of the 'disguised infidels' who – it was later claimed – responded to the periodical's promise of free discussion by swamping the editors with deist propaganda.[7] Writing under the pseudonym of 'A Deist, Pentonville', he engaged throughout 1812 in a heated debate with Thompson and Coates. He disputed their acceptance of Christian evidences and supernatural intervention and, with an impressive display of philosophic learning, used Hume, Voltaire and Bolingbroke to demonstrate the invariability of the laws of nature.[8] This defence of deism unearthed a kindred spirit and fellow correspondent in William Burdon, a prosperous mill-owner, former Cambridge don and trenchant rationalist.[9] Together, they assailed Freethinking Christian theorists for stopping short of deism (and even atheism), and for failing to support the veteran Jacobin publisher, Daniel Isaac Eaton, when he was prosecuted in 1812 for publishing Paine's *Age of Reason*, part III.

Cannon thought himself entitled to lecture the sect on their timidity; when Eaton's court defence faltered in the face of persistent interruptions from Lord Ellenborough, the young trainee lawyer came to the old publisher's aid by bellowing legal advice into his near-deaf ears.[10] By early 1813 Cannon's and Burdon's criticisms over this and other issues were so outspoken that the editors decided to stop printing their letters.[11] The

Freethinking Christians would no longer accept contributions from inveterate enemies of Christianity, who, they said, were more deserving of a spell in the pillory than of inclusion in their magazine.[12]

Cannon's brief encounter with the Freethinking Christians and championing of Eaton not only shows his rationalism, but also hints at his ambition to become a philosopher and man of letters. He had only just started training as a solicitor when he plunged himself into literary and philosophical controversy. The source of this ambition remains hidden. Could his father have been the one-time Methodist minister, Thomas Cannon, who about the time of George's birth was preacher at a small independent chapel in Grub Street? Thomas Cannon later gave up his religious calling and opened a 'classical academy' in Kentish Town,[13] which would explain George's educational attainments. Or perhaps young Cannon became interested in literature and philosophy at Staple Inn. The chambers he was to occupy – number one – had only a few years earlier been a gathering place for a brilliant circle of artists and literati headed by the Principal of the Staple, Isaac Reid.[14] Cannon might have benefited from this tradition and here acquired the formidable liberal education which magistrates were later to remark.

Rev. Erasmus Perkins, philosopher and man of letters

Cannon's break with the Freethinking Christians had actually been caused by his warm support for another infidel work published by Daniel Isaac Eaton. This was Baron d'Holbach's *Ecce Homo, or, A critical inquiry into the history of Jesus Christ.*[15] The publication of the work had been financed and sponsored by the wealthy radical freethinker, Timothy Brown. Brown owned a bank in Lombard Street, a brewing business in partnership with Whitbread, a country estate near the Isle of Wight and a large London house called Peckham Lodge. He had been a regular member of Horne Tooke's Wimbledon Common circle which met over Sunday dinner for more than twenty years and gathered up a glittering array of radical talent.[16] By 1812–13 a series of deaths brought the circle's activities to an end; over the next few years Peckham Lodge replaced Wimbledon Common as a nursery for young radical literati.

Brown's fascination with religion and philosophy ensured that those who attended gatherings at Peckham Lodge had a strong interest in freethought as well as radicalism. The circle included J.B. Baverstock, another prosperous brewer and freethinker; William Burdon when he was in London; Joseph Webb, a radical bill-broker, and, surprisingly, the so-called 'churchman' William Cobbett.[17] As well as encouraging the purchase, reading and discussion of freethinking works, Brown financed their publication through the near-bankrupt Eaton. Early in 1813 Brown learnt that a down-at-heel young radical journalist from Scotland, George Houston, was negotiating with Eaton to publish a new edition of *Ecce Homo* (which had been published in small numbers in Edinburgh in 1799).

Brown was rapturous. *Ecce Homo* had been written by the most thoroughgoing sceptic and materialist amongst the French philosophes. It both disputed the divinity of Christ and – unlike any other infidel work popularly available in England – used the scriptures to make lewd insinuations against his morality.[18] Brown threw the full weight of his wealth and influence behind its publication. He encouraged and entertained Houston ceaselessly – even at 'his parties for pleasure'. He subsidised the printing and publishing of the work. He read and commented on the proofs. And he worked hard to promote the circulation of each of its four parts. In September 1813 a sceptical article in *Cobbett's Political Register* inspired him to approach its famous editor to give similar publicity to *Ecce Homo*.[19] The article which gave Brown this idea was written by George Cannon.

Cannon's appearance in the *Political Register* arose indirectly out of his dispute with the Freethinking Christians. Noticing early in 1813 that Cobbett was also debating with this argumentative sect, he evidently decided to lend support. The MP William Smith had proposed a Trinity Bill for extending toleration to rational Christians of the Unitarian type: Cobbett claimed sympathy with those who held the scriptures to be sacred and with those who rejected them altogether – Smith's bill he called 'a little piddling palliation' which satisfied neither position.[20] William Coates – representing the Freethinking Christians – retaliated by calling Cobbett 'the very refuse and offal of Deism', and a disguised infidel.[21] This last accusation was close to the mark. The self-proclaimed churchman, Cobbett, was flirting with infidel ideas and contemplating a public change on this as on other previous positions.[22]

Cannon intervened in the debate with a deviousness which was to become his hallmark. Between September 1813 and January 1814 three letters appeared in the *Political Register* obviously written by the same pen but under the separate pseudonyms of 'Gulielmus', 'Churchman' and 'A Lover of Truth' – all professing to be from scholars defending religious toleration. Although these letters took the ostensible form of Christian apologias, their real purpose was to exacerbate the religious doubts of Cobbett and his readers by ridiculing the Established Church and the Christian religion.[23]

Whether or not Cannon had previously been known to Cobbett and Brown, these letters marked him out as someone worth cultivating. He became a frequent visitor to Peckham Lodge and part of the circle later described by Houston as 'literary men who took pleasure in such controversies'.[24] With Cobbett's connivance, these men peppered the *Political*

Register with pseudonymous letters which advertised and defended the contents of *Ecce Homo*, and which urged the merits of deism against Freethinking Christian opponents. Cannon wrote as 'A Lover of Truth, London'[25] and Houston as 'Observator'.[26] 'Varro' was probably Brown himself,[27] and 'Veritas' might either have been Burdon or possibly Baverstock.[28]

Initially the results of their efforts matched Brown's hopes. Sales of *Ecce Homo*, which had been quiet, increased sharply.[29] And Cobbett, with covert assistance from the Peckham circle, was brought to the verge of admitting his conversion to deism. He conceded that *Ecce Homo* had raised serious 'doubts and difficulties' in his mind.[30] But moves by the government to prosecute Eaton and Houston checked this impetus. Brown and Cobbett became worried about their own safety. The latter was also warned that his sympathy for infidelity had alienated supporters. In November 1815 Houston was convicted of blasphemous libel and sentenced to two years' imprisonment in Newgate plus a £200 fine. Even then, Cobbett and Brown did not back off completely: a month later the *Political Register* carried the first of a series of eight lengthy articles in defence of religious toleration. They were written at Brown's persuasion by George Cannon, under the pseudonym of Rev. Erasmus Perkins.[31]

Cannon's adoption of this pseudonym marks an important point in his social and intellectual development. At one level his use of the name and title was simply a prudent move to avoid discovery and prosecution. Throughout a long literary life Cannon never published a single word under his real name. And as a disguise it was not implausible. The freethought historian, J.M. Robertson, believed that Perkins was who and what he pretended to be – 'a cultured dissenting minister of large experience and liberal views'.[32] Some of Cannon's contemporaries evidently thought the same.

'Rev. Erasmus Perkins' was also Cannon's most persistent and elaborate alias – and so gives some clue to his character. 'Erasmus' represented his aspirations to be a scholar-humanist, social satirist and religious reformer. 'Perkins' had indigenous associations; it was intended to remind readers of the legacy of William Perkins, the great Puritan theologue, don, preacher and social critic.[33] Friends like Brown and Cobbett no doubt relished Cannon's joke, especially because general readers could not be certain of its falsity. However, the pseudonym may hint at real elements of Cannon's background such as a connection with Dissent. It probably also reflected his social ambitions and fantasies: he was to take out a dissenting minister's licence within a year.

Erasmus Perkins professed to be a middle-aged dissenting minister with a scholarly and rational concern for religious toleration. He claimed to have been moved by Houston's prosecution to write an apologia on

Christian principles for complete freedom of religious opinion, including that of deists, pagans and millenarian enthusiasts. His articles contained – at one level – exactly the kind of arguments, authorities and preoccupations one would expect from an author steeped in the 'Real Whig' or Commonwealth-man tradition. They were prefaced with patristic quotations in support of religious freedom and drew heavily on the writings of ecclesiastical historians such as Tillemont, Dupin and Mosheim. They attacked the principle and practices of established churches – with their tithes, steeple-houses, 'popish ceremonies and pantomimical mummeries' and their 'adulterous union of church and state' which led to the evils of political priestcraft. They stressed mankind's need to return to the tolerant spirit of primitive Christianity. They invoked Puritans such as Penn and Milton in support of the principle of voluntarism. They cited 'Real Whig' fathers like Toland and were hostile to monarchy – to Charles I in particular.[34]

At least one reader of the *Political Register* suspected that Rev. Erasmus Perkins was not what he claimed to be. The issue of 25 March 1815 contained a letter which declared that the articles were 'particularly dangerous'. 'Verax' of Sheffield detected in them a 'mischievous tendency, inasmuch as they are tinctured with a *profession* of religion, when they are evidently aimed at the very foundation of it'. He believed that Perkins was not actually a tolerant Christian, but an infidel, or philosopher, who had shown himself to be 'a decided enemy of revealed religion' and an exponent 'of almost every sceptical writer who has flourished since the birth of our Saviour'.[35] Given Cannon's love of dissimulation we cannot, however, rule out the possibility that he wrote this critique himself as a devious means of advertising his wares.

In any case it was a pretty fair summary of the underlying intent of his articles. Beneath the battery of Christian scholarship and the measured rational tone we glimpse a clever, cynical young man who was thoroughly hostile to religion, who relished his own guile and who itched to show off his mastery of sceptical theory. Behind Erasmus Perkins lurked the young Voltaire or perhaps a libertinist coffee-house wit like Rochester. He disingenuously cited anecdotes of the Christian Fathers so as to make them seem far more bigoted and ignorant than pagans. He innocently listed scores of Christian atrocities – including those committed by the revered primitive Christians. He enunciated core doctrines of Christianity in a tone of unctuous mock-piety, and with enough distortion to make them seem ludicrous:

We ... believe that the great Author of Nature, in order to redeem his creatures from a portion of the disgrace entailed upon them, in consequence of their first parents eating some fruit from a forbidden tree, he begat, in a natural manner, a son upon the body of a young woman, who was betrothed to an old man. That this immaculate conception was brought about by the instrumentality of the Holy

Ghost, an incorporeal spiritual personage, sometimes represented as appearing in the shape of a Dove, and sometimes in various other forms. We believe also in a doctrine called the Trinity, said to have been established about the third century of Christianity, which represents the Father, the Son and the Holy Ghost, to partake equally of divinity, and in fact to be three Gods and One God at the same time ... It is true our enemies ridicule this ineffable mystery of our holy religion, but we implicitly believe it, though so inscrutable that we cannot comprehend it.[36]

As if inadvertently, Perkins showed that deists had always possessed a lofty morality and a tolerant attitude toward other religions. He repeatedly touted, while affecting to decry, the sceptical works of Paine, Voltaire, Volney, Mirabaud (Holbach), Helvetius, Toland and William Burdon. He insinuated leading infidel doctrines into his articles in such a way that they appeared both unexceptionable and persuasive. Readers were introduced to the law of necessity, the material basis of the universe, the sensationalist psychology of belief and utilitarian natural morality.[37]

Sometimes, however, Perkins could not help abandoning his Christian persona. 'Philosophers', he claimed, were men 'whose works breathe nothing but the most unbounded philanthropy and benevolence' and 'whose labours have been devoted to the improvement of mankind, whose dispositions have been most amiable, and whose lives most exemplary'. To them he offered – in an article of 7 January 1815 – the fruits of an alleged twenty years of labour: a proposed biography 'of all those persons denominated infidels' since the birth of Christ.[38] A week later, in another burst of candour, he disclosed an even larger philosophical ambition. By comparison with French philosophes, English efforts at spreading enlightenment had been hampered by the isolation of her philosophers. The 'republic of letters' in England urgently needed a 'medium of communication for Theology, Metaphysics and Moral Philosophy', particularly one that was open to disciples of nature, followers of Pyrrho and 'Latitudinarians of every class'.[39]

Cannon's new philosophical journal followed closely on this hint. The first number appeared in March 1815, claiming to be 'conducted by Erasmus Perkins, assisted by several eminent literary characters'. Its title encapsulates Cannon's philosophic pretensions: the *Theological Inquirer; or, Polemical Magazine; being a general medium of communication on Religion, Metaphysics, and Moral Philosophy – Open to all Parties – containing Free Discussion – Criticism – Original Poetry – Selections and Reprints and scarce and curious works connected with theology, ontology and ethics.*

Without considerable financial and literary help Cannon could not have launched so costly and ambitious a project. That he did so says much for his powers of persuasion and for his reputation as a budding philosopher and man of letters. Much of the support came from literary contacts made over the past three years. These included some of the more literary minded Freethinking Christians whose own magazine had closed in December 1814.[40] But the Peckham Lodge circle provided the backbone: Cobbett gave Cannon several letters left over from the *Ecce Homo* controversy for inclusion in the new journal;[41] 'Varro' became a regular correspondent, as did William Burdon under the initials 'W.B.' – and both were probably substantial financial contributors. A correspondent using the initials 'W.D.' might have been the former diplomat turned philosopher, Sir William Drummond, whose privately printed work, *Oedipus Judaicus*, had also been publicised by the *Ecce Homo* controversialists.[42]

One of the contributors to the *Theological Inquirer* was to acquire genuine literary eminence, though Cannon could only have guessed it at the time. A month before publication of the first issue, he visited the Shelleys in London and left his 'papers' for them to examine and discuss.[43] How he came to make this acquaintance we cannot say for certain. Intriguing snippets of information in the Home Office show that Shelley was implicated in clandestine radical and infidel activities during the years 1811–15.[44] He might have learned of Cannon through the controversy in the *Political Register*, or through some connection with the Peckham Lodge circle – Shelley had acquired and was reading a copy of *Ecce Homo* in 1813.[45] Moreover, in September of that year a correspondent in the *Political Register* (who was almost certainly Cannon) revealed detailed knowledge of Shelley's infidel past.[46] Perhaps the two met at the Pimlico freethinking circle which Shelley was attending at this time.[47] Shelley's litigious financial disputes with his father could also have brought him into contact with Cannon – they took him to Staple Inn on 29 October 1814.[48] Equally, the two might have met through Thomas Jefferson Hogg, co-author of *The Necessity of Atheism* and Shelley's constant companion in 1814–15. Hogg was then a law student at Gray's Inn, the fellowship most closely connected to the Staple, and he was also present when Cannon's papers were received and discussed by the Shelleys. Perhaps it was Hogg, too, who persuaded them to assist the project, even though they did not take to Cannon.

They probably did not need much inducement. Both P.B. and Mary Shelley were in a militantly anti-Christian frame of mind at this time. Mary's *Journal* records that she was reading – mostly at Shelley's direction – Louvet de Couvray's libertinist and anti-clerical memoirs (later translated and published by Cannon), William Drummond's *Academical Questions* and/or *Oedipus Judaicus*, Gibbon's *Memoirs* and *Decline and Fall*, Voltaire's *Candide*, and *Zadig*, Holbach's *System of Nature* and others in the same vein.[49] Above all, Cannon's proposed periodical offered Shelley an opportunity to ventilate his own buried infidel writings. The first number of the *Theological Inquirer* in March 1815 carried instalments of two previously unpublished works by the young poet-philosopher – 'A Refutation of Deism' and 'Queen Mab'.[50]

'A Refutation of Deism', published in full in two parts,[51] was exactly the kind of work Cannon would have found appealing. Shelley had borrowed David Hume's (and more directly Drummond's) cunning device of using a mutually destructive dialogue between a Christian and a deist, leaving atheism the implied victor. It was Voltairean in the savage wit of the first dialogue and Holbachian in the trenchant philosophical materialism of the second. The latter also reproduced (for the first time in popular form) David Hume's ingenious arguments against design and causation from the *Dialogues Concerning Natural Religion*. However, the *Refutation* was perhaps too advanced for readers of Cannon's periodical, many of whom would have read little beyond Paine's deist primer, *The Age of Reason*. The only explicit response to the work was a rejoinder written by the Freethinking Christian 'Mary Ann' (Coates, née Thompson).[52]

Correspondents responded more enthusiastically to 'Queen Mab' even though it appeared only in expurgated extracts with an accompanying commentary by 'F', a young shoemaker-poet and friend of Cannon called Robert Charles Fair.[53] Readers might have been predisposed to favour its benedictory tone, sacramental imagery and visionary format through their earlier acquaintance with Bunyan and, more directly, with Volney's *Ruins of Empires*. One of the reasons that the *Ruins* and *Queen Mab* went on to become formative popular radical texts was their shared Gothic–Romantic sensibility.[54] Fair certainly extolled the poem and later imitated it at tedious length. His only regret was that he did not dare to publish those dangerous portions which proved Shelley to be 'a philosopher of the first rank' and the equal of Paine, Voltaire and Volney.[55]

Even aside from Shelley's contributions, the *Theological Inquirer* was an impressive rationalist production and one that deserves attention from literary and social historians. In the retrospective preface to the bound volume, written in August 1815, Cannon claimed to have brought to the republic of letters a genuine 'theatre for free inquiry'. True, its overall complexion had turned out to be 'decidedly sceptical'. Nevertheless, the only restrictions placed on correspondents had been that they use language commensurate with 'the dignity of philosophy and polite literature', and that they 'write as philosophers and enlightened Christians instead of bigots and angry zealots'.[56]

The journal's contents over its six months of publication show that given these provisos Cannon had been reasonably open-minded. He gave generous space to the writings, doctrines, practices and proceedings of both Freethinking Christians and their Unitarian opponents. His reviews of recent publications by Samuel Thompson, and by Unitarian leaders, Robert Aspland and Thomas Belsham, were models of judiciousness. He published criticisms by Christians of infidel works like *Ecce Homo*. And he made an effort to redress the journal's sceptical bias by featuring a lengthy exposition on Danielic prophecy, and by inserting some brief anti-infidel extracts from evangelical magazines.[57]

Still, it was as an organ of infidel philosophy that the *Theological Inquirer* excelled. Standard sceptical philosophes like Paine, Volney, Voltaire and Holbach were well represented, but Cannon also managed to include much rarer infidel extracts, summaries and works. Many readers would have had their first chance to read the ideas of infidel and 'Real Whig' predecessors like Peter Annet, Matthew Tindal and John Toland.[58] A lucid summary by Burdon made accessible Anthony Count de Gebelin's massive and erudite *Primitive World Analysed*. A range of contemporary free-thought speculation also found its way into the journal. Contributions came from Burdon, Drummond, George Ensor, Belsham and Shelley, as well as lesser talents such as Brown, Fair, Mary Ann Coates and Cannon himself under a maze of pseudonyms. And in a nice reversal of anti-infidel propaganda, readers were offered inspirational biographies and tranquil death-bed affirmations of freethought martyrs and heroes. The *Theological Inquirer* of 1815 was, the editor boasted, a complete philosopher's hand-book.

In the same year Cannon entered the Law List as a solicitor of 1 Staple Inn, and became legally entitled to call himself 'Reverend' through having taken out a dissenting minister's licence under his own name.[59] His real and fantasy careers seemed to have aligned.

Infidel Spencean

Surprisingly, Cannon also began in these years to inhabit the shadowy underworld of the Spenceans. He probably joined the society around 1813 or 1814 – before Spence died, since he was one of the half-dozen former associates whom Place approached for recollections when compiling material for Spence's memoir in 1831. Two of the others, Wedderburn and Fair, were friends and literary collaborators of Cannon: they became Spenceans in mid-1813.[60] Cannon was certainly a senior member of the society by 1816. The idea of such an urbane and intellectual young man – a lawyer, philosopher and clergyman – frequenting the same milieu as and sharing the aims of a group of degraded artisans, Jacobin revolution-aries and millenarian enthusiasts is initially disconcerting. Yet once we re-examine Cannon's actions and achievements over the years 1812–15, he begins to look less respectable, successful and intellectually superior than he liked to pretend.

For a start his legal career looks shaky. When Cannon joined Staple Inn in 1812 it was already in decline. Its longstanding affiliation with Gray's

Inn had been severed the previous year; thereafter the old Inn of Chancery lost status rapidly. A mid-nineteenth-century Royal Commission described it as little better than a dining club: chambers could be purchased, seniors had long since abandoned their educational responsibilities and degrees were no longer offered.[61] George Cannon might have been an early casualty. Years later the scholar-bibliographer Henry Spencer Ashbee referred to him in a brief biographical note as having been a lawyer's clerk.[62]

If Cannon did become a full solicitor as the Law List of 1815 suggests, we still need not attach too much significance to the qualification. He was included for that year alone and I have found only one instance of his practising openly – and that in 1816. Two years later *The Triennial Directory of London, Westminster and Southwark* (1817–19) did not list him as a solicitor. London's gutters, garrets and pot-houses were crammed with over-educated and under-employed solicitors and attorneys whose lives were barely distinguishable from those of their struggling clerks. When they lacked capital or influence, solicitors – along with surgeons, apothecaries, teachers, preachers, bill-brokers and journalists – occupied a position of social and economic marginality similar to artisan intellectuals.[63]

Men of this type drowned their sorrows in places like the Three Herrings in Temple Bar, where Place's father used to drink with dissolute attorneys and barristers and conduct drunken burlesques of House of Lords proceedings.[64] In the 1830s the doyen of Judge and Jury clubs, Renton Nicholson, generated a lively correspondence in his periodical, the *Town*, when he published stories and articles suggesting that lawyers and law-clerks were, with bakers' boys, mechanics and artisans, the backbone of London's drunken free-and-easies, cider cellars, cock and hen clubs and blackguard taverns.[65] One correspondent, though keen to defend the reputation of the legal profession, had to admit that it often attracted men who were 'of good family, and educated for a higher situation in society, but, by various casualties, have become reduced, and the legal profession being more congenial to their ideas than a mechanical business have chosen to follow its path'.[66]

This path often led them also into radical and freethinking circles and clubs. The spy Barlow furnished detailed reports of the activities of two such clubs in Liverpool, 1797–9, showing that they were made up almost equally of artisans, clerks and small merchants, many of whom also exercised their literary bent by composing tracts, elegies, odes and songs.[67] Another spy, Milner, who was watching the LCS and United Movement free-and-easies at Furnival's Inn Cellar in 1797, reported that 'Many of them appeared to be either Hackney writers or attorneys' clerks'.[68] Evans's colleagues Owen Savage and Jones, both law-clerks, were probably among these.

Milner's equation of law-clerks and hackney writers hints at the frequency with which marginal or failed legal men attempted to construct alternative literary careers amongst a horde of aspiring Grub Street writers and *philosophes-manqués.*[69] Social desperation might have fuelled Cannon's drive to become a philosopher, theologue and man of letters over the years 1812–15. Viewed in this light, his portrayal of Rev. Erasmus Perkins seems as wistful as it was satirical. His donnish and clerical affectations – the mannered style, pedantic wit and weight of pseudo-scholarship – also hint at his being an insecure intellectual.

Cannon's links with wealthy, respectable or genteel literary men were not necessarily made as a social equal. Radical literary circles like those of Horne Tooke and Brown often added a leavening of intellectual artisans and lower middle-class sorts. Houston's prison testimonies on the *Ecce Homo* affair show that he, the publisher Eaton and the printer Charles Mitcham were men of this type. Though they dined at Peckham Lodge, they looked on Brown and Cobbett as patrons and employers rather than friends and equals. Houston was typical of many young Scots of humble background who migrated to London at around this time in the hope of acquiring fame and fortune. Before the publication of *Ecce Homo* he had been without adequate work for eight months and was struggling to feed his large family.[70] He would not have been out of place in the literary underworlds of the eighteenth century. In prison he was to turn informer and, according to Richard Carlile, to swindle an innocent woman of £300.[71]

Brown's intervention of 1813 had lifted Houston's fortunes and ensured the completion and temporary success of the *Ecce Homo* project. He provided the necessary injection of capital to enable printing and publication, drummed up publicity and sales through Cobbett and other friends and helped distribute the work under the protection of privileged franks. In the process he entertained Houston lavishly, introduced him to influential literary figures, and helped get him the editorship of Cobbett's *Political Register.*[72] Brown had dispensed 'dinners and money' equally freely to Gwillam Wardle and his radical associates during the Mary Anne Clarke affair.[73]

Cannon was probably in a similar position to Houston. He did not belong to the cabal of wealthy freethinking literati intimate with Brown, but to an aspiring fringe expected to take the direct risks of publication and publicisation in exchange for patronage opportunities. He was 'encouraged and flattered'[74] by Brown into joining the controversy. One of the reciprocal benefits of writing the *Political Register* articles was assistance in launching and running his own periodical. His frequent and lavish praise of William Burdon's writings might also have been prompted by hopes of patronage, as was his visit to the Shelleys in 1815.

The return demanded by such patrons could be heavy. In spite of Brown's wealth and philosophical ardour he expected a commercial profit from the *Ecce Homo* venture and drove a hard bargain to ensure it. Despite Charles Mitcham's rationalist credentials and genuine poverty, Brown did not hesitate to threaten him with prosecution when the hard-pressed printer delayed work through shortage of funds. Brown and Cobbett kept Houston constantly at their beck and call, paying him little and expecting 'utmost devotion in return'.[75] They also insisted that the struggling young journalist take sole responsibility for publishing *Ecce Homo* – amounting in this case to two years' imprisonment and a heavy fine.

Cannon managed to get literary contributions from the Shelleys, but not social respect: 'vile beast', Shelley recorded, 'it is disgusting to see such a person talk of philosophy. Let refinement and benevolence convey these ideas.'[76] Shelley conceded Cannon's talents but could not forgive his pretensions. Men like Cannon and Houston carried the stigma of inferior social origins even amongst fellow radicals and freethinkers. Like so many of the *philosophes-manqués* of pre-revolutionary France, Cannon and Houston discovered that the 'republic of letters' still contained its plebeians. Birth and wealth counted in the world of infidel-radical letters as it did in the 'corrupt' society at large. Aspiring philosophes could find themselves as dependent and expendable as chattels.

We do not know what Cannon thought in private about the Shelleys. He could hardly have failed to notice their condescension. Houston's resentment of his dependence on Brown and Cobbett grew into hatred by the time he had languished in Newgate for sixteen months. He came to feel that he had – like Eaton before him – been 'deceived, abandoned and betrayed'. In an effort to get revenge and extricate himself from his plight, he offered the government detailed information on the role of Cobbett and Brown in the *Ecce Homo* affair. In return he probably received a free passage to the United States where he recommenced his career as an infidel pressman.[77]

Untrustworthy patrons were not the only hazard for the would-be man of letters in early nineteenth-century London. An expansion of the reading public and growth in popular journalism had improved the conditions and prospects for some categories of professional writer since the days of the Grub Street 'Dunces',[78] but it was still a fiercely competitive and fragile trade for those lacking capital and social standing. Cannon's new career as a littérateur was as risky as the legal one he had relinquished. To the continuing threat of bankruptcy was added the menace of libel suits. John Bone, William Hone and Sir Richard Phillips were amongst the more talented radical publisher-booksellers to become bankrupt at around this time. An article in the *Scourge* of 1812 claimed that such men were well off compared with the writer whom they employed: 'while the bibliopolist is basking in affluence and accumulating wealth by the product of the man of genius, the latter is often (too often, alas!) left to pine in hopeless

7 *Perils of the hack: writing for a pittance; imprisoned for libel.*

misery and anguish, with nothing to console his cold and comfortless existence, but the airy and fantastic visions of future fame and glory'.[79]

The distressed writer was a stock figure of eighteenth-century popular caricature. George Cruikshank might almost have had Houston and Cannon in mind when he produced his series of engravings of 1813 entitled *The Pursuits of Literature* (Ill. 7). Number one shows the down-at-heel hack surrounded by his clamorous family, being badgered for copy; number three depicts him a little later, alone in a prison cell, having received a libel sentence. When defending Houston in the *Political Register* in 1814, Cannon wrote feelingly of 'the extremely precarious emolument derived from literary pursuits,' and pointed out that imprisonment meant ruin and starvation for such a man with a large dependent family.[80] He was to make exactly the same plea on behalf of himself and his seven children in a court defence of 1831.[81] The failure of an expensive publishing project could also deposit a marginal littérateur in the gutter or prison alongside the indigent and unrespectable. The *Theological Inquirer* closed after only seven months and Cannon's proposal to publish a 'Theologica sceptica' of rare philosophe reprints foundered with it.

His decision to take out a dissenting minister's licence at the end of 1815, two months after the closure of the *Theological Inquirer*, was not inconsistent with someone in a marginal or declining position. Overt religious motives are unlikely to have played much part in the decision since his writings show that he was vehemently anti-Christian and probably an atheist. But he did relish the clerical role. He flaunted his ministerial title at every opportunity and was later given the nickname in Spencean circles of 'Brown Friar'.[82] As a fellow correspondent in the *Freethinking Christians' Magazine* pointed out, the social benefits of possessing a clerical title were numerous: 'don't you know that people think something of you', he quoted a recently licensed weaver-preacher as saying, 'it looks something above the common run and I can get credit for anything now'.[83] Cannon was probably tempted to bolster his status in this way after the failure of his most ambitious literary undertaking.

A clerical title might even help to sell books. Dissenting ministers had been a feature of the Grub Street literary underworld of the eighteenth century. One of the most notorious London hacks, John Dunton, had also manufactured a clerical persona not unlike the Rev. Erasmus Perkins in order to sell his seedy wares.[84] H.S. Ashbee, the great nineteenth-century bibliographer of erotica, claimed that Cannon began selling obscene works in 1815, the year that he became a minister.[85] Still, there is no firm evidence to connect these events, nor to confirm Ashbee's date. If Cannon did begin selling obscene literature at this time, he did not become a serious pornographer until much later. Perhaps he had not by the end of 1815 crossed the grimy threshold of Grub Street, but his aspirations to become a man of letters had received a definite setback and he was showing signs of social uneasiness.

Political uneasiness probably also contributed to his decision to take out a dissenting minister's licence. Cannon was shrewd enough to realise that the increased legal toleration granted to Unitarians through the Trinity Act of 1813 would give considerable protection to an infidel who licensed himself as a minister of that faith. The failure of his periodical meant that he was reduced to moving regularly in a more exposed and less respectable infidel-radical milieu where the dangers of prosecution and imprisonment were incomparably greater.

The man at the centre of this milieu and at the frontier of infidel-radical agitation in London during these years was Daniel Isaac Eaton. After returning from exile in America, the battered old Jacobin publisher spearheaded a popular infidel-radical revival during the years 1810–14. His bookshops – in Cornhill Street, then Ludgate Hill – served as headquarters for political and religious debate, and as outlets for infidel propaganda. His prosecution and imprisonment in 1812 also aroused popular sympathy.[86] The *Scourge* – by no means a radical periodical – expressed a common view when it asked why the government 'did not employ the ample means rested in their hands for the punishment and suppression of titled prostitutes, exalted gamblers, official adulterers, and noble swindlers in the courts and squares of the West End of town, instead of confining their endeavours to the humble purlieus of Grub Street and Paternoster Row'.[87] The London mob gave their verdict by turning Eaton's spell in the pillory into a triumph.

Cannon might have made his original contact with Eaton's circle through the Freethinking Christians. A close friend of Eaton's, Dr William Hodgson, author of the *Commonwealth of Reason* and original English publisher of Holbach's *System of Nature*, seems to have been a member of their congregation in 1810.[88] Charles Mitcham, one of their deacons and printer of their magazine, was also printer of Eaton's infidel works and a member of the Peckham Lodge circle. He contributed towards Eaton's triumph in the pillory by printing a set of scathing anti-government handbills, then distributing them amongst the crowd.[89]

Whatever way they met, Cannon knew Eaton well enough by 1812 to advise him in court and to support him in print. Cannon's *Political Register* articles also drew on the infidel works which Eaton published between 1810 and 1813: Helvetius's *True Sense and Meaning of Nature*, Nicholas Freret's *Preservative against Religious Prejudices* and *Moseiade*, Paine's *Age of Reason*, part III, and of course *Ecce Homo*.[90] It was probably in Eaton's shop, 'The Ratiocinatory', that Cannon met many of his future infidel-radical associates. These included men connected with the Peckham Lodge circle like Houston, Mitcham and Joseph Webb, as well as others suspected by the government of treasonous political activities.

For all his courage, the ailing, debt-ridden Eaton did not cut a respectable figure during the last few years of his life. Not only his patron, Brown, but also his colleagues, Houston and Mitcham, became irritated at his financial unreliability.[91] But this did not deter Spenceans Thomas Evans and George Cullen, both of whom organised subscriptions for Eaton in

1814. So, too, did veteran bookseller-publisher M. Jones of Newgate Street,[92] the same man who published Margarot's *Thoughts on Revolutions* in 1812, and Cannon's *Theological Inquirer* in 1815, and who sold 'Spence's Plan' in early Regency years. Another, more portentous, figure whom Cannon probably met in this circle was Arthur Thistlewood: around 1812 'the Captain' had begun to fraternise with 'those who were in the habit of assembling at the shop and house of Daniel Isaac Eaton'.[93] Eaton's followers overlapped with the mysterious 'Jacobin party' which attempted to smuggle Margarot to France, and to launch the *Political Censor* in 1813. It was intended that the periodical should be financed by Thistlewood, printed by Mitcham and edited by Houston, with the assistance of 'several well-known literary characters attached to the cause'.[94] We would not be guessing wildly to suggest that Cannon was amongst them.

Radical debating clubs were another milieu where Cannon might have come into contact with the Spenceans during these years. Whether as covers for sedition, agencies of radical propaganda, centres of plebeian conviviality or forums for aspiring philosophes, such clubs pervaded the early Jacobin agitation in London. The Seditious Meetings Act of 1795 which restricted the size of public meetings and required a magistrate's licence for debating halls temporarily silenced most clubs – including the Westminster Forum run by the quasi-professional Jacobin debater, John Gale Jones.[95] By 1806, however, the deterrent effects of the act were starting to wear off; Gale Jones opened a new radical debating club in Poland Street, called the British Forum. Three years later it was being rivalled by the Athenian Lyceum, the Philomathic Institution, the new Robin Hood Society, run by radical journalist Peter Finnerty, and the London Institute in Old Jewry – as well as several lesser-known clubs meeting at the Russell Rooms in Brunswick Square and the Leverian Museum near Blackfriars Bridge. What these clubs had in common – according to the *Satirist* in 1808 – was their attendance by 'the most notorious infidels and Jacobins of the age' and the substance of their debates which 'carefully blended the usual routine of scepticism in politics and religion'.[96]

A long retrospective memoir published in Benbow's *Rambler's Magazine* [1822], and almost certainly written by him, described the attraction of debating clubs to young aspiring philosophes. Benbow depicted himself as a young man who 'had obtained a glimpse of past things and generations, and looked forward to futurity with the hope that I, obscure as I then appeared, might one day be numbered amongst the renowned and illustrious of the earth ... I was seized with a mania, common to many, of attending and exhibiting at these popular arenas, termed *debating clubs*'. There he had mingled with well-educated but down-at-heel professional debaters like Gale Jones and Jack Wright, as well as 'the Spenceans' with whom they debated regularly.[97]

The *ROBBING* Hood Debating Society.

8 The Robin Hood debating club satirised, 1809.

The British Forum became so notorious that Gale Jones was hauled
before parliament in 1810 and eventually given a twelve month sentence
for criminal contempt.[98] As a result radical debating clubs shifted back to
less vulnerable informal tavern venues. Typical of these was Jonathan
Wooler's Socratic club, held at the Mermaid tavern, and the Polemic club
which, as we have seen, was probably founded around 1811–12 at the
Cock in Grafton Street. As well as attracting veteran Jacobins and Spenceans, the latter club appealed to young artisan autodidacts like Thomas
Preston. He described it as a literary-cum-debating society of 'philosophical tenor' (freethinking) whose members gave him 'kindness and attention' when he was in need.[99] Other recruits almost certainly included
shoemaker-poet Robert Fair and Cannon himself. And though little is
known about the character of the Polemic club during these early
Regency years, we can be reasonably certain that it met secretly at low
taverns in an atmosphere of convivial revelry, and that it was not the sort
of philosophical society that men like Brown, Baverstock, Burdon, Cobbett
or Shelley would have attended.

If, on re-appraisal, Cannon's social and economic circumstances around
1814–15 seem more compatible with the Spencean milieu, his religious
outlook still presents a problem. Enthusiastic religion afforded Rev. Erasmus Perkins and his philosopher friends with a fund of amusement and
derision between 1812 and 1815. They consistently represented it as the
antithesis of rational philosophy; 'fanaticism' was the one attribute that
brought exclusion from the columns of the *Theological Inquirer*.[100] A good
example of the sort of attitude we might expect from such philosophers

may be seen in an article printed in Wedderburn's *Axe to the Root* [1817].
The pseudonymous correspondent, describing himself as 'one of that numerous class of society called Seekers, who spend our leisure in inquiries
into theological, moral and political creeds and opinions', ridiculed the
editor for underestimating the importance of rational free inquiry and for
presenting his Spencean doctrines in an 'enigmatical' and incomprehensi-
ble manner. Wedderburn was accused of being like Joanna Southcott:
'continually offering to our imagination the promised Shiloh, that is to
produce so much happiness, but when or how, or by what means is
entirely left out of consideration'.[101] Yet it was this same enthusiast,
Wedderburn, whom Cannon was to select as his key literary collaborator
over the next five years.

Explaining the actions of someone as protean and devious as Cannon is
difficult even when there is some evidence. In this case we can only guess
at his motives. Perhaps he decided, cynically, that the Spenceans' blend of
revolutionary and eschatological ideas made them a potent anti-establishment force which could be exploited at little personal risk. 'Jew' King had
evidently reached this conclusion earlier, though his millenarianism
seems to have had a genuine basis. Cannon and Houston had been manip-
ulated in the freethinking cause by Brown and Cobbett; now perhaps it
was Cannon's turn to play the manipulator. Reid's claim that 1790s'
religious enthusiasts were often 'Punchinellos, whom those who held the
wires behind the scenes might play off, as best suited their purposes'[102]
has understandably never been taken seriously. The careers of men like
King and Cannon make it seem more credible.

In February 1815, for example, Cannon devoted a full article in the
Political Register to a discussion of the new millennial doctrine of our
prophetess, Joanna Southcott. Under a pretence of urging toleration for
Southcottians he used the sect's extremism to ridicule Christianity generally. He was delighted to be able to embarrass orthodox religion from
within the Christian fold and to exacerbate the widespread fears which
Southcottians evoked in respectable society.[103] When, as in the case of the
Spenceans, sectarian energy was linked to an overt social and political
radicalism, it must have seemed doubly attractive.

Cannon was also aware of the superior popular appeal of vital religion
over philosophical rationalism. He attributed this to the ability of enthusiasts to play on the emotions, and to their greater use of 'extemporaneous
preaching'.[104] In a later pamphlet (issued under Wedderburn's name but
substantially written by Cannon), 'learned men and philosophers' were
explicitly criticised for preaching 'to the understanding instead of the passions', and for being 'deficient in that ardent zeal for proselitism which
distinguished those whom the world calls enthusiasts and fanatics'.[105]

Any sort of an acquaintance with Spence and his followers must quickly

have convinced Cannon that they were excellent examples of what Reid
had called infidel 'auxiliaries'. Some were already convinced freethinkers,
others were partially infidel in their outlook or displayed anti-clerical attitudes compatible with infidelity. We have already seen that Spence himself
qualified as an infidel of an eccentric kind. He had absorbed the rhetoric of
truculent political anti-clericalism which was so much a part of the popular dissenting outlook. He was heir to the strange blend of social prophecy,
popular materialism and scepticism which had surfaced in the writings
and utterances of plebeian sectarians like the Ranters and Seekers. And he
had ingested elements of enlightenment rationalism through his reading
of philosophes like Volney.

Moreover, Spence possessed a paradoxical ability to mirror the aspirations and outlooks of an artisan Jacobin like Evans, and a plebeian millenarian like Wedderburn, and a philosopher-littérateur like Cannon.
Spence's claim to the last title rivalled that of Rev. Erasmus Perkins. As a
young man in Newcastle, he had been a schoolmaster and an active
member of a philosophical society. He had founded a debating club and
participated in the vital autodidact culture which generated Bewick's engravings and Spence's own phonetic works, including the pioneering
Grand Repository of the English Language (1775).[106] This last, along with
his other contributions to English orthography and language, are now
acknowledged as significant works of scholarship as well as agents of
linguistic levelling.[107] Like Perkins (Cannon) he was steeped in the fertile
literary and philosophic traditions of the English Commonwealthman and
radical dissenter. He reproduced extracts from and used the ideas of thinkers like Harrington, More, Milton, Sidney, Lyttleton, Berkeley, Locke, Joel
Barlow and Price.[108] He borrowed, too, from Augustan utopian and satirical writings like those of Defoe and Swift, to whose ironic style Erasmus
Perkins was also heavily indebted.

Spence thought of himself above all as an educator, and drew the
admiration of the great radical publicist William Hone for his 'fearless
thinking and printing'.[109] In perhaps his most widely circulated work,
Spence promised to further the millennium, golden age, or age of reason
in a fashion dear to the heart of any philosopher, 'by the Progress of
Reason, aided by the Art of Printing'.[110] Over the period 1801–14 he
operated debating clubs more consistently than any other metropolitan
radical. And the explanatory subheading of his last publication, the *Giant
Killer*, could just as easily have been appended to Cannon's *Theological
Inquirer* a year later.

This weekly miscellany, besides supporting its title as to Politics, will comprise
Humorous and Instructive Essays, Remarkable Adventures, General Anecdotes,
Moral Tales, Historical and Biographical Sketches, Poetry both original and from
the Works of the best Authors, frequently accompanied with appropriate Remarks

and Observations. Being on the whole a general Repository of elegant, useful and entertaining literature.[111]

The Irish bill-broker George Cullen has left signed annotations of several freethinking works in the British Library which leave us in no doubt that it was possible to be an infidel philosophe like Cannon as well as an ardent disciple of Spence. Holbach's discussion of the formative powers of early education led Cullen to describe how he had acquired and lost his faith:

we suck in the belief in God, with our Mother's milk. no person can remember when he hard the name of God first mentioned. I remember my mother whipping my arse for only asking the second time what God was. She was a Roman Catholic and notwithstanding she was a very religious woman she was almost allways in poverty and trouble and for many years I never mised a day but I went to church or chappel to worship God. and now I am convinced there is none.

To demonstrate his further credentials as a philosophe, Cullen summoned other authorities in support: 'the great Lord Chancellor Bacon' to endorse the notion that 'Atheism leaves to Man Reason, Philosophy, Laws, representation, and everything that can serve to conduct him in virtue'; and 'Our great poet, Thomson' to declaim against 'Religion mild, a yoke to tame the stooping soul, a trick of state to mask their rapine and to share their Prey'.[112] Another philosophe tract, which he attributed to Thomas Paine, moved him to write: 'greater truth, or better Information were never written. May his memory live for ever'.[113] Significantly, he bound it side by side with his copy of Spence's *Important Trial*, in which he wrote: 'I am proud to say, I was one of his [Spence's] bail, and when Sir Richard Ford asked me if I would be answerable for his appearance ... I answered Yes, in ten thousand was I worth it'. With men like Cullen to appeal to, it is no wonder that George Cannon saw an opportunity to demonstrate his literary and philosophical talents among the Spenceans.

It would not be fair to conclude this survey of Cannon's odyssey from cultured philosopher to Spencean infidel without suggesting the possibility that deeper, less calculated impulses were also at work. His life and career between 1812 and 1815, as far as we can piece it together, conform in many ways to Weber's model of the typical sectarian. In Weber's analysis the incipient religious radical often experiences a similar pattern of relative deprivation through such factors as failed ambition, declining status and economic position, or disturbing changes in occupation. For all Cannon's urbanity he could well have been one of those pariah intellectuals from the lower middle class who – along with their artisan counterparts – found themselves attracted to radical religious sects which promised to transform the social order.[114] If so, George Cannon, renegade lawyer, preacher, philosopher and littérateur, came to Spenceanism not only as an infidel-radical machiavel, but also – like Evans and Wedderburn – because it met a deep personal longing.

If Cannon was no longer able to enjoy the companionship of respectable literary freethinkers, he could at least find a substitute satisfaction alongside those with humbler attainments, and amongst whom he must have seemed a luminary. The insecurities of an increasingly precarious existence were also eased, perhaps, by being shared with others in equally difficult situations. Solace, if not hope, were to be found in their revolutionary schemes. They offered comradeship-in-arms and a shared outlet for social resentments and intellectual fantasies. Their underworld might also have been titillating to someone who evidently enjoyed the spice of clandestine activity. Without it, his life threatened to become increasingly drab and dispiriting.

PART 2

THE UNDERWORLD INSURGENT, 1815–21

5

Spence's successor, 1814–17

More than twenty years ago E.P. Thompson called the mass reform movement which sprang up during the post-war distress of 1816–20, 'the heroic age of popular radicalism'; it has continued to fascinate historians ever since – whether as the 'forcing-frame' of working-class consciousness, the cradle of Chartism or the flash-point of an English revolution that never came. Because of their reputation as proto-socialists and revolutionaries *manqués*, the London Spenceans of this period have received a fair share of attention in recent years, yet their character, purpose and influence remains surprisingly misunderstood.

Confusion over the identity and aims of the Spenceans goes back at least as far as the *Report from the Committee of Secrecy* of February 1817 which equated Spenceanism with London ultra-radicalism as a whole. It described the Spencean society as a large, covert metropolitan organisation with extensive provincial contacts and a commitment to violent republican and infidel revolution including the equalisation of property and extinction of landlords and fundholders. It also blamed the Spenceans for the Spa Fields uprising of 2 December 1816, which it depicted as a premeditated insurrection.[1] As in the 1790s, Francis Place initiated a counter-historiography. He claimed that the *Report* had purposely confounded 'Spenceans, reformers and the rabble of all sorts' in order to justify legislative and judicial repression: 'the poor harmless Spenceans with their library consisting of an old bible and three or four small publications, a high priest under the title of Librarian and some forty or fifty followers were held out as a bugbear to all men of landed property'.[2] Modern historians lean towards the Secret Committee's account of the insurrectionary milieu of 1817; they tend to ignore Evans's society or accept Place's dismissive evaluation of it. Even studies which purport to unravel the complex strands of London's post-war radicalism often perpetuate old confusions by failing to distinguish consistently between Spenceans and related ultra-radical coteries.[3]

Admittedly, the intricate and fissiparous character of post-war London radical politics makes such lapses difficult to avoid. A recent historian has

noted the addiction of London's leaders to squabbles, splits and realign-
ments. It prompted Hazlitt to call them 'a collection of atoms whirled
about in space by their own levity'.[4] But factionalism was encouraged by
the social and economic complexity of the metropolis and gives some clue
to the *sui generis* character of its radicalism. Moreover, petty differences
over personalities, ideology and tactics sometimes portended far-reaching
social and political divergences and developments.

Insufficient attention to this factionalism has certainly led to gaps and
distortions in the historiography of post-war London popular radicalism.
Historians have underestimated the significance of Thomas Evans as a
radical leader, and his Spencean society as a strategic and cultural organisation. Evans has been overshadowed by sometime associates like Watson,
Thistlewood and Preston – more colourful, sanguinary and fateful figures.
A publication projected by Evans in 1821 through which he hoped to set
the record straight seems never to have appeared.[5] He makes only a
fleeting appearance in accounts of 'the heroic age', even though the Home
Office placed him under intensive surveillance in 1816, then imprisoned
him for twelve months in 1817 on suspicion of high treason. At the time
the government saw him as the immediate father of the post-war ultra-
radical revival and a devious leader responsible for nurturing an underground of revolutionary activists, practices and ideas. Spies and Home
Office officials did not make the modern mistake of presuming that Evans's
Spenceans disappeared or were absorbed into the ultra-radical followings
of Watson and Thistlewood in the winter of 1816.

Spencean leader, 1814–16

The man who led London's ultra-radicals out of the wartime wilderness in
1815 had none of the personal, oratorical or literary attributes of popular
heroes like William Cobbett and Henry Hunt. But charisma does not always
depend on flamboyance; radical social movements often call for more subtle
or prosaic leadership skills.[6] Evans chose to rest his claim to ultra-radical
leadership mainly on the credentials of his predecessor, Thomas Spence.
Had Evans seen the 1815 intelligence report which referred to his organisation as 'disciples of Spence' he would probably have been pleased. Long after
Spence's death he continued to present himself as chief disciple in a body
dedicated to the memory, principles and methods of the little bookseller.
Those who wished to join his Society of Spencean Philanthropists were
obliged, as in United Britons' days, to undergo a formal 'test' (which he
often administered from memory). Intending members had to affirm that
the land was the people's farm, that the Spencean system was founded in
divine justice and would 'restore peace, liberty, security, happiness and
society', and to declare their willingness to spread these ideas.[7]

Like an aspiring chief anywhere Evans made skilful use of symbol, ritual and ceremony to forge emotional links with his predecessor. Spence was buried in September 1814 with 'due pomp'. His body was carried in procession down Tottenham Court Road to the new burial ground of St James's, Hampstead Road. Several followers, 'to testify their sense of his [Spence's] upright intentions to serve mankind with inflexible integrity and purity of life, ... carried ... scales as the emblem of Justice ... containing an equal quantity of earth in each scale, the balance being decorated with white ribbons, to denote the innocence of his life and example'. Other supporters distributed stamped medallions to onlookers; listened in silence to the formal panegyric, then ceremonially cast Spence's favourite tokens into the grave[8] – an intricate display of symbolism which evidently made a deep impression on several new recruits.[9] Evans also continued the tradition, initiated in 1812, of holding anniversary tavern dinners on the 21st of June each year to honour Spence's birthday – an occasion for reminiscences, memorial toasts and commemorative ballads. 'The Memory of Spence', composed by Evans and sung to the tune of 'Auld Lang Syne', reminded followers:

> His books and songs for forty years,
> He's published many ways;
> For which he oft was sent to jail;
> Grant him your meed of praise,
> And never let him be forgot,
> Though he is gone from hence,
> But drink a bumper o'er the tomb,
> Of old Tom Spence;
> Here's old Tom Spence, my boys &c.[10]

Sculptor (and spy) George Edwards was also commissioned to make fifteen busts of Spence as a memento for followers.

Evans's self-effacement can lead us to overlook the originality of his contribution to the shape of the new society. Spence's free-and-easies of 1801–14 were loose, informal affairs. Some moves had been made to formalise the following in 1812, but Evans developed a systematic organisation. Informality had been one of the great strengths of the free-and-easy; he was careful to preserve as much of it as possible. But too much informality could lead to purposelessness – one of the reasons historians have largely discounted the 'tavern group' as a radical form.[11] Evans's society combined elements drawn from the traditional plebeian free-and-easy, the more formal radical debating club, the Jacobin-style political society and the trades or benefit lodge. He retained the traditional location, atmosphere and fraternal rituals of the free-and-easy. He borrowed from the LCS the idea of 'joining' and 'quarterly' operating fees (of a shilling each), as well as minimum regulations of conduct. He incorporated a set of debating procedures like those of the British Forum, and he used a benefit club system of dividing the society into federated 'lodges' under rotating chairmen.

In 1815 four such lodges (later called sections) met in taverns on different nights of the week: on Mondays at the Nag's Head, Carnaby market; on Tuesdays at 8 Lumber Street, Borough; on Wednesdays at the Cock, Grafton Street, Soho; and on Thursdays at Johnson's Mulberry Tree tavern, Moorfields. Soon after, these were joined by an energetic fifth lodge which met at the Northumberland Arms or Golden Key in Bethnal Green (and during the tumult of 1816 by several other more ephemeral lodges in Spitalfields). Using secret ballot each lodge elected a chairman of the evening debates, as well as two delegates to a 'corresponding committee' and to a central coordinating or 'conservative' committee. The latter then elected three executive officers – a secretary (Edwards senior, later young T.J. Evans), a treasurer (John Hooper for a short time, then Seymour) and a librarian (Thomas Evans) whose nominal job was to purchase and lend books, newspapers and pamphlets. Spies also mentioned a quarterage committee headed by shoemaker Charles Jennison, which seems to have been intended to police the payment of quarterly operating fees. Thanks to Evans's experience and pragmatic skills the Spencean society thus entered the post-war period with a structure that was appealing, reasonably efficient and tactically flexible.[12]

Allocating himself the position of librarian symbolised Evans's role as keeper and interpreter of the Spencean principle. He was not the only Spencean ideologue in post-war years,[13] but he was certainly the leading one. In the year following Spence's death he proved it by publishing the *Address of the Society of Spencean Philanthropists* and a series of letters to the *Independent Whig* outlining his version of the Spencean critique and plan. These he elaborated into a lengthy 1s 6d pamphlet of 1816, called *Christian Policy, the Salvation of the Empire.*[14]

The new manifesto was designed to combine Spence's ideas with Evans's own theoretical advances. This is not to say that he developed Spenceanism into a land nationalisation programme as is sometimes claimed.[15] The practical details of his plan continued to derive very literally from Spence. In essence, Evans wished to transfer 'all the land, waters, mines, houses, and all feudal permanent property to the people, to be held in parochial (or other small) partnerships' (p. 25). These were to be administered, as Spence had decreed, through a parochial leasing system. In some ways Evans actually softened rather than toughened the original creed – a point made by one of his otherwise severest critics, Robert Southey.[16] The new Spencean plan 'would not disturb the relative classes of society', and it would retain a monarch, a pensioned and titled (but not private landowning) nobility and a paid, established clergy (p. 33).

The title of *Christian Policy* meant exactly what it said. Whereas Spence had been eclectic in borrowing sources, analogies and settings for his plan, Evans encapsulated his critique and plan within a systematic Christian model, language and historiography. Like Spence, Evans derived his land plan from a state of nature and traced its historic origins back to the Mosaic Jubilee of Leviticus 25. However, he gave a new emphasis to the reviving and purifying role of Jesus Christ, represented as an inspired Jewish Spartacus who had ushered in the Christian epoch 'on the broadest republican principles' (p. 8). Evans even approved of the polities of the Roman Catholic and Orthodox Greek churches because they held property in common and elected their ministers and functionaries; though he condemned their junction with the secular state and their elevation of Christ into a divinity. He also contended that the original principles and practices of parochial land partnership had been revived by the Christian King, Alfred, who destroyed feudality in the soil only to have it brutally restored by the Normans.

This nostalgic historiography contains obvious echoes of Cobbett. Evans's economic analysis owed him still more. Several recent studies have drawn attention to the 'populist' character of Cobbett's radicalism, which in turn owed much to Bolingbroke's critique of eighteenth-century courtier parasitism, as well as Paine's savage dissection of the English financial system and Major Cartwright's democratic Saxon constitutionalism.[17] Many of these same features are present in Evans's writings, 1815–18. For example, he held the typical populist belief that a parasitical financial elite had conspired to ensnare the people in a mesh of debt and dependence. Both he and Cobbett derived this aspect of their radical critique from Paine's still underestimated tract of 1796, *The Decline and Fall of the English System of Finance*.[18]

Evans's version argued that the long and unjust war against France had been financed by an explosion of useless paper money. This created spiralling inflation and a massive foreign debt, from which fundholders, foreign courts and agricultural monopolists alone benefited. High prices and rentals, coupled with grinding taxation to meet the national debt, caused a serious slump in consumption – the motor of all domestic and foreign trade. Once the wartime agricultural monopoly was broken, England could no longer compete with countries like Russia and America. 'We are all in debt to one another and have no money to buy for our own use', he complained, (p. 4) 'The causes of all the evils are debt and taxation' (p. 28). Again this anticipates later populist underconsumptionist economic theory.[19]

Evans's indictment of English landlords exceeded even Cobbett's demonological litanies:

Has it not been you, the oligarchy, the land-monopolists, of these realms, that have caused all the troubles, wars, and distractions in Europe and America, for these last fifty years at least; while you have made the crown, the stalking-horse, the scape goat? Are not all the horrors of the colonies, of slavery, of men hunted down by bloodhounds, – of wars on the continent of America, scalping, burning, and hanging – of India, war, rapine, and famine – of Ireland, rebellion, executions, persecution, degradation, military coercion, and every species of oppression – of England, exactions, debt, taxation, deprivation, pauperism, bankruptcy, &c. to be attributed to you; that you might enjoy, by extension of wealth and power, secured to your families for ever in fields of blood? [pp. 23–4]

He linked this financial-landowner elite with despotic foreigners conspiring to deprive the English people of their peace, liberty, trade and capital. And he echoed Cobbett in his purple appeals to English patriotism:

Is the sun of Britain's glory setting for ever? Shall this noble, generous, industrious nation expire, writhing and agonized at every pore, under the torturing domination of the Pagan flesh-mongers of the Continent? – This nation, to whom the modern world owes so many and such great obligations – the parent and nurse of liberty, civil and religious – the radiance of whose brightness has pierced all corners of the earth, extending a knowledge of the blessings of freedom; all the present enlightenment of mankind emanates from this small spot, this England, as from a divinity. [p. 7]

Worst of all was the greedy, tyrannical Russian empire which had burgeoned during the war at England's expense,[20] particularly through its capture of Poland, 'the granary of Europe', on which England had depended for twenty years or more (p. 3).

Several other lesser aspects of Evans's manifesto seem also to belong to the populist mould. He harked back to a pastoral and racial golden age of Saxon democracy.[21] He idealised small-scale individual enterprise, particularly of a rural kind.[22] He deployed emotional pietistic language.[23] And he showed an autodidact's fervour to dislodge true knowledge or enlightenment from the grip of the ruling elite.[24]

However, analogies with populism will take us only so far; Evans's writings also deviate in important ways from Cobbett-style radicalism. He did not share Cobbett's demonological hostility to paper money, but believed paper currency to be 'as good a circulating media as any other provided the public have sufficient guarantee to give it confidence'. This would come, he argued, by eliminating the debt, funding and taxation systems, by stimulating consumption and by supporting the currency with earnings from popular parochial rental (p. 45). Though limited as an economic analysis, it was considerably more sober and consistent than Cobbett's. Even Southey admitted that *Christian Policy* propounded 'a distinct and intelligible system', and warned that agrarian radicalism was not 'so foolish, or so devoid of attraction that it may safely be despised'.[25]

More important, Evans rejected the key-stone of Cobbett's 'Old Corruption' critique: 'It is not the expenses of government (so loudly declaimed against) of placemen and pensioners, (so reviled and abused) that oppress the people. No: their claims on the public are but a drop in the ocean, compared with exactions of landlords and stocklords that destroy the industry of the people, by cutting them from the land' (p. 24). Consequently, his manifesto contained no detailed list of the names of placemen, pensioners and sinecurists – something which has been seen as *sui generis* to early nineteenth-century radical populism.[26]

Many of Evans's economic ideas mirrored the specific local experiences of artisans and small masters in wartime and post-war London – men struggling to survive as producers and consumers in the face of burgeoning commercial and mercantile capitalism, pressing indirect taxation, high food prices, currency fluctuations and erratic trade cycles.[27] And despite his muscular patriotism and splenetic Russophobia, Evans showed no trace of the anti-semitism that tainted Cobbett's populism.[28] Nor was the emotional pietistic language of *Christian Policy* deployed in the interests of Protestant bigotry. Like Spence and other plebeian radicals of the period, Evans tried to give old language new dimensions.[29] The epithets of anti-popery took on novel, often opposite, meanings. 'Pagan', his most common term of abuse, signified any religious or secular organisation that abandoned the ideals of parochial land partnership. 'Jesuitism' was a political term, used not against the Roman Catholic church, for which he had considerable sympathy, but against the monarchical congress system of Europe (p. 7). In castigating 'atheists', he did not mean infidels (whom he said often possessed a lofty natural morality), but 'supporters of assumption and undefined power' (p. 13).

Whether or not Evans's manifesto was really populist, he reshaped Spencean ideology in ways that greatly extended its attraction for urban artisans and lesser professionals. *Christian Policy* passed through two editions in 1816 and possibly another the following year. Spies reported that it sold briskly at Spencean free-and-easies in 1816 and that Evans was pleased with the sales.[30] Preston helped give the pamphlet a wider constituency by selling it in rougher, non-Spencean alehouses around Spitalfields. Cobbett and William Hone read it, as did Evans's critics Place and Southey.[31] Thomas Malthus – one of Evans's targets – gave *Christian Policy* publicity by attacking it in the 1817 edition of his famous *Essay on Population*.[32] And several Spenceans later confirmed its influence within the society. Preston's autobiography (1817) echoed Evans's denunciations of the Corn Bill, foreign traders, fundholders, Property Tax and Malthus.[33] Ideas and phrases from *Christian Policy* were reproduced in Wedderburn's two periodicals of 1817 and in his anonymous poems and tracts of 1818. All these blended millenarianism with attacks on the war, taxation, the national debt, landlords, Malthus and the oppression of the Irish.[34] Twenty years later Allen Davenport's *Life of Spence* contained both evidence and a fulsome acknowledgement of his intellectual debt to Evans.[35] So integral were Evans's ideas to Spencean ideology by 1817 that both the Committee of Secrecy and the Attorney-General at Watson's trial cited Spencean opposition to fundholder profits as a principle second only to their denial of private landownership.[36]

Evans's actual personality remains tantalisingly elusive. Most accounts are hostile. Place depicted him as a seedy fanatic; Bamford thought him pompous and opinionated; government spies found him exasperatingly crafty. Yet we glimpse occasional contrary views. An associate of Sidmouth who interviewed Evans in prison in 1817 found him 'a man of strong acute mind and who has read a great deal'.[37] William Hone not only thought Evans the embodiment of a manly English artisan, but also respected him as a fellow Jacobin with an impressive campaign record and many battle scars. Evans was never reticent about jogging people's memories on this score: the introduction to *Christian Policy* laid out his patriot and veteran credentials at length. It described the sufferings he and his family had endured during his imprisonment in the infamous 'Bastile' of Coldbath Fields; his patriotic, intellectual and domestic qualities as a Jacobin martyr; his willingness to suffer for England's freedom without thought of reward; and his links with the glorious reforming traditon of Chatham.[38] All this was calculated to impress both old and new generations of radicals. In accordance with his veteran status, Evans's name often stood at the head of radical subscription lists in the immediate postwar years. On one such list eleven of the twenty names below his can be identified as former Jacobin associates[39] – indicating both the continuity and the status of the old cadres.

Being an old campaigner had other advantages too: by 1817 Evans had been participating in metropolitan radical politics for some twenty years, and working as a tradesman in the Strand for nearly as long. Inevitably he had accumulated a substantial body of friends, business connections and relatives, as well as political associates. The role of such personal, family and community networks in binding and perpetuating radical groupings deserved closer investigation from historians. Attention to this kind of material could disclose for radicalism, as it has done for an eminent nineteenth-century aristocracy of intellect, 'the generations of men and women who were born, married and died, and perhaps bequeathed to their descendants some traits of their personality, some tradition of their behaviour, which did not perish with the passing of the years but persisted in their grandchildren and their grandchildren's children'.[40] Despite the scanty evidence available within plebeian radical milieux, spy reports indicate that Evans's family, business and social ties were important in his construction of the Spencean society, 1814–18, and in reinforcing his role within it.

We have noted that many who gravitated to Spence's circle in the years after 1803 had previously been associated with Evans in the LCS and the United movement. By post-war years some of these had in turn added sons, brothers or other relatives to the society. William Clark jnr, Thomas John Evans, James Watson jnr, Robert George (son of John) and Sadgrove jnr were all active Spenceans, and probably of a similar age.[41] The sailor and gold-lace weaver George Pickard was probably related to Evans's old LCS colleague James Pickard.[42] The Savage brothers were possibly members of the large family group of that name who belonged to the Freethinking Christians,[43] and might also have been related to law-clerk, Owen Savage, who was arrested with Evans in 1798. Other sets of brothers included the Cormacks, the Jennisons, the Keenes and of course William and George Edwards.[44] Many of these family pairs also belonged to the same trades, usually shoemaking, weaving or tailoring.

In addition to ties of kin, there were those of business or neighbourhood. It was reported in 1818 that William Edwards was 'connected with Evans by way of business' and that young Robert George worked as Evans's shopboy.[45] From the George family came another possible link: a Mrs George of Enfield was 'Dr' James Watson's aunt. But the explanation for Watson's recruitment given by a friend, Whitfield, around 1815–16 is probably sufficient. He claimed that 'so late as the last peace' Watson had been an ardent conservative who painted loyal devices at considerable expense and who illuminated enthusiastically. However he had established a 'connection' with his neighbours, the Evanses (probably around 1810), and this 'turned his politics'.[46]

This kind of 'connection' was probably influenced crucially by the wives or mothers of radicals. We have noted that Thomas Evans was lucky to have so politically committed and forceful a wife as Janet. A landlady and two servants testified in 1817 to the centrality of Janet's role in establishing a network of domestic ties between the Evans, Thistlewood and Watson families over the years 1814–16. Janet accompanied and recommended the Thistlewoods when they moved to nearby premises in Southampton buildings. Thereafter, she visited them regularly and cared for their son Julian when Susan Thistlewood returned briefly to the country.[47] The male Evanses and Watsons were also frequent visitors to Southampton buildings. Other reports of 1816–17 noted that Thomas John Evans was young James Watson's 'chief intimate', and that young Charlotte Watson, aged sixteen, was part of this circle of friends.[48] When Watson senior was unable to look after Charlotte early in 1816 he sent her to the Thistlewoods to stay, though she eventually ended up in the charge of the Evanses. Young Julian Thistlewood was only eleven years old, but he too became part of this radical community. Thomas John Evans corresponded with him after returning from France in 1814, at which time Julian was living in the same street as the Evans family. Four years later – after Thistlewood senior had broken with the Evanses – he wrote to his son warning him to avoid their pernicious influence.[49]

By the end of the war Thomas Evans's combined organisational, ideological, symbolic and social attributes had established him as unquestioned leader of the London Spencean society. Its continuity with the Jacobin past made this small tavern grouping, numbering probably little more than fifty or sixty members, the torchbearer of metropolitan popular radicalism. Had the Committee of Secrecy reported then, instead of in 1817, they would have been substantially right when they equated Evans's Spencean society with London ultra-radicalism as a whole.

The Spa Fields split of 1816

Evans's writings of 1815 anticipated England's economic collapse due to paper inflation, the weight of national debt and taxation, and trade failures associated with the end of the wartime corn monopoly. Ironically, the apparent fulfilment of his predictions early the following year had the unforeseen effect of putting his radical leadership under pressure. Demobilisation, poor harvests and a trades' slump (following the cessation of war contracts) generated widespread distress amongst both metropolitan and provincial artisans, and rekindled hopes of a mass radical revival. In the autumn of 1816 Watson, Preston and Thistlewood began pressing Evans to move the Spencean society out of its restricted tavern club format and to adopt tactics capable of translating the emerging discontent into some form of political mobilisation and insurrection.

Evans's reluctance encouraged his three colleagues to take independent action. Inspiration for this arose out of Preston's connections with disgruntled trades' societies in the East End. Election to the position of secretary of an anti-machinist committee of trades' delegates encouraged him, along with Watson and Thistlewood, to form a separate radical committee of 'distressed manufacturers, mariners and artisans'. An engine-weaver and trades' leader named John Dyall was made nominal chairman; John Hooper, treasurer; and Preston, secretary. They sent out letters asking prominent radicals to speak at a metropolitan mass meeting. Only one replied, but he seemed perfect for their purposes. Henry Hunt of Bristol was a brilliant, pugnacious orator with a substantial provincial following, an unequivocal commitment to radical reform and ambitions to supplant the Whig-Radicals in Westminster. After preliminary correspondence and discussions, he agreed to address a mass meeting at Spa Fields on 15 November which would petition parliament and the Prince Regent for radical parliamentary reform. True to their title, the committee worked to rally support amongst the metropolitan distressed. Young Watson put his recent sea-faring experience to good use amongst discharged sailors around Wapping and Horsley; Preston extended his trades contacts amongst the hard-hit Spitalfields weavers and other East End trade societies; and he, Watson senior and Thistlewood combed alehouses around Paddington, Shoreditch, Longacre and Drury Lane recruiting unemployed navvies, coal-heavers, porters and carmen, masons, iron workers and disbanded soldiers.[50]

Evans disapproved of this independent political activity from the outset, but it was Hunt who precipitated the first open breach between the new Spa Fields committee and the Spenceans. He agreed to speak at the meeting only if the petition's resolutions in favour of parochial land reform were dropped (before long he was publicly describing the Spencean plan as 'chimerical and fanatical').[51] The committee complied: of the three leaders only Preston was deeply committed to Spencean principles, and he was willing to waive these temporarily rather than lose Hunt's support. From this moment Evans began working to keep his Spencean followers from involvement in the Spa Fields meetings – a point which historians have not made clear.

This is not to say that Evans immediately broke with his former colleagues or had them expelled from the society. He was still sufficiently friendly with Thistlewood to dine with him on the eve of the Spa Fields uprising in December, and he allowed notices advertising the first meeting to be displayed at Spencean debates at the Cock. However, spies reported that he worked hard to dissuade Spenceans William Clark jnr and John Keenes from associating with the Spa Fields committee.[52] The *Polemic Fleet* of November 1816, a 'who's who' of leading Spenceans, omitted the names of Watson, Thistlewood and Hooper, and censured young Clark for his backsliding. Only the equivocal Preston remained on the roll-call.[53] We do not know how many Spenceans attended the first Spa Fields meeting on 15 November – which turned out to be both large and peaceable – but its chairman, young William Clark, was the only erstwhile member, apart from Watson, Preston and Thistlewood, to sign the petition.[54]

Evans's concern to distance himself from his former colleagues was probably influenced by pique at their challenge to his leadership. The success of the meeting on 15 November indicated that he had lost control over the metropolitan ultra-radical movement. But there is reason to believe that he was also genuinely incensed at the committee's abandonment of Spencean principles and strategies. In spite of the many points in common between his ideas and those of other ultra-radicals, there were important differences. We have already noted his rejection of the central plank of Cobbett's 'Old Corruption' critique, namely that popular distress derived primarily from the gross expenses of government. Evans and Spence had also come to believe that the French Revolution failed because it was not grounded in a thoroughgoing parochial land reform. The failure of both the mass and underground Jacobin movements in England had underlined this view.

In opposition to post-war radicals of almost all shades, Evans held that economic inequities caused political corruption rather than the reverse: 'It is property and property alone that gives power and influence, and wherever the people are wholly deprived of property they are slaves.' Mass mobilisations to intimidate parliament into conceding universal suffrage, or to force a similar result through armed violence were useless: 'Without the restoration of land ... reforms and revolutions are unavailing: they are ... effusions of madness, which rise like a mob, and subside, or are put down like a mob, and the oppression continues or returns with redoubled force.'[55] The debating topics at the four main Spencean taverns in the winter of 1816–17 pointed in the same direction: 'Meetings for Parliamentary reform, do they mislead or inform?'; 'Do the expenses of Government cause the miseries that surround us?'; 'Would the practical establishment of the Spencean system afford a complete and desirable remedy for the present distresses?'. As Evans intended, debaters invariably concluded that mass meetings were useless, and that radical reform was a 'farce' and a 'half-measure, exchanging one set of thieves for another'.[56]

Evans also wanted the Spenceans to avoid the Spa Fields meetings because, as he warned the Mulberry Tree section on 14 November, his former colleagues had 'desperate projects in view'.[57] These projects did not materialise until the second meeting on 2 December, but Evans knew for some time that the proposed armed uprising was being organised secretly from Preston's house at 9 Greystoke Place. His warning to Mulberry Tree members did not arise from intrinsic opposition to the use of violence. Like most ultra-radicals, he regarded force as a stock part of his repertoire – to be used in self-defence against government attack, or to complete a prepared revolution. The government spy Vincent Dowling described him as 'd – bly violent'. But Dowling and other spies admitted that Evans was evasive on the subject of armed uprising and that he was having no part of the 1816–17 plots. Talk of violence was discouraged at Spencean debates in the winter of 1816 and there were mutterings in the society about formally expelling Thistlewood for his extremism.[58]

The government concluded after the attempted storming of the Tower led by young Watson on 2 December that Evans had dissociated himself from the plotters because he lacked their courage and thought the timing of the uprising 'imprudent'.[59] His close friends Galloway and Moggridge certainly believed the impulsive riot to have been premature; both expressed the opinion around this time that revolutionary impetus had to come from the North.[60] Evans's refusal to join the plot probably stemmed as much from realism as cowardice. He knew enough of the proposed plan, the conspirators' personalities and the government's intelligence system to guess that abortive riot and draconian repression were the likely outcomes.

The Watsonites' plan to capture the Bank and Tower in 1816 has been likened to Despard's proposed coup of 1802, but they lacked the earlier movement's military connections and the underpinning of Irish and French revolutionary support. Despite its French revolutionary trappings, Spa Fields savoured much more of a plebeian uprising like that of Masaniello or Wat Tyler. Much of the time, money and effort of the leaders went into making revolutionary talismen – black flags, banners, ribbons and tri-coloured cockades – in the apparent hope that these would have the quasi-magical effect of 'arousing' the London mob and causing the authorities to capitulate.[61] Evans knew full well that none of the leading plotters possessed any experience in the Jacobin underground; and that some, like Preston, were inclined to be drunken and garrulous, or, like Thistlewood and young Watson, to be 'wild' and impulsive. He also doubted old Watson's stamina and resolve under interrogation.[62] During his interrogation Preston confirmed that young Watson was drunk when he led the charge to the Tower in the name of Wat Tyler. Watson senior also admitted that he had never been able to control his son who had once been treated in Bath for insanity.[63]

Watson and Preston were probably exaggerating the young man's volatility in order to deflect attention from their own involvement in the plot. Still, Evans was well aware that this sort of conspiratorial milieu was a perfect recruiting ground for spies and informers. He had been duped himself by a spy in the late 1790s, and had then seen his friend, Colonel Despard, executed in 1803 as a result of the government's intelligence system. In contrast to the inexperienced Spa Fields plotters, Evans's vigilance during the winter of 1816–17 was exemplary. Several spies reported that he was suspicious of their motives, as well as cagey about discussing armed insurrection.[64] He had good reason for caution. Watson introduced the seedy spy John Castle into the Spencean society in October 1815, and then into his own conspiratorial organisation, on the strength of nothing more than a casual prior acquaintance.[65] In the winter of 1816–17 the Spencean society and the plotters were being watched by more than a dozen spies and informers.[66] Scores of informal or irregular informants also volunteered information to the Home Office and other authorities.

Given the intensity of the surveillance, remarkably few of Evans's Spencean followers were compromised in 1816–17. Surprisingly, one of the few seemingly to be trapped into an indiscreet conversation was George

Cannon. A mysterious informant, 'NN', persuaded him in February 1817 to disclose a good deal of information about the Spa Fields conspiracy. We cannot rule out the possibility, however, that Cannon talked deliberately, either to underline his own innocence, or to vindicate his legal clients Preston and Hooper, or to confuse the government intelligence network. Another spy had reported a few months earlier that a 'crafty man' named Cannon appeared to be responsible for disseminating coded and anonymous hoax-letters containing threats and false reports of plots and agitations.[67] This was exactly in character, and is one of the rare instances of an early nineteenth-century radical taking deliberate counter-measures against Sidmouth's spy system.

The story that Cannon told 'NN' sounded wild enough. He claimed that Watson, Preston and Hooper had become unwitting 'tools' of enemies of the Bourbon regime in France. He himself had recognised a notorious revolutionary agent from France standing in the wagon at Spa Fields. Cannon believed that young Watson's impetuosity had spoilt a carefully planned uprising intended to spark simultaneous eruptions in France, Belgium, Ireland and elsewhere in Britain. He also claimed that the conspirators had received secret funding for their legal and other expenses from France, from Irish agents in London and from some very respectable London radicals, including Lord Cochrane and the Regent's rakish playmate W.A. Miles.[68] There was at least a germ of truth in all this. Watson and Preston did not deny the details when approached by 'NN' for confirmation; though they cursed Cannon for his indiscretion. The veteran United Irishmen envoy, William McCabe, whom Thistlewood had met in France in 1814, had indeed crossed secretly to London and been present at the attempted uprising of 2 December. He was arrested soon after in Belfast.[69] Raids on the plotter's premises uncovered at least one £10 bill from Lord Cochrane[70] And W.A. Miles had by this time become sufficiently disenchanted with the Regent to have written several blackmailing pamphlets about him. Miles was also a close friend of radicals like Hardy, and might well have given secret financial encouragement to the conspirators.[71] Perhaps he was the rich gentleman whom, Watson claimed under interrogation, had provided them with money and had promised to spirit them to the United States if the plot failed?[72]

Whether Cannon was genuinely deceived or playing a devious game, his statement confirmed the non-involvement of Evans's Spencean society in the plot. A defence counsel during Watson's trial for high treason in 1817 made the point that none of the 250 witnesses called by the government had been members of the Spencean society. Two of the most influential radical journalists in the metropolis, Hone and Cobbett, both ran articles in winter 1816–17 exonerating the Spencean society from any connection with the conspirators. Cobbett pointed out that Evans had

9 *Alehouse ultra-radicals: Hunt, Thistlewood, Watson and Preston planning the Spa Fields uprising.*

been advocating his plan for eight years, and that it was a perfectly constitutional scheme based on Christian brotherhood.[73]

Cannon probably asked his old friend Cobbett to publish this timely dissociation at a time when the Spenceans felt themselves under grave threat from the government dragnet. In private, however, the Spenceans made some efforts to defend the conspirators from government retribution. When Preston was arrested during the riot by the City authorities, Cannon appeared as his solicitor. He persuaded the Lord Mayor to alter the charge from a felony to the lesser, bailable, offence of 'party to the riot'. He did the same also for Hooper, though the person whom Cannon proffered as Hooper's bail turned out, typically, to be fictitious.[74] Cannon might also have had a hand in dredging up dirt on the chief government witness (and spy) John Castle, who possessed an embarrassing record as a thief, forger, blood-money informer, bigamist and pimp. These disclosures persuaded the jury to acquit the conspirators of high treason and certain execution. Other Spenceans, such as young Evans, Moggridge and William Carr, helped in various ways to hide young Watson, and subsequently to smuggle him out of the country to the United States.[75] Even Thomas Evans was prepared to head a subscription to pay for the legal defence of the conspirators.[76]

These moves did little to heal the breach between the Spenceans and their former colleagues (with the exception of the equivocal Preston). Though Watson senior agreed in 1817 to testify to the Evanses' innocence of any involvement in the riot, he and the other plotters subsequently felt betrayed by them. Mutual suspicion soon turned to outright hostility.[77] Recent studies have rightly stressed the 'watershed' effect of the Spa Fields meetings of 1816. Westminster radicals of all shades recoiled from Hunt's mobbish oratory at the mass meetings, and still more from the attempted uprising. They were frightened that the government would use the latter as a pretext to reinstate an anti-radical legislative and judicial terror similar to that of the 1790s. After the failure of the conspiracy, the Spa Fields ultra-radical leaders are usually represented as having divided along two broad strategic lines. Dr Watson, in alliance with Hunt, concentrated on developing the 'constitutionalist' but intimidatory tactic of the mass radical platform. This could also serve as a springboard for national insurrection, or as a means of convening a national convention and anti-parliament. Thistlewood, Preston and Hooper cooperated with Watson but committed themselves also to the underground 'politics of violence': they simultaneously planned an armed coup d'état designed to spark a national insurrection.[78]

These accounts of post-Spa Fields radical developments neglect to say what happened to the true Spenceans – that band of London ultra-radicals who remained committed to the leadership, ideals and tactics of Thomas Evans (and his predecessor). Their numbers were small, perhaps no more than a few hundred at peak, but they left their mark on the evolving character of London popular radicalism. The Spencean society continued after 1816 – as it had done during the war years – to provide a training ground for future ultra-radical leaders and propagandists. It served as a point of contact between Westminster reformers like Galloway and the world of tavern ultra-radicalism from which they are generally supposed to have been estranged. Through Spence's plan of parochial land reform Evans's society perpetuated an important sub-strand of ultra-radical ideology. And it continued a vital radical strategy and cultural form – the tavern debating club.

6

Tavern debating clubs: Spencean strategy and culture, 1815–17

The Spenceans' preference for the tavern debating club as a radical organisation and strategy linked them with long-established popular traditions. The English alehouse had been a pivotal institution in plebeian life since the sixteenth century. By the eighteenth it served as labour exchange, house-of-call, trades' headquarters, benefit club, strike centre, pick-up joint, unlicensed theatre and drinking place. Groups of seventeenth-century sectaries had gathered in taverns and alehouses to debate and enact profane and blasphemous rituals. There they had likely rubbed shoulders with turbulent young trades' apprentices who met in clubs for recreational, fraternal and occasional political purposes. The irreverent post-Restoration coffee-house and tavern club culture had rapidly encompassed urban artisans, shopkeepers and lesser professionals, as well as patrician intelligentsia. Alehouse clubs had also proved to be stubborn centres of Jacobite popular resistance.[1] But the 'true parent' of the popular radical debating club was – according to W.H. Reid – the Robin Hood Society founded in a tavern of that name in Butchers Row around 1742 by the schoolmaster Peter Annet. Its debating modes, convivial practices, social composition and blasphemous-seditious proceedings established a pattern that was widely imitated in London and the provinces, particularly during the American Revolutionary War and the Wilkite agitation.[2] According to Reid, most of these alehouse clubs in London had been absorbed into the democratic agitation of the 1790s, helping to make them a staple Jacobin form. The United movement underground exploited their inspirational and insurrectionary potential during the years 1797–1802, and Spence relied on their defensive and educative properties to preserve his following from 1803 to 1814.

Strategy

None of these lessons was lost on Thomas Evans, which is why he founded his Spencean society along tavern debating club lines in 1814 and why he persisted with this form in the face of rival strategies. Events in the immediate aftermath of the Spa Fields uprising seemed to vindicate his decision. The jailed plotters faced what looked like inevitable high treason convictions and Hunt prudently reined in his London activities for fear of being implicated. Ultra-radical initiative thus passed back to Evans; between December 1816 and February 1817 his Spencean society flourished as never before. The twice-weekly alehouse debates at Soho, Moorfields and the Borough were packed to capacity and fresh members enrolled at every meeting. New debating sections opened at the Commercial rooms in Whitechapel, the Golden Key in Spitalfields, the Northumberland Arms in Bethnal Green, as well as at Richmond, Bath, Leicester and Birmingham.[3] In January 1817 Hampden club delegates from Leicester and from Manchester (in the person of shoemaker William Benbow) attended the Cock on several occasions. They promised to circulate 1000 copies of a new edition of Evans's *Address*.[4]

The success of Evans's tavern debating clubs presented the government with a vexing problem. We have seen that section fourteen of the Seditious Meetings Act of 1795 had proved reasonably effective against Jacobin debating halls like Gale Jones's British Forum. But less formal convivial debating clubs held in the tap-room, parlour or club-room of a low alehouse or tavern had been harder to suppress. Provided tavern clubs kept their numbers reasonably small and avoided corresponding, they dodged the provisions of the 1795 Act. It was next to impossible to frame legislation that did not at the same time attack innocent alehouse recreational clubs. The right to meet in alehouses to debate public affairs had, a *Leeds Mercury* correspondent noted in 1802, 'long been claimed by free Britons and acknowledged by all administrations'.[5] Such clubs were regarded as part of an Englishman's birthright, along with the ale that lubricated them. The anti-radical legislation of 1817 could do nothing more than renew 1795 provisions. The relatively open character of Spencean clubs (as well as Evans's avoidance of treasonous plots) largely nullified their penetration by spies and informers. Action against individual debaters for using seditious, blasphemous or treasonous words was hampered because spies and shorthand writers were liable to be detected in such small, close-knit gatherings. Moreover – as we shall see – alehouse debaters could convey anti-establishment sentiments in elliptical ways that were difficult to prosecute in the law-courts.

In order to suppress this type of informal club the government had to rely on traditional alehouse licensing powers exercised by Justices of the Peace at quarter sessions. After 1795 these powers had been used increasingly to close down or frighten public alehouses that hosted LCS sections. Even so, JPs had not been completely effective. In London, unlike Manchester, publicans did not always cooperate (a Society of United Publicans was formed to protest against the 1795 legislation).[6] Because of the relatively unsystematic harassment London radicals could sometimes keep ahead of local officers by moving from alehouse to alehouse; Reid's Jacobin debating club had moved to seven different locations before establishing itself for a time at Hoxton, beyond the jurisdiction of City magistrates.[7] Particular alehouses also became focal points for resistance. Ousted LCS sections were advised to concentrate at places like the George in East Harding Street, the Fleece in Windmill Street, the Green Dragon in Fore Street and the Cecil in St Martins Lane.[8]

Significantly, all these alehouses were to recur as radical venues in later years, though it is unclear why. Some might have been unlicensed and hidden in obscure alleys and courts. Most were located in centres of depressed artisan trades, in Spitalfields, Finsbury and Soho, and probably developed strong traditions of trades and radical support. The Fleece in Windmill Street which harboured Spence's free-and-easies between 1803 and 1811 was still a noted house-of-call for tailors in the 1840s.[9] But it was probably the individual publican's politics and degree of commercial independence which really determined whether an alehouse could resist harassment. William Tilly who kept the Swan in New Street where Spence's followers had met in the early Regency years was himself a fervent Spencean. And the chief haunt of Evans's Spenceans in the postwar years, the Mulberry Tree in Moorfields, was kept by the Johnsons who were radicals and Spencean sympathisers. They also owned the freehold on their premises.[10] One report of Spencean tavern clubs in 1817 complained that landlords were frequently 'in league' and signalled if any strangers approached.[11]

There is evidence that Sidmouth was urging JPs to take more systematic and intensive action against Spencean alehouses early in 1817,[12] but this was only a supplementary tactic. Since he could not legally prohibit Spencean tavern debates, nor implicate the society in the Spa Fields affair, he decided to move against the Spenceans by arbitrary arrest of their leaders. Early on Sunday, 9 February 1817, Evans and his son were arrested at their house on a warrant asserting suspicion of high treason. A series of recommittals and re-examinations kept them in Coldbath Fields until the Suspension of Habeas Corpus passed through parliament on 4 March. Thereafter, they were detained in prison for a year without ever being charged.

A few weeks after his arrest Evans wrote a petition to the government expressing astonishment and outrage at the extremity of this action. He claimed the Spencean society was 'not a political institution' but a 'club of individuals' whose discussions were intended only for instruction and amusement.[13] The post-war government was sceptical, and official correspondence in the Home Office files, 1815–18, shows that they were not simply being paranoid. Suspicion of Evans's Spenceans appears to have been based on a realistic appraisal of their debating club activities. The exaggerations and confusions of the *Report from the Committee of Secrecy* of February 1817 were – one suspects – tactical. Place felt that 'it ... purposely confounds Spenceans, reformers, and the rabble of all sorts'.[14]

Even so, the government had many reasons for doubting the harmlessness of Spencean debating clubs, not least because they could be used as instruments of riot or national insurrection. Significantly, Watson and Thistlewood did not altogether reject the use of convivial debating clubs after Spa Fields, they simply wanted to adapt them to the new circumstances of post-war mass unrest. Throughout 1816–18 they continued to use alehouse clubs as a supplement to their insurrectionary strategy. Preston and a former United Irishman, Doyle, were deputed to stage free-and-easies at alehouses like the Waterman's Arms in Bethnal Green, at Doyle's own King's Head in St Lukes, and at the Red Lion and Spotted Dog in Spitalfields. They still hoped to mobilise rough, unemployed canal navvies, soldiers, sailors and dockworkers. Convivial tavern clubs were a favoured recreational form of such masculine groups. Preston often extolled the alehouse free-and-easy in 1817 as 'the best way of getting the men together to see if they would come', but his ambitious plan to establish twenty all over the city as flashpoints for an uprising was lost in a blur of alcohol.[15]

Evans never spoke openly of any intention to use Spencean debating clubs for insurrectionary purposes. The government interpreted this as simply another indication of his craftiness. Most spies thought he was biding his time until the country was properly prepared – he had, after all, federated the debating sections so that their activities could be coordinated. In *Christian Policy* he had promised 'to form affiliated societies in every parish and street'. By January 1817 he had made a promising start.

Culture

Even if Evans did not intend to use the debating clubs as insurrectionary sections, the 'instruction' which took place in them was hardly as innocent or as apolitical as he claimed. A good deal of the society's energies between 1815 and 1817 went into disseminating radical and rational knowledge in the manner of the LCS. The numerous cheap publications – 'swivels against established opinions' – which Reid had seen strewn over alehouse tables in the debating clubs of the 1790s also featured at Spencean meetings. Typical examples included copies of Paine's *Rights of Man* (sold by one Houndsditch printer only to Spencean members); Evans's manifestos, *Christian Policy* and *Address and Regulations*; Spence's *Important Trial* and *Spence's Songs*, parts I–III; and Wedderburn's periodicals,

Forlorn Hope and the *Axe to the Root*. These were accompanied by penny, twopenny and threepenny handbills, satirical posters and broadsheets like the *Polemic Fleet*, Hone's political litanies, and printed copies of the previous week's song (often composed by Spence, Evans or Wedderburn). Printing was usually done by Arthur Seale and paid for by a small fee levied on attendants. Issues of Cobbett's *Political Register*, White's *Independent Whig* and Wooler's *Black Dwarf* were also read out occasionally for those unable to read or afford publications.[16]

For people in these last two categories especially, the weekly debates were the chief source of 'instruction'. Under Evans's leadership, debates were openly didactic. Most debating questions echoed the arguments of *Christian Policy*: they aimed – as we have seen – to unify the Spenceans against other ultra-radicals. In practice, however, few speakers bothered to stick to the topic, let alone address Evans's theories or conform to the debating rules laid out in the *Address and Regulations*. The favoured Spencean debating style was polemical – symbolised in their occasional alternative title of 'Polemic Club'. They delivered their speeches in combative and dramatic style – a mode of political instruction still preferred by working-class Londoners in the late nineteenth century.[17] Wedderburn's speech at the Nag's Head on the topic 'Is the American government to be applauded or condemned for the means they have taken to civilize the Indians by giving them a portion of land?' was described by one spy as 'the most blasphemous, inflammatory, incoherent harangue I ever heard'. Wedderburn had asserted among other things that

Ignorance was better than knowledge, Barbarism better than Christianity, even the Father of Christianity had declared that he came to set Father against son and son against Father. He sincerely hoped that if there was a God he would prevent Christianity from getting among the Indians, give us nature and we don't want to know God we can worship the Sun.[18]

Wedderburn's rather garbled version of Holbachian rationalism probably mattered less than his tone and language. He spoke plebeian profanity in the voice of someone who was himself barely literate. Robert George, debating the crucial Spencean question of whether 'the expenses of government cause the miseries that surround us?', showed a similar disregard for ideological nicety. Instead, he described a royal procession of that day where nobody had cheered 'except a guinea-pig in a tree, but the people soon took care to beat the powder out of his head'.[19] These were just the kind of 'extemporaneous effusions' that Reid had observed in nineties' tavern debates.

When speakers did use Evans's theories, they usually rendered them in a cruder, demonological style. At the Cock on 15 January 1817 Preston typically exclaimed:

though the landholder was a monster who must be hunted down there was a greater evil namely the fundholder, it was that system that separated between Prince and People, that destroyed our vitals, these were the rapacious wretches that took from us 15d. out of every quartern loaf, and who received it, why the government, but though they received it with their right hand, this system forced them to pay it with their left.

On other occasions he fulminated against the Bank of England: 'it is in that building that is concentrated most of our evils' – thereby twisting Evans's ideas in much the same way that young Watson had done when he had told members of the Lifeguards in 1816 that the government intended bringing out 50,000 Russian soldiers to serve in their stead.[20] All this was closer to the sentiments, tone and temper of William Cobbett than Evans would perhaps have liked.

Songs and ballads – one of the oldest political expressions of the English poor – also featured prominently at Spencean debating club meetings, just as they had done in Jacobin taverns during the 1790s and at Spencean free-and-easies during the war years. This kind of political singing alarmed the establishment almost as much as plebeian debating. George II had legislated against Jacobite singing in 1730; Hannah More churned out loyalist ballads in the 1790s in an effort to counter Jacobin tavern songs. The *Report from the Committee of Secrecy* of 1817 cited the Spenceans' 'profane and seditious songs' as one of the chief justifications for suppressing the society, a fear which Chartist Thomas Frost later satirised in his novel, *Paul, the Poacher*.[21] The *Satirist* explained in 1808 that people like Hannah More were alarmed because the song possessed a special, deeply rooted 'magic power' in English popular culture.[22] Songs could convey anti-establishment sentiments in an appealingly traditionalist form and – like debates – act as conduits for carrying political ideas to the less literate.

Most published Spencean songs were heavily didactic: 'The Propagation of Spensonianism' to the tune of 'Lilies of France', or 'A Song to be Sung at the Commencement of the Millennium' to the tune of 'God Save the King'. Evans's lugubriously titled 'The Inefficacy of the French Revolution' must have been almost impossible to sing, however instructive the lyrics. But when Spence, Tilly or Evans refrained from tampering too much with the original folk-ballad forms, their adaptations had the rousing qualities of good political hymns. Some were also humorous or whimsical: Evans's 'Address to the Fair' to the tune of 'Lass of Richmond Hill' has a catchy simplicity, and 'The Rose and the Shamrock', the rollicking Irish jollity of a good drinking song.[23] This would probably have suited the regular Spencean singer Thomas Porter, noted for an ability to sing 'loud' and for always doing so in the white apron of his trade as stone-cutter. However, he, Edwards and Savidge were usually asked to sing the more general radical favourites, 'Ça ira', 'Quivedo' and 'The Hog of Pall Mall'. Edwards's

version of the last was a comical and blood thirsty tilt at the Regent and
Royal Family:

> Tis in Pall Mall there lives a Pig,
> That doth this Mall adorn,
> So fat, so plump, so monstrous Big,
> A finer ne'er was born.
>
> This Pig so sweet, so full of Meat,
> He's one I wish to kill.
> I'll fowls resign on thee to dine,
> Sweet Pig of fine Pall Mall.[24]

Porter's rendition of 'Quivedo' offered infidel as well as political instruction:

> When Quivedo went down to the region below
> He met with the Devil a sort of a bow
> Then scraping his hoof with a comely like grace
> Made an offer to him to show him the place
>
> Far and wide they ranged over torterous crimson
> And on every side saw millions of damned
> Each profession locked up in a separate cell
> Like the pews in a Church that is inside of hell
> Dam'd lawyers, dam'd priests, dam'd knaves
> Dam'd patriots, dam'd –, dam'd time serving slaves
>
> Dam'd bishops, dam'd – [unintelligible]
> With the rest of the *** set toasting their noses
> There was Peter, Mahomet, and Aran and Moses …[25]

This ballad hints at the Spenceans' interest in religious subjects – one of
the reasons Evans felt entitled to make his disingenuous claim about their
non-political character. But the society's critics found their religiosity
neither convincing nor consoling. Spencean communitarian and millenarian ideals were regarded as a masquerade for political sedition and
economic levelling. Their plebeian anti-clericalism was thought to
threaten a pillar of the country's constitution and social order, and their
blasphemous rationalism to undermine popular moral restraint as well as
deference to traditional authority. After attending his first debate at the
Cock in 1816, James Hanley, who was less preoccupied with Spencean
infidelity than some other spies, reported that 'the principal instigators of
these proceedings are not only avowed enemies to Revelation but do not
scruple to deny the Existence of the Deity himself thereby striking at the
root of all moral obligation and perverting the minds of those young men
who are so unwary as to connect themselves to so dangerous a faction'.[26]

The Solicitor-General, Robert Gifford, gravely reported this finding to Sidmouth who had one of Evans's former friends questioned closely on the Spencean leader's 'atheistic' views.[27] These were also the target of a pamphlet written in 1817 by a clergyman who took exception to the underlying deism of *Christian Policy* and to its use of scriptural passages to support the Spencean creed.[28] Another pamphlet, written in the same year by loyalist Thomas Williams, claimed that Spencean 'alcoholic clubs' combined intoxication, advocacy of sexual promiscuity and blasphemous rituals. He predicted that their brand of irreligion would, if unchecked, produce 'footpads' and 'dissolution of government and disorganisation of society'.[29] The *Report from the Committee of Secrecy* (1817) concluded similarly that 'the minds of those who attend their meetings are tainted and depraved; they are taught contempt for all Decency, Law, all Religion and Morality, and are thus prepared for the most atrocious scenes of outrage and violence'.[30]

By contrast, Evans claimed in his petition that Spencean emphasis on conviviality was proof of their harmlessness; tavern gatherings merely provided 'entertainment' for members. Up to a point this was true. Spy reports show that participants often enjoyed themselves immensely. Here is a summary of a typical meeting held at the Watermans Arms, Castle Street, Bethnal Green, in late September 1817.

The spy John Williamson reported that he arrived at the tavern around 7 p.m. and drank and chatted in the tap-room for an hour whilst the long-room upstairs filled up. He then went upstairs, paid the landlord three halfpence at the door for tobacco, and found a place in a room crammed with around 140 people. Thomas Porter took the chair, opening proceedings with a song against the Prince Regent 'about a fat pig in Hyde Park'. A great many other anti-government songs followed, all punctuated by toasts drunk in porter. The chairman's was 'May the Skin of the Tyrants be burnt into Parchment and the Rights of Man writen upon it'. Each toast was received with shouts, claps and other acclamations. At this point the landlord appeared, urging caution because some officers were downstairs. Some of the company dispersed immediately; those who stayed covered with a 'merry-making song'. Soon after this, Preston arrived (having been called by a sailor) and tried to drum up a debate by delivering a speech against 'those damn'd infernal villains'. No one seemed willing to follow, so the company concluded at about 11 p.m. by giving three cheers with their hats off. Williamson, Preston and a sailor then went down to the bar for gin.[31]

Most of the evening's convivial practices resembled those of any early nineteenth-century free-and-easy or convivial club such as William West described in his *Tavern Anecdotes* of 1825. Samuel Bamford experienced something similar in 1817 when he visited a London trade club meeting addressed by Preston and Watson. Taverns also provided the Spenceans with recreation outside of their formal meetings. Thomas Pemberton, boot-closer, former Despardian and frequent chairman of the Mulberry Tree section in winter 1816–17 spent many of his non-working hours in the tap-room. He drank and chatted with the publican Johnson and his wife, played checkers with other Spencean colleagues and perhaps waited for trade custom.[32] The Mulberry Tree was his neighbourhood pub – the pivot of his working and social life, as it was for so many of London's working classes throughout the century. Men like Pemberton treated the tap-house as their private parlour and looked to the Spencean debating club to provide the same kind of entertainment as a concert hall or plebeian theatre. They expected to relax and gossip with friends in a convivial atmosphere, to be stimulated by dramatic, fantastic and humorous performances, and to participate in the ritual 'hullabaloo' of singing, toasting, chanting and cheering. Free-and-easies gave them a chance, in Crabbe's words, 'to be kings and heroes of the night'.[33] Some Spenceans probably attended them for purely expressive purposes – to enjoy the social ritual and to experience a release of tensions.[34]

Not all aspects of Spencean entertainment were escapist, however. Most of the convivial proceedings were intensely political in their aim. They continued and extended the eighteenth-century popular practice of expressing anti-establishment sentiments in symbolic or ritualised forms.[35] The alehouse debating club was a perfect vehicle for protest of this sort. Much of its vitality and popularity as a radical structure and strategy derived from its ability to mediate radical politics through traditional recreational customs and rites. As in Wilkes's day, Spencean toasts, debates and songs were intended both to entertain and to puncture dominant symbols of social and political authority. Their tavern meetings worked to eliminate social deference: this is why priests were favourite targets of abuse and why speeches were so often blasphemous and profane. Speakers like Wedderburn enjoyed being deliberately shocking, using a type of verbal iconoclasm to break down taboos. They resembled those seventeenth-century Ranters who had met in taverns to swear and blaspheme in 'a symbolic assertion of freedom from moral restraint'.[36] Reid had noted the same sort of outrageous behaviour in Jacobin tavern clubs. The Spencean debating meetings of 1816–17 sometimes give an impression of deliberately flouting respectability. Contrary to the usual image of artisan radicalism, participants made no effort to mask roughness of speech, conduct and appearance – again reminding us of John Wilkes's tavern saturnalia. John Castle reported, for example, that anyone who turned up to debates at the Cock 'finely dressed' was accused of being a spy.[37]

Castle was himself an exponent of that famous radical toast: 'May the last of the kings be strangled with the guts of the last of the priests.' Spies

lapped up this sort of stuff, but they had no need to invent it – Spenceans
vied to produce the funniest or most shocking toasts. Here, too, they drew
on an old tradition. Plebeian satirical toasting had originated as an inver-
sion of loyalist ceremony in the populist alehouses of the late sixteenth
century.[38] Men like Pemberton practised the art with toasts like: 'May the
guillotine be as common as a pawnbroker's shop and every tyrant's head a
pledge.'[39] More typical still was the toast given by Edwards at the Mulberry Tree on 16 January 1817: 'May the Spencean Hogs never cease
their grunting till they have got their rights' – an indication that plebeian
radicals were redeploying Burke's infamous phrase, 'the swinish multitude', in spoken as well as written propaganda.[40]

Another way of breaking down the cultural mystique of the establishment was to lampoon its sacred offices, texts and ceremonies. In spite of
recent interest in the Queen Caroline affair, and the satire it generated,
humour remains a neglected facet of nineteenth-century radicalism. Spencean debating clubs revelled in it. Spence himself had signalled this by
advertising in his 1801 free-and-easy 'to treat all the swine with a jest' –
itself a jest given the Jacobin redefinition of the word 'swine'. Popular
radical delight in irony, satire and parody had been inherited from diverse
sources. Traditions of urban literary and political satire associated with
sceptics, wits and libertines like Rochester, Blount, Woolston and Wilkes
reached artisan and lower middle-class radicals through Grub Street pam-
phleteering, popular theatre, graphic caricature and, of course, tavern and
coffee-house debates. In Spencean circles this probably merged with a
more demotic tradition of anti-authoritarian raillery derived from broad-
sides, chap-books, prints and almanacks, and from the customary recreational practices of fairs, festivals, holidays, elections, taverns and chari-
varis.[41]

Many Spencean tavern entertainments were cast in the shape of truculent and ribald 'counter-theatre',[42] or, more properly, of low burlesques.
Loyalist pamphleteer Thomas Williams wrote in 1817 that Spenceans
deliberately turned religion into a 'jest' and 'burlesque' by mixing 'sacred
devotions with the revelry of the tavern and alehouse'.[43] The traditional
free-and-easy closing ritual of 'harmony' provided the occasion for most of
the Spenceans' satirical practices. Because Cannon could not sing, he
conducted harmony by intoning 'an obscene paraphrase of the 1st Psalm',
a performance that must have been especially piquant since he was a
licensed dissenting minister. Old Evans – always the most pedagogic –
devised a type of land reforming catechism; he shouted out phrases like
'The land is the people's right' and the company chanted in agreement.
His son preferred to read out the questions from Hone's *Political Litany*,
with the debaters again chanting the responses – a practice which the
Committee of Secrecy singled out for mention.[44] The countrywide popu-

larity of Hone's political parodies of the Anglican litany and catechism – even before his triumphant court acquittals at the end of the year – was probably due in part to their advertised suitability to being 'said or sung' in alehouse meetings of this kind.[45] Mass Observation reported that satirical litanies were still popular with London pub gatherings in the 1940s.

Lord Ellenborough had in 1810 accused Gale Jones's British Forum debating club of being a 'mock tribunal'. He was referring to the ancient and socially irreverent popular custom of mock-trials practised by rural recreational groups and urban fraternities such as trade, apprentice, underworld and social drinking clubs.[46] Ritual mockery of this kind no doubt served various social purposes, the most obvious being to undercut traditional authority by ridiculing its roles, functions and symbols of distinction. Spencean tavern clubs often had an element of the mock-tribunal about them. Like tavern judge-and-jury clubs of mid-Victorian times, they mimicked parliament, the church, or other weighty institutions. Spenceans also gave each other grandiose and ironic nicknames like 'Black Prince' (Wedderburn), 'Bishop' (Preston), 'Brown Friar' (Cannon), 'Count' (Perrin), 'Poet of the Court of Acquity' (Clark jnr) and 'St Matthew' (Pemberton).[47]

Nicknaming and chanting could also serve other symbolic functions such as demarcating Spenceans from other radicals and inspiring them with feelings of group solidarity – especially important during periods of government repression or radical recession, when morale was low. Spence extolled this aspect of free-and-easies in his 'Address to Mankind' of 1811: 'Do not men when they meet encourage each other and resolve each other's doubts and thus build one another up in their opinions?'[48] We recall, too, how Evans had gathered together a group of former state prisoners and United men at the Green Dragon in 1802 and 'proposed to have meetings of the same kind often to keep a sett of persons united together'. Convivial drinking rituals were easily adapted to such purposes. Temperance campaigner John Dunlop wanted tavern associations suppressed in 1839–40 because in them 'Men are ... attracted, allured, drawn together, wound around by the chains of habit, of vitiated appetite, social encouragement, and in many cases conventional restraint.'[49] At a time when Thistlewood was making followers swear secret oaths of loyalty on the Bible, Evans was achieving a similar effect through the ritual mutuality of his tavern meetings. John 'Snip' Keenes's evidence at a government interrogation of December 1816 confirms how seriously Spencean bonding ceremonies were taken. He denied having been a real Spencean on the grounds that, though he had attended their meetings for some eight months, he had never stayed back for 'harmony'.[50]

Christopher Hill detected an affinity between the rough tavern meetings of Puritan sectaries and 'communal love feasts'. Evans's attraction to the tavern club might have been based in part on its ability to serve as a surrogate outlet for religious longings. The central promise of his writings of 1815–16 was that Spenceanism would restore 'the harmony and brotherhood so necessary to the well-being of society'[51] – a closely knit tavern fraternity represented at least a partial implementation of these ideals. Tavern debating clubs belonged to the category of radical organisations which aspired to push 'beyond democracy to consensus'.[52] In this they resembled religious sects. Men with such strong popular dissenting and communitarian backgrounds as Evans and his followers naturally found tavern clubs appealing because – like sects – these convivial groups represented Spence's utopian community in microcosm.

Sects were also known for their capacity to fortify members during times of dislocation and persecution. During the first half of 1817 Spencean tavern clubs had their fraternal bonds and defensive properties tested. The arrest of the Evanses under suspicion of high treason, the vehemently anti-Spencean findings of the Committee of Secrecy, the passage through parliament of the Suspension of Habeas Corpus and four other anti-radical measures, the arrest and execution of the Derby rioters and the intensified pressure from JPs on Spencean taverns: all these combined to recreate an atmosphere of terror and repression akin to that of 1795–1803. Most Spencean sections stopped overt political debating for fear of compromising themselves or the Evanses (in prison). Some of the weaker sections closed down within weeks, and the lively Bethnal Green group led by Fair and Clark lasted only a few months. The main Mulberry Tree section survived but suffered the defections of the regular chairmen Pemberton and Savidge, though not before they had advised their colleagues to stop political debating and singing.[53] A few of these defectors joined Thistlewood's insurrectionists who resumed their plots and castigated the Spenceans.[54]

Considering the difficulties that beset the Spenceans, they proved strikingly resilient. Instead of disintegrating under the immediate impact of the repression of winter and spring, the society generated a series of interim leaders whose tactical acumen nearly equalled Evans's own. John Baxter resumed a role of fifteen years earlier when he had operated radical free-and-easies in the teeth of the government repression of 1801–3. He urged the society to purchase a copy of the Habeas Corpus Suspension Act and organised for members with legal expertise to explain its ramifications. One result was the abolition of formal office-bearers so that the Spenceans no longer constituted a society in law. Baxter seems also to have initiated the new Mulberry Tree debating strategy of casting debates in religious form.[55] Wedderburn helped him by devising new debating topics and volunteering to take over Evans's task of superintending sections, particularly 'young' ones like the Golden Key in Shoreditch. He also pressed members to pay outstanding quarterage fees in order to meet printing costs and enable Mrs Evans 'to go on'.[56]

Janet Evans's ability to go on was another crucial factor in the society's survival. As in 1798–1801, she displayed indomitable qualities. She supported her husband and son in gaol, kept the business running and acted as a Spencean organiser and propagandist in her own right. Soon after the arrests, one spy reported that she was 'more furious than ever and bids open defiance. She sells the Spencean pamphlets which are much sought after.' She also wrote petitions to the government, and letters to radical periodicals like the *Reformist's Register*, *Independent Whig* and *Forlorn Hope*. They cited her own difficulties and denounced the unconstitutional imprisonment of her husband and son. Spies complained also that she was adept at smuggling political information in and out of prison, including versions of the Spencean plan which were then sent off to *The Observer* and the *Independent Whig*.[57]

At the beginning of winter she was mentioned as being one of the moving forces (along with Wedderburn, Jennison, Savidge, Moggridge, and Galloway) behind a Spencean revival.[58] A small group of debaters had probably continued to meet at the Mulberry Tree throughout summer and autumn, protected by the publican Johnson's commercial, political and geographic independence. No reports of these meetings survive, probably because spies had switched their attention to Thistlewood's renewed plotting at this time. By early winter 1817, however, debates at the Mulberry Tree were attracting sufficiently large crowds to provoke renewed government concern, and several spies resumed their attendance.

By this time, too, there had been an interesting change in tactics. The spy Hanley reported that the Spenceans had carefully studied the rulings on constructive treason at Jeremiah Brandreth's trial in order to evade them. Other spies commented on the debaters' care to frame topics in religious form. The society had also hidden its Spencean allegiances under the title of the Polemic debating club. As in early Regency years this entailed more than a name change: the Mulberry Tree section broadened its scope to attract a popular front of non-Spencean radicals. Professional orators from the British Forum, such as Wright and Steele, became regular speakers and attenders – as did a number of the Freethinking Christians who were meeting nearby at a Worship Street chapel (coincidentally named Evans's chapel).[59]

Beneath the surface the lineaments of the old society survived. Wedderburn was a star attraction as speaker. Spies reported that his ferocious anti-clerical and radical polemics ensured that the large room, easily capable of taking 100 persons, was 'every debate night crowded to suffocation principally by unthinking young men whose minds are too easily alienated and become enemies to order and religion'.[60] They also noted his

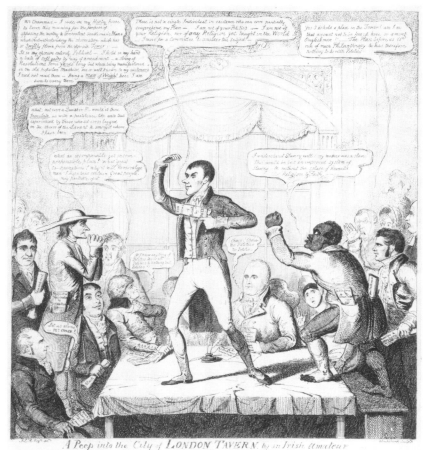

10 Wedderburn argues with Owen, 1817.

adoption of other leadership functions. He arranged the topics for discussion, he organised the annual supper to commemorate Spence's birthday at the Cock in June and he boasted of his intention to reopen debating sections throughout the town and countryside. Most important, he substituted for Thomas Evans as an ideologue.

Probably with financial help from Galloway, Wedderburn joined with Jennison in autumn to publish the *Forlorn Hope*, which he followed in winter with his own more substantial *Axe to the Root*. Small and shortlived as these periodicals were, their sale and distribution at Mulberry Tree meetings helped keep Spencean ideas alive against the rival claims of radicals such as Wooler, Burdett, Hunt and Cobbett.[61] Wedderburn extended his criticisms to the new cooperative doctrines of Robert Owen. Ill.10 shows the ragged mulatto preacher, armed with a Bible, shaking his fist at Owen during one of the celebrated August meetings at the City of London tavern. Wedderburn also published a letter in the *Forlorn Hope* warning Owen that 'the lower classes are pretty well convinced that he is the tool of the landholders to divert the attention of the public from contemplating on the obstinacy and ignorance of their governors'.[62] By December the Mulberry Tree had debated 'Owen's Plan' and agreed that it was destructive to social happiness.[63]

When it was announced after a debate on the evening of 20 January 1818 that the Evanses had been freed unconditionally that day, there were over seventy supporters at the Mulberry Tree to toast their health and welcome their return with a three times three.[64]

7

Blasphemous chapels: the preacher as insurrectionary, 1818–20

One of Thomas Evans's first actions after leaving prison in January 1818 was to announce his intention of reorganising the Spenceans 'on a better system'. He had decided to reconstitute the society along the lines of an independent dissenting sect. Some time in spring or early summer he and Wedderburn took out a joint licence to operate a dissenting chapel in a large basement backroom at 6 Archer Street – a small Haymarket laneway. The 'Christian Philanthropists', or 'Enquirers after Truth' as they sometimes called themselves, met three times a week. On Sundays, for no charge, Evans lectured in the morning and Wedderburn in the afternoon. On Wednesday evenings preadvertised debates or 'Conferences' were held at a cost of three halfpence at the door or by monthly ticket for sixpence. Young Evans usually took the chair, his father and Wedderburn gave the main speeches, the secretary James Mee issued the tickets and the treasurer, Seymour, collected the money. As in 1815, Thomas Evans accompanied the reorganisation with a new manifesto.[1]

Spies soon reported that despite the external changes Spencean blasphemy and sedition continued as before. They believed that the new format was purely expedient.[2] Their scepticism was understandable. Evans had spent twelve months in prison, and had seen the metropolitan radical movement decimated by repressive legislation. His attenuated Mulberry Tree section survived the magistrates' campaign against tavern debating clubs only because Johnson was a committed radical who owned the freehold on his premises, and perhaps because licensing authorities were lax in the Moorfields area. Even so, the Polemics had believed themselves in danger throughout the winter. In contrast, just around the corner from the Mulberry Tree stood the licensed meeting-house of the Freethinking Christians who had operated a radical-cum-rationalist debating club since 1798. Their attendance at Wedderburn's crowd-pleasing religious debates in December 1817 had drawn attention to their long immunity. Evans and Wedderburn decided to counter the state's apparatus of repression by sheltering the Spencean society behind the broad oak of religious Dissent.

It was notoriously easy to procure licences for both dissenting ministers and their chapels. Sidmouth had, as we have seen, failed to pass legislation tightening up their administration. By 1817 at least four leading Spenceans had taken out dissenting ministers' licences, most under the title of Unitarian. Archer Street chapel, with Wedderburn as its official 'Unitarian' preacher, pioneered a new model of ultra-radical debating club. It was soon widely imitated. Sidmouth experimented with draft formulae to seal this dangerous chink in the state's legislative armour, but found that he could not again risk offending Nonconformist interests.[3] The Six Acts of 1819 were to do little more than re-enact earlier provisions against formal debating clubs. The Home Office could act against radical and blasphemous chapels only by prosecuting speakers for libel on the basis of informers' transcriptions.

Wedderburn's success with religious debates at the Mulberry Tree in winter 1817 also reflected a general climate of interest in radical preaching and sectarianism. For most of 1817 the millenarian spy John Shegog was minister to a congregation of 'Christian Believers' in Mile End, before he transferred to the Borough Road chapel were he preached 'under the care and observation of Thistlewood and Preston'. He also passed information to the government about a supposedly seditious group of ex-Methodists who met every night in Holborn, and about the 'dreadful judgements' being preached in Spitalfields by the American revivalist Lorenzo Dow and his prophet associate, Dorothea Ripley. Evans's old friend, partner and Jacobin colleague, John Bone, was also operating a meeting-house in High Holborn where he preached to audiences of around 300, Wedderburn and Watson among them. Bone's assertion that Jesus was a reformer and his system a commonwealth led Wedderburn to suggest that he become a Spencean. Christian communitarianism had always been integral to Evans's Spencean society, but a prison reading of John Melish's American travels pushed Evans further in this direction. He discovered how the simple communal life of the Rappite sect at Harmony had 'produced freedom, equality and happiness as perfectly as nature will permit'. Perhaps he saw Harmonite 'fraternal Christianity' as an extension of the Spencean tavern ritual of 'harmony'. His new manifesto of 1818 was more sectarian than earlier writings in its support for the idea of small Christian societies 'abstracting themselves from surrounding error'.[4]

The new sectarian format also offered Evans a chance to reassert control over Spenceans who were showing signs of being tempted by other radical leaders. Thistlewood and his insurrectionary wing posed little threat: Evans believed that 'the Captain' had become deranged enough to 'knock someone off their hooks',[5] a judgement confirmed soon after when Thistlewood was sentenced to twelve months in Horsham gaol for challenging Sidmouth to a duel. On the other hand, Dr Watson's stature as an ultra-radical leader had grown apace since his acquittal in 1817. His decision to

exploit the mass radical platform in alliance with Henry Hunt greatly
increased his metropolitan support and provincial contacts. He organised
mass meetings at Spa Fields in May 1818, and at Palace Yard in
September. He also formed a series of radical unions which attracted a
wide following. Despite some economic improvement during 1818, his
weekly summer meetings at the White Lion in Wych Street (later the
Falcoln in Fetter Lane and the George in East Harding Street) were packed
to capacity. Out of them emerged a new group of talented organisers with
contacts in the provinces and in metropolitan trade societies. By winter
Watson was also beginning to attract some of Evans's Spencean followers,
including Wedderburn. Early in November Evans managed to persuade
the fiery preacher to resign his week-old membership of Watson's committee. A few days later it was the turn of veteran Spencean, John George, to
be warned off; Evans advised him to set up an affiliated Spencean chapel
instead.[6]

Evans's earlier concern to separate his Spenceans from Watsonite ultra-
radicals had by 1818 gained a new dimension. Then, it had been mainly a
matter of ideology and tactics, now it also involved style and social standing. At least from the time of his release in January Evans determined to
prove the superior *respectability* of the Spencean society over the rival
ultra-radical following of Watson and Thistlewood. This interest in adopting a more respectable and moderate radical stance can be traced in part
to the influence of Alexander Galloway. If worldly success had not
lessened Galloway's sympathy for radical reform, he had by 1817 grown
hostile to 'mobbish' political methods and socially unrespectable behaviour. Moreover, Galloway's interest in Spencean respectability was personal as well as tactical. His fondness and ambition for his nephew, young
Thomas John Evans, has been noted. William Hone described young
Evans in 1816 as 'a well-read studious youth, very modest in his demeanour and of good speech'; Galloway did not want these qualities endan-
gered by association with political undesirables.

There are signs, too, that the Evanses were coming to share his views on
respectability even before their arrest in 1817. After a debate at the Nag's
Head in January that year, young Evans provoked an uproar by announc-
ing that the Conservative committee 'had determined to abolish smoking
in their societies'.[7] This might have been the beginning of an intended
campaign to improve the image of the Spenceans; if so, it was arrested
with the Evanses. Symptoms of internal dissension on related issues nevertheless persisted at the Mulberry Tree in the winter of 1817. Wedderburn
was rebuked on several occasions for vulgar and intemperate speeches by
the genteel looking John Wright and his supporters.[8]

The imprisonment of the Evanses had also increased their reliance on
Galloway and other Westminster colleagues. Samuel Brooks presented

Thomas Evans's first petition; Galloway collected subscriptions and helped Janet Evans keep the business going. (Evans was later to reciprocate by voting for Westminster committee candidates at the by-election in 1818.) The family's links with respectable Westminster reformers were dramatically confirmed when a subscription committee headed by Galloway and Brooks allocated them close to half the total sum of £1450 collected for the 'Relief of Sufferers under the Suspension of Habeas Corpus'. The Spa-Fields leaders received nothing. This incident, and the acrimonious public dispute that followed, widened the gulf between Westminster reformers and Watsonites, and dealt a serious blow to the prestige of the Evanses in ultra-radical circles. Even old friends and followers like Moggridge and Carr were incensed by the apparent favouritism.[9]

Evans's attempt to impose a more respectable and moderate stamp on proceedings at Archer Street chapel precipitated the Spencean society's last and fatal split. When Wedderburn agreed to act as partner and preacher at the chapel, he probably assumed that the debating atmosphere would be similar to tavern club days. In fact, spy reports show that smoking, drinking, toasting, singing of vulgar songs and performing of burlesques no longer took place. Speeches were delivered from a pulpit and the congregation sat on benches. Evans was described as 'well-dressed' and his manifesto and speeches displayed a new note of restraint. Significantly, he announced in November 1818 that women were henceforth to be admitted to the chapel free – the very intention of attracting women showed how far the Spenceans had moved from their former alehouse patterns. Janet Evans might have been behind this move to rid Spencean convivial club radicalism of its rough masculinity. Wedderburn later hinted as much in a bitter attack on his former leader (published in 1819) in which he represented Janet as a 'Dulcina' who wore 'the breeches' and was responsible for Thomas's backsliding.[10]

Not all the Archer Street congregation were happy with the move towards respectability. Evans could rarely attract more than a dozen listeners to his measured Spencean lectures on Tuesday mornings; Wedderburn's ferocious rhetoric in the afternoon regularly gathered around sixty. Tensions generated by these conflicting impulses led to quarrels between Wedderburn and other members. By 2 November 1818 Hanley was reporting that 'Wederburn the Spencean was at the George last night. I understand this Mans Language is so Horridly Blasphemous at Archer St every Tuesday afternoon – that the Spenceans themselves are aprehensive of a Prosecution – some of them wish him to withdraw his name from their Society.'[11] When he did eventually leave the society and chapel some months later, it was in typical style; he took the benches with him. He was delivered over to a constable as a felon after a scuffle in the street with Evans and some of his followers. It was a pyrrhic victory; most

of the driving force of the Spenceans left with him. After trying vainly to
start another chapel, Evans and a tiny rump of debaters returned to the
Mulberry Tree. Wedderburn published a poem in the spring of 1819,
describing Evans as 'a half-baked cake' which 'Spence's God doth me
command to turn'.[12] His way of obeying the command was to open a
radical chapel of his own.

Wedderburn's new chapel, registered on 23 April as a Unitarian meeting-house for religious worship, resembled its predecessor in many ways.
It consisted similarly of two back-rooms, and was located nearby, on the
corner of Hopkins and Brewer Streets in Soho. The new building – co-
owned by a friend and follower of Thistlewood – was possibly a trifle
shabbier, the main room being actually 'a ruinous hay loft' capable of
holding around 300 people who reached it by stepladder. The preacher
used a desk instead of a pulpit, and there were no benches for the congregation. Tickets cost one shilling and admitted the bearer to the twice-
weekly night debates and Sunday afternoon lectures for a period of a
month.[13]

Many of the former Archer Street congregation were attracted to Wedderburn's new chapel. Longtime Spenceans and Haymarket locals featured amongst the signatories of the licence. Evans's oldest cronies –
William Carr, Robert Moggridge and John George – defected, still angry
over the Westminster relief committee. Other Spenceans were impatient
with Evans's growing moderation. Wedderburn's new chapel promised
more to a man like Davenport who boasted in October that he 'studies
politics all day, writes on politics, dreams politics and stands here twice
weekly preaching blasphemy and sedition'.[14] His friends, Charles Neesom,
a tailor, and Henry Medlar, a carpenter, seem also to have transferred, as
did 'Dr' Brown, a painter, printer and vendor of Cow Cross Street, Perry, a
shabby elderly veteran, and some of the rougher characters who had
attended Preston's free-and-easies in 1817–18, including Porter, George
Pickard and Robert George. Several government informers moved across
to Hopkins Street as well – Banks as a regular attendant, Hanley, Williamson and Edwards more intermittently.

Other members of Wedderburn's new congregation had no previous
connections with the earlier Spencean chapel. Hopkins Street debaters
were not only more numerous (often 200 or more), but they were also less
respectable; one observer described both orators and auditors as 'with few
exceptions persons of the lowest description'. They included a large
proportion of Watsonite ultras, particularly those disposed to favour
Arthur Thistlewood's insurrectionary plans. This was the group spies
called 'desperate' or 'fighting' radicals. They were men like William 'Black'
Davidson, an unemployed cabinet-maker reduced to turning the handle at
the Marylebone poorhouse mill. He and his friend, James Hartley (alias

Hartnet), an ex-soldier and unemployed servant, were desperate enough to commit footpad robbery in the radical cause. John Harrison, a ferocious unemployed baker and ex-Lifeguardsman, had been forced to steal sheep for survival during the previous winter. John Hill, a journeyman tailor, had fled from Manchester after taking a shot at the notorious radical hunter, Deputy Constable 'Joe' Nadin. The 'fighting' title was appropriate, too, for men such as Dennis Shaw, a veteran of the Irish Rebellion (with a strong following amongst Lambeth Irish iron workers) and his fellow countryman, Pinley, a leader amongst the former rebels, navvies and iron workers who met at the White Horse tavern.[15]

The three most extreme Watsonite pressmen of 1819 also attended Wedderburn's chapel. E.J. Blandford was a down-at-heel hairdresser, poet and occasional printer with Spencean sympathies. Thomas Davison was a journeyman printer who did most of the work for Thistlewood's coterie and became one of London's leading ultra-radical publishers in 1819–20. Samuel Waddington, a tiny, effervescent shoemaker who had established himself in 1818 as a trades' society and Watsonite activist, soon became a celebrated radical printer, billsticker, court defendant and Hopkins Street orator.[16] Two other members of the congregation were also destined to become notable radical propagandists in their own way – the future pornographer, William Dugdale, who was a tailor and migrant from Stockport, and the future spy, Abel Hall, a tailor and migrant from Plymouth. (Ironically, it was Dugdale whom Thistlewood suspected of being the spy because of the violence of his speech.) Finally, there was the shadowy orator and preacher, George Cannon, whose influence as a covert publicist was to touch and surpass them all.[17]

The chapel as political cell

Aided by Hunt's charisma and influence and Wedderburn's defection from the Spenceans, 'Dr' Watson became unrivalled leader of London's ultra-radicals. Through the efforts of Waddington and Gast he gained a considerable following amongst London trades during the winter of 1818. Dennis Shaw brought him an influx of Irish labouring support. Dugdale, Hill, and an ex-Luddite, William Washington, established new links with Lancashire radical organisations. The ultra-radical periodical, *Medusa*, founded in February 1819, provided a propaganda outlet, and Davison, Blandford and Waddington did any necessary printing. Watson also persuaded Thistlewood to give up armed conspiracy temporarily in favour of the ambiguous 'constitutionalist' tactics of the mass platform. Watson argued that a series of countrywide mass meetings to petition for reform would mobilise enough people to force reform or a confrontation (possibly armed), from which a national convention would follow.[18]

Wedderburn's chapel was intended to be an integral component of this strategy. He became a leader, and the chapel a section, of Watson's new radical union formed around April. In this capacity the 'Hayloft Preacher' helped to plan a successful meeting at Smithfield on 21 July, at which Hunt and Gast spoke forcefully in favour of the non-payment of taxes. A few weeks later Wedderburn chaired a Watsonite meeting at the George in East Harding Street where he announced the distribution to Ireland (and the English provinces) of several thousand printed copies of Hunt's speech, *Address from the People of Great Britain to the People of Ireland*. Around this time Watson elaborated his London organisation into seven parochial divisions, each with a president and secretary: at Seven Dials, Cripplegate, St James, Shoreditch, Clerkenwell, Lambeth and Soho (Hopkins Street chapel).[19]

Of all these divisions, Hopkins Street was the hardest for Watson to restrain in the summer months leading up to Peterloo. At a general committee meeting at the White Lion on 5 August Wedderburn's followers angrily called for armed resistance, while he himself made a ritual request to 'be placed in the front rank' and 'martyred' as an example to younger radicals. A few days later Harrison and Wedderburn were again amongst the few Watsonite ultras urging physical force – a pointer to the way they would speak on the Hopkins Street question of the following evening: 'Is it any sin to kill a tyrant?'[20] On the evening of Peterloo Wedderburn was actually in prison charged with blasphemous and seditious libel; Sidmouth had promised the Prince Regent on 12 August that the 'notorious firebrand' would be silenced by prosecution.[21] Under the substitute chairmanship of Cannon, the chapel nevertheless debated the question: 'Is it possible for the government to be extracted from the accumulating perils with which it is daily surrounding itself?'[22] Even without news of the massacre (which did not reach London immediately), the answer was negative.

Naturally the shock of Peterloo greatly strengthened the hand of Watsonites who favoured arming for mass meetings. Wedderburn, free on bail, was present at the George tavern when the news of the massacre was reported to a group of 160 ultras – nearly half of them Irish. One informer claimed Wedderburn to be the 'ringleader' of those advocating violent retribution, though Hartley was considered the most dangerous.[23] For the first time since his release Thistlewood also aired plans for a four-pronged London uprising. Over the next few weeks arrangements were made for the manufacture of pikes, weapons were raffled, and ammunition was purchased and stored. The Hopkins Street division openly urged members to attend the forthcoming London meeting of 25 August, armed.[24]

Even amongst these hotheads, arming was still presumed to be defensive. The change of venue from Kennington Common to the better protected Smithfield market place made this clear. Thistlewood himself proposed not to carry weapons there, but to have a brace of pistols hidden nearby in case of attack. In the event the meeting was so peaceful that Watson wrote to Mayor Atkins praising his restraint.[25] As long as Watsonites could still feel themselves part of Hunt's national radical campaign, they remained essentially committed to constitutionalist tactics. After Smithfield all their energies went into organising Hunt's magnificent triumphal entry into London on 17 September – an occasion which saw cooperation between a broad front of radicals, including Watson, Thistlewood, Galloway, Evans, Carlile, Wooler, Cobbett and Burdett.[26] But Hunt had grown wary of his connection with the London ultras: he deliberately snubbed Thistlewood and Watson, and later published letters implying that they were provocateurs.[27]

Wedderburn was quickest to announce a change in strategy. He declared after the Hopkins Street debate of 15 September that 'Hunt's principles would not suit their purpose which must be nothing short of revolution'. London ultras, he claimed, had 'sufficient force to carry out their own plans independent of the Huntites and Burdettites, the greater part of whom were ready to join them'.[28] After this, Watson stopped trying to rein back Thistlewood and the fiery Hopkins Street circle. Most Watsonites were disgusted by Hunt's cautious policy of relying on legal redress through the courts. They believed that the government was on the point of suspending Habeas Corpus and launching a systematic attack on radical leadership. The time seemed ripe to take advantage of the national outrage over Peterloo through armed mass meetings staged simultaneously all over Britain. Such meetings could have three possible results: provoke an armed confrontation between the people and government which the people would win; grow to such a proportion that a national assembly could be summoned; or force the government to capitulate and pass a radical reform of parliament.[29]

This strategy was endorsed by several ultra-radical delegates from Manchester. Early in September, a leader of the Manchester female radical union, 'Mrs Wilson', visited the Watsonites to raise subscriptions for arms and to found a London branch of the female union. She left them in no doubt as to their backwardness compared to the North. She attended meetings at the White Horse tavern with a loaded pistol tied up in her handkerchief and threatened to use it on several occasions. She also scorned London female reformers for their timidity, and openly became John Hill's lover, provoking his wife to inform.[30] A few weeks later another delegate called Tetlow arrived from Manchester under the alias of Westwood or Wedgwood. He attended meetings at Watson's house, various taverns and Hopkins Street chapel, confirming northern support for armed simultaneous meetings aimed at dethroning the Prince. He also urged London radicals to form branch unions subdivided into sections of a dozen members with overall management entrusted to a secret committee of five.[31]

Details of Watsonite organisation at this time are murky, but an attempt seems to have been made to implement Tetlow's advice. Hopkins Street chapel became the location and Wedderburn the 'Captain' of the sixth and most militant of the new sections. Over the next three weeks Wedderburn (who had been acquitted of seditious libel), Hartley, Waddington and 'Black' Davidson harangued crowded chapel meetings on the need to arm and drill. Congregations were directed to prepare for armed confrontation at the forthcoming Finsbury meeting of 1 November – to be held simultaneously with others all over the country. Some of the oratory was no more than the ritual rhetoric of vengeance which also filled ultra-radical periodicals in the charged atmosphere of October–December 1819. But there was a more practical side also. Wedderburn stressed that the loyalties of soldiers could be bought: corporals were promised a piece of land; sergeants, a double allowance of pay; and officers, benefits according to their rank. Some members of a recently disbanded militia were brought into the chapel and given a subscription on the spot. Such policies, Wedderburn said, would induce the army to treat the Prince Regent as they had Charles I – 'to spit in his face and cut him off'. Waddington also claimed to have invented a 'drag with spear' for dismounting cavalry. And Hartley assembled a cache of 2000 pike-heads.[32]

Wedderburn stressed that acquiring and learning to use a weapon was only the first step. He had been taught how to prime, load and fire the 'big gun' on a man-o'-war, and how to handle small arms on the top station of a privateer, but still thought it necessary to practise drilling and manoeuvres. 'We must learn how to form the solid square', he told his cheering Hopkins Street audience, 'and from that to extend our centre' – much as the Irish had done at Vinegar Hill. His section drilled in the chapel after debates and – with other 'fighting radicals' – before dawn on Sundays at the back of Primrose Hill, at Chalk Farm, and at Harrow Road near Paddington. They stored their arms and pikes at Hartley's house. Thistlewood declared at the White Lion on 18 October that 'he depends more on Wedderburn's division for being armed than all the rest' – Davidson, Hartley and Wilson even robbed a man near Regent's Park at pistol-point to raise money for arms.[33]

For most of October the Watsonites held high hopes of provincial support. Thistlewood visited Leicester to collect money and to forward the policy of simultaneous meetings. He also corresponded with Nottingham, Derby and Manchester. Waddington's 'Saracen's Head' division contacted Yorkshire, and Blandford visited Norwich.[34] But as the date of the proposed meeting drew near, Hunt's public opposition to simultaneous meetings began to take its toll. By the end of the month Watson reported that some dozen centres had decided against meeting on 1 November. News that a pro-Hunt faction had prevailed over Tetlow and William Walker in Manchester was the greatest blow. These defections disturbed Wedderburn particularly. He warned Watson and Thistlewood that the Hopkins Street section now believed that no armed uprising should be attempted until parliament actually suspended Habeas Corpus. He feared that in the absence of provincial support London ultras could muster no more than 2000 men, not all of them armed.[35]

Wedderburn's fears proved well grounded, even down to his estimate of the numbers who braved the thick mud and biting cold to attend the meeting at Finsbury Market Place on 1 November. Although some of the fighting radicals turned out with arms and Hartley openly sold pike-heads at 1s 3d each, the meeting was not attacked. Wedderburn gave a speech – according to *The Times* 'fraught with the beauties of Billingsgate slang' – advising the crowd to attend the next scheduled meeting of 15 November with 'harms'. But after all the preparations, the meeting was clearly a failure and a crushing disappointment to Watsonite hopes.[36]

About this time Arthur Thistlewood began to make serious plans to assassinate members of the government. Dwindling provincial and local support as a result of worsening weather, the opposition of Hunt, fear of government action and improving economic conditions suggested that the simultaneous meetings of 15 November could also fail. Above all, Thistlewood was hurt by Hunt's widely publicised spy accusation. 'From this time', claimed a contemporary observer Alexander Richmond, 'he seemed imbued with the opinion that he should perform some bold and daring act to wipe away the imputation.' Wedderburn's speeches at Hopkins Street shared this anger and frustration. He claimed to be goading his sons to violence by taunting them with their degradation and their cowardice in enduring it. Hopkins Street chapel and the Scotch Arms in New Round Court became nerve centres for those prepared to countenance Thistlewood's assassination plans.[37]

However, on the fitting date of 5 November the conspirators decided to stop using Hopkins Street as a conspiratorial centre because reports of late night drilling had reached the press and a raid was expected. This threat, combined with rumours of the impending government bill, led them to debate the question on 15 November: 'Is the Design so plainly evinced by his Majesty's Ministers, to prevent the People from possessing and learning the use of Arms necessary for the Preservation of Public Peace, or is it a daring and unconstitutional attack upon the Rights and Privileges of Englishmen?' In spite of this defiant debate, James Hanley reported a week later: 'a body of ultras at Hopkins Street chapel, Soho, who are considered as the most determined for carrying of the government by force of arms have quarrelled with each other and are broke up'.[38]

It is not clear exactly why this happened or what it meant. Rumours of impending government legislation had been causing unease in ultra circles for some time. The Hopkins Street section had anticipated a raid ever since the publicity of 5 November. When the new legislation was passed they could expect to be one of the government's first targets. Under these circumstances some members probably wanted an excuse to defect. Towards the end of November John Hill returned secretly to Manchester because his wife had informed on him and he expected to be arrested. Spy reports around this time reveal an increasingly tense and paranoid atmosphere amongst the 'fighting radicals'. By the end of December Hartley had resigned and gone into hiding; the spy Williamson had left for the Cape to join a band of armed Methodists; Banks, another spy, had also gone underground after Robert George denounced and tried to shoot him; and Harrison was so nervous that he offered to inform.[39]

Wedderburn himself did not defect. On the evening the Six Acts were introduced into parliament he held a crowded debate on the question: 'Seeing that his Majesty's Ministers have ordered all Pices of Ordinance and Military Stores which are in the possession of private individuals, to be deposited in their own Depots, would it not be advisable for them to take down all the Iron Pallisading throughout the Empire, and to Destroy the Gas-Works to prevent the Radicals making use of them in case of Civil War?' The following day he and Waddington attended a meeting designed to organise a further mass meeting in association with Manchester. Within a week both men were in gaol, charged respectively with seditious and blasphemous libel. Attempts by a White Lion subcommittee to raise immediate bail for Wedderburn (and for Watson, who had also been arrested for debt) failed. Debates continued for a time under Cannon, but a spy reported a few months later that the chapel had closed, and that Wedderburn's imprisonment had devastated his followers. They could only console themselves with the thought that when 'Their Black Prince' regained his liberty, he would be even 'more staunch'.[40]

Whatever caused the quarrel in the Hopkins Street section in late November, Thistlewood continued to regard Wedderburn as one of his trusted conspirators. When Hopkins Street closed he re-formed some of the old members as a new fourth section under the leadership of the spy Banks.[41] And on the day before Christmas, when he had already formulated his plan to assassinate government ministers, he reacted jubilantly to a report that Wedderburn had been released on bail. '[That] would be one to our strength', he told the informer Edwards, 'for Bob always says he will be in the front rank.' Had it not been a false rumour, Thistlewood might well have been right. Wedderburn was never short of courage, and he felt himself near the end of a hard, bitter life. He would almost certainly have joined Thistlewood at Cato Street with the intention of 'plunging a dagger into the heart of a tyrant'.[42]

'Temple of blasphemy and sedition'

It would be easy to regard Wedderburn's chapel as simply a cover for ultra-radical plots. Neither his opponents nor attendants took this view. If anything, the government seems to have been more alarmed by the chapel's propaganda than by its activities as a covert section. Archer Street debates had led Sidmouth to consider outlawing such chapels in 1818, and it was for preaching seditious and blasphemous libel that Wedderburn was prosecuted in 1819 and 1820. On the second occasion, in February 1820, the Solicitor-General commented that Hopkins Street had attracted the attention of magistrates because of the 'extraordinary freedom' with which political and religious topics were handled. He and the judge who sentenced Wedderburn stressed that blasphemous ideas delivered in vulgar and extreme language to an audience of the lower orders were 'particularly dangerous'. If unchecked, they would lead to a sapping of popular morality and social respect.[43] Having read through the Committee of Secrecy papers soon after Peterloo, William Wilberforce concluded similarly that ultra-radicals were shifting to irreligious propaganda because it undermined the social edifice 'more effectually'.[44]

Notorious criminals and radicals were often interrogated about their exposure to infidel doctrines and encouraged to recant as an example to others. Wedderburn's Cato Street colleagues aroused particular interest. The chaplain of the Clerkenwell House of Correction, Rev. David Ruell, investigated their religious tenets in detail because he thought it vital 'to the interests of Society and religion … to ascertain what were the professed principles of men who could calmly meditate such a crime'. His predictable conclusion was that infidel ideas had caused them 'to cast off the fear of God and [they] were thus fully prepared for the commission of any crime'.[45] Ruell's reports, coupled with the conspirators' defiance on the scaffold, confirmed Sidmouth's fears about the dangers of places like Hopkins Street.

Twice a week for six months Wedderburn's chapel attracted 200 or more of the most extreme and impoverished radicals in London. It did so, moreover, at a time when many of the attenders believed England to be on the verge of a national insurrection. Why did they put so much time and energy into chapel debates? No doubt there were many individual reasons. For some the chapel might have offered a flight into dramatic fantasy in response to political impotence. But the broad answer seems to be that Hopkins Street in 1819, like the Mulberry Tree tavern in 1816–17, offered uniquely appealing instruction and entertainment. Allen Davenport boasted that Hopkins Street chapel was unsurpassed in the world for the kind of questions that were proposed and argued there.[46] Debating topics were often suggested by members of the audience and reflected their plebeian understanding and concerns. No rules of decorum prevailed other than to shout down speakers who attempted to read from books or written material. Wedderburn – by his own admission 'a low vulgar man' who could scarcely write – claimed that every speech he made at Hopkins Street arose 'on the spur of the moment'.[47] Spy reports show that his language was always coarse, violent and colloquial.

Such anti-intellectualism or 'parochialism' is more commonly associated with the poor than with artisan autodidacts.[48] Wedderburn, many of the other speakers and most of the audience, probably belonged to an especially poor and casualised sector of artisans and lower middle-class sorts. Hopkins Street chapel was one place where 'ragged radicals' – to use Dr Watson's self-description – could hear and express political sentiments relevant to their own understandings and experiences. The result was popular radical ideology in its most unvarnished form. Regular reports from the spy Banks, as well as the detailed transcriptions of specially commissioned 'manifold writers', help us to gain some idea of what these sentiments were and how they were conveyed.

Off-the-cuff utterances accentuated the populist strain observable in some early nineteenth-century radical pressmen. Like Cobbett, Hopkins Street ultras derived their rough theoretical framework from eighteenth-century 'Country Party' critiques of political corruption and exclusion. Tacked to this were fragments of Major Cartwright's saxon constitutionalism and of the natural rights agrarianism of Paine and Spence. In general, however, Hopkins Street debaters eschewed theoretical or abstract analyses. As in earlier tavern days, theirs was less a systematic ideology than a rhetoric designed to arouse emotion, to debunk authority through shock, pathos or humour, and to impel action. Wedderburn and his followers are usually seen as republicans, deists and Spenceans – descriptions they sometimes used themselves – yet Paine or Spence would probably not have recognised the ideas expressed at Hopkins Street chapel. Speakers worked within the broad paradigm of 'Old Corruption', but transformed it into something very like a folk demonology. Their rhetoric drew heavily on allusive traditional symbols, motifs and beliefs, disregarding most literary sources or authorities apart from the Bible. More than anything else, Hopkins Street oratory echoed the 'ideology' of London's rioting crowd – that truculent plebeian-populist outlook which Rudé, Thompson and others have delineated so well.

The virulent anti-clericalism of almost every transcribed speech drew on a very old popular political language. During the sixteenth and seventeenth centuries anti-papal caricatures had evolved into a type of political shorthand – to the extent that both sides of the Civil War enlisted its imagery to their cause. The militant anti-clericalism which erupted amongst plebeian sects during the revolutionary decades had been fed by traditions of English erastianism, by lay movements originating with the Reformation and by 'an ancient folk distrust of clerical ambitions and ... hatred of priestly domination, corruption and greed'.[49] During the eighteenth century no-popery rhetoric was a staple of the volatile populism of the London crowd. Images of bishops and priests in political caricatures acted as a type of barometer of opinion.[50] Jacobinism added a measure of Gallic venom to this essentially Nonconformist anti-clericalism and helped to give it a wider political perspective.

Hopkins Street debaters used the traditional image of the fat-gutted parson as a symbol of theft, corruption and mystification. However they laid equal stress on the role of established clergy as state propagandists, prosecutors (Society for the Suppression of Vice) and clerical magistrates.[51] Older demotic prejudices also surfaced. A debate of 29 November asked: 'Which of the three professions is most calculated to harden the human heart, the Hangman, the Grave-digger, or the Parson?' All three were perceived to have a crucial relationship to plebeian death and burial since they could determine whether the poor met a dignified end, or one that was untimely, brutal and degrading. For Wedderburn's followers these were realistic fears: some were destined to die at the hangman's hand, and many others to receive squalid pauper's burials. All agreed that the 'fat-gutted parson' had the least compassion for the suffering, death and proper burial of the poor.[52]

And although Hopkins Street speakers called themselves republicans, they were, a month after Peterloo, still holding to the old popular nostrum that the King (Prince Regent) was the dupe of evil advisers. They referred to the Prince being 'led by the nose' by corrupt ministers. Wedderburn represented him as a fool who could be induced to say anything if bribed with 'plenty of wine and two or three whores'.[53] Talk of dethroning made no mention of the irrationality of monarchy as an institution, only of the Prince's personal forfeiture of the trust and confidence of the people. Traditional xenophobic libertarianism – the 'dark side' of populism – also showed itself in frequent claims that 'ugly cut-throat Russians' and 'barbarians' were to be brought over to defend George's throne as they had been in the early days of 'Dutch William'.[54] Even lingering Jacobite sympathies surfaced occasionally. Wedderburn was immensely proud of his Jacobite grandfather, and one occasional Hopkins Street informant reported rumours that a member of the Pretender's family was hiding out near Staines.[55]

When they did air republican sentiments, speakers often referred back to the seventeenth century. Wedderburn was fond of saying that the people should serve the Prince Regent 'as Charles I's soldiers did'.[56] A group of sailors who attended Hopkins Street believed in early 1820 that portents showed another Cromwellian 'reformation' to be imminent. They also recalled a favourite republican model of Wedderburn's which does not appear in most analyses of post-war radical ideology. This was the story of 'Masaniello', 'Masinello', or 'Tom Angelo' as they remembered him, the fisherman of Naples who managed to usurp government for a few hours.[57] The idea of such a 'low and obscure character' momentarily turning the world upside down had impressed both W.H. Reid and Spence in the 1790s;[58] Wedderburn probably heard of it at the free-and-easies at the Cock in 1813–14.

Wedderburn also invoked the example of a better-known fisherman-republican:

Jesus Christ, by the new testament, taught the Christian religion; but what did he teach us, what did he say? 'acknowledge no king', now every king is a lord: every parson is the same … as he lords over us … Jesus Christ says acknowledge no rabbi (no priests); no! he knew their tricks, and says stand it no longer.[59]

The scriptures had manifold use for chapel orators; Wedderburn and Waddington claimed to know 'many passages therein to suit the reformers' purposes'. The ancient symbol of the levelling Christ, beloved of folk rebels and Jacobins alike, was easily given ultra-radical topicality. Hunt's entry into London and Carlile's blasphemy trial both drew equations with the life of Jesus. Wedderburn explained:

Times were bad then and Christ became a Radical Reformer. Now I never could find out where he got his knowledge but this much I know by the same book that he was born of very poor parents who like us felt with him the same as we now feel, and he says I'll turn Mr Hunt – and then when he had that exalted ride upon the Jackass to Jerusalem the people run before him crying out HUNT FOREVER! for that was the same as crying out Hosanna to the son of David.[60]

Wedderburn and other speakers rarely outlined detailed agrarian reform proposals, but they often cited Spence's Levitical justifiction that 'God gave land to the children of men, then why should we suffer it to be taken from us?' They also drew scriptural support from Exodus and Daniel for throwing off slavery and killing tyrants.[61]

Debaters were conscious that scriptural symbols and language carried weight in the society at large. Waddington upstaged his prosecutors in court on 1 September 1819 by drawing a Bible from his pocket and telling the jury that he relied on 'an authority much higher' than legal precedents. He went on to display a skill with scriptural texts that earned him a succession of court acquittals. When prosecuted for sedition in September 1819 Wedderburn also escaped conviction by claiming his right to practise an ancient English folk tradition – 'the true and infallible genius of prophetic skill'. This he demonstrated with a mixture of scriptural citations and descriptions of his 'sleeping visions'.[62]

There is no doubt that Wedderburn and Waddington used their biblicism to influence the courts. They succeeded because London jurymen shared their respect for the idiom of the scriptures and its political applications. Much has been written about constitutionalist rhetoric as part of the tactical and ideological armoury of popular radicalism, but historians have been less disposed to acknowledge the similar function of scriptural symbols. Puritan rebels had made the Bible an emblem of truth and William Hone deployed this legacy brilliantly in his celebrated court defences of 1817.[63] He and Cruikshank featured the Bible conspicuously beside Magna Charta and the Bill of Rights as part of 'the Wealth that lay in the House that Jack Built'. In Thomas Preston's opinion anyone who failed to resist oppression was 'a rebel to his God'.[64] Speakers at Hopkins Street used scriptural rhetoric automatically because it was for them a familiar and versatile political trope, just as it was for many scholarly millennialists. Waddington even mimicked the device of figurative exegesis. He claimed that the text 'Woe to the nation whose Prince is a child' referred to the Prince Regent brought up in the lap of luxury; and the passage 'if the right hand offend cut it off' applied to the Prince because he was the right hand of the people.[65]

Their rhetoric also exhibited a typically artisan (and populist) anger at the erosion of community and craft values, standards and ways of living. In numerous ways speakers attacked the ruling classes for abandoning traditional social responsibilities (versions of moral economy). The debating topic for 26 October 1815 asked: 'Is it not probable that the Loyal Cordwainers will be driven to the necessity of becoming Radical Reformers, seeing that the Prince Regent's Boot and Shoemaker refuses to give regular wages, and gets his work done in the poor-houses?' Degraded artisans like Wedderburn and Waddington felt themselves victimised both as producers and consumers. The passing of the Corn Laws and the Property Tax was 'a blow struck against us poor devils … while they are feasting their fat guts, ours are griping'. Landlords, they claimed, now cared for nothing as long as they could extract rent from their tenants: 'The Poor can go to hell for all they care'. Parsons, likewise, were willing to bankrupt and imprison small farmers by demanding tithes, yet neglected their traditional social obligations of charity and help to the poor.[66]

Behind this broad populist explanation for distress and oppression – the theft, corruption and mystification practised by an elite of kings, priests and lords – were some differences of emphasis. Those with a Spencean background tended to see land theft and monopoly as the root cause of popular misery. In response to the question 'which of the two parties are

likely to be victorious, the rich or the poor, in the event of a universal war',
Wedderburn explained that two classes of people had arisen because 'the
land was held by about 400 families alone'.[67] Along with most speakers,
he divided society into social classes based on haves and have-nots – 'the
very rich and very poor' – rather than employing the usual radical distinction between productive and parasitic classes. Those at Hopkins Street
clearly felt themselves to be without property, resources or respectability.
Wedderburn spoke from the bitter experience of a rejected beggar when he
exclaimed: 'the rich are always enemies of the poor, they despise us, they
not only despise us themselves, but they teach their servants to do so'.
Shortly before the Cato Street attempt, Thistlewood similarly attacked
London shopkeepers as 'a set of dammed aristocrats' and claimed not to
believe that any man worth more than £10 could be good. Even radicals
were not exempt from such criticism. Speaker after speaker asserted that
propertied and titled radicals could not be trusted. Money might be accepted from 'great ones' like Earl Fitzwilliam or Coke of Norfolk, but such
men should be kept 'in the background' and shot or 'cut off' if they showed
signs of betraying the people.[68]

Speakers tended to view politics from a personal and local perspective.
The symbols of 'Old Corruption' were turned into flesh and blood villains
and located in a social and geographical setting familiar to their ragged
Soho audience. When Wedderburn wanted to demonstrate clerical vice he
did so by reminding his listeners of John Church's behaviour at the Vere
Street homosexual brothel, or of the Vicar of St Martin's Parish who had
signed a loyal address promising to cooperate with magistrates to put
down sedition. He named local clergymen who had stolen from the communion plate or double-charged their Parish for black mourning cloth at
the time of Princess Charlotte's funeral. He told of attending a sailor's
wedding where the curate had begged for wine and food because his entire
fee went to the vicar. He described how, as a prisoner in Coldbath Fields,
he had seen a poor, hardworking Welshman sacked from the job of prison
chaplain and replaced by a 'fine dress'd man, powdered and of polished
language'. 'I knew he would get it', Wedderburn told his packed congregation bitterly, 'because he could tell us poor devils a pack of dammed lies.'[69]
If some of these examples seem crude and trivial, they nevertheless convey
an undeniable feeling of plebeian authenticity. We sense that the Hopkins
Street auditor experienced this populist rhetoric in much the same way
that the pre-revolutionary Parisian had read his *libelles*: 'the villains and
heroes were real to him; they were fighting for control of France. Politics
was living folklore.'[70]

How integral was religion to this political folklore? We know that some
Chartists evolved a species of radical 'counter-Christianity' (with infidel
affinities),[71] but whether we can apply the same notion to Hopkins Street

is uncertain. Men like Wedderburn tended to merge sacred and secular ways of thinking.[72] And like many with far greater pretensions to being systematic thinkers, they were often ambivalent or plain inconsistent in their stance on religion. We cannot say whether Thomas Preston really believed in the levelling promise of Judgement Day, or whether he simply thought it an appropriate idiom for addressing threatening letters to Lord Sidmouth.[73] On the same day that 'Dr' Watson wrote a letter to his brother full of the ecstatic millenarian language of the coming Jubilee, he published an article denying the immortality of the soul and espousing a commonsense materialism (it also cited a declaration from Solomon).[74] What are we to make, too, of the character of Wedderburn's belief (let alone of the message conveyed to listeners) when he could assert that 'reason and commonsense' rather than scripture should be man's sole guide, then immediately cite Exodus 21.16 in support of putting slave-stealers to death.[75]

We can be a little more confident, however, about the religious convictions of some members of the chapel circle. Irishman Dennis Shaw used intensely religious language in both speeches and letters, and it was his Lambeth Irish followers who insisted that Thistlewood administer a sacred oath of silence.[76] Some Hopkins Street extremists, including Robert George, 'Black' Davidson, Harrison, Hartley and Firth, also attended Thomas Hazard's 'school' in Queen Street, Edgware Road, where the prevailing sentiments were unequivocally religious, as well as treasonous. Hazard, an old crippled school-teacher, and his leading disciple, Emmanuel Francis, were breakaway Wesleyan Methodists and extremely enthusiastic.[77] 'Black' Davidson's Methodist sentiments were probably in abeyance at this time (though they re-emerged in the Tower), but Firth still occasionally visited a Methodist chapel in Hinde Street and was deemed by Rev. David Ruell to be 'under religious impressions'. The conspirators, Richard Bradburn, James Gilchrist and Charles Cooper were also declared to be firm believers in revelation. And when the spy Williamson defected, he joined a band of Methodists bound for the Cape. Perhaps the ultra-radical Manchester delegate, 'Sailor Boy' Walker, was right when he remarked at the White Lion in November 1819: 'there are not many of us is Radicals over Religions'.[78]

Some of the most outspokenly infidel of Wedderburn's associates seem also to have believed in a mixture of folk magic and Christian supernaturalism.[79] Affecting to be personally sceptical, Preston nevertheless boasted of the prediction of a Brentford cunning woman that he was destined to be a celebrity and to prevail over great perils, including prison.[80] Williamson left for the Cape partly because he feared the fulfilment of a fortune-teller's prediction that he was destined to great trouble in his thirty-sixth year.[81] Some of the apparently reckless behaviour of Thistlewood and his fellow plotters between 1817 and 1820 might have derived from their belief in the power of magical forces such as omens, prophecies and portents. They cherished a scrap of torn flag with the words 'die' on it as a talisman of good fortune, and seemed convinced that certain flags or symbolic actions would automatically 'rouse the people'.[82] Thistlewood rejected revelation, yet believed in providential interventions. He and Wedderburn both described the death of Princess Charlotte as 'a judgement from God' over the execution of the Derby insurrectionists.[83] And the ferocious Cato Street conspirator, John Brunt, thanked God on hearing news of the impending Cabinet dinner: 'he has called all the Ministers together for us to murder them'.[84] In the same month the spy J. Brittain claimed he had spoken to a group of Wedderburn's followers who 'declared they was never so happy in their lives, for it appeared that God was on their side'. They saw portents of a coming revolution in: 'A Dead King, A Dead Duke and a Foolish Prince and a suffering nation'. And they ascribed these judgements to the corruption of the ministers.[85]

Rationalist texts and theories were rarely if ever mentioned in Hopkins Street speeches. Much of the alleged infidelity reported by spies and loyalists was not scepticism of a systematic or theoretical kind, but crude plebeian blasphemy. Observers did not bother to make the distinction: all that mattered was that Hopkins Street debaters 'set at defiance everything holy, everything sacred'.[86] As in Mulberry Tree days, speakers deliberately tried to shock. After one particularly torrid piece of blasphemy, Wedderburn admitted that 'he had been endeavouring to offend that they might ring it in the ears of Kings, Lords, Princes and Commons'. He claimed that the timidity, superstition and deference of the common people – learned from priests and patriarchs – had to be jolted out of them. 'We should think none greater than ourselves' he told his congregation in a debate entitled: 'Is the Bible the Word of God?' To prove it, he called Moses a 'whoremonger', and David a murderer like the Manchester magistrates. These were typical examples of his blasphemous exegesis. Intellectual rationalists might concentrate on exposing the historical or philological inconsistencies of the scriptures, Wedderburn simply gave them new meaning by translating actors, events and doctrines into the speech and settings familiar to his hearers. In a sermon of 29 November he described the prophet Zacharias as a 'liar', Balaam as a 'fortune teller' worthy of the Bridewell, God as 'a molloch', Joshua as a 'liar and fool' for commanding the sun to stand still and 'the author of the Bible' as a murderer because he had had John the Baptist's head struck off 'to gratify the desire of a whore'.[87]

Modern readers must stretch their imaginations to understand why this kind of plebeian profanity could have seemed politically dangerous, as well as immoral. One of the more reliable of the Home Office spies, Spitalfields artisan James Hanley, suggested that blasphemy had the effect of making ultra-radicals 'better fitted for ... acts of desperation'.[88] It is difficult to take such claims seriously. Yet why else would desperate men like Thistlewood and his associates have bothered to listen to Hopkins Street blasphemy? 'Butcher' Ings – perhaps the fiercest of the conspirators – hinted at his reasons when he vowed shortly before Cato Street that 'he would not have anything to do with any man who feared God or the Devil, Heaven or Hell, or who went to Church and Chapel'.[89] (Presumably this did not include blasphemous chapels.) The ringleaders of the conspiracy all prided themselves on being infidels in the Wedderburn mould, and – with the exception of Davidson – died on the scaffold unrepentant.

Broader, more speculative, aspects of religion were discussed at Hopkins Street with little reference to ideas of fashionable published theorists (Volney, Voltaire, Paine and Holbach). However familiar debaters might have been with such infidel philosophy, their spoken irreligion was closer to a tradition of English folk scepticism which went back at least as far as the sixteenth century. At bottom was a strong plebeian distrust of abstract and enigmatic religious doctrines, a scepticism which often took the form of practical materialist doubts about the physical reality of immortality, Heaven and Hell. This kind of 'commonsense' was exactly Wedderburn's touchstone of disbelief. It informed his first reported excursion into infidel philosophy at the Cock in 1817, when he had argued: 'We were all born the same way and must all perish alike – we were but animals, we might talk of the immortality of a Principle within us, but what was it, he never saw it, never felt it, nor did he believe a word of it.'[90] His congregation voted in 1819 to reject the idea of the existence of the Devil because it 'could be of no use except to the clergy of whom he was the principle support', and they regarded future punishment as 'silly and ridiculous'.[91] The sorts of earthy doubts which Waddington and Wedderburn customarily expressed about the Balaam's Ass and Witch of Endor stories seem to have been widespread amongst plebeian exegetes. Spence had ridiculed these incidents, and the millenarian preacher, John Church, explained them (in the same way as Hopkins Street debaters) as the work of conjurers and magicians.[92] Wedderburn wanted to know, amongst other things, whether the reincarnated Samuel was walking around in Heaven or Hell, whether these places were made of matter, and, if not, what they were made of.[93] It was the intangibility of much religious doctrine that worried hard-headed artisans. The Cato Street conspirator John Strange could not bring himself to believe that God had 'really made a revelation of himself', and Richard Tidd told the Rev. David Ruell: 'I have met with no *facts* to prove Christianity true.' Neither man, Ruell believed, had abandoned Christian belief altogether, but they held sceptical ideas that were 'inconsistent with a rational profession of it'.[94]

Like their folk predecessors, many Hopkins Street debaters seem to have been led to doubt over social or moral concerns. They usually perceived the Christian God and many of his followers to be cruel or unjust. The horrors of Hell so luridly presented by evangelicals – particularly when associated with crude notions of predestination – seemed pointlessly vindictive. George Cullen expressed this sort of view in one of his tangential annotations to *Christianity Unveiled*: 'What do you think of the *justice of God* who first permitted the French Revolution and then destroyed millions of lives to prevent its effects, ask yourself that Mr. Christian ... If he [God] has the power of doing everything, he can prevent evil, now if he don't prevent it, it is a proof that he likes it.'[95] Many at Wedderburn's chapel were outraged at the way that professed Christians (the Vice Society) had persecuted Richard Carlile: 'Black' Davidson claimed that it had turned him from doubt to outright rejection of Christianity.[96] When questioned by Ruell, 'Butcher' Ings began by echoing Wedderburn's words that 'some parts [of the Bible] are very well', but then furiously interrupted the priest's homilies to ask 'whether a good Providence ever intended a person should starve in a land of plenty'. Neither he nor fellow conspirator Brunt could see what the Creator had ever done for their kind.[97] Wedderburn sounded uncharacteristically poignant when he made the same point at Hopkins Street on 10 November: 'God lend us better days, we cannot have worse but God I think as nothing to do with us, he to has forsaken us altogether'.[98]

One also gets the impression that Hopkins Street scepticism was primarily negative and critical. Rarely, if ever, did speakers mention the beneficial aspects of 'Nature'. It is of course possible that spy reports omitted this side of infidelity. Equally, these 'desperate radicals' might not have had any clear notion of an alternative natural morality, beyond some rough idea of social justice for the poor and down-trodden. Their slender understanding of the philosophical tenets of deism did not mean they were insincere. Evangelicals liked to cite the stoicism of Christian martyrs as proof of their depth of faith. By the same test the Cato Street conspirators were not found wanting. In spite of intense pressure from Ruell, only William Davidson sought religious consolation on the scaffold. The others were content to face death sustained by their strange blend of blasphemous scepticism and radical counter-Christianity. Even critics admitted that these infidels showed a dignity in dying which had eluded them in life.

At the same time there was a lighter side to Hopkins Street blasphemy. As in Mulberry Street tavern days, debates functioned as a form of theatre intended to ridicule authority and entertain listeners. Part of the chapel's notoriety derived from the reputation of its leading speakers as performers. Wedderburn believed that many had come to see and hear him because 'his name had gone abroad as a strange curious sort of fellow'. He had, in

Richard Carlile's words, developed 'a powerful eccentricity of manner'.[99] His coarse and profane language; his colour and physique (often described as stout); and the spectacular events of his life – the slave background, rejection by his wealthy family, experiences as a fighting sailor, criminal and pauper – were, to say the least, arresting. He displayed the traits characteristic of many populist leaders – physical bulk, roguery, flamboyance, bombast, emotional religiosity and a thirst for martyrdom.[100] And whether consciously or not, his speeches and performances echoed styles, themes and motifs fashionable in contemporary English and French melodrama.[101] A description of a similar 'irreligious service' conducted at Pratt Street in November 1819 confirms that histrionics were part of the blasphemous preacher's role. In this case the preacher began by feigning drunkenness, adopted 'the posture of a fighter', poured out a 'torrent of abuse' against the clergy, then finished with a series of blood-curdling prophecies. All this, he 'interspersed … with humorous anecdotes'.[102]

These, too, were a feature of Hopkins Street speeches. References to the noise from Balaam's Ass, to Castlereagh's desire for an 'unnatural union' between England and Ireland, to the ministers making 'a rod for their own bottoms', and to the Witch of Endor having 'slip't wind' indicate the delight taken in ribald word-plays.[103] The doyen of this blasphemous buffoonery was the remarkable shoemaker-printer Samuel Waddington, or 'little Waddy'. If Wedderburn's performances bring melodrama to mind, Waddington's evoke the world of pantomime. His role was that of the 'imp of mischief' or 'genius of nonsense' portrayed in contemporary pantomimes such as John Rich's 'Harlequin and the Red Dwarf'; or more pertinently, he personified Wooler's radical literary imp, 'The Black Dwarf' (another of Waddington's nicknames).[104]

Waddington belongs to a long tradition of Englishmen who specialised in radical and anti-clerical theatrical buffoonery, including the Puritan sectary Samuel Fisher, the radical jester John Wilkes and the celebrated 'Garrat election' radicals, Sam House and 'Sir' Jeffrye Dunstan.[105] His resemblance to Dunstan is particularly striking: Waddington possessed all the grotesque and saturnalian characteristics needed to succeed in the carnival atmosphere of the Garrat mock-election had it still been functioning. As a shoemaker he was an undoubted plebeian; at around 4 foot in height he qualified as a dwarf (like Dunstan); and his proclivities for drink, brawling and lechery were to earn him prosecution and imprisonment in the 1820s (for assault and for rape). Like Dunstan, too, Waddington became a popular celebrity by using his eccentric appearance and behaviour to lampoon the establishment. He composed and printed hoax placards, bills and letters; he paraded through Spitalfields in boards blowing a horn to proclaim an ultra-radical meeting. He kept watch on John Stafford's house decked out in women's clothes; he attended the Smithfield meeting dressed in a white apron with a huge pistol in his belt; he had courtroom crowds, juries, and sometimes prosecutors rocking with laughter during his numerous trials. It was his custom to sit on the edge of the bar in a white top hat with Bible in hand, conducting cross-examinations in a cocky, mock-menacing fashion.[106]

To take Waddington's blasphemous and bloodthirsty speeches at Hopkins Street absolutely literally, as one historian has done, is to miss the point; his appearance, persona and reputation was that of a buffoon, and he drew laughter whenever he spoke.[107] Waddington was a committed and able radical, respected by associates and opponents alike, but his style of radicalism was saturnalian and burlesque. As in Mulberry Tree tavern days, the proceedings at Hopkins Street resembled the blasphemous theatricals of de-Christianisation in parts of revolutionary rural France (what Richard Cobb has called 'schools of demystification').[108] Wedderburn and Waddington were a comic team, similar to Dunstan and House (also stout). Together 'The Black Dwarf' and 'The Black Prince', a shoemaker-dwarf and a black rascal-preacher – the dregs of society – convulsed their audiences and turned the world upside down. At one level they were engaged in deliberate 'mock-worship' using biblical texts and prophecies. An observer at a Hopkins Street 'service' on 29 November disgustedly witnessed the 200 young men in the audience cheering violently and standing 'with hats on' – an ancient gesture of popular protest and defiance also practised by Marian martyrs, Ranters and French sectionnaires.[109] In much the same Rabelaisian spirit Thomas Preston supposedly attended a Sunday service in late 1819 at St George's Church, Borough (a favourite target of Wedderburn's attacks), and deliberately drank all the wine in the communion cup.[110]

All this humour and burlesque in no way diminished the seriousness of purpose of the Hopkins Street chapel congregation. Wedderburn's bloodthirsty followers were shattered by his arrest in December (followed soon after by that of Waddington).[111] Cannon – whom another spy mis-identified as Rev. George Cummings, a Methodist preacher – kept the chapel open for a time and was reportedly even more violent, but he lacked the black's populist talents and courage. Soon he moved the congregation to a new and secret venue, then he closed down the chapel altogether, probably around February/March 1820.[112] This, coupled with the government's decisive enforcement of the Six Acts and the seizure of the Cato Street conspirators, seemed to spell the end of Wedderburn's insurrectionary congregation. Almost, but not quite: in April Wedderburn was released briefly on bail. Several informers reported sighting 'Dr Wedderburn ... the Hayloft preacher' with a radical dissenting minister (who resembled Cannon) visiting a 'little low public house' in Clements Lane. This was the Spotted Dog, where the remnants of London's ultras were meeting under

Preston's leadership. An informer followed Wedderburn in there on 19 April and watched him work to restore the group's morale with the old tavern rituals. After singing several 'diabolical songs', including 'Ça ira', the company joined hands with their hats off and chanted 'we will die for liberty'. They then parted hands and drank the toast: 'May the barren land of our country be manured with the blood of our Tyrantry.'[113]

On 10 May, however, it was the blood of their own Cato Street colleagues which manured the earth; a day later Robert Wedderburn was sentenced to two years' imprisonment in Newgate gaol.

8

The ultra-radical press: philosophes and populists, 1819–21

To turn from the pungent oratory of Hopkins Street chapel to the literature that came from the same quarter in 1819 is on the whole a disappointing experience. For though many London ultra-radical tracts and periodicals emerged in the heat of the Peterloo crisis, their rhetoric often fails to bite. Time and again their analyses seem overburdened by an abstract and theoretical freethought derived mainly from the European Enlightenment. We might expect to find a difference in the language and content of published works as against extempore speeches, but in this case the gulf seems great. True, an addiction to 'the rationalist illusion' was characteristic of artisan autodidact culture. At its best this culture was mutualist, fiercely libertarian and genuinely democratic; at its worst, blindly individualistic with a naive faith in the mechanistic power of reason.[1] Even so, there seems to have been an exceptional adherence to this type of rationalism on the part of London ultra-radical pressmen of the post-war years. It has been suggested that they were less politically engaged and more remote from the roots and sources of their radicalism than later counterparts in the 1830s,[2] but we do not know why.

The sophisticated 'philosophic' character of many ultra-radical publications is especially puzzling given the milieu from which they originated. How did men, like Wedderburn who was nearly illiterate, or Thomas Davison who had 'a meagre formal education',[3] or William Benbow whose letters from prison in 1817 were barely coherent, manage to write the erudite rationalist works that appeared under their names in 1819 and 1820? Indeed, why should they have wished to write such works? Equally, how could Wedderburn – a ragged jobbing tailor – Davison – a wretchedly poor journeyman printer – and Benbow – a demobbed soldier-shoemaker – afford to print, sell and distribute these publications? In the 1830s, type and compositing cost around £14 per thousand copies; an old hand press, around £30; paper, between 15s and 1 guinea a ream; and rent on bookselling or printing premises, around £40.[4] Modest as these costs sound, they were well beyond the reach of the three artisans mentioned above.

Rancière's recent analysis of a similar literary milieu – that of utopian worker-poets and journalists in 1830s' France – doubts that their writings reflected the pure and authentic voice of artisan culture. By abandoning artisan trades and becoming intellectuals 'at the frontier of encounters with the bourgeoisie', French worker-journalists developed a discourse that was neither purely artisan nor bourgeois, but compounded of both.[5] Of course men like Wedderburn tended to be poorer and less educated than Rancière's worker-poets, though arguably this could increase the need for direct patronage and literary help. And in fact a covert patronage system operated by middle-class intellectuals and entrepreneurs underpinned much of the writing and publishing of London ultra-radical pressmen in the post-war years.

Radicals like Wedderburn and Davison were not, however, ciphers or men of straw. The degree of independence, equality or reciprocity in their dealings with 'patrons' varied according to individual and moment. Their relationship could be one of client to patron, employee to employer or agent to sponsor; and sometimes it could take the form of a genuine collaboration between friends. In every case it entailed some kind of symbiosis of dependence. There were multiple and uneven levels of participation in the business organisation of the radical book trade during the post-war years – between capitalist-sponsors, editors, printers, publisher-proprietors, booksellers, writers and vendors. Their complex relationships helped shape the character of post-war radical literary production and ideology. George Cannon's role in this trade between 1819 and 1821 uncovers some of the hidden connections between artisans and a marginal middle-class element within popular radicalism, and indicates some of the diverse influences which contributed to plebeian radical discourse in this period.

Philosophes

We can never hope to trace all of Cannon's literary strings, but a study of the output of three salient ultra-radicals – Robert Wedderburn, Thomas Davison and William Benbow – confirms his secret influence. Wedderburn, for example, was the supposed author and publisher of at least three tracts in 1820–1 that were largely ghosted, and probably financed, by Cannon. Two of them, addressed respectively to the Archbishop of Canterbury and the Chief Rabbi of England, took the form of mock-pleas from the unlettered preacher for help in answering sceptical questions raised by his congregation.[6] The other borrowed its format from Shelley's *Refutation of Deism*. It took the form of a specious, mutually destructive, dispute between the Christian Wedderburn and the deist Perkins that left atheism triumphant.[7] All were written in Cannon's ironic, scholarly style and deployed the same patristic and ecclesiastical authorities, as well as Greek and Hebrew citations, used in his earlier *Political Register* articles. They contained footnotes to the *Theological Inquirer* and passages duplicated from a theistic tract (published under the Perkins' pseudonym in 1820) advocating a materialist-sensationalist psychology of the mind.[8]

Cannon's influence over Thomas Davison was less overt, but still significant. He probably helped to write several rationalist pamphlets that appeared under Davison's name, particularly the sly, donnish parody of Leslie's famous work, *A Short Way with the Deist [1820?]*, and *Plain Questions to Trinitarians* (1821), which bears a close resemblance to Wedderburn's *Letter to the Archbishop*.[9] But Davison is best known as a pressman rather than pamphleteer: modern historians believe him to have been editor-publisher of at least three ultra-radical periodicals of 1819–20: *Medusa*, *London Alfred* and *Deists' Magazine* – and publisher of others, such as the *Cap of Liberty* (edited by James Griffin) and *Theological Comet* (edited by Robert Shorter).[10] There is no doubt that Davison was involved to varying degrees with all these, but Cannon and other middle-class figures were also important contributors and string-pullers. Numbers of the rationalist articles, extracts and letters contained in these periodicals had earlier appeared in Cannon's *Theological Inquirer* (1815).[11] The *Deists' Magazine, or Theological Inquirer*, [1820] – occasionally subtitled *Polemical Magazine and Theological Inquirer* – was almost a reincarnation of the 1815 periodical. Substantial portions of the original were incorporated unchanged, including its opening manifesto and numerous extracts from sceptical philosophe writings.[12] Much of the new material in the *Deists' Magazine* also reveals Cannon's influence. Several articles and all reviews were written under the Perkins' pseudonym. Letters from correspondents appeared under pseudonyms familiar from 1815, such as 'Varro' and 'W.D'. In short, the two periodicals dispensed an identical scholarly rationalism; there was nothing in the *Deists' Magazine* to show that it had emanated from a violent artisan political milieu. Cannon almost certainly edited (and probably financed) it, whilst Davison, who was imprisoned halfway through the periodical's run, acted as the legal publisher.[13]

Davison's chief sponsor and financier (if not writer) was, however, a well-to-do master printer and radical named William Mason. Mason had been printing and publishing in the radical cause since 1809, distinguishing himself in 1811–12 as a pro-Caroline propagandist. He resembled Cannon in both political and religious disposition, being sufficient of a Commonwealthman to write a *Life of Hampden* in 1819 and sufficient of a rationalist to have once belonged to the Freethinking Christians. In 1819 he was operating a substantial printing works at 21 Clerkenwell Green; Davison worked there as a journeyman printer and overseer. Several spies sent to investigate Davison in the summer of 1819 reported that he was desperately poor, and that he was Mason's 'tool', being 'put forward as an inferior person'.[14] The claim cannot be proved absolutely, but Mason was certainly allowing Davison and other of Thistlewood's associates to use his presses after hours without charge in order to produce handbills, posters and other propaganda material.[15] Mason published and printed the *Radical Reformer* and the *London Alfred* (which contained factual reports of Thistlewood's public meetings during winter 1819). He was also printer of almost all the tracts and periodicals attributed to Davison, Wedderburn, Griffin and Perkins (Cannon) in 1819–21.

After Wedderburn and Davison were imprisoned in 1820, Cannon needed new agent-collaborators to peddle his philosophy. He located ideal candidates in two struggling bookseller-publishers, William Benbow and James Griffin.[16] Benbow had set up premises in the Strand around 1818 with the assistance of William Cobbett for whom he was working. However the Cobbett family soon accused him of fraud, and he was probably only too happy to find a fresh patron-sponsor in Cannon. Their most important joint production was a cheap portable edition of *Queen Mab* which appeared under the false imprint of William Baldwin, New York, in 1821. Cannon already possessed the text from a copy given to him by Shelley in 1815, but he produced a new, more rigorously atheistical, translation of the notes.[17] In return, Benbow probably agreed to accept legal liability should their ruse be uncovered. At much the same time he also launched a philosophical and literary periodical, the *Radical Magazine*, to which Cannon (as Perkins) contributed substantially.

Their next joint production, a *Philosophical Dictionary* (1822), was even more recondite. It was not Voltaire's famous work, but a more substantial dictionary written by the Austrian medical man and philosophe, François-Xavier Swediauer. When first published in London in 1786 it had been described by the *Monthly Review* as 'the quintessence of impiety'.[18] Benbow's new and anonymous 10s 6d edition, advertised as 'a valuable library in itself', boasted 'original articles written purposely for this work by the editor'.[19] Given that these included entries on Cannon's sceptical favourites Burdon, Helvetius and Hartley, we may guess that this revised dictionary was the closest he came to producing his proposed 'Collectanea sceptica'. In the same year Cannon also translated, wrote the preface and provided the plates for Benbow's new four-volume edition of the libertinist-freethinking classic, *Amours of the Chevalier de Faublas* by Louvet de Couvray. This collaboration brought Benbow several prosecutions for obscene libel.[20]

Why were Benbow and his artisan radical colleagues prepared to risk and endure prison sentences on behalf of middle-class intellectuals and entrepreneurs like Cannon and Mason? One incentive might simply have been a wish to transcend the marginality, low status and onerousness of artisan occupations. Wedderburn often complained of his inadequate education and of the hardship and poverty he experienced as a jobbing tailor. He had always wanted to be a scholar and theologian, but lacked the learning to master rationalist theory and language. In a breathless, semi-incoherent essay on the printing press published in 1818, he noted wistfully that a philosophical education 'opens an inexhaustable source of entertainment ... and qualifies men for acting with propriety in the most important stations of life'.[21] By 1820, thanks to Cannon's pen, he could boast of being 'Dr Wedderburn, V.D.M.', a member of 'the republic of letters'.

Nominal authorship of these scholarly theological pamphlets dignified Wedderburn's efforts to leave behind the grubby tailoring bulk in St Martins Court and become a dissenting minister, chapel proprietor and moral-theological lecturer. The tracts enhanced his claims to the benefits of clerisy. Richard Carlile often compared the freedom of a radical pressman's life with the mindless petty tyrannies he had endured as an apothecary's assistant, apprentice tin-plate worker and journeyman tinman. During his leisure time in 1804 Allen Davenport could temporarily forget the drudgery of working as a 'dishonourable' London shoemaker by joining with his employer's children in an amateur 'little academy' of poetry, painting, music and literature.[22]

The legendary eighteenth-century Grub Street milieux of London and Paris had been partly created by influxes of educated provincial artisans who burned to become philosophes. By the early nineteenth century this trend was being exacerbated by the rapid increase in elementary popular literacy and the rising status of the professional man of letters, particularly the young, romantic poet-philosopher made fashionable by Byron, Shelley and Keats.[23] Testimonies to this fever abound: it infected young Richard Carlile in the quiet Devonshire village of Ashburton; Allen Davenport in Ewen, Wiltshire; Thomas Dolby in Sawtrey, Huntingdonshire; William Dugdale in Stockport; and William Benbow in Manchester. Dolby, the son of a farm labourer, typically acquired his 'ardent desire to be a scholar' in the small village dame school. Spies reported that Dugdale was already a 'tolerable scholar' steeped in Paineite deism when he arrived in London at the age of eighteen with ambitions to enter the book trade. The son of a Quaker tailor-bookseller in Stockport, he had been educated at a Quaker school and had worked briefly as a tailor and basket-weaver before trying his luck in the metropolis. His future employer, Benbow, had by the age of fifteen 'imbibed the spirit of the romances and chronicles of ancient days', which inspired an eventual move to the metropolis 'as the goal of all my hopes, the stage whereon I was destined to appear before an admiring and grateful world'.[24]

Nowhere are the attractions and perils of the career of radical letters better illustrated than in J.A. St John's self-conscious manuscript journal, 'Memoir [*sic*] d'un philosophe' (1821-2). St John, the son of a shoemaker, was educated at a village school in Langhorne, Caernarvonshire, and then migrated to London at the age of sixteen in search of literary fame and fortune. Here he became a friend of Cannon and also worked briefly in winter 1819 as stand-in editor of Carlile's *Republican*. As Carlile later recorded, 'distress as well as profession of love of principle brought him to me'. By 1821 St John had become editor of a radical newspaper in Plymouth and was berating himself for failing to make better progress in attaining the philosophe ideal:

I am now 26 – have acquired more knowledge – perhaps, than most gentlemen of my age – have thrown off the yoke of every prejudice that degrades the mind – have travelled, and thought, and written, more than some authors have during their whole lives – but notwithstanding all this, I perceive I have been wandering in the wrong path. From my earliest youth I determined to acquire *fame*; not through the vulgar desire of being *talked of*, I know that its breath was the breath of ignorance, but on account of the real advantages that accrue from reputation.[25]

He concluded that he had read too indiscriminately, and so lacked the depth and focus of a true philosophe. To become 'profound and eminent' he needed to undertake an intensive three-part programme:

Politics:- requires a knowledge of Greek, Latin, Italian and French – ancient and modern. Geography – History – the Present State of all the Kingdoms of the World, and their Relations.
Philosophy:- requires a knowledge of the most celebrated theories of the Human Mind, as well as its actual nature – as much of physical nature as possible – the nature of Government and everything that concerns Man.
Poetry:- requires a knowledge of the beauties of inanimate nature – properties of animals – passions, weakness and follies of man. [p. 16]

Above all, he hoped that success in the 'literary lottery' would gain him an introduction to Byron, Moore, Hobhouse, Leigh Hunt and Shelley, though 'I fear I was born too late – these great men will have formed their circle before I can possibly be admitted'. Had he asked Cannon he might have been told that it was not so much being born too late as too lowly that led to exclusion from such circles.

   For someone like St John to succeed he had to be prepared to snatch any opportunity. Many *philosophes-manqués* of lowly background found that their best hope lay in the patronage of a better-off radical littèrateur. By allowing Davison to use his presses without charge, Mason enabled the impoverished printer to accrue enough capital to set himself up in business. For an unemployed hairdresser like E.J. Blandford and a ragged shoemaker like Waddington, access to Mason's presses meant the chance to learn new compositing skills and subsequently to take out printers' licences themselves. Mason might also have been the unnamed benefactor who lent Waddington £172 in 1819 to acquire a press, type and premises (from which he sold radical pamphlets, pikes and beverages).[26] A similar loan probably helped Davison to open businesses, first, as an independent printer at Portman Square in September 1819, then as a publisher-bookseller at 10 Duke Street, Smithfield (in conjunction with another mysterious partner or patron, Rhoda Helder).[27]

Career assistance of this kind seems to have been a common 'perk' in exchange for protecting radical patrons or employers from legal liability. Young William Sherwin, a Nottingham migrant, used profits accumulated as a minor beneficiary of 'Old Corruption' to establish a radical printing and publishing business in post-war London. However, he began to grow nervous of prosecution in 1817 under the combined pressures of marriage, an impending legacy and the government's gagging legislation of 1817. By mid-April the fearless pamphlet vendor Carlile was 'filling the gap' between Sherwin and any would-be prosecutors by managing his bookshop and publishing his periodical. Carlile went on to become one of the most distinguished radical pressmen of the nineteenth century. Two other radicals whom Sherwin employed to write for his *Political Register* – William Clarke and ex-Jacobin pamphleteer, Dr William Hodgson – also became independent printer-publishers soon after. So successful was Sherwin at masking himself from prosecution that some radicals suspected him of having a secret connection with Castlereagh.[28]

Successful career take-offs of this kind often began new chains of patronage, clientage and advancement. Carlile was able to employ St John when the latter was 'hungry enough to snap up whatever came his way'. Later, he helped establish bookselling-publishing careers for several young provincial artisans who had joined his Zetetic movement in the 1820s. Benbow, once an agent of Cobbett, later himself employed Dugdale in the same capacity. Dugdale in turn permitted Wedderburn to print and publish from his premises in 1823–4. Without 'some kind friend, or generous patron to take them by the hand' even talented autodidacts like Allen Davenport had little hope of making a permanent transfer into the world of professional letters. As a result, Davenport never progressed beyond part-time writing. Dolby, however, thanks to a £40 loan from an employer, was able to give up working as a gentleman's servant and open up a profitable radical bookselling and stationery business in 1808.[29]

Self-improvement was not the only motive for entering into collaboration with middle-class 'pushers'. Although artisan radicals like Wedderburn could not command the literary style and learning of their patrons, they believed just as strongly in the politically liberating powers of reason. It would be hard to find a more ardent tribute to reason, and its agent the printing press, than Wedderburn's crude little essay on the subject in

1818. He argued that the press would 'ere long change the face of the universe', and that without rational knowledge (or freethought) man would still be mired in priestly tyranny, bigotry and ignorance: 'thanks to philosophy! since the revival of learning, through the aid of science, and of in particular, that memorable gift of celestial genius the PRESS, Yes – Philosophical writers are the sages who have arrested and disarmed this epidemic disease, more dangerous than the most dreaded calumnies'.[30]

No wonder he was happy to foster and protect the philosophic sage, Cannon – a man who might conceivably help the poor mulatto to become something of a sage himself. The preface to Benbow's *Radical Magazine* (1821) – probably also a cooperative effort with Cannon – argued similarly that the task of literature was to benefit society by teaching the people to reason and think properly, thereby cultivating and enlightening their minds upon moral and political subjects. The results would be to dissipate ignorance, error, tyranny, corruption and selfishness.[31]

Accepting patronage usually had a cost. Dugdale, writing in 1843 when he had long ceased to be an agent of other men, nevertheless envied the father of philosophes, Voltaire, because he 'never felt the misery of being obliged to abandon his liberty that he might procure subsistence, ... nor to flatter the prejudices, or the passions of a patron'.[32] Davison and Benbow both incurred hefty prison sentences through taking responsibility for Cannon's works; Wedderburn's prison sentence of 1820 was greatly increased for the same reason. That they accepted these penalties uncomplainingly is probably explained by Cannon's willingness to give support when his agents got into trouble. Not all radical patrons were as considerate: Cobbett and Brown had washed their hands of Houston and Eaton in 1813 and Dolby was abandoned by Maginn, the sponsor-proprietor of *Pasquin*, as soon as the periodical was threatened with prosecution in 1821.

Ironically, Cannon's help proved counter-productive for his unfortunate clients, Wedderburn and Davison. He wrote the learned philosophical pleas for toleration that were read out in court as their legal defences and mitigation pleas.[33] In Wedderburn's case this evidence of 'a perverted and depraved talent' led the sentencing judge to over-rule the jury's recommendation of mercy and impose a two-year gaol term for 'aggravated offence'. Davison's clever rationalist defence so infuriated Justice Best that – in spite of an intervention from the floor by Mason and a legal affidavit from Cannon[34] – he imposed contempt fines totalling £100 on top of a two-year gaol sentence and good behaviour sureties. Cannon might have been a svengali, but he at least had the grace not to abandon his unfortunate agents once they were behind bars. He ran Wedderburn's chapel for a time, edited both men's trials and several of their tracts, advertised their works and their plight in prison, and helped organise subscription funds for their beleaguered families.[35]

From the patron's point of view the most important attraction of such collaborations was legal protection. Cannon, Mason and Sherwin were never prosecuted during these years. To men of their professed respectability and cultivation, prison was a frightening prospect: it damaged social standing, disrupted business and, as the genteel ex-clergyman Robert Taylor was to discover in 1828, it was personally gruelling. But their ragged agents accepted such afflictions stoically. 'If your dungeon is ready, My Lord', Davison responded to one of Justice Best's splenetic interruptions, 'suffer me to give you the key.' Wedderburn, faced with two years in Newgate, told the court: 'I am so extremely poor that prison will be a home to me and as I am so advanced in life I shall esteem it an honour to die immured in a dungeon for advocating the cause of truth.'[36]

No doubt radical patrons also hoped to make money out of these literary collaborations – we have seen that this was Timothy Brown's intention when sponsoring *Ecce Homo* in 1813. Sherwin profited from Carlile's boldness in 1818–19, though he seems to have ploughed some of this back into assisting the latter's own publications. The Cannon–Benbow editions of *Queen Mab* and the *Amours of Faublas* were probably commercial successes, if only because of their notoriety and risqué associations. However, it is doubtful whether the lavish, erudite edition of Swediauer's *Philosophical Dictionary* repaid its outlay. Healthy profits could be made on radical periodicals, but *Medusa, Deists' Magazine* and others of that stable did not attain a high enough circulation, nor last long enough to have earned much.[37] One suspects that most of the recondite freethinking works that Cannon dispensed through Wedderburn, Davison and Benbow lost rather than made money. Perhaps he was able to offset such costs by charging agents or other radical bookmen for services as a translator, editor and writer – this was certainly the practice of down-and-out intellectuals like 'Dr' William Hodgson and Jack Mitford, who in effect hired themselves out as hack writers.

For Cannon the attraction of these collaborations might in any case have been more psychological than financial. Throughout a long, diverse, literary career he consistently played the role of trickster, always deploying new masks and laying false trails. Here, as in other ways, he resembled London's wits, jesters and libertines of a century earlier. One suspects that he loved placing his corrosive learning at the disposal of ragged and violent roughs like Wedderburn and Davison. There were multiple deceits and ironies to be enjoyed. In 1820, for example, he was writing (in a periodical of which he was secret editor) glowing pseudonymous reviews of works which he himself had ghostwritten. 'We do not remember to have seen a more Jesuitical, hypocritical and insidious performance', he gloated over one of Wedderburn's ghosted tracts. It only went to prove – he claimed – that persecution led people to become 'more subtle ... in evading the law'.[38]

And if Cannon was to fulfil his own declared ambition of spearheading a 'republic of letters', he probably had little choice other than to cultivate aspiring artisan intellectuals. Having failed to establish a secure foothold in the circles of freethinking literati around Timothy Brown and Percy Shelley, he evidently decided to replicate those circles at a less respectable level. Like the earlier Encyclopaedists, whom he revered, he hoped to build a secularist salon. Amongst men like Wedderburn, Davison, Griffin and Benbow, who looked up to him as sage, he could renew his attempt of 1815 to create a theatre of free inquiry. A 'society of infidel publicists' which he claimed to have formed in 1820 was one result. It aimed to counter the activities of the Society for the Suppression of Vice, and met at places like the Patriot Coffee House, Soho, and at Griffin's premises in Holborn.[39] Members disseminated deist propaganda and probably simulated and parodied fashionable literary salon life. As secretary of the Patriot House Society, Cannon wrote to Benbow's *Radical Magazine* saying that he had been instructed to switch their subscription from *Blackwood's Magazine* to Benbow's periodical because they were sickened by *Blackwood's* political toadying, unprincipled scribbling, sensationalism and failure to live up to 'the dignity of polite literature'.[40]

Although this letter shows Cannon indulging in his usual love of irony, it also reflects an underlying dilemma that confronted *philosophes-manqués* of his type. Despite his frequent disparagement of enthusiasm, superstition, sensationalism and so on, he seems to have realised the limitations of 'polite literary traditions', if only from a pragmatic and commercial perspective. He admitted in a pamphlet ghosted for Wedderburn that 'learned men and philosophers' needed to discover how to tap the ardent popular passions generated by unlearned enthusiastic preachers.[41] By recruiting men like Wedderburn, Davison and Benbow, he was trying to do exactly that – to make use of their plebeian and vernacular credentials. Cannon probably did not really want to merge plebeian-populist radicalism of the Hopkins Street type with his own scholarly rationalism, but he wanted to give that impression. Someone of Wedderburn's colour, notoriety, courage and eccentricity could guarantee excellent publicity.

However, there were limits to the pliability and passivity of artisan spokesmen. The concerns, forms and language of a native plebeian-populist culture sometimes broke through the polite rationalist crust that patrons like Cannon sought to impose. The threepenny squib, *Cast-Iron Parsons*, composed by Wedderburn in Dorchester gaol and published by Davison in 1820, is one such example. For once Cannon's role seems to have been confined to editing and polishing Wedderburn's words. With due allowance for this polishing, the tract contained the kind of earthy, blasphemous, anti-clerical sentiments of Wedderburn's Hopkins Street chapel speeches.

He claimed to have been inspired to compose the pamphlet by the facetious remarks of an old female apple-seller in Shadwell. She had convinced him that the labour-dispensing machinery which was supplanting (and starving) labourers and artisans ought to be extended to the Established Church. Cast-iron automata could provide a cheap and appropriate substitute for lazy, greedy, heartless and corrupt clergy. By contrast, mechanisation could never replace the doctrines of 'the meek and lowly Jesus', nor the passion, zeal and energy of lowly dissenting preachers.[42] The pamphlet's robust vernacular style – its use of personal anecdote, burlesque humour, 'Old Corruption' and radical Christian rhetoric: all owed more to Cobbett than to Cannon. The latter made an explicit editorial criticism of its 'Cobbettisms'. He also gave it only a perfunctory review compared with Wedderburn's other, more rationalist pamphlets.[43]

However much Cannon disliked Wedderburn's excursion into independent radical journalism, he went along with it – a sign, perhaps, that *Cast-Iron Parsons* suited the prevailing literary climate. For the eruption of the Queen Caroline affair during the second half of 1820 had brought the plebeian-populist voice of the radical press into sudden and strident prominence, temporarily drowning out its polite rationalist counterpart and, in some instances, reversing the relationship between patron and agent.

Populists

The Queen Caroline affair of 1820–1 continues to occupy an uneasy, ambiguous position within labour historiography. True, the period of early neglect or positive dismissal has ended; some important revisionist studies have emerged.[44] Nevertheless, there seems to be a lingering wish to explain away the supposed capitulation and failure of popular radicals during this extraordinary episode. A thoughtful recent study has argued, for example, that the real (and rational) political purpose of England's popular radicals was overwhelmed and subverted by the diversionary gothic-romantic aesthetic which the affair generated. Popular radicals are presumed to have been – at least initially – exempt from this maudlin and loyalist populist discourse.[45] No doubt some were. Richard Carlile, that most principled republican, was at first sceptical of Caroline's bid to defend her name and crown; he intended only to make anti-monarchical capital out of the affair. And though Carlile eventually became as fulsome a supporter of the Queen as any, he did ultimately regret the inherently trivial and diversionary aspects of the affair.[46] But Carlile's early and later doubts were exceptional amongst London's ultra-radical pressmen. Rather than being overtaken by the loyalist-populist mythology of Queen Caroline, most radical pressmen helped create it.

The Queen Caroline affair is usually dated from the time of its mass

eruption in summer 1820, but its origins as a popular radical cause go
back much earlier. Caroline became an issue in radical – as well as Whig –
politics and propaganda during the years between the 'Delicate Investigation' scandal of 1806 and her exile in Europe in 1814. Over this period
numbers of London radical pressmen, including some who were again
prominent in 1820–1, helped to define and publicise the essentials of the
pro-Caroline/anti-Regent mythology. When Caroline landed in Dover on 5
June 1820 the framework of the populist aesthetic already existed; it had
only to be reactivated. In the eyes of many ultra-radicals, Caroline was
already a wronged woman, already the heroine of a gothic-romantic fantasy.

William Cobbett was of course a key figure in laying the literary foundations of Caroline's popularity. He was invited to take a leading place in
Caroline's campaign of 1820 because of the impact of his earlier press
writings in her favour.[47] Several more obscure radical journalists and
publishers had also played a crucial propagandist role during the early
Regency years. Their muckraking between 1808 and 1813 helped to link
the royal sons with endemic financial, political and moral corruption. By
the beginning of the Regency, English political caricature was already
registering a shift in popular perceptions by depicting the Prince as the
bloated, lecherous and whiskered old dandy[48] so familiar in the post-war
works of William Hone and others. Of the many scandals between 1802
and 1814 the one that most damaged George in popular esteem was the
'Delicate Investigation' of 1806. Not only did it become widely known that
the report, or 'Book', had exonerated Caroline of having produced an
illegitimate child (as her husband had claimed), but it was also known
that the Prince and Perceval's government had tried to prevent publication of the report.

Much of the sentimental literary propaganda generated in favour of
Caroline during the early Regency years derived from pirated or fictional
versions of 'The Book'. One of the most influential of these was an anonymous three-volume work published in 1811 under the title: *The Spirit of
'The Book'; or, memoirs of Caroline, Princess of Hasburgh*. It had been written
in Newgate in six weeks by the dissolute, blackmailing hack, Captain
Thomas Ashe, who had earlier worked for several sensationalist newspapers of varying political hues. A talented scribbler, he also penned smut
on behalf of – then against – Perceval; and was eventually recruited to
write for Caroline's party.

Ashe claimed *The Spirit* to be factual, but subtitled it *A Political and
Amatory Romance* and cast it in the epistolary form of popular romance.
His fictional correspondence between Caroline and her 'adored' daughter
Charlotte stressed the forced separation of mother and daughter – a major
element in the later Caroline myth. The letters told a lurid and sentimental

gothic tale. The innocent young princess had fallen in love with a hand-some Irish noble, Algernon, but was forced to marry the profligate, adulterous Prince Albion in exchange for her lover's freedom (he had been locked in a black tower). After forcibly ravishing Caroline on their wedding night, the depraved Albion gave himself over to vice with a series of gross, whoring, courtier mistresses. Before long these harpies instigated a plot to humiliate the ingenuous princess and to poison Albion's mind with lies about her infidelities. The 'Delicate Investigation' was attributed to the arrest of a stranger near the palace carrying Caroline's locket. In accordance with romantic convention, this handsome stranger turned out to be Algernon pining for a glimpse of his lost love.[49]

The Spirit contained all the romantic, melodramatic and quasi-pornographic elements which resurfaced in the pro-Caroline literature of 1820–1. However ludicrously fictional, Ashe's story was an immediate success. A knowledgable printer-publisher – himself a central actor in the affair of the suppressed 'Book' – claimed that *The Spirit* made £3000 profit for its publisher in the first twelve months of publication. It also inspired a host of imitations: 'the drudges of Grub Street and the presses of St Giles ... obtained full employment in the production of fabricated tales and scandalous inuendos'.[50] A cheap 'concise abridgement' of *The Spirit* was printed and published in 1812 by none other than William Mason. This edition was prefaced by a romantic woodcut (see Ill.11) and its relative brevity helped accentuate the fairytale aspects of the original.[51] Other versions followed thick and fast, particularly from the radical presses of John Fairburn, Effingham Wilson and J. Johnston. E. Thomas, a regular Spencean printer, brought out *The Book Itself, or Secret Memoirs of an Illustrious Princess ... A Political, Amatory and Fashionable Work*; Mary Anne Clarke incorporated the gothic plot against Caroline into her suppressed memoir; and Ashe himself, working both independently and for Caroline, produced new romances developing the original theme.[52] All of these works adopted or embellished aspects of Ashe's fantasy mixed with factual details of Caroline's history gathered from newspapers or from portions of the suppressed report.

As early as 1816 William Hone floated a rumour in one of his chapbooks that the 'Delicate Investigation' was about to be renewed.[53] Both the Milan Commission which began sifting evidence the following year and the Bill of Pains and Penalties of 1820 were widely interpreted as revivals of the original investigation. Not surprisingly, much of the radical and populist propaganda of 1811–14 was also revived or incorporated into the flood of new publications of 1820. William Mason republished a sixpenny edition of one of Ashe's many versions of *The Spirit* – this one called *Algernon and Caroline, or the Spirit of the Spirit*. It sported a highly coloured romantic woodcut and passed through seven editions within a few months. The radical Holborn Hill printseller and publisher John

A CONCISE
ABRIDGMENT
OF THAT POPULAR AND INTERESTING WORK,
THE
SPIRIT
OF
"THE BOOK,"
OR
Memoirs
OF
CAROLINE,
PRINCESS OF HASBURGH,
A Political and Amatory Romance.

"THE BOOK."—Any person having in their Posses-
sion a certain Book, printed by Mr. Edwards in 1807, but
NEVER PUBLISHED, with W. Lindsell's Name as the Seller
of the same on the Title-page, and will bring it to
W. Lindsell, Bookseller, Wimpole Street, will receive a
HANDSOME GRATUITY.—*Times Newspaper, March 27, 1809.*

LONDON:
PRINTED AND PUBLISHED BY W. MASON,
21, Clerkenwell Green:
AND SOLD BY
T. JOHNSTON, 98, CHEAPSIDE.
And by all Booksellers.
1812.

See p. 6

11 *Romaticising Caroline, 1812.*

Fairburn republished his edition of 'The Book', as well as other Ashe-influ-
enced works. Effingham Wilson reprinted several of his earlier pro-Caroline/
anti-Regent tracts, including one written by the hack George Daniel which
had been 'bought up' by the Prince in 1812.[54] The Cheapside printseller
and publisher Johnston, who had launched his radical publishing career
during the Mary Anne Clarke affair, recycled his earlier attacks on the
'Delicate Investigation' plotters. Titillating and scandalous accounts (both
true and imagined) of George's mistresses, Fitzherbert, Jersey, Hertford and
Conyngham, were also borrowed from earlier writings and incorporated
into the pro-Caroline canon. They found their way into the publications of
quasi-pornographic Grub Street entrepreneurs like William Chubb and
William Lowe, as well as those of the austere republican, Carlile.[55]

The more sentimental and melodramatic elements of the Caroline myth
were also taken up by the gutter-press entrepreneurs of St Giles and Seven
Dials, Jem Catnach and Johnny Pitts – both of whom are said to have
made fortunes out of the affair.[56] Their numerous balladsheets and chap-
books stressed the theme of Caroline as a wronged mother exiled from her
child in 1814. This last was a vintage motif of the chap-book genre, and
seems to have evoked an especially strong response at a time when
working-class families were experiencing intense strains from urbanisa-
tion, industrialism and social change. Allen Davenport was one of several

aspiring radical littérateurs whom Pitts hired to versify on the subject. Davenport's bathetic verse chap-book, *Claremont*, presented Caroline's plight through her dead daughter's eyes:

> But oh! thou had'st a Mother long exiled
> From thou her Daughter and her only child.
> And, O, what pleasure arises in one thought,
> That thou has practis'd what thy Mother taught!
> One cloud hung o'er thy mind, – Thy Mother's fate
> From which distilled (Felicity's alloy)
> A tear, that oft obscured a beam of joy.

Another of his ballads, set to the tune of the old martial hymn of the United movement, 'Erin go bragh', concluded with the words:

> We who have loved the daughter, will cherish the mother,
> The lawful, legitimate Queen of the Isles.[57]

Although Cannon's new collaborator William Benbow had scarcely established his publishing business in the Strand when the Caroline affair erupted, he made devastating use of the 'Delicate Investigation' smut. His success derived in part from employing the veteran pro-Caroline hack, Jack Mitford. A scion of the Redesdale family, Mitford possessed an appropriately bizarre history. After distinguished naval service as a commander under Hood and Nelson, alcoholism and a strain of eccentricity 'amounting to insanity' had blighted his naval career. To free him from the navy, the current Lord Redesdale had paid for Mitford to become 'a parlour boarder' in Thomas Warburton's fashionable Whitmore House lunatic asylum. Whilst he was in there a distant relative, Viscountess Perceval, briefed and hired him to write in Caroline's cause (see Ill.12). Under such pseudonyms as 'Matthew Bramble' and 'Justicia', he proved to be a master of scurrility. However the Perceval-Caroline connection was uncovered in 1814 and the Viscountess tried to exonerate herself by suing Mitford for libel (unsuccessfully).[58]

By 1820 Mitford was a hopeless alcoholic and derelict, yet he was still a brilliant hack satirist with an intimate knowledge of the Royal domestic politics of the previous decade. With the re-emergence of the Caroline affair, opportunistic radical pressmen such as Benbow, J.L. Marks and Johnston immediately hired him to be a literary 'caterer'. Lying in a bed of nettles at the old waterworks near St Giles, he would scribble verse until his usual payment, a blacking bottle of gin and 2d worth of bread, needed replenishing.[59]

One result was the squib, *A Peep into W-r Castle, after the Lost Mutton* (1820), published initially by quasi-pornographic Soho caricaturist and publisher, J.L. Marks (who also worked for Benbow for much of 1820).[60] It

12 *Conspiring for Caroline, 1814: Lady Perceval and Jack Mitford composing.*

was immediately 'bought up' by the Palace for £35, only to be republished by Benbow as a shilling pamphlet under the provocative subtitle of 'The Suppressed Poem'.[61] Its theme was simply John Bull's search through Windsor Castle for the Regent – 'mutton' being a word-play on the way George was represented by caricaturists as a ram-like creature with mutton-chop whiskers (see Ill. 13) and on the gutter colloquial connotations of 'mutton' as female pudenda or whore. What made the squib so embarrassing to the Palace, apart from the more than passable satirical verse, was its wealth of intimate reference to Royal sexual intrigues during the early Regency, and its brilliant demonological image of the Regent:

> For the good of the people this carcase so brawny
> I fatten with Turtle and mullogatawney.
> For the good of the people I spend on a –
> What else would be wasted on ten thousand poor.

Nor did Mitford pull his punches:

> John boldly flung open the huge folding door
> And step't where few persons had stepped before.
> Stretched at length on a sofa, with fat bloated face
> He saw the 'Lost Mutton' of Br – k's lost race.
> … Whilst over him bended, to sympathy true
> The voluptuous form of the fam'd Mrs Q.[62]

13 Benbow's version of petticoat government: George IV and Lady Conyngham.

Such was the success of the pamphlet that the adventures of the 'mutton' and Mrs Q (Harriette Wilson) were soon being sung by ballad-chaunters all over London.[63] Pirate editions and imitations – some more scurrilous than the original – were brought out by radical gutter pressmen like Johnston, S.W. Fores and Wilson.[64] True, most of these publishers were willing – as in 'Delicate Investigation' days – to accept hefty payments from the Palace to suppress their smut, yet this did little to stem the flow. During 1820 Benbow received more than £200 from Carlton House in separate instalments; he and his associate, Marks, usually pocketed the money and published anyway, often boasting of the 'suppression'.[65]

Benbow was a shrewd recycler of earlier pro-Caroline and anti-Regent propaganda, but he also influenced the populist-radical aesthetic of 1820–1 in original ways by his skilful use of traditional plebeian street genres such as sensationalist posters and popular prints. Both were urban art forms that could be sophisticated or 'crudely blunt and obscene';[66] Benbow's productions fitted the latter description. His prints were rivalled in obscenity only by those of Fores and John Marshall. A notorious Benbow print represented the Milan Commission – which had been appointed to collect and sift evidence of Caroline's amours in Italy – as a black, bloated and excremental leech. The House of Lords Committee of Scrutiny he depicted as 'Doctors, Bishops, Judges, Generals and Statesmen at Hard work, or a Shitting Committee': they were shown excreting into a rank, bulbous, green bag used for collecting state evidence (while soldiers and farm labourers ridiculed them in the background).[67] The green bag, long a symbol of repression in radical circles, thus took on broader populist associations as the repository of state plots against Queen Caroline.

Herein lay Benbow's talent: he was amongst the crudest of the gutter pressmen, but he also had a knack of conveying a radical political message by deploying traditional iconographic symbols of popular London protest. We see this in the print *K – g Cupid in the Corner – Playing Bopeep*, where he revives the Wilkite mob symbol of petticoat government by showing the old mutton, George, peeping out from under Lady Conyngham's scanty underclothes (see Ill.13). *The Blanket Hornpipe* (Ill.14) skilfully weaves together several popular political threads: 'blanket hornpipe' was a slang phrase for fornication; tossing in a blanket, a traditional folk sanction against transgressors of accepted moral codes. Women are shown rebelling against the Regent's promiscuity and hypocritical attack on Caroline's virtue. Moreover, these are women of the street – gross plebeian 'actresses' from the Theatre Royal – who are turning George's world upside down. Egging them on in the background are common soldiers flanked by the institutions of government – opulent, barred and booby-trapped to exclude the people. No wonder Benbow's Strand premises were reckoned by spies and loyalists to sell the most profane and seditious prints in town.

14 The Blanket Hornpipe: *defending Caroline's honour.*

Officials of Carlton House, the Treasury Solicitor's office, and the newly founded Constitutional Society visited regularly with bribes or threats of prosecution.[68]

Benbow's sensationalist posters became equally notorious. They translated the visual messages of his caricatures into bold print headlines. Here again he tried to integrate xenophobic, patriotic and libertarian elements of London crowd ideology with the specifically radical critique of 'Old Corruption'. The poster *Character of the Queen* represented Caroline's sybaritic travels of 1814–20 as the chivalrous, romantic and pious odyssey of an exile. *Glorious Deeds of Women* situated her in a pantheon of liberty-loving heroines. *Brutal Abuse of the Queen* and *Proposal to Murder the Queen* used the rantings of the loyalist press to make it appear as if a plot had been laid to stab, boil or behead Caroline – a piece of pre-tabloid journalism that some readers took literally. It probably became one of the many wild rumours that flashed through London's streets in 1820.[69]

Benbow did not hesitate to tap the unsavoury, xenophobic side of metropolitan populism. At their first arrival he described the crown's Italian witnesses as 'such wretches as go about with dancing dogs and monkeys, white mice, tame snakes'. His poster *Swearing more Profitable than Fighting* claimed that wily, grovelling seamen-spies from Italy were being given

15 *William Benbow in his shop, 1820.*

huge bribes to perjure themselves against Caroline – money stolen from the just labours of English soldiers and sailors who had defended their country from foreign despotism. He, Fairburn, Dolby and other radical publishers churned out anti-Italian songs, slogans, jokes and prints (see Ill.16). Most had some political point. Count Majocchi and his associates were represented as the latest recruits to an army of spies and provocateurs paid to attack the people's liberties.[70] According to some actual members of this spy system, Benbow and Fairburn employed men and boys to blazon the metropolis and surrounds with these subversive posters – copies of Benbow's were seized in Essex, Yarmouth and Wisbech.[71]

Often the posters carried advertisements or excerpts from Benbow's larger shilling squibs and pamphlets (usually illustrated with lurid woodcuts in the fashion that Hone and Cruikshank made famous). Though Benbow was not as prolific a producer of pro-Caroline squibs as Dolby, Fairburn, Wilson and Hone, he published some celebrated examples such as *Horrida Bella, Sultan Sham and his Seven Wives* (see Ill.15), *Khouli Khan*

16 *Anti-Italian scurrility from Fairburn, 1820.*

and *Fair Play, or Who are the Adulterers, Slanderers and Demoralizers?*. They
were hardly more restrained than his posters. In *Fair Play* he described the
Italian crown witnesses as 'a horrid lazaroni, picked out of the dregs of
society, in the most profligate part of the world', and he asserted that
'there is not a jury in the United Kingdom, would believe the filthy testimony of the filthy witnesses, arranged by the filthy junta, employed for the
base, unmanly and iniquitious purpose of dethroning a Queen'.[72]

This pamphlet – published under the pseudonym of Shandy Sinecure
esq., FRS – and most of Benbow's other large works of 1820–1 also
contained detailed listings of beneficiaries of 'Old Corruption'. Such specific
lists have been described as the most important and distinctive contribution of early nineteenth-century popular radicalism.[73] If so, Benbow's
works deserve recognition alongside the better-known *Black Book* of John
Wade. Benbow cleverly linked 'Old Corruption' with Queen Caroline's
cause by exposing her accusers' crim. con. and adulterous records, by
listing the salaries, pensions and sinecures of those who opposed her in the
House of Lords, and by recording the moral and financial 'crimes' of
clergymen who had taken the King's side.[74] Benbow admitted that this
kind of publication entailed 'much painful research', and he probably
relied on his scholarly collaborator Cannon for some of it. The underlying
purpose of these lists was naturally to expose the workings of the old
unreformed parliament so as to bring about radical reform. Benbow rated
his twopenny House of Lords exposé, *Peep at the Peers* (which sold an

alleged 100,000 copies), as his greatest contribution 'in stirring up public opinion in behalf of her late gracious Majesty' and 'freeing her from the fangs of her blood-thirsty enemies'.[75]

Clearly, London's ultra-radical pressmen helped to manufacture the Queen Caroline 'aesthetic'. Populism did not overwhelm anterior radical theories because it was already an intrinsic element of these. The same holds true if we turn from the domain of radical propaganda to that of action. Here too we find that the Queen's affair encouraged those plebeian-populist traditions of counter-theatre and saturnalia that had been conspicuous at Hopkins Street chapel. Had Wedderburn been free from gaol he would probably have revelled in the chance to deploy his flamboyant and theatrical skills in Caroline's cause. Other former Hopkins Street colleagues, however, were able to take up the challenge.

The Queen's affair offered Cannon a wonderful chance to play the prankster and machiavel, though we will never know how many of the masses of anonymous pro-Queen satires originated from his pen (or of others like him). One focus for literati of his type was the Liberal Alliance formed in the second half of 1820; it attracted such pressmen as Mason, Dolby, Griffin and Davison. The Liberals, as they were known, were a broad-based radical literary and debating group who organised subscriptions, meetings, spectacles and propaganda in favour of the Queen.[76] Cannon's habitual secrecy allows only one glimpse of his activities during the affair – though this proved typical. In August 1820 a raid on a turbulent pro-Queen crowd in St James captured three leaders, one of whom escaped from custody before he could be identified. This appears to have been Cannon. Home Office officials eventually uncovered that he had written the savagely ironic declaration to the King which had been read out on the day. It had implied (in much the same vein as Benbow's works) that the conspiracy against the Queen was being financed by huge secret bribes taken out of the people's taxes. When questioned, Cannon admitted authorship but refused to name the printer (who was probably either Davison, Benbow or Waddington).[77]

Samuel Waddington was as visible as Cannon was covert. The loyalist newspaper, *John Bull*, named him on 7 January 1821 as a leader of the radical 'drivellers'. This prominence derived from his trades' connections, especially with the influential John Gast; from his prestige as one of the few survivors of Hopkins Street and Cato Street; and, most of all, from the way that the Caroline furore suited his burlesque talents and appearance. G. Humphrey's print of February 1821, *Grand Entrance to Bamboozl'em* (Ill.17), captures the Rabelaisian flavour of the pro-Caroline plebeian radical campaign. It depicts Caroline as Columbine at the head of a procession of Italian carnivalians. They are meeting up with an equally theatrical procession of radical revellers, among whom is the dwarfish Waddington

17 Radical Carnival: Waddington and the radicals meet Queen Caroline.

carrying a placard, Burdett in harlequin-like electioneering favours and
Matthew Wood represented as a drunken sailor and master of ceremonies.
In the background the mob performs a charivari.

This portrayal of Waddington was accurate as well as symbolic. He
appeared at pro-Caroline meetings held in trades' alehouses at Goswell
Street and the Barbican wearing a Huntite white hat and carrying a green
bag on a pole, with a mob of boys around him shouting 'Waddington for
ever'.[78] His penchant for extravagant and chivalrous gestures in the
Queen's cause, such as invading the Mansion House and declaring himself
a prisoner, or attacking loyalists who tried to deface his billposters, earned
him the ironic nickname of the Queen's 'Champion' (Ill.18). It was a title
to which he could fairly lay claim, if only because of his continued successes in the courts.[79] He and Benbow also publicised and helped enforce
illuminations in support of Caroline's victory after the Bill of Pains and
Penalties was abandoned. They joined the broad-based radical committee
to subscribe Caroline silver plate (as befitted her status as Queen), and they
were leading members of the Patriotic Benevolence Society which helped
to organise the popular demonstration at her funeral procession. Fittingly,
'Little Waddy' marched with 'Dr' Watson at the head of the last metropolitan ultra-radical mobilisation of the post-war years, a procession – replete
with trades and radical pageantry – to bury two labourers killed when

18 *Little Waddy: the Queen's Champion.*

trying to ensure that Caroline's body received its due popular homage. And as late as September 1821, Waddington attracted notoriety by attempting to present a cheeky address of sympathy to the King for the loss of his 'uncrowned, calumniated and persecuted wife'.[80]

By this time, however, 'Waddy' was something of a lone voice in the wilderness; the Queen's affair subsided as quickly as it arose. There have been many explanations for this rapid demise: Caroline's errors of judgement and untimely death; the withdrawal of Whig and City leadership on which the popular democratic movement still depended; the intrinsic weakness of the metropolitan radical movement due to its diverse constituency and the crippling effects of the Six Acts; the typically ephemeral and self-destructive character of populist political causes; and, of course, the 'diversionary' popular aesthetic which the affair generated. Richard Carlile made a point similar to the last in December 1820 when temporarily closing down the *Republican*. He blamed fellow radical pressmen, not for their adulation of Caroline in which he had shared, but because their propaganda had taken trivial forms. Squibs and pasquinades could amuse and annoy but not influence serious political change.[81]

Modern students of popular mentalities would not necessarily agree. Robert Darnton's brilliant study of low-life literature in eighteenth-century France argues persuasively that the Old Regime incurred serious political damage from the flood of scurrilous *libelles* that engulfed Paris before the revolution.[82] It has been said that England's censorship was less severe than France's, and her monarch George IV more tolerant, but both these points can be exaggerated.[83] The Queen Caroline affair erupted just after the imposition of severe legislative restrictions on the popular press and at a time when government and voluntary societies were conducting fierce prosecuting campaigns. Censorship broke down temporarily in 1820 only because it could not cope with the volume of smut.

George and his government were remarkably sensitive to popular ridi-cule and caricature. In the same month that Carlile denigrated satirical radical literature, Sidmouth and his officials were racking their brains for ways to counteract the 'deadly weapon' of popular caricature.[84] Between 1819 and 1822 Carlton House spent at least £2600 in a vain attempt to buy off radical caricatures. Wellington believed that the King's dislike of popular ridicule was his most vulnerable point, and as late as 1823 George wrote to Peel complaining that print and bookshops all over London were depicting him in an indecent or ridiculous manner: 'This is now become a constant practice, and it is high time it is put a stop to'.[85] It was probably the shock of the Queen Caroline affair, as much as the permeation of evangelical values, that initiated the reformation of Royal and aristocratic public morality during the early Victorian years.[86]

And there can be no doubt that the Caroline affair and its literature touched sections of the London population that were ordinarily indifferent or hostile to the appeal of popular radicalism. For example, there was the prostitute who in June 1820 warned a roomful of soldiers at the Crown alehouse that if they saluted the King 'you shall not come to bed to me. I am for Caroline. I am a whore and if she has had a whore's stroke is that any reason she is not to be Queen?'[87] Who can say that some thread of deference had not been irreparably broken in this case? Thirty years later Mayhew interviewed a crossing-sweeper who recalled of Caroline: 'She was a woman, she was. The yallers, that is the king's party was agin her.' Street patterers also told Mayhew that Jem Catnach had made upwards of £10,000 from the sale of street literature on Caroline, particularly from whole sheet 'papers'.[88]

Nor can we presume that because the politics of the Caroline case became entwined with elements of popular romance and fantasy that its anti-establishment effects were negligible. Gothic melodrama and domes-tic romance were two of the pre-eminent forms of English working-class fiction,[89] and the incorporation of Caroline's history and grievances into the framework of their fictional aesthetic immeasurably increased her popular appeal. Moreover, both literary forms were characterised by a powerful Manichean moral structure well-suited to conveying intense anti-establishment feelings. True, the emotions which ultra-radical theatricals and propaganda worked to inflame, with their overtones of xenophobia, patriotism and chivalry, could be dangerously volatile or double-edged. They might eventually have led plebeian Londoners to iden- tify with the Chartists against THEM – the oppressive and corrupt state – or equally, to idolise the girl-queen Victoria. Either way, the populism of the Queen Caroline affair cannot be ignored.

Its radical legacy was equally ambiguous. In the long term it probably helped to show up the fallibility of the ruling classes and to demonstrate the justice of radical demands for a reform of the 'Old Corruption' machine that had plotted against her. In the short term, as Humphrey's print indicates (Ill.17), Caroline provided a 'rallying point' for metropolitan popular radicalism when the movement was badly fractured as a result of the Six Acts and the post-Cato Street dragnet. True, the renewed alliances and restored morale did not endure, but the boost that the Queen's affair gave to ultra-radicalism was to help it to survive through the difficult decade of the twenties. The effect on some of London's ultra-radical pressmen was less happy. Although it launched or invigorated the literary careers of philosophes and populists like Cannon, Benbow and Fairburn, it also set many of them on the path of a new, more dubious branch of the trade.

PART 3

Underworld culture, 1821–40

9

The ultra-radical march of mind: politics, religion and respectability

In a series of intelligence reports filed towards the end of the 1820s the government's most reliable and conscientious spy, Abel Hall, pronounced the death of the old Spencean ultra-radical underworld. Hall, a Finsbury tailor and ex-Cato Street conspirator who had been recruited as a spy in prison in 1820, reported that his former 'dangerous' associates of ten years earlier had changed their dispositions, opinions and principles. Not only had they become preoccupied with earning a living like everyone else, but they had also ceased plotting 'revolution or riot' in the old way. Instead, they met openly in coffee-houses to read and discuss the news of the day.[1]

On the face of it this information is unsurprising. Labour historians since Francis Place have noted that overt political radicalism declined and disappeared during the 1820s. This quiescence is attributed to the draconian anti-radical repression of 1819–22, to the improvement in economic conditions in the early and middle portion of the decade, to the more liberal reforming disposition of the Tory government and to the widespread popular diffusion of the values of respectability and self-improvement. The execution of the Cato Street conspirators in 1820 and the death of Queen Caroline in 1821 are seen as having marked the end, respectively, of the old Jacobin-style conspiratorial coup d'état and of the old ribald satirical culture associated with Regency popular radicalism.[2] Spencean ultra-radicals as foremost practitioners of both could be expected to have fared especially badly during the decade that followed.

Their relative poverty and roughness also threatened to make them obsolete. Francis Place and his contemporaries encapsulated the character of the twenties in the phrase 'the march of mind' – so called because of the massive drive on the part of artisans and lower middle classes for intellectual, social and moral self-improvement. Place believed that the stability (or prosperity) enjoyed by many trades and small businesses accelerated a transformation in popular manners and morals that had begun with the moderate LCS radicalism of the 1790s.[3] By the 1820s this drive for respectable self-improvement was showing itself in a host of popular educational institutions – Zetetic societies, mechanics' institutes, mutual improvement societies, trades' newspapers, reading circles and Sunday schools. Hall's reports from the late twenties would have delighted but not surprised Place; at exactly the same time he was gathering evidence designed to prove that the shift by artisans from taverns to coffee-houses was a major cause and effect of popular self-improvement.[4]

Since the publication of E.P. Thompson's *Making of the English Working Class* twenties' self-improvement has come to be viewed as a crucial and 'formative' phase in nineteenth-century labour and radical history. During this decade, Thompson argues, popular radicalism took the form of a vital intellectual culture which – in spite of its sober and self-improving character – contributed to the making of a new socialistic working-class consciousness and ideology.[5] True, subsequent historians have doubted whether this culture was as uniform in its character and effects as Thompson claims. They have connected it with forms of class consciousness, ideology and political action characteristic of an emerging labour aristocracy, or of small producers being proletarianised, or of an uneasy 'middling class' of philosophical radicals, or of an individualistic radical-liberal sector of the working class.[6] Nevertheless, recent scholarship has confirmed that new anti-capitalist theories and practices did emerge in London's ultra-radical press during the later twenties and early thirties.[7] This would seem to challenge the survival of the old Spencean ultra-radical underworld from a different direction. The radical march of mind – self-improving and/or socialist – appeared to present veteran ultras with a crisis of adaptation.

Respectability and radical culture

Of all those connected with the post-war Spencean ultra-radical underworld, the Evanses (particularly young Evans) were the best attuned to the self-improving mood of the twenties. We have noted that Thomas and Jane Evans and Alexander Galloway had determined that the boy should receive a good education and a respectable upbringing. Their success can be gauged by the fact that Francis Place, Thomas's bitterest enemy, nevertheless admitted in 1818 that young Evans was 'a very worthy young man'.[8] His assessment might have been influenced by signs that the Evanses were trying to improve the style and image of their Spencean society. We have noted their growing ties with Galloway and Westminster radicalism, the effort to abolish smoking at tavern debates and the new moderation and gentility of the Archer Street enterprise. Place was probably impressed, too, when the Evanses decided in November 1818 to open a coffee-house and reading-room at 20 Long Alley, Moorfields.[9] They were 'routed out of it', but the attempt, combined with their shedding of Wedderburn and his extremist supporters, was a further mark of respectable aspirations. Consequently, Place joined with Galloway to secure T.J. Evans the editorship of the *Manchester Observer* in February 1820.[10]

In some senses this new position signalled young Evans's attainment of the ideal of respectability. It showed that he had acquired an impressive level of education and some influential patrons. In view of his background, the job also represented a considerable step towards self-advancement. He also took out a printer's licence and used the *Manchester Observer* premises to print, publish and sell radical tracts. None of this denoted any dilution of ultra-radical political ideals. Under his editorship the newspaper was reported to have become far more 'inflammatory'. True, it did not openly espouse Spenceanism, but young Evans freely admitted that his father had been a friend and associate of Thistlewood. He also used the newspaper and its premises to campaign strongly in the cause of Queen Caroline. He published pro-Caroline squibs and addresses; he worked in collaboration with ultras in London and he masterminded the celebratory illuminations in Manchester and its environs.[11] Meantime, Evans senior began work on an admiring life of Spence which he published from Manchester in 1821. He also worked with his son to establish close links between Manchester and London radical groups, a task which involved them in collecting and administering relief funds for victims of political harassment such as young Samuel Bamford.[12] Before long all these activities were attracting the keen attention of local magistrates and loyalists. In August 1820 T.J. Evans was indicted for seditious libels in the *Manchester Observer*: a group of drunken soldiers had brutally attacked five radicals in Oldham; Evans used the occasion to mount a scathing attack on the standing army and the bullies of Peterloo. This earned him twelve months in Lancaster Castle plus a further six months for libelling a clergyman whom he had accused of having sexual intercourse with a servant.[13]

T.J. Evans's imprisonment seems to have marked a turning point in his career. Like so many young radicals during this period he used prison as a college, adding Spanish to the four languages he already knew. The Evanses' previous spell of twelve months imprisonment in 1817 had influenced them to moderate their political image, but a further eighteen months in Lancaster Castle seems to have been more sobering still. With his father elderly, unwell and unemployed, and the radical movement in ruins, young Evans faced a precarious situation when the family returned to London in 1822. Two early actions signalled a determination to accelerate his advance along the path of respectable self-improvement. One was his prompt and eager involvement (along with Evans senior) in the London Mechanics' Institution founded by Joseph Robertson in 1823; the other was his decision in the same year to appeal to Francis Place for a loan and for help in finding respectable work.[14]

We should not overstrain the significance of these two actions. They did not mean that the Evanses had ceased to be radicals, nor that they had become members of what John Stuart Mill was in 1833 to call the 'English Gironde'.[15] Both Evanses continued to be active in London radical politics at least until the mid-twenties. We know, too, that many artisan/middling radicals joined self-improving educational institutions in a spirit of militant independence. They aspired to liberate themselves from social condescension and to obtain what were regarded as the universal, humane and civilising benefits of rational knowledge.[16] Nor can we interpret T.J. Evans's attainment in 1823 of a job as parliamentary reporter with the *British Press* newspaper – in the 'uneasy' middling ranks of early nineteenth-century society[17] – as a sign of impending or actual embourgeoisement.

Nevertheless, respectable self-improvement could in some instances and over time modify the political and social outlook of individual radicals. The liberal values at the heart of this self-improving radicalism were – notwithstanding any militancy of expression and intent – sometimes compatible with those of middle-class reformers.[18] Carlile's brilliant young volunteer shopman, Richard Hassell, complained in an essay of 1826 that working men tended either to be too ignorant to benefit from mechanics' institutions or to use them as a way of raising themselves to superior social situations.[19] We have been reminded too that the mutual instruction societies of the 1820s, including the London Mechanics' Institution, often did 'purvey knowledge of the dominant culture'.[20] Speaking at the end of the twenties, Galloway described the 'march of improvement' as a popular triumph against Tory reactionaries like Lord Eldon, yet he also championed the London Mechanics' Institution because it taught industrial skills, habits of work-discipline and the means to self-betterment.[21] There are indications, moreover, that this particular organisation became more orthodox as the twenties progressed; it certainly attracted an increasingly large number of clerks rather than artisans.

Nor can we afford to overlook the symbolic implications of young Evans's approach to Place in 1823. Twenty years earlier Thomas Evans's action in using money he had borrowed from Place 'for a dishonest purpose' had led to a bitter feud between the two men. Place's willingness in 1823 to give young Evans a loan and to find him a job indicated a belief that the boy had redeemed the sins of his father. Place's readiness to help young Evans a second time in 1830 also suggests that the young man had consolidated that trust during the remainder of the twenties. By this time old Evans was almost certainly dead and the quarrel could be laid finally to rest. Young Evans was also able to support his plea for help by citing an impressive list of intellectual achievements, including having earned Canning's praise for earlier work as a parliamentary reporter.[22] Once again

Place obliged – this time finding Evans a position with the *British Traveller*. Thereafter, T.J. Evans drops out of sight. Perhaps he remained an active radical, but I have found no record of political involvement after the mid-twenties. What does seem certain is that respectable self-improvement had removed him far from the milieu and traditions of his father's Spencean ultra-radical underworld.

Before the Evanses withdrew from the arena of radical politics they had helped in 1822 to organise metropolitan support for Richard Carlile's nascent campaign for freedom of publication and religious opinion – the only overt popular radical movement to function through the first half of the decade. Carlile stubbornly refused to allow his imprisonment for blasphemy in 1819 to force the closure of either the *Republican* or his publishing-bookselling business in Fleet Street. The former, he continued to edit from Dorchester prison; the latter, he staffed with volunteers, initially from his own family, then from all over England. In an effort to defeat the government and prosecuting societies, men and women streamed to the London shop prepared to martyr themselves in the courts and to jam the prisons. They were supported by a countrywide network of freethinking reading clubs known as Zetetic societies which furnished bookshop volunteers, subscription funds and reader-writers for the *Republican*.[23]

Early in 1822, when the Fleet Street volunteers were being fast depleted by a spate of prosecutions, Samuel Waddington enrolled in 'Carlile's Corps'. By April he had taken out a printer's licence and opened a shop in the Strand, where he began selling Carlile's deistic publications using the ingenious 'clockwork' method devised by earlier volunteers.[24] Waddington exchanged both books and money by means of a bag on a rope which he operated through an upstairs spouting, unseen by the purchaser. The window of his shop also sported cheeky placards addressed to the Constitutional Association and the Society for the Suppression of Vice: 'To the forces of the Bridge Street and Essex Street gangs, Samuel Waddington sells nothing seditious or blasphemous but he has a strong suspicion that somebody under his roof does.' Beneath it another placard boasted that 'Paine's *Age of Reason* and Palmer's *Principles of Nature* are now selling behind the Curtain, Price 5s each. No connection with Waddington the Fanatic'.[25]

By hiding in the upstairs room of a neighbouring tobacconist, informers from the SSV eventually managed to witness Waddington selling a copy of Elihu Palmer's trenchant deistic tract, *Principles of Nature*. He was tried for blasphemous libel in October and – despite a typically boisterous defence – his conviction was a foregone conclusion. He was confronted with a packed and hostile special jury and the prosecution undermined his usual appeal to scriptural radicalism by citing passages from Palmer which denounced the scriptures as forgeries and Jesus as 'nothing more than an

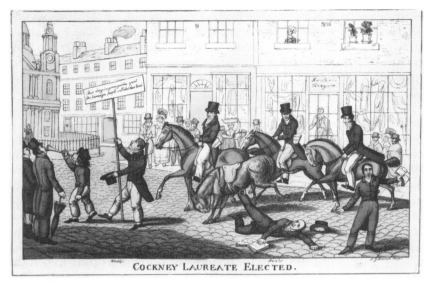

COCKNEY LAUREATE ELECTED.

19 Bentham ousted: Little Waddy leads the march of mind.

illegitimate Jew … hopes of salvation through him rest on no better foundation than of Fornication or adultery'. He was sentenced to twelve months' imprisonment in Coldbath Fields.[26]

On the face of it Waddington seemed to have made a successful transition from the old conspiratorial underworld radicalism of the post-war years to the more respectable intellectual modes of the 1820s. A satirical print of 1821, *Cockney Laureate Elected*, depicts him as a harbinger of the popular march of mind (see Ill. 19). Carlile's Zetetic movement of which he had become a member represented the *ne plus ultra* of the twenties' radical intellectual culture. The word 'Zetetic' denoted the search for knowledge, and the London branch was no exception. The rules and regulations of 1822 stressed its learned and respectable character, symbolised in the encouragement of women members. It offered lectures on theology, art, science and history, and devoted the monthly shilling subscription to the purchase of a library.[27] In his fearless volunteering, his bold defence speeches and his publication of two defiant prison tracts, Waddington seemed to typify the spirit of Carlile's Zetetic martyrs. Both Jonathan Wooler and the cantankerous Carlile himself heaped praise on the 'little billsticker' in the winter of 1822.

But Waddington's acceptance as a member of 'Carlile's Corps' was shortlived and, in retrospect, illusory. Compared with the majority of the volunteer shopmen and women, he was an incongruous – even embarrassing – figure. Most were young artisan autodidacts driven by a powerful urge for intellectual and social self-improvement. Like young Evans, they used prison as college and finishing school, and – with the help of Carlile and other patrons – often went on to become substantial bookseller-publishers.[28] Whether in bookshop, courtroom or prison, they were characteristically sober, serious and morally intense. 'Little Waddy' was none of these. He could not help treating Carlile's cause in his old burlesque style. Only a few days after volunteering in January 1822 he was proposing to 'laugh down' the prosecuting societies and government by constructing life-size paste dummies of Castlereagh and Sir William Curtis. Since he was 'but a little man', he intended to animate them from inside like a comic puppeteer.[29] In the courtroom he eschewed the scholarly rationalist defences which Carlile provided for most of the volunteers, preferring to rely on the same combination of buffoonery and radical biblicism which had secured his acquittals in Hopkins Street days.

He was still able to produce gales of laughter in the court, but, according to *The Times*, the Chief Justice found his defence so eccentric that he asked the prosecution whether the little man was deranged. Waddington compounded this impression by attempting to run out of the court after being convicted. When he came up for sentencing in November 1822 he drew a Bible from his pocket and warned the judges:

they must one day appear before the God of the Universe to answer for what they were going this day to do. Then when the great book of crimes should be opened, they might find that they had sold the righteous man, and oppressed the poor, and might hear passed on them the awful sentence, 'Depart ye wicked into everlasting fire prepared for the Devil and his angels ...'.[30]

His gaol publications were also vastly different from the writings on materialist atheism, feminism, birth control and political economy produced by Carlile's shopmen in the *Newgate Magazine*, 1825–6. Waddington's works consisted of a half-satirical *Letter to the Editor of the 'Traveller'* complaining that the prison authorities had been unable to furnish him with a Bible on his first committal, and a semi-incoherent parody entitled *The People's Universal Prayer*. A typical verse of the latter went: 'Be first, Daniel, with some lying tale, thou forging *Courier*, thy Danish, or thy Mrs Q's blue eyes and dubious breasts compose; and with veal cutlets and curacoa thy hopeful baby please; cram him well, and glut thy deluded slaves with lies'.[31]

Carlile might have been willing to tolerate Waddington's old-fashioned enthusiasm and levity but he could not pardon the little radical's failure to meet the standards of moral respectability expected of Zetetics. A month after his initial indictment on the blasphemy charge, a bruised and battered Waddington appeared at the Westminster sessions, having tried to assault a watchman who was arresting him for a drunken disturbance in

Windmill Street. On this occasion Waddington's comical talents gained him an amused and indulgent acquittal from the chairman of the court.[32] However, Waddington's next outbreak of rough behaviour proved the opposite of amusing. In 1823 he was convicted of an attempted sexual assault on an eleven-year-old girl who was delivering laundry to his prison cell. This put him beyond the pale of Zetetic ethical codes and of common folk morality. He complained that fellow prisoners tossed him in a blanket and hurt his back, and for some time after his release from prison in the late twenties he was forced to avoid former radical colleagues because of the obloquy attached to his crime.[33]

Waddy's old comrade Robert Wedderburn appeared to be another casualty of twenties' self-improvement. Early in 1828 a handbill announced that a 'New Assembly Room' was shortly to open at 12 White's Alley, Chancery Lane, where Rev. Robert Wedderburn would deliver 'theological and moral lectures' on Tuesday mornings. The charge was 3d and 'much singularity, novelty and originality' was promised. Hall anticipated that Wedderburn would do well; infidel chapels were one of the few forms of radicalism to be flourishing in 1828. The Christian Evidence Society and Association of Universal Benevolence run by renegade Anglican clergyman, Robert Taylor, had blossomed since its establishment in London in 1824. And although a blasphemy conviction put Taylor out of action in 1828, a former Stepney radical, Rev. Josiah Fitch, was attracting good crowds to a new Christian Universalist chapel in Grub Street, Cripplegate. Hall thought that Wedderburn would eclipse Fitch: the black's proposed new chapel was bigger and cheaper, and Hall could remember the Hopkins Street success.[34]

Shrewd as he was, Hall had failed to notice how much the infidel chapels of Taylor and Fitch differed from those of 1818–19. Hopkins Street chapel had been an insurrectionary radical section and a blasphemous debating club; the twenties' chapels represented themselves as places of deist religious worship. Their preachers issued liturgies outlining 'forms of public worship' and made use of a variety of religious rituals and ceremonies. Taylor's *Holy Liturgy* unashamedly borrowed its 'Canticles, Creed, Lessons, Thanksgiving and Collect' from the Anglican service. Attendants were encouraged to regard themselves as a congregation; the conductor of the service was instructed to 'wear such decent ornaments and scholarlike apparel pending his initiation as may become the dignity thereof'.[35]

Why this format proved attractive during the twenties is difficult to say. The ability of a sect to gather its followers into a close-knit brotherhood during unpromising times might have been one reason. We have seen that Spence and Evans dabbled with sectarian forms when trying to hold the Spenceans together during the troubled war years. Evans and Wedderburn had turned to chapels in 1818–19 more out of tactical expediency than a wish to keep their disciples from the world. But when (in 1821) E.J. Blandford, Benbow, Cannon and other ultras, impressed by the example of the Carbonari in Naples, formed a shortlived Anglo-Carbonarian Union based in Soho, they recast the old radical-Spencean rhetoric of Hopkins Street into devotional language and accompanied it with a deistic catechism. A supporting article in Benbow's *Radical Magazine* hoped this would usher in the time when 'religion itself will, sooner or later, be restored to its native purity, loveliness, and simplicity'.[36]

Deistic sectarianism was also an expression of the early nineteenth-century appetite for heightened feeling and emotion, reflected in romanticism and popular evangelicalism. In view of Taylor's later cynicism, it is worth noting that when he founded his infidel society in London in 1824 he still believed 'in God, in Providence and the immortality of the soul'. He was also steeped in literary romanticism. He plagiarised the Anglican service because of 'its majestic rythmns ... and declamatory grandeur', and he stressed that it had been altered 'in philosophy only and not in piety'.[37] Chapters from Volney's *Ruins of Empires*, and later, *Queen Mab*, were read aloud at deist services for the same reasons. 'This book [Volney's *Ruins*]', wrote Richard Carlile in 1830, 'is admirably suited to the taste and temper of the present time, and is truly prophetic.'[38] Such readings, when combined with deist catechisms and ceremonial, could induce something very like ecstatic conversation. After attending one of Taylor's services in 1830, a young architect's clerk, William Knight, filled several manuscript pages with his new-found afflatus: 'in vain my pen attempts to express the throbbing joys which fill my heart, no tongue can utter and no Christian's mind can imagine the pleasures which fill my Soul ... Be still my heart for thou art free! thou cans't reach the Heavens.'[39]

Interest in the cult of Theophilanthropy of late revolutionary France had been based in part on a belief that the structure and ceremonial of religion helped to inculcate or reinforce natural morality. Similar moral yearnings had induced some correspondents to espouse sectarian forms of deism in the post-war radical press and probably led others – like Henry Hetherington – to join the Freethinking Christians during the 1820s.[40] Cannon claimed in 1822 to be responding to popular demand when he produced a new translation of the *Manual of the Theophilanthropists*. Though doubtful about Theophilanthropy as a 'kind of castrated Christianity', he admitted that many people found 'certain exterior practices' helpful in bringing them 'more frequently and efficaciously to the principles of natural religion'. The *Manual*, he claimed, would prove useful for fostering in children the universal principles of 'piety, Charity, Concord and Tolerance'.[41] This concern to teach the strenuous but supposedly natural principles of enlightenment morality was shared by all the deist preachers of the twenties. Roland Detrosier's moral creed has been described as elevating 'bootstraps into a religion'; Taylor's *Moral Catechism* for children and *First to Thirteenth Moral Discourses* advocated virtues like 'moral fortitude' and 'government of temper' (along with more unorthodox ideas on sexuality and the family).[42]

Morality was only one aspect of the education taught at the deist chapels. Hopkins Street had doubled as an insurrectionary political section; Taylor described his chapel as 'a school'. 'Hither we come to learn', he told his Salter Street congregation, 'to have new capacities of knowledge unbarred'. Carlile hoped that the Sunday School of Free Discussion which he opened at the same time as Wedderburn's new chapel in 1828 would 'produce a lever to move the intellect of the earth'. Fitch had once been a schoolmaster and he continued at Grub Street chapel to teach such subjects as elocution and astronomy. Detrosier was equally dazzling whether he lectured on theology, political economy, literature or chemistry, though his breadth of scope was nearly matched by Taylor who had been a fellow with the Royal College of Surgeons in 1807 and taken a BA at Cambridge in 1813. He accompanied his critiques of Christian evidences with 'experiments and facts in demonstration of the surprising efficacy of merely physical causes to correct the constitution and to give vigour to the mind'.[43] The excitement which young men like William Knight felt in listening to such services was partly that of the autodidact discovering the boundless possibilities of knowledge.

William Knight's occupation (architect's clerk) was also fairly typical of those who made up the deist congregations of the twenties. They were drawn overwhelmingly from the respectable 'middling sort' – ambitious artisans, small shopkeepers and lesser professionals. Taylor's and Fitch's main financial backers comprised William Devonshire Saull, a prosperous Aldersgate wine-merchant; John Brooks, a publisher-bookseller; Pummell, a Walworth fishmonger; Room, 'a gentleman'; Freeman, a Nonconformist preacher and Joseph Brushfield, an oilman/silk weaver. They helped Taylor – who had begun his London career preaching in tavern back-rooms – to acquire his own Salter's Hall chapel (or 'Areopagus') in autumn 1826, at the cost of £1850. Subscriptions for the Christian Evidence Society cost 1 guinea a quarter, and shares for the Areopagus, £5 each – another indication of the background of Taylor's supporters.[44] Carlile thought that the high proportion of well-dressed and respectable young women who attended Taylor's lectures were 'fashionable ladies' attracted by the ex-clergyman's suave manners and looks.[45] More likely, they were socially frustrated 'gentlewomen' from middle-class backgrounds like Eliza Macaulay who lectured at Fitch's chapel and Carlile's own future wife, Eliza Sharples, who was to lecture on feminist and freethinking subjects at the Rotunda in 1831–2.[46]

All this was a far cry from the type of infidel chapel that Robert Wedder-burn had operated in 1819; and there are some signs that he tried in 1828 to adjust to the prevailing twenties' mode. At Hopkins Street he had represented no particular religion or denomination; at White's Alley he presented himself as founder of a sect of 'Christian Diabolists, or Devil Worshippers'. Carlile helped him to produce a liturgy cast in inflated devotional language.[47] Naming the chapel 'The New Assembly Room' and advertising 'moral and theological lectures' also smacked of deist preachers like Taylor and Fitch.

In reality, Wedderburn had no chance of matching these two apostles of the march of mind. He had tried to use the two years' solitary confinement in Dorchester gaol 'to learn to read and write', but was too old and poorly grounded to emulate the feats of prison autodidacts like T.J. Evans, Richard Carlile and most of the Zetetic shopmen. At the end of the twenties Wedderburn was still barely literate, and probably as little versed in rationalist theory as he had been in 1819. It is doubtful whether he was even a thoroughgoing deist, let alone an atheist like many Zetetics. At one level he never ceased to be a radical Christian with millenarian leanings. He always attended religious services in Dorchester and Carlile had mis-chievously tried to get him appointed prison chaplain. Carlile's insistence in 1828 that Wedderburn's new sect of Christian Diabolists was a serious deist undertaking 'with nothing bordering on jest' in the liturgy was not exactly persuasive given its burlesque title.[48]

Once the chapel opened, it was evident how little had changed from 1819. The signpost over the door saying 'New Assembly Room' could not disguise the fact that the chapel was actually a roughly converted, unlit, carpenter's shop. According to Hall, who rarely exaggerated, Wedderburn delivered his lectures 'in the most vulgar manner that could possibly be imagined'. Ostensibly addressing the question 'whether the world had a beginning or not', the preacher made an incoherent attack 'without any main point' on the first few chapters of Genesis. Before long, this lack of what Hall called 'a regular system' caused the meetings to degenerate into nothing more than 'abusive conversation'. We can sense Hall's realisation that Wedderburn's style of infidelity had become obsolete. The qualities which had made the hayloft preacher a success in 1819 were contributing to his failure in 1828.[49] The clergyman, Dr Evelyn, in *Tremaine* – R.P.Ward's anti-infidel novel of 1825 – could almost have had Wedder-burn and Taylor in mind when he contrasted the old-fashioned, relatively harmless exponent of 'vulgar blasphemy' and 'indecency', with the new style of 'well bred ruffian ... who silently approaches and undermines the heart'.[50] During the two months that it operated, Wedderburn's chapel rarely attracted more than a few dozen supporters, in spite of his lowering of the admission price to 1d. By the end of June, 1828, he was forced to announce the chapel's closure; he could no longer afford the 5s weekly rental on the premises.

Another reason for the failure of Wedderburn's chapel in 1828 was the extreme unrespectability of most of those who sponsored and attended it. Before it opened, Hall predicted that it would be 'less respectably' attended than Fitch's, but he was still surprised at the roughness of the congregation. He described one service as 'the worst fracas' he had seen; the congregation had behaved as vulgarly as the preacher, with 'no sort of decency exhibited by anyone as to being uncovered'. This recurrence of blasphemous Hopkins Street rituals was to be expected given that Wedderburn's backers and supporters at the new chapel were, according to Hall, 'all very poor who have long known him'. They included veterans William and John Dugdale, 'Old' Palmer, Thomas Jeffryes and William Edgar, as well as a 'Mr Cameron' – possibly another mis-identification of Cannon.[51]

By the end of the twenties men of this sort were regarded as embarrassingly unrespectable in artisan and middling radical circles. This was not necessarily because they were poor, but because of the way they behaved and made their livings. In 1819 Wedderburn's criminal past had added to his stature at Hopkins Street; by 1828 such things were better hidden. When it was revealed the following year that William Edgar had been secretly operating a business pimping for his own wife, he was immediately 'discarded' by infidel-radical associates.[52] In winter 1830 Robert Wedderburn was sentenced to two years' imprisonment with hard labour for a similar connection with a 'bawdy house'.[53] His old ally Little Waddy had just completed his long spell in Coldbath Fields prison, but was still shamefacedly avoiding old radical-infidel friends. Wedderburn's other major supporters at the new chapel were little better. In 1828 the Dugdale brothers and George Cannon made their livings by publishing and selling pornography, and by 1831 Cannon, like Wedderburn, was behind bars; he had been sentenced to twelve months' imprisonment in Tothill Fields gaol for obscene libel.[54]

The fact that Wedderburn and Edgar began operating petty brothels around 1829–30 is not so surprising when we recall their backgrounds. Both men had been reared in the 'old blackguard' artisan culture of late eighteenth-century London. By Place's account, bawdiness and casual promiscuity had been the norm in this milieu. He remembered several of his father's tradesmen friends who had sold their daughters or female relatives. As an apprentice Place kept company with whores and had casual sexual affairs with tradesmen's daughters. Such practices had been commonplace and, he believed, harmless, because they carried no opprobrium. Most of the girls subsequently married and became exemplary wives.[55] Petty prostitution – sometimes in association with wives or mistresses – was one way for poor artisans (and their families) to supplement their income. The practice of part-time brothel-keeping was probably re-garded as no more deviant amongst rough artisans than stealing from employers, for which Wedderburn had earlier been imprisoned. The whitesmith and informer John Castle had pimped in this fashion around 1816. Christopher Harris, who also belonged to Thistlewood's ultra-radi-cal coterie, admitted in 1819 to operating a brothel from the same prem-ises that he used for selling seditious publications. Men as poor and un-skilled as Wedderburn had to scratch a living as best they could; it was probably debts incurred from the failure of the chapel in late 1828 that caused him to open a bawdy house. The fact that he and Edgar both did so (independently) suggests that this was still a reasonably common practice amongst degraded artisans at the end of the twenties. What had changed by then, however, was that brothel-keeping was no longer acceptable behaviour for an ultra-radical.

Not all ultras failed so spectacularly to adapt to the new imperatives of the 1820s and 1830s. Allen Davenport and his close friends Charles Neesom and Charles Jennison moved easily into step with the march of mind. Though Davenport did not become one of Carlile's volunteer shopmen, his intellectual development during the twenties overlapped with the Zetetic movement. When Davenport's friend and employer, W. Bainbridge, launched into building speculation in 1822, he appointed Davenport over-seer, caretaker and salesman of a group of new cottages at Tollington Park, near Hornsey Road. There followed six years of comfort, leisure, prestige and pastoral inspiration, enabling Davenport to broaden his education and renew his boyhood literary ambitions. Over the next dozen years he pro-duced a stream of articles and poems for the periodical press – particularly the *Republican* – as well as several published volumes of poetry, a play, a biography of Spence and some unpublished fragments of novels.[56]

These writings show Davenport making the same speculative advances as Carlile and his bolder supporters. Shelley's *Queen Mab* was a decisive text. It filled Davenport with the romantic afflatus and provided a model for his own radical odes. Its necessarianism and lengthy Holbachian notes also carried him in the direction of materialist atheism and sowed his first doubts about orthodox sexuality. Davenport, like Carlile, soon became a keen supporter of the courageous feminist shopworker Susannah Wright; an advocate of contraception; and a fierce critic of orthodox Christian marriage as repressive and exploitative of women. Like Carlile, too, he dabbled with political economy – supporting Hector Campbell's theory of a bread wage standard against Francis Place in 1826. In the later twenties he seems also to have been influenced by Robert Taylor's critique of the scriptures as a repository of astronomical and zodiacal myths.[57]

By the mid-twenties he and his immediate circle of friends had also come under the sway of another, more far-reaching, influence. In a letter to the *Co-operative Magazine and Monthly Herald* of 1826, Davenport announced his conversion to Owen's new 'social system'. It advanced beyond Spence's plan in embracing 'all the powers of production and distribution, as well as holding the lands in common'. (He later admitted that Spence's ideas tended to fall into neglect at this time in the face of the new Owenite promise of political and social regeneration.) Believing firmly that he would live to see 'the universal establishment of that paradisiacal system', he became an ardent practical and theoretical disciple. In 1830 he joined the pioneering 'First London Co-operative Manufacturing Society' which held its weekly meetings at Jennison's Old Street premises. Here, as superintendent, storeman and overseer of the boot and shoe department, he helped his colleagues to produce and exchange goods in proof of 'the superiority of the co-operative principle over that of competition'. Even when 'the customs, habits, and influences of the old society' brought down their small community, his faith remained unimpaired. He, Jennison, James Mee and John Hunter – all former Spencean ultras – joined the important British Association for the Promotion of Co-operative Knowledge around this time. In 1831 he and Jennison shifted premises to be closer to Owen's Grays Inn Road Exchange. A few years later he wrote a 'co-operative' play called *The Social Age* which was performed at the Charlotte Street Exchange before audiences of 300, including Owen himself on one occasion.[58]

When he looked back over his life in 1846, Davenport was struck most by the growth of educational institutions catering for working people. As well as generating new social and economic ideas, the Zetetic, deist, sectarian and Co-operative movements of the twenties were important agents of this messianic popular drive for intellectual and moral improvement. Davenport believed that they helped to transform the minds, manners and whole social demeanour of their members. He recalled festivals and balls held at the Grays Inn Road Exchange where the surrounding avenues had been brilliantly lit by Grecian lamps. Bands containing more than a dozen musical instruments had accompanied ladies and gentlemen as they sang celebrated airs to the

admiration and applause of five or six hundred supremely happy individuals, the greater part of whom, were attired in the most fashionable dresses, and bedecked with costly jewellery, which blazed in the light, and shed a glory around, which had no parallel, but in the fairy scenes of poetical romance. And many there were, whose accomplished manners, and gracefulness of deportment, would not have disgraced the drawing room of the most fastidious nobleman, in this polite kingdom.[59]

At around this time he joined reading and discussion circles at the Cornish coffee-house, Bunhill Row, and the Hope coffee-house (also attended by Place and Galloway). Later he was elected president of the Tower Street

Mutual Instruction Society and the Gould Square Mechanics' Institute, as well as honorary member of the Finsbury Mutual Instruction Society in Bunhill and of Lovett's National Association for Promoting Social and Political Improvement. No wonder this dogged autodidact radical described himself at the end of his life as 'one, whose ruling passion has always been to acquire knowledge, and to impart it to those of his order, who might happen to be placed at a still greater distance from the wholesome and cheering rays of that bright intellectual sun'.[60]

Survivals and revivals

There is no doubting the importance of all these 'changes' which Hall observed in his colleagues during the twenties. At one level they would appear to corroborate recent claims that the drive for respectability reached a poorer, more unskilled sector of the nineteenth-century working classes than is generally believed,[61] at another, to illustrate the penalties of failing to keep up with the march of mind. But nineteenth-century respectability was a multi-faceted phenomenon capable of leading in a variety of directions. Other scholarship has questioned whether the values and behavioural patterns associated with 'roughness' and 'respectability' were fixed and mutually exclusive cultural absolutes, preferring to see them as a fluid and overlapping repertoire of roles which could be deployed in calculated ways.[62] Significantly, by November 1830 Abel Hall was beginning to doubt whether the new-found respectability of his ultra-radical colleagues was as fundamental or permanent as he had earlier thought.[63]

In addition to the imperatives of respectability there were other reasons why ultra-radicals shifted to coffee-houses in the 1820s. A lowering of excise duties around this time made the tavern staple of porter relatively expensive compared with coffee and gin. Coffee-houses began assuming many of the social and recreational functions of alehouses and taverns, except for the provision of liquor which could be bought cheaply at gin-shops and one-room dramhouses.[64] Coffee-houses were also relatively cheap, easy to establish and free from the control of licensing justices and conservative brewers. As early as 1817 some of Thistlewood's followers expressed a preference for them over public houses because they could stock seditious publications without interference. This probably explains also why such ultra-radicals as Evans, Ings (the Cato Street conspirator), Whittaker and Walker opened up coffee-houses in 1818–19. The last two were used by Preston and his colleagues as venues for formal commemorations of their Cato Street friends. The ceremony was additionally dignified at Walker's coffee-house (in Union Street, Spitalfields) by a black-bordered portrait of Thistlewood which hung on the wall. By spring 1821 the spy Shegog was naming these places, as well as the Patriot Coffee Shop in Soho (frequented by Cannon), the Chapter and the Sun in the Barbican and Williams's coffee-house in St Martin Le Grand, as 'the most successful auxiliary the seditious and corrupt press have'.[65]

Whittaker's, Walker's and the Sun survived to form part of a network of twenties' coffee-houses situated in the old Spencean ultra-radical tavern strongholds of Bethnal Green, Finsbury and Soho. Around the corner from Walker's stood Sampson Elliot's Coffee Shop in Old Street, St Lukes, and not far away, the Phoenix in Grub Street, the Cambridge in Shoreditch and the Albion in Lantern Wall. Hall's reports from the first half of the twenties are unaccountably missing, but retrospective comments from him and another spy, Isaacson, as well as other fragments of evidence, indicate that 'Old Spenceans' met at these coffee-houses throughout the twenties in groups of around forty to debate pre-arranged political topics. Hall named the leading veteran attendants as Preston, Medlar, William Millard, Stanley, Carr, Blandford, Keenes, Kenney, Hunter, John Palin and Robert George.[66] They might not have plotted violent revolution, but they did perpetuate other ultra-radical traditions. A probably exaggerated confession of 1830 from a horse-thief named Charles Brophy gave details of a secret federation of West-End coffee-house clubs centred in Mayfair and linked to Walker's coffee-house in Spitalfields. Brophy listed numbers of veteran ultra-radical members and linked the organisation with a republican and land-nationalising programme. He even provided half-persuasive examples of their secret cipher.[67]

More reliable glimpses of the old underworld during the later twenties are to be found in accounts of the British Forum debating club which met at Lunts coffee-house, Clerkenwell Green, under the leadership of Gale Jones and – for a short time – of Thomas Evans. The British Forum was opened five times a week for reading, singing and debating; its republican, infidel, agrarian reform and anti-slavery debates attracted old and new ultras.[68] Wedderburn and members of 'that school' were regulars.[69] Part of their impetus – and that of the British Forum generally – probably came from the revival of the anti-slavery movement in 1823, whose impact on twenties' popular radicalism has been insufficiently appreciated. Wedderburn and Davidson's anti-slavery polemics at Hopkins Street had attracted the keen attention of abolitionists – so much so that Wedderburn received a sympathetic visit from Wilberforce in prison. This seems to have inspired the black radical – on his release – to publish an exposé of his slaver father in Bell's Weekly. A year later he incorporated this into an autobiography, The Horrors of Slavery, which testified to the persistence of his political ardour: 'I am still in the same mind as I was before and imprisonment has but confirmed me that I was right'. At commemorations of Paine's birth-day, 1822–4, British Forum members denounced 'the foul and infamous traffic in slaves', drank toasts to the republicans of St Domingo and to future insurrections in the West Indies, and sang the 'Lament of the Negro'. All this helped to inspire a new generation of radical leaders with ultra and anti-slavery sympathies.[70]

The new ultras included Carlile's ex-shopman James Watson, young G.J. Harney, 'the Devil's Chaplain' Robert Taylor and the eccentric 'Reforming Optimist' Pierre Baume. At Lunts William Lovett heard all these, as well as the veteran republican-freethinkers Gale Jones and Carlile.[71] The British Forum overlapped with the earlier-mentioned debating-cum-literary group known as the Liberals. It attracted numbers of former Jacobins and Spenceans and Watsonites, including 'Dr' Watson himself, as well as Cannon, Hunter, Moggridge, Millard, Stanley, Medlar, Beckwith, Preston (occasionally) and the two spies Hall and Brittain. They met through most of the twenties at the Mercer's Arms, Longacre, and often joined with British Forum members in annual tavern commemorations of Paine's birthday. Here they continued the old traditions of 'friendly hilarity' – toasting, chanting, burlesquing the coronation and singing 'Scots wha ha', 'Quivedo', the 'Marseillaise', Evans's 'Charter of Kings' and the Jacobin ballad composed by Joseph Gerrald whilst sailing to Botany Bay.[72]

As poor harvests, trade slumps and democratic political movements in France and Ireland began to generate conditions of mass political unrest similar to the post-war years, Hall also noted a renewal of old ultra-radical strategies. In 1829 Palin – whose mail was being intercepted by the government from 1825 – and Kenney, both former members of the same Cato Street division, persuaded disaffected shoemakers to form a radical committee based at the Cheshire Cheese. Preston was already working to capitalise on the 'angry feeling' of unemployed Spitalfields weavers; two years later he formed a 'Committee of Observation' so that ultra-radicals might be 'ready to be called into action'.[73] As in 1803–15, an apparently innocuous debating club culture had kept intact a group of experienced ultra-radical leaders. It had also perpetuated a body of programmes, practices, ideas and strategies, and provided a springboard for renewed mass political action.

By October 1831 the Tory *Age* was reporting that 'the old incendiaries are at work, getting up petitions, spouting treason and fomenting civil discord, who created such alarm in 1818 and 1819. We could name a baker's dozen of these same worthies, many of whom have already been incarcerated, and all of whom ought to be again.'[74] In the decade that followed Spencean ultra-radicals underwent a revival in prestige and influence which enabled them to leave a significant impress on metropolitan mass radicalism up to the early Chartist years. They dominated debates, occupied key offices, influenced programmes and determined strategies of a succession of important working-class radical organisations.

John George became a leading member of the Huntite Radical Reform Association of 1829; Hunter, Mee, Millard and Walker, of the Metropolitan Political Union of 1830. And when the pivotal National Union of the Working Classes was formed shortly after, it was joined by a string of old ultras, including Benbow, George, George Petrie, Warry, Mee, Neesom, Preston, Low, Davenport, Medlar, Jennison, Hall, Gast, Mills, J. Clements, Charles Davis and 'Dr' Brown. The NUWC was the broadest-based, most effective metropolitan radical organisation of the early 1830s, and these men led its debates, moved many of its resolutions, occupied class leader positions and comprised most of the militant Finsbury division. Out of this last came the Finsbury Forum of 1834–5 and its successor, the East London Democratic Association (later the London Democratic Association) of 1837–41, whose importance as a crucible of London Chartism is now being recognised. Again, veteran ultras featured amongst the leaders, notably Davenport, Neesom, Mee, John George, Preston, Gast, Jennison, Blandford, the Savage brothers and Waddington (who had emerged from his disgrace). Finally, we should note that several ultras, including Mee, George, Neesom and Davenport also joined the more moderate London Working Men's Association and gave new zest to its rank-and-file and local activities in 1839–40.[75]

As in post-war years these groups met mainly at public houses, chapels and coffee-houses – some of them old and familiar haunts. Benbow's Commercial coffee-house at Temple Bar, the Albion coffee-house in Shoreditch and Lunts were favourite venues of old ultras in the NUWC and ELDA. Equally prominent in the mid-thirties were a series of blasphemous radical chapels: the Philadelphia chapel in Windmill Street, the old Borough chapel in Chapel Court, Benbow's chapel at 8 Theobald's Road and the Bowling Square chapel in Bethnal Green. Public houses also regained much of their old attraction after the Beer Act of 1830 spawned a multitude of small, cheap and laxly controlled beerhouses all over the metropolis. The Green Dragon in Fore Street, an intermittent radical haunt since W.H. Reid's day but now apparently re-licensed as a beerhouse, hosted the LDA council during winter 1838–9, and ramshackle beerhouses like the Spotted Cow in Old Kent Road and the Standard of Liberty in Brick Lane were gathering places for several LDA sections.[76]

Like their earlier counterparts, most of these venues functioned as educational and educative centres, as well as political sections. The Philadelphia chapel which had been opened by Henry Medlar for Universalist preaching in the mid-twenties was revived by Baume in 1829, then taken over by James Watson in 1831. Under these last two it served as a radical and freethinking debating hall, as well as the headquarters for Class 73 of the NUWC – a section which contained many veterans of the post-war chapels. Later, under the title of the Finsbury Forum, this lively debating club moved to the Bowling Square chapel where Classes 40 and 42 of the NUWC also met. Two of the management committee, Mee and Neesom, had formerly been officials at Archer Street chapel, and a third, Medlar, was also a veteran of post-war years. Likewise, Lunt's coffee-house served as headquarters for the LDA Clerkenwell district committee, whose 'factotum' was none other than 'Little Waddy'. A lecture by William Cobbett at Benbow's Theobald's Road chapel in June 1832 showed that the tactical *raison d'être* of these chapels had altered little from 1818–19. He praised radical chapels as the best political strategy of the times and declared that if the Whigs attacked the radical reform movement he would immediately take out a preacher's licence, hire a large chapel, collect money in the manner of a religious service and use the Bible as his radical text.[77]

Throughout the 1830s these veteran ultras campaigned incessantly in favour of the Watsonite post-war tactics of simultaneous mass meetings leading to a national convention or anti-parliament. To Place's dismay the idea even surfaced within the moderate NPU at the instigation of a Mr Perry, probably the old Jacobin and Hopkins Street orator. After it was rejected, Benbow and his Commercial coffee-house coterie denounced the NPU as shopocrats and aristocrats. Benbow, like many of his post-war predecessors, believed that it was necessary to arm NUWC mass meetings with staves for 'defensive' purposes. His famous 'Grand National Holiday' proposal of 1833 also had its roots in Spencean ultra-radical rhetoric and strategies – encompassing simultaneous meetings, a cessation of labour, 'a moral rising of the people' and a national convention. Place believed that Benbow's scheme and its supporters nursed a further underlying aim of seizing the land and dividing it among the people. The NUWC's Coldbath Fields meeting of May 1833 was summoned by veterans Petrie, Lee, Mee, Preston and George, who were incensed at the Whigs' betrayal of the people in the Reform Act; they called for a national convention and condemned the private ownership of land. The ferocious ex-soldier Petrie also wanted to use the occasion for a Spa Fields type attack on the Bank and Tower.[78]

Petrie had long been an advocate of armed drilling and insurrection. Though more outspoken than others of his circle, he was not alone. In 1834, during the declining days of the NUWC, a spy reported that Benbow and Preston were discussing assassination plans in Hoxton alehouses.[79] At numerous private and public meetings of the LDA during 1838–9 Preston, Waddington, George and others invoked the insurrectionary tactics of Watsonite, Cato Street and even Queen Caroline days (the funeral battle). In the charged atmosphere of 1839 most of these die-hards seem to have contemplated an armed uprising of some kind, whether arising from mass simultaneous meetings and strikes, from a Spa Fields (or Babeuvist) style of attack or from the type of desperate assassination coups planned by Thistlewood between 1817 and 1820. In May 1839 Samuel Waddington was captured with a handful of armed LDA leaders in the supposed Shipyard conspiracy, occasioning no surprise in policemen who knew him to have been implicated in the Cato Street affair. The following month he presided at a turbulent meeting at Clerkenwell. In November, after he had been acquitted of the Shipyard conspiracy through lack of evidence, he issued an inflammatory summons to a Smithfield meeting, the real purpose of which was to support the Newport uprising. The response was poor, but rumours of armed plots persisted. Early the following year Charles Neesom was arrested with a cache of arms at the Bethnal Green Trades Hall – allegedly part of a planned LDA uprising to save Frost from execution.[80]

When not engaged in plots these 1830s' ultra-radicals espoused political ideas and programmes that often resembled those aired in taverns, chapels and coffee-houses over the previous thirty years. Naturally, both veterans and tyros had been influenced, sometimes deeply, by the new theories, prescriptions and practices of the 1820s. Yet we should take care not to exaggerate or misunderstand this impact. As Abel Hall discovered, the 'changes' were not necessarily as fundamental or as permanent as they first appeared. Scholars have long noted the persistence of 'old' postwar ideological elements alongside the 'new' unstamped critiques of the 1830s, and a trenchant recent study has also demonstrated the basic continuities between these two radical analyses.[81] Hostility to capitalists and competition did not alter the basic Paineite idea that the English social system had evolved out of plundering, cheating and oppression. And although the emergence of a popular socialist and anti-capitalist political economy in the 1820s has been charted in detail, its historian admits that the radical working-class press lost interest in this critique after 1834.[82] In a sense this is not surprising: the aggressive, interventionist policies of the Whig government during the 1830s revived and confirmed the longstanding radical belief that the plight of the working class, and of the people generally, derived from the activities of a corrupt, monopolistic political state.[83]

By the later thirties it was clear that Owenite socialism had not extinguished older Spencean ideas. From the outset many ultras had regarded the two creeds as compatible and reinforcing; like William Hone they viewed Owenism as Spenceanism 'doubly dipped'. Owenism had appealed to a diversity of existing artisan radical concerns and aspirations: nostalgia for land and community; desire for social and economic independence; hunger for moral and intellectual improvement; and a yearning for a form of religion that was independent, socially relevant and visionary. Some ultras (like Benbow and Petrie) who became 'co-operators' in the late twenties actually did so in opposition to Owenite organisations. Even men like

Davenport who admitted to having been dazzled by 'the golden calf' of Owenism had regarded the system as an improvement rather than a complete supercession of Spence's plan.[84] Desire for agrarian reform had been a continuing strand of artisan radicalism since the 1790s, and its protagonists added to, adapted, or fluctuated between, a variety of schemes. Thomas Preston and his friends were reported in March 1834 to be enthusing over Alex Milne's *The Millennium or Social Circle* because it improved on both Spence's and Owen's schemes by going 'straight to capital and income'.[85] Nevertheless, the land reform proposals that Preston himself put forward in 1834, 1840 and 1845 were essentially derived from Spence. Preston, Davenport and Lee were probably chiefly responsible for the revival of interest in Spencean doctrine that was being noted in the *Northern Star* in June 1838.[86] At the same time they and other ultra-veterans were to become enthusiastic supporters of the Chartist Land Plan even though its proposal to purchase and rent out small allotments diverged from both Owen's and Spence's prescriptions.

Throughout the 1830s the speeches and resolutions of the NUWC and the (E)LDA echoed those of 1819. 'Citizen' George harked back to Evans's Saxon agrarian Commonwealth, citing fifty-four years of radical service as his authority; Preston denounced fundholders with his old ferocity; Davenport tirelessly advocated Spencean 'agrarian justice', and Waddington reminded listeners at Kennington Common in May 1839 that he had been arrested at the same spot for urging exactly the same resolutions twenty years before.[87] He was scarcely exaggerating. The NUWC's resolutions for their Coldbath Fields meeting in 1833 attacked primogeniture and individual appropriation of the soil; the funding system; and the 'hereditary and exclusive legislation' which had engendered massive taxation and debt, and parasitical aristocratic, clerical and monarchical establishments.[88] True, the language of the LDA constitution of 1838 carried a new, more class-conscious note. It attacked the profits of the employing classes as well as landlords. The term 'proletarian classes' also replaced that of 'people' at one point, but the actual definition remained much the same – 'the multitude ... possessing no fortune and property'. The list of LDA objectives, too, displayed an essentially Jacobin outlook. They wished to institute Cartwright's suffrage and electoral provisions, to repeal the New Poor Law and the restrictions on the press, to reduce work hours and support rational trades' combinations, to promote the diffusion of political knowledge and to unite 'all classes into one bond of fraternity'.[89]

The programme and rhetoric of the LDA were familiar because they mirrored the grievances and aspirations of essentially the same social groups from which the old radical underworld had been recruited – mainly 'dishonourable' yet proud artisans from traditional handicraft trades that were experiencing acute degradation. Above all, these consisted of shoemakers, tailors, carpenters, cabinet-makers and weavers (and a sprinkling of lesser professionals) concentrated in the old stamping grounds of Islington, Hackney, Shoreditch, Bethnal Green, Finsbury and Spitalfields, and in pockets around Holborn, Marylebone and Soho, and across the river in Lambeth and Southwark.[90] By the late 1830s their situation was at least as bad as it had been in the immediate aftermath of the war, but their consciousness had grown. Now they chose to define themselves specifically against 'the respectables' or 'men who, being raised above the common lot of their order, do not experience their privations, and therefore cannot sympathize with their sufferings'. But their overall promise – 'the poorer, the more oppressed, the more welcome' – was exactly that of the men of 1819.[91]

It was not only their political language that was familiar. The chapels, coffee-houses and taverns of the thirties also resounded with variations of the old blend of radical Christianity, millenarianism and infidelity – all given fresh zest by the kindred sectarian, rationalist and messianic impulses of Owenism. Between 1830 and 1834, Mee, Davenport, Lowe, Gast, Medlar and Benbow conducted weekly lectures and debates at the Philadelphia, Bowling Square and Theobald's Street chapels on such subjects as: 'Materialism', 'Is the Bible the Word of God' (with the ex-Southcottian watchman Sibley), 'Deism', 'The Signs of the Times', 'Raphael's Prophetic Almanack' and 'Prophecy'.[92] In 1831 the crippled shoemaker John 'Zion' Ward, whose social and spiritual evolution so resembled Wedderburn's, was preaching a theology at the Philadelphia chapel which merged elements of social radicalism, Southcottian eschatology and Carlilean infidelity. He could feel the minds of the hearers 'stirred up like a troubled ocean'.[93] His regular venue at that time was the Borough chapel where the Antinomian, John Church, and the spy, John Shegog, had preached during the post-war years. On being imprisoned in 1832 Ward was succeeded there in turn by a fiery young Scots ex-Presbyterian and Wroeite, James Elishama (Shepherd) Smith. Smith preached in company with Gast, George, Davenport and Harris to crowds of 700–800 people on such subjects as: 'The Fallacies of the Christian Religion' and 'The Prophecies of Old and Modern Times' (where he defended Brothers, Dark and Southcott).[94] And if some of this millenarian (and infidel) language was being put to 'new psychological and political purposes',[95] some of the new vocabulary of Owenism was also being put to old psychological and political purposes. Just before he died in 1846 Davenport still looked forward to the 'approaching storm' that he had prophesied in Hopkins Street speeches. It was to be a 'moral earthquake which will shake the world and convulse Europe from its centre to its circumference'.[96]

Even remnants of the old fraternal conviviality and Rabelaisian theatricals persisted into the new age. Allen Davenport was 'amused and instructed' during the 1830s in much the same way that he had been at the Mulberry Tree tavern during the post-war years. At the Cornish coffee-house in Bunhill Row he 'met with that kind respect and brotherly love, among the friends who are in the constant habit of meeting there to amuse themselves by public discussions and private conversations, which is so calculated to bind man to man, in the sacred bonds of friendship and of love, that I have always considered this house a sort of second home'.[97] We may guess that some of the amusement there consisted of the old counter-theatrical performances. The way the NUWC flouted the 1832 Fast Day with satirical placards, a rowdy march and ostentatious eating and drinking certainly had much of the Garrat Election about it. Little Waddington, 'commonly called the Black Dwarf', continued to excite laughter with his saturnalian radical antics at Owenite Social Union gatherings, Borough chapel debates and Chartist meetings at Kennington Common. And though his audiences were now sometimes described as 'respectable', his behaviour was not: a Clerkenwell Green meeting in August 1839 broke up in confusion after he began openly brawling with another radical.[98]

Wedderburn's chapel of 1828 might have been a failure because of its roughness, yet in 1832 the Finsbury ultras Thomas Bull, Barrett and Kingsmill revived old memories when they opened a 'Loft Chapel' which charged 1d for entry and served up 'vulgar' abuse of the Gospels.[99] Moreover, Wedderburn's style of blasphemous burlesque had deeply impressed the new doyen of London radical freethought Robert Taylor, who began in the thirties to emulate it increasingly. Taylor's infidel services at Theobald's Road chapel in 1834 were conducted in lavish costume and accompanied by a full Swiss Orchestra and a group of young women who strummed guitars and sang. But the 'buffoonery', 'coarse remarks' and 'excremental jokes' of his sermons would not have been out of place at Hopkins Street. The spy George Ball wrote in February 1834 of a typical service: 'He [Taylor] very jeeringly and theatrically ridicules all the forms of the Christian religion and drinks cold gin and water which he says is as good as the blood of Jesus Christ who he was sure was half-seas over when they say he walked on water.' Appropriately, the last recorded sighting of Wedderburn was when the elderly black 'and others of that school' visited the chapel a month later to hear Taylor preach in language which Ball described as 'the most impious I have ever heard'.[100]

10

Grub Street Jacks: obscene populism and pornography

The authorities caught up with George Cannon for the first time in October 1830. Early the following year, after two separate prosecutions, he was sentenced to a total of twelve months' imprisonment in Tothill Fields, not as we might expect for blasphemy or sedition, but on charges of obscene libel. By the end of the 1820s Rev. Erasmus Perkins was editing, translating and publishing books which discoursed on 'the philosophy of birch discipline' and sported such pseudonyms as 'Philosemus', 'Mary Wilson' (a notorious contemporary prostitute) and 'Abdul Mustapha'. The last was the false imprint he used on *Festival of Passions* (orig. c. 1830), one of the three works for which he was convicted in 1831. The others were Baron Vivant's *Point de lendemain* (1777), translated by Cannon as *The Voluptuous Night: or, ne Plus Ultra of Pleasure* (1830), and another work so explosive that he did not dare translate it from the French. This was *Juliette, ou les prospérités du vice*, the first of the Marquis de Sade's writings to surface in England.[1] Some time in the mid-twenties Cannon had transferred from infidel to obscene publications.[2] For the next thirty years he worked as a pornographer from successive premises in Covent Garden, Leicester Square and St Martins Lane.

Prosecution records, as well as erotica collections and catalogues, show that he was not alone. Half-a-dozen of those also snared for selling obscene publications in the early thirties had been radical pressmen during the post-war years. They were – with Cannon – to become legends in their new trade. John Benjamin Brookes of Hanover Square, later the Opera Colonnade, had been one of the pro-Caroline publishers bribed by Carlton House in 1820; a decade later he was publishing crude plagiarisms of de Sade. John Duncombe had been convicted of selling the *Republican* in 1819 (he and his brother Edward were still agents of this and other radical periodicals in the mid-twenties). By the end of the thirties they had also accumulated a string of convictions for publishing works like Cleland's *Fanny Hill*. Another pair of brothers, John and William Dugdale, were beginning to rival them in output and notoriety. William, the young 'fighting radical' who began his literary career working on Watson's

Shamrock, Thistle and Rose, was to become the most prolific pornographer of the nineteenth century, operating under a maze of aliases from premises in Drury Lane and Holywell Street.[3]

Other post-war radical pressmen who dabbled more or less deeply in the obscene publications' trade during the 1820s included the Holborn publisher-bookseller John Fairburn; James Griffin, who occupied Middle Row premises next door to John Duncombe; Fores and Marks, two of the most scurrilous pro-Caroline caricaturists; and the man who had commissioned much of their work, William Benbow. SSV prosecutions for obscene libel forced Benbow in 1822 to move to lesser premises near Cannon in Leicester Square, though 'The Byron's Head', as he called the new shop, gained welcome notoriety when Southey described it in print as 'one of those preparatory schools for the brothel and gallows; where obscenity, sedition and blasphemy are retailed in drams for the vulgar'. Benbow and Edward Duncombe also used Jack Mitford's craving for gin to harness him to obscene hackery. Other former radical associates like Joseph Glover, Robert Wedderburn and John Jones seem to have worked as occasional agents in the trade, though Jones later went on to publish obscenity in his own right, as did John Ascham, Thistlewood's former friend from the Kings Bench debtors' prison.[4]

Populists, libertines and pornographers

For some of these pressmen, involvement with obscene publications arose out of practices and traditions that had been commonplace in earlier milieux. Bawdy songsheets, chap-books, squibs and prints had been a feature of urban plebeian culture throughout the eighteenth century and long before. We have seen that Thomas Evans made a living in the 1790s from colouring what were probably bawdy prints. H.D. Symonds, one of Paine's earliest publishers, sold obscene works as a sideline – according to Francis Place an almost universal practice amongst booksellers at that time. Bawdiness or obscenity had entered naturally into the political idiom of Regency radicals, informing their songs, toasts, speeches, writings and drawings. The tradition reached its zenith during the Queen Caroline affair, and it is notable that Benbow, Fairburn, Fores, Marks, Chubb and Wilson were foremost producers of pro-Queen smut. When the market for radical literature contracted after 1821, it must have been tempting to continue or expand a style of publication which had appealed to circles far beyond those of the usual radical public.

Some of the material published by these pressmen in the early twenties does seem to have been an outgrowth of this radical tradition. It continued to display a type of bawdy or obscene populism, which, whatever its commercial objectives, intended to amuse, shock or disgust readers by exposing the crimes, vices and hypocrisies of the ruling classes. In style, tone and price it also borrowed heavily from traditional street literature. Throughout the 1820s scandalous and satirical memoirs, confessions, squibs and prints were still produced in significant numbers by pressmen like Benbow, Fairburn, Marks, Fores and Chubb. Most of their targets were familiar from post-war years: Lady Conyngham and her hapless husband; the Countess of Guernsey; Lord Castlereagh and, of course, the King. It was probably the many ribald and grotesque portrayals of George's sexual exploits on royal visits to Scotland and Ireland that provoked his angry demand for government action in 1823.[5]

The sensational 'crimes and horrors' genre which William Hone had harnessed to the radical cause during the Regency years also continued to flourish in the twenties, albeit with a more obscene emphasis. Benbow and Mitford produced a typical example in 1825 which claimed, among other things, that warders at Thomas Warburton's private mad-house were in the habit of sexually exploiting female inmates. Mitford, speaking from personal experience, asserted that the mad-house was under the personal protection of Lord Sidmouth.[6] Benbow's earlier enterprise of cataloguing priestly crimes received a startling boost, too, when the news broke in August 1822 that eight witnesses had caught the Anglican bishop of Clogher, Percy Jocelyn, in a sexual act with a guardsman in the back-room of a London alehouse. The incident proved a godsend to the increasingly beleaguered radical press. Gutter pressmen produced salacious prints and tracts filled with puns about the 'arsebishop' (see Ill.20). Serious-minded Carlilean freethinkers who were suffering a judicial onslaught from the prosecuting societies raked up a fund of additionally damning information about Clogher. Not only was he supposedly a vast pluralist, but he had also brought about the imprisonment, transportation or death of an 'innocent' man who accused him of homosexuality in Ireland in 1811. Best of all, Clogher was allegedly a prominent member of the SSV. Official complicity was hinted at when he was allowed to escape without trial (he moved to Scotland under an assumed name). Though he was never convicted, Clogher's notoriety seriously embarrassed the SSV and government. James Byrne, the man whom Clogher had prosecuted for blackmail in 1811 was feted as a radical hero. Street balladeers sang of

> Divines who against Deists plod
> That our faith may not swither
> Now hang their heads and cry – by God
> We're b-gg-r'd a'thegither.[7]

Predictably, the Clogher affair triggered a mass of further exposés of clerical vice and crime. Initially this material took the form of listing specific local names and incidents, most of which were eventually gathered in

20 The Arse Bishop Josling a Soldier: *Percy Jocelyn, Bishop of Clogher, compromised.*

Benbow's comprehensive two-volume work of 1823, *The Crimes of the Clergy, or the Pillars of priest-craft shaken.* But having exhausted the English scene, Fairburn turned to French and Irish newspapers for details of 'atrocious acts of Catholic priests'.[8] From there it was not long before he and his colleagues began to tap the altogether richer vein of anti-clerical obscenity derived from indigenous no-popery works of the seventeenth century, and from the vastly larger corpus of related French writings.[9] Their resulting popular translations and plagiarisms displayed a style of anti-clericalism that was markedly more lurid, fantastic and pornographic. Typical examples included: Benbow's new mid-twenties' edition of Gabriel d'Emilliane's *Frauds of Romish Monks and Priests* (1691); Fairburn's *A Peep at Popes and Popery*; Brooke's *The Seducing Cardinal* (c. 1830) and Dugdale's gross three-volume version of the French novel, *Les Nonnes Lubriques*, entitled *Nunnery Tales*.[10]

The emergence of works of this type in the later twenties indicates that not all the obscene publications emanating from radical pressmen can be explained, or explained away, as outgrowths of plebeian political satire and bawdry. Local demand for obscene anti-popish literature probably increased during the Catholic Emancipation controversy; still, the real provenance of works like *Nunnery Tales* was *le libertinage érudit* – the literary and philosophical tradition of European, and especially French, libertinism. Scholars have found libertinism a mercurial concept, but there is broad agreement about several of its features: it originated in sixteenth-century Europe and peaked two centuries later; it reflected a revolt in thought and deed against orthodox customs and morals; and it entwined itself with sceptical rationalism.[11] The last point is especially important. Libertinism and freethought shared a kindred antagonism to religion and religious establishments as enforcers of moral laws and codes of conduct. The body of Enlightenment ideas which spread to English artisan and lower middle-class circles in the latter part of the eighteenth century had always contained a libertinist or sexually libertarian aspect.[12] Pressmen like Cannon, Benbow and Dugdale who prided themselves on being sophisticated philosophes could hardly fail to be touched by this underside of the Enlightenment. Their attempts to give philosophical credence to various obscene publications might have been shallow, inconsistent or self-justificatory but they were anchored in the tenets of libertinism.

Dugdale was content to cite the words, as well as the 'protean and ductile' example, of Voltaire to justify his right to publish heterodox religious and sexual works.[13] Cannon, however, expounded his views 'on love' with a greater philosophical rigour. His opening article in Benbow's *Rambler's Magazine* outlined the libertinist (and Epicurean) notion that sexual appetite was an imperative of nature, describing it as 'the secret spring of sexual desire, which nature has implanted in us, that as creatures of necessity, we should, in spite of ourselves, do her journeywork'. To yield to love's dictates was, he argued, simply a way of 'subscribing to the religion of nature'.[14] His pseudonymous serial, 'The Life, Adventures, Amours, Intrigues and Eccentricities of Gregory Griffin', went further in linking philosophical freethought with the morally nihilist values of libertinism. In it, a typically libertinist femme fatale, Madam St Clair, plots the best means of seducing an innocent young priest, Gregory Griffin, from both the church and the path of virtue. She rejects Volney as too slow acting, Holbach as too serious and verbose, Boulanger as too vague and declamatory and Helvetius as too arduous. Instead she confronts him with an obscene burlesque, Evariste de Parny's poem 'La Guerre de Dieux'. Instantly he is emancipated from 'the trammels of education ... and terrors of superstition'. Further exposure to Ovid's love poems and Jean-Baptiste D'Argens' erotic classic, *Thérèse Philosophe* (1750), leads him to embrace both Madame St Clair and a full-blown libertinist philosophy:

It was then that he first began to suspect that all virtue and honour among women, were only appearances – that all principle among men, was but a mask – and that, as the world was divided into slaves and enslavers, he would unite himself to the strongest and most oppressive party. What is religion but an imposition to terrify men? What are morals but masks for the rich to gratify their vicious inclinations? What are laws but a robbery of the poor, and protection of the great? No wonder that a man like Gregory Griffin who had read the explanations of the philosophers against society, and who knew something of the depravity which history exhibits in its pages, should entertain such dangerous opinions.[15]

This passage is typical of much late libertinist literature in that a concern with philosophical freedom has been displaced by interest in deception and perversity. This perhaps reflects Cannon's own philosophical progression, and certainly illustrates the type of text on which he and his associates drew. Anything from the French libertinist canon – 'classic' or 'hack' – was eagerly translated or plagiarised, then published under new titles and pseudonyms to suit English tastes. Cannon's and Benbow's 1822 edition of Louvet de Couvray's *Amours of the Chevalier de Faublas* was an early example. In the preface Cannon described it as a romance written from the perspective of a democrat who 'defended liberty at the peril of his life', and which laid bare the 'foibles and vices' of priests and aristocrats.[16] But it was the book's ribald anti-clericalism, transvestism and boisterous copulation scenes which caught the attention of the SSV and brought Benbow an obscene libel conviction. He had reproduced portions (with suggestive illustrations) in *Rambler's Magazine*, alongside extracts from 'Le Muet Babilard', Voltaire's *L'Ingenu*, *The Golden Ass of Lucius Apuleius* and Rabelais's *Diogenes and his Tub*.[17] Cannon might have failed to produce his 'Collectanea sceptica' but he advanced a good way towards a collectanea erotica. By the end of the 1830s he had translated and published (mostly in the name of Mary Wilson) more than twenty anonymous French libertinist texts, including works from de Sade, Chorier, Mirabeau, Vivant and M'lle Théroigne. Brookes, Ascham, and the brothers Duncombe and Dugdale also produced versions and adaptations from de Sade, de la Bretonne, Nerciat and d'Argens,[18] some of which were re-exported to Paris – indicating that the underground book traffic between the two capitals flowed both ways.

France was not the exclusive source of libertinist literature. The roots of the tradition went back to classical antiquity whose dissolute literary influence was deplored both by Place, as a student of popular morals, and William Acton, as a medical writer. William Dugdale, Mitford and Cannon – all at various times described as tolerable classical scholars – were well placed to exploit this legacy. Cannon sold some obscene works untranslated from the Latin; most fellow pressmen produced popular editions of Ovid's love poems; and Benbow published a new cheap version of *Basia*, a risqué piece supposedly translated from Catullus and Secundus.[19] R.P. Ward's *Tremaine* had its protagonist become an infidel and sensualist mainly through his exposure to Epicurean ideas. It was not altogether a caricature; one of the last books that Dugdale's hack writer Edward Sellon produced before he shot himself was called *The New Epicurean; or the*

21 Reviving Rochester – Dugdale style.

Delights of Sex, Facetiously and Philosophically Considered. Cannon had declared himself a follower of Lucretius and Epicurus in some of his earliest
writings. The philosophical implications of such a position were spelled
out most fully by the rakish infidel-preacher, Robert Taylor, whose *Moral
Discourses* to the Christian Evidence Society in 1826–7 attacked orthodox
Christian ethics in favour of the 'speculative laxity' of pagan morals. The
young radical lawyer, Henry Cooper, pressed the same theme so vigor-
ously in his courtroom defence of Benbow's *Faublas* that the Lord Chief
Justice reminded him acidly: 'We do not take our morality from Greece
and Rome.'[20]

These pressmen also drew on an indigenous libertinist canon going
back at least as far as the Restoration. It was manifested in luridly illustrated editions of Rochester's poems (see Ill.21) and probably in plagiarisms of blasphemous and obscene works from Grub Street predecessors
like Ned Ward, John Dunton and Thomas Brown. Benbow's *Rambler's
Magazine* of 1822 and 1824 revived a late eighteenth-century genre of
similarly titled 'bon ton' or 'galanterie' miscellanies which had recounted
stories and scandals of fashionable libertines. Benbow interspersed the
latter with more plebeian fare, including accounts of popular theatre,
poetry, politics, sport and 'crim. con.' trials. A more direct radical-libertin-

ist lineage could be traced through works like Woolston's *Discourse on the Miracles* (condemned as blasphemous and obscene in the 1720s), Peter Annet's deistic and sexually speculative *Social Bliss* of 1749 (reprinted by Carlile's shopmen in 1826) and, of course, John Wilkes's *An Essay on Woman* (c. 1763). Dugdale and company reintroduced Wilkes's obscene parody to a new audience in the nineteenth century and laced many a work with accounts of the blasphemous orgies of Wilkes and Wharton at the Hell-Fire Club and Medmenham Abbey. They also produced new editions and scores of plagiarisms of the greatest classic of English libertinism, Cleland's *Fanny Hill: or, Memoirs of a Woman of Pleasure* (1750).[21] Cannon might even have had some ancestral connection with the radical freethinker Thomas Cannon who was outlawed for a time in the late eighteenth century for publishing an obscene work on pederasty.[22]

The core intellectual ingredients of libertinism – hostility to religious authority and belief in a hedonistic morality which stressed instinctual sexuality – also gained fresh impetus from the accession of certain elements of romanticism. 'Poetry as cannon shot', is what one scholar has called the extensive pirating by these radical pressmen of selected works of Shelley, Byron and Southey, rightly representing it as part of a wider twenties' campaign for press freedom.[23] The infidel-radical character of these pirated works has been noticed – particularly *Queen Mab* and *Cain* – but not their associated sexual dimension. Prosecutors of pirate editions of *Queen Mab* were as worried about its immorality as its irreligion, though they failed to prevent it from circulating extensively during the twenties and thirties, and from converting some artisan and middling radicals to Shelley's unorthodox sexual ideas. Byron's works, particularly *Don Juan*, were pirated even more avidly. Not only had the Don Juan legend been a key-stone of literary libertinism from the seventeenth century, but Byron had also combined in his own writings, person and life all the elements from which the tradition had been forged – notably liberalism, anti-clericalism and eroticism. Benbow called *Don Juan* 'a masterpiece' and praised Byron as a man without hypocrisy who wrote 'in the true spirit of an epicure and a libertine'. Of course these attributes helped to make the poet immensely saleable as well. Radical pressmen encouraged this by illustrating their pirate editions with suggestive plates and by publishing obscene and fantastic accounts of Byron's *Voluptuous Amours* written by Jack Mitford (who claimed to have been a personal friend). At the same time young radical printers like Thomas Frost were idolising Byron's deeds and imitating his raffish dress styles.[24]

Over and above any ideological connections, libertinist and infidel literature shared a kinship of illegality and persecution. Richard Carlile's popular freethought movement of the twenties in defence of press freedom has overshadowed the simultaneous drive by the SSV and police to stamp

22 *The libertinist literary canon.*

out obscene publications.[25] To men like Cannon and Dugdale – as well as their opponents – obscenity and blasphemy could be represented as part of a common cause, a battle on a different front against the same enemies as Carlile's Corps. 'We have not flattered hypocrites and scoundrels that we might share in their dishonest plunder', wrote Benbow typically in the preface of *Rambler's Magazine*: 'To unmask these has been our object and with what effect let the Vice Society tell.' Court defences and writings hammered the class message that the Vice Society was 'a gang of reverend hypocrites' who confined their attention to the immorality of the labouring classes, for political rather than religious reasons. Old radical troupers like Benbow, Dugdale and Cannon knew how to arouse libertarian sympathies in juries by playing up the SSV's use of 'common informers' in both obscenity and blasphemy prosecutions.[26] And though Carlile himself was no friend to obscene literature, he was tempted briefly during the mid-twenties to give it qualified support on a variety of now familiar libertarian grounds. He argued that there was no clear legal definition or standard of obscenity, so that perfectly healthy material describing the natural act of intercourse was proscribed as obscene (he was writing a birth-control pamphlet at the time). He denied that obscene literature could injure morals since it was read only by the aristocracy who were already depraved. Finally, he claimed that prosecution merely stimulated sales and drove the trade underground. If necessary, he was 'prepared to war' on these issues.[27]

Cannon and company, however, were not prepared to martyr themselves for freedom of publication. Every clandestine skill learnt as ultra-radical pressmen was deployed to evade prosecution and imprisonment. They hired nominal risk-takers; they laid a maze of false imprints; and they perfected new techniques to baffle the police and Vice Society. One of Cannon's 'secret dealings' was to employ agents – probably posing as laundry women – to throw obscene books over the walls of girls' boarding schools as an enticement to later sale. He also developed a system of 'lending' obscene books to clients, proceeding only to sale when convinced of their bona fides. The same legal expertise that had gone into writing court defences for blasphemous libel in the post-war years he now directed towards evading obscene libel convictions – leading one magistrate to regret that a man of such liberal education and talent could end up in so sordid a trade.[28]

Sordid trade it undoubtedly was, or at least it had become so. This magistrate's concern about Cannon stemmed from the fact that by the 1830s legal authorities, police and prosecuting societies regarded Cannon, Brookes and the brothers' Duncombe and Dugdale as professionals in what we would call the hard-core pornography trade. For these particular radical pressmen obscene publication was not an under-the-counter side-

line as it had been for several generations of predecessors; they were not
simply dabblers in obscene publication out of necessity; and their pornography was not an expression of their political commitment, though it
might have originated that way. By the 1830s pornography had become
their business.

During the middle years of the 1820s most, if not all, London radical
pressmen seem to have experienced a trade crisis which probably encouraged some to experiment with pornography. Broad structural
changes in technology and labour processes no doubt played their part
in this crisis, though evidence is hard to come by. Steam presses were
gaining ground after their introduction in 1814 and few radicals would
have been able to raise the capital to make such a transition.[29] Yet
Thomas Dolby who had made a substantial investment in technology
still went under.[30] Moreover, many radical pressmen continued to use
small-scale hand presses profitably throughout the 1830s.[31] Actually
the immediate cause of the mid-twenties' crisis seems to have been political; namely, the judicial repression stemming from the Six Acts of 1819.
A decrease in popular unrest associated with some trade improvement
also lessened the demand for radical publications. This slump probably
hit all the harder because the Queen Caroline bonanza had tempted new
entrants into the trade and had encouraged old hands to over-extend
their stock and equipment.

The radical booktrade had always been hazardous but never more so
than in the 1820s. Cannon's talented and ambitious young friend J.A. St
John was reduced to working on obscure provincial newspapers and
churning out travel books. He confided to his journal: 'to a philosophical
mind, society is a monster'.[32] Other *philosophes-manqués*, such as the self-
educated shoemaker, Benjamin Offen, and failed clergyman-schoolmaster,
Gilbert Vale, migrated to the United States where conditions were more
congenial. They joined George Houston in setting up a flourishing popular
freethought movement around New York during the later twenties.[33]
When Jonathan Wooler was forced through declining sales to close down
the *Black Dwarf* in 1824, he attempted – in a reversal of Cannon's career –
to enrol as a law student at Lincoln's Inn. He was refused and had to be
content with working as a prisoner's advocate in the police courts.[34] By
this time, too, William Hone had dissipated his substantial post-war earnings. He was arrested for debt in 1826, after which he subsisted mainly on
the popularity of his folklore miscellanies.[35] Thomas Dolby experienced
several disabling prosecutions in the early 1820s; his business also suffered
because of falling sales, a loss of control over the cost and quality of paper
and his inability to raise capital to buy new stereo-type plates. By 1825 'a
total stagnation in trade' meant he could no longer meet the interest
payments on his premises and his ten Stanhope presses. Two years later he

was completely bankrupt.[36] Financial losses due to prosecutions in 1821-2 also forced Benbow out of his Strand shop into much less salubrious premises.[37]

Under these circumstances the temptation to take up obscene publication must have been strong – even for those who had not previously published bawdy or libertinist literature. The growth of erotic and pornographic literature in Western Europe from the seventeenth century remains something of a mystery. It has been linked with the same cluster of social and economic forces which produced the novel, and with the emergence of new psychological needs in the bourgeois male associated with the strains of 'individuation' and changing patterns of family life.[38] Whatever the cause, there is no doubt that the demand for pornography intensified during the early nineteenth century. So did the drive to eradicate it. By the end of the twenties, prosecutions by the Vice Society and police were causing a sharp contraction in outlets of supply.[39] There seem to have been two consequences. First, obscene publications became more profitable, and hence more attractive to marginal bookseller-publishers. Second, as the trade was driven underground, it passed increasingly into the hands of specialists willing to employ covert methods to evade prosecution and imprisonment. Taken as a whole, these developments help to explain both why some ultra-radical pressmen like Benbow, Griffin and Fairburn were tempted into publishing a variety of bawdy, obscene or libertinist literary works, and why others – such as Cannon, Brookes and the brothers Duncombe and Dugdale – gradually became professionals in this trade.

By 1830 any radical populist or libertinist element in the publications of this last group was largely incidental. Their main aim was to produce and sell literature designed to create sexual arousal. Cannon's speciality was flagellation literature, an elite pornographic sub-genre noted for its stylistic sophistication, high cost (usually between one and three guineas a book) and upper-class readership (Cannon mentioned aristocrats, judges, admirals, generals and lawyers). He was responsible for such typical titles as *Birchen Bouquet*, *The Exhibition of Female Flagellants* and *Elements of Tuition and Modes of Punishment* – all filled with domineering 'mamma' figures, blooming nosegays, green birch rods, crimson orbs and blood running down to the heels.[40] Whether producing translations of French flagellation works, adaptations of de Sade, gothic-byronic travesties, pseudo-medical treatises or pirated contraceptive manuals, Cannon and company usually added erotic plates and sometimes expurgated genuinely philosophic or technically informative elements. The biting anti-clericalism and moral nihilism of the libertinist canon was often reduced to ludicrous burlesque: Dugdale's version of *Nunnery Tales* has the hero reflect at one point:

This is rather a strange predicament for a young man – To find himself in girls' clothes riding the Lady Superior of a Strict Convent, and which lady is his own Aunt. And at the same time witnessing his Mother being outrageously fucked in the same room by her Father Confessor whom I firmly believe to be my own bodily father.[41]

Contemporary observers of all kinds – including the pornographers themselves – declared that material of this kind was not bought by the working classes but by elderly male aristocrats and professionals (see Ill.23) as well as servicemen, fast clerks, journalists and country visitors.[42] These were the kinds of people who were later to attend the mid-Victorian *poses plastiques* and sing-songs at places like the Coal Hole and Cider Cellars, and who could afford the substantial price tags on pornography. Some might also have acquired a taste for flagellation at public schools or in the services. When Cannon's premises were raided for the last time in 1853, officers confiscated 2115 obscene prints, 9 copper plates and 81 obscene books, all selling at high prices[43] (compared with hauls from Dugdale's premises this was modest). The profitability, or at least viability, of these businesses is shown in their longevity. Apart from short closures owing to imprisonment, they operated from the late 1820s until the deaths of their proprietors: Brookes in 1839, Cannon in 1854 (his wife continued the business for a further ten years), Edward Duncombe in 1859 and William Dugdale in 1867.

One likely penalty for profiting from unrespectability was the loss of respect of former political associates. By the end of the twenties, it must have been difficult to be a professional trader in pornography and to retain credibility in radical circles. During the latter part of the decade Place and Carlile, as well as some of the latter's Zetetic followers, had publicly criticised orthodox sexuality, but the theoretical and practical result was more libertarian than libertine. Their support for contraception, female equality and even freelove was embedded in liberal enlightenment ideas of individual freedom and social utility, and did not challenge prevailing artisan or middle-class beliefs in moral respectability.[44] Their new sexual values did not extend to licence or promiscuity. In spite of his equivocation of 1825, Carlile generally hated pornography and what it stood for. In 1822 he attacked Benbow's obscene publications as 'mischievous to public morals', regretting 'that they should emanate from the same shop as the works of Paine'. He also quarrelled with his former shopman, J.W. Trust, and his elder sons, Alfred and Thomas Paine Carlile, when they took up the trade; and he denounced Cannon in 1826 as 'a bad character'.[45] Why some radical pressmen took Carlile's libertarian path during the twenties; others, Cannon's libertine-pornographic one, is difficult to say. It was not solely a matter of economics. Carlile and some of his supporters endured poverty and persecution attempting to practise their

23 Four Specimens of the Reading Public, *1826*.

calling as infidel-philosophers yet were never tempted into obscene publications. The explanation for the divergence probably goes back to family and childhood experience. Young artisans like Carlile seem often to have led solitary, bookish and sexually isolated lives during boyhood,[46] perhaps very different from those of men like Cannon and Benbow. The poem 'Epitaph on Grub Street Jack' published in Benbow's *Rambler's Magazine* was probably more than a little autobiographical:

> ... A pretty girl and flowing bowl;
> These were the poet's chief delight,
> And first induced his pen to write.[47]

Admittedly, Benbow seems to have given up his flirtation with obscene literature during the 1830s, and so retained his foothold in ultra-radical circles. It is doubtful whether the same can be said of Cannon, Dugdale and Duncombe; like their brothel-keeper associate Edgar they were probably 'discarded' by other radical-infidels. One suspects that the lives of London's professional pornographers increasingly took on the quasi-criminal shape of earlier Grub Street hacks like Dunton and Edmund Curll, or Bruzard de Mauvelain and Charles Théveneau de Morande in pre-revolutionary France. By the mid-thirties, Cannon, whose address had once been 1 Staple Inn, was living and working in the rabbit-warren of Great Mays buildings, St Martins Lane. Dugdale was helping to make Holywell Street

24 Holywell Street in 1851.

synonymous with pornography (see Ill.24). Thomas Frost, who at one time worked for Dugdale as a compositor, has left us with a vivid portrait of the dingy, cobwebby backroom at 37 Holywell Street where eight fellow compositors were busily engaged in laying out smut.[48] The SSV and police gradually forced these pornographers to cluster in professional ghettos centred around Holywell Street and Wych Street, St Martins Lane and Russell Court, and Leicester Square and its surrounds. These were the kind of milieux that William Dugdale charted in his first obscene publication, *Yokel's Preceptor*, an underworld directory of smut shops, brothels, thieves' dens and gambling hells.[49] Cannon and company had passed during the twenties from a radical to a sexual underworld. Cannon's imprisonment in 1831 for selling pornography was a literal and symbolic expression of his failure as a radical-infidel. Nothing better illustrates the pariah path he and Dugdale had chosen than the fact that both men were eventually to die in prison whilst serving sentences incurred through selling pornography.[50]

Revivals and survivals

By the 1830s most respectable radicals might have felt bound to condemn the practice of pornography, but the worlds of popular radicalism and Grub Street obscenity were not completely divorced. Some pressmen evidently succeeded for a time in living dual lives as pornographers and radicals. The devious Cannon comes as no surprise in this company. At one level he was a typical contributor to the march of mind. During the 1820s he belonged to the Society for the Promotion of the Arts, Manufacture and Commerce in the Adelphi; he subscribed to the *Newgate Magazine* run by Carlile's most talented and militant shopmen; he attended the Liberals' reading and debating club meetings at Longacre; and he served as secretary of the Patriot coffee-house Literary Society. All this time he also churned out pornography under the cover of a 'foreign bookseller'. Similarly, William Dugdale – with his brother John – was giving active support to Wedderburn's 'New Assembly' chapel about the same time that he also became a pornographer. William Dugdale was still sufficient of a freethinker in 1843 to issue a new edition of Voltaire's *Philosophical Dictionary*. During the political excitement of 1848 a *Times* correspondent commented to Thomas Frost that, judging from Dugdale's shopwindows, the literature of the working classes consisted of 'a mélange of sedition, blasphemy and obscenity'.[51]

True, such double lives could not survive frequent and notorious convictions for selling pornography. But even if individual publishers ceased to be acceptable in radical circles, this does not mean that their whole literary output became unacceptable as well. Most of these Grub Street pressmen also published genres of literature that were bawdy or obscene but stopped short of the pornographic. These works usually retained a populist or anti-establishment character and were sold at prices aimed to attract members of the working classes, including both older and newer generations of London radicals. Like their pre-revolutionary Parisian counterparts, Dugdale and company were thus 'carriers' of cultural strains which deserve closer scrutiny from historians.

The resemblances between Regency veterans like William Dugdale, Benbow, Fairburn and the Duncombes, and the new unstamped pressmen of the 1830s like Hetherington, John Cleave, Strange, George Berger and

Benjamin Cousins were closer than we might expect. In 1834 the fiercely respectable Hetherington produced a broadsheet periodical called *Two-penny Dispatch* which promised 'fun and frolic ... Police intelligence ... Murders, Rapes, Suicides, Burnings, Maimings, Theatricals, Races, Pugilism'.[52] This was only one of many similar crime and crim. con. periodicals produced by unstamped pressmen. It was from works like these (and during this period) that the muckraking Sunday newspaper originated. Even the heroic *Poor Man's Guardian* figured indirectly in this tradition. The bohemian bookman Gilbert A'Beckett served out his literary apprenticeship on Hetherington's famous radical paper. He went on to edit the earthy *Figaro in London* and to produce numerous catchpenny scandal-sheets of his own, such as the *Wag, Thief, Penny Trumpet* and *Gallery of Terrors*. Gruesome and bawdy works like *Annals of Crime, Caskets of Mirth* and Duncombe's racy *Minor British Drama* tracts also featured (along with *Don Juan*) on lists of stock sold at Hetherington's shop in 1834.[53]

Sometimes there were direct links between older and newer generations of pressmen. During the course of their long careers Cannon, Dugdale and company employed scores of printers, writers, agents and shopmen, some of whom went on to become notable radical publishers in their own right. Exactly how many such people came under Dugdale's influence over the years will not be known until his seedy career has been charted in full. We have seen that Thomas Frost was one. He started his literary life writing freethought, Owenite and Chartist works, but after working for Dugdale went on to produce two obscene anti-establishment novels, a sensationalist crime collection and the muckraking *Penny Punch* (1849) which nearly earned him a public ducking. Charles Grieves (alias Young) printed Dugdale's pornography for many years before establishing himself as a publisher-bookseller in Russell Court. The well-known unstamped pressman George Vickers was Dugdale's next door neighbour in Holywell Street, which may explain why he became involved in smutty publications – including G.W.M. Reynolds's *Mysteries of the Court of London* which at one time was selling 40,000 copies a week.[54]

As well as pornography, John Duncombe published a vast corpus of popular theatre and melodrama scripts. In the late twenties he befriended Douglas Jerrold and hired him as a hack writer. Duncombe introduced Jerrold to two other young pressmen employees who quickly became close friends and collaborators – Laman Blanchard and Kenny Meadows. Together they wrote for *Punch in London* (1832–3) where they 'hit hard ... at peers and royal dukes' and parodied the court circle, especially Cumberland. Around the same time they also contributed to the *Monthly Magazine* which, though not overtly political, 'had a clear relation to social politics' in its wit and satire.[55] The proprietor of this last paper was none other than William Clarke, the pro-Caroline radical pressman who had issued a pirate edition of *Queen Mab* in 1821. Between them Duncombe and Clarke were important patrons and friends of this circle of London literary bohemians. It included figures like Henry and Thomas Mayhew, George Augustus Sala, Henry Vizetelly and Blanchard Jerrold, all pioneers of a lively mid-Victorian cockney literature comprising burlesques, comic writing, melodrama, satire and spicy fiction.[56]

Benbow's *Rambler's Magazine* might well have influenced John Cleave, a close political associate whose similar ribald style helped make *Cleave's Weekly Gazette* an immense popular success between 1835 and 1841. The connection is more certain in the case of G. Berger. After working as Benbow's agent in the 1820s, he opened up premises in Holywell Street, from which he became a major publisher, bookseller and newsagent. He and several other young printers turned radical pressmen – Vickers, G. Purkess, Benjamin Cousins and William Strange – were agents and publishers of a new crop of bawdy 'bon ton' periodicals in the 1830s, including the *Quizzical Gazette* and *New London Rambler's Magazine*, each edited for a time by Benbow's old employee, Jack Mitford.

Strange and Berger, who were both eminent unstamped pressmen, occupied premises virtually next door to each other in Holywell Street, not far from Dugdale. There is no doubt that Strange, at least, lived up to the street's reputation. Around 1836 he published probably the first edition of *The Confessional Unmasked*, an obscene anti-popish work which was to have a long publishing history in militant Protestant circles. Another of his ribald productions, a tilt at Prince William and Queen Adelaide, reached the convict colony of Van Diemens' Land where it was confiscated by an indignant Governor Arthur. And in May 1857 Strange was prosecuted at the same time as William Dugdale for selling *Paul Pry* and *Women of London*, works which the judge Lord Campbell described as 'obscene and disgusting'.[57]

Obscene and disgusting they might have been, but neither work could really be called hard-core pornography. More than anything else publications like *Paul Pry* echoed the ribald genres and motifs of Regency radical journalism. Here was another line of continuity between old and new generations of pressmen. The bawdy and satirical literary traditions of Regency radicalism are supposed to have disappeared during the 1820s,[58] but a mass of related populist-style material continued to flow from radical presses throughout the twenties and thirties. A typical example was the genre of *chroniques scandaleuses* – usually cheap, paraphrased versions of the confessions (real or spurious) of famous courtesans. The lineage of such works professed to go back at least as far as Nell Gwynn (whose 'memoirs' were revived by Fairburn and others during the 1820s), but it was probably only after the Mary Anne Clarke affair of 1809 that they acquired an explicitly radical association. From this time radical pressmen

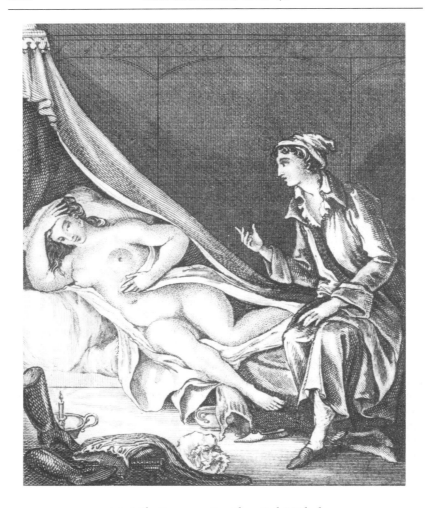

25 A Sly Peep: *prurience from Jack Mitford.*

were quick to take advantage of courtesan confessions as vehicles for
exposing upper-class vice and corruption (and for making money in the
process). The most important examples in the 1820s centred on the
figures of Madame Vestris (wife of the actor Charles Mathews) and the
notorious Harriette Dubochet, better known as Harriette Wilson or Mrs Q.
As in Queen Caroline's day the familiar crew of Benbow, Dugdale, Duncombe, Mitford, Chubb, Fairburn and Mason churned out numerous 1s
and 2s 6d editions of these 'memoirs'; some pirated, some plagiarised, some
imagined.

26 Harriette Wilson blackmailing the establishment.

Whatever their differences in detail these *chroniques* usually ran to a familiar pattern. The courtesan 'authors' – invariably from humble but respectable backgrounds – began by describing how they had been tricked by aristocratic or royal libertines into parting from their true loves. They had then been seduced and forced into prostitution. Thereafter they had become mistresses to a succession of corrupt, perverted and cruel aristo-crats, against whom their only recourse was – like Madame Vestris – to play one conquest off against another, or – like Mary Anne Clarke and Harriette Wilson – to turn private sexual knowledge to blackmailing/pub-lishing advantage. The latter tactic could be devastatingly effective. When Harriette Wilson announced the impending publication of her memoirs in the mid-twenties, she sent tremors of panic through governing and royal circles. The King himself was aghast at the news; Jack Mitford claimed that the popular sensation exceeded that of the Sacheverell affair in the previous century. Harriette and her sponsor, the shrewd commercial por-nographer John Stockdale, are said to have netted some £10,000 from a combination of excision fees at £200 a time, and from sales of the memoirs describing her amours with aristocratic notables like Wellington who had defied her to publish. Radical pressmen could not benefit directly from the blackmail exercise, but they exploited the voracious demand for Harriette Wilson material that chronicled the supposed depravities of the King, the Duke of Argyll, Frederick Lamb, Wellington and 'most of the Nobility of the Present Day'[59] (see Ill.26).

The Harriette Wilson affair jogged memories back to Queen Caroline. In part this was because Harriette's escapades with the Prince Regent had featured regularly in the pro-Queen propaganda of Benbow and company. The mythology which had grown up around Caroline in the Regency years also found echoes in the populist-libertinist themes of Harriette Wilson's *chroniques*. Ashe's gothic-romantic fable of Queen Caroline and Prince Algernon found its way into Renton Nicholson's bohemian periodical the *Town* in October 1837.[60] The following year a some-time radical publisher William Emans produced an enormous quasi-fictional memoir entitled *The Murdered Queen, or Caroline of Brunswick*. It combined blood-curdling accounts of vampires, vaults, tortures and seductions with an immensely detailed record of 'the infernal plot' against Caroline – so detailed in fact that it took 586 pages to get Caroline to the shores of England in 1820.[61]

Ruling-class vice and corruption was also satirised or excoriated in a variety of other gutter genres which resembled those of Queen Caroline's day. Place, a keen collector of later eighteenth-century bawdy ballads and flash chaunts, would probably have recognised the ribald, pro-criminal sentiments, if not some of the actual songs, contained in the scores of sixpenny songsters published during the early Victorian years by Fairburn, Dugdale, Duncombe and William West. True, as their titles often indicate, many of these songsters were designed to entertain the rough or bohemian groups of servicemen, journalists and sporting bucks who frequented seedy nightspots like the Cider Cellars and Coal Hole.[62] Yet even the smuttiest miscellanies, such as John Duncombe's *Fal-Lal Songster* [c. 1833], Fairburn's *Social Songster* [c. 1842] and West's *Cuckold's Nest* [c. 1860], usually contained a sprinkling of irreverent lampoons like 'Parson Stump', 'Genealogy' and 'The Slashing Costermonger'. A recent study has identified at least twenty-three different London street songs which satirised Queen Victoria's marriage to the German Prince Albert.[63] Shilling squibs delighted in the same theme: William Dugdale's *Royal Wedding Jester: or, All the Fun and Facetiae of the Wedding Night*, though levelled at Victoria and Albert, was a recognisable descendant of the anti-Regent scurrility of 1820–1. Dugdale was just as quick to exploit any whiff of scandal associated with the new young Queen and her courtiers. The quarrel between Victoria and one of her ladies-in-waiting, Flora Hastings, over the latter's alleged pregnancy (in fact a tumour from which she died) brought an exposé from Dugdale containing the sententious warning: 'A vicious aristocracy, babbling courtiers, slandering beldames, jealous "rough decrepit hags", and ambitious maidens, if left without the compass of good example … will soon make the court of even a maiden queen a national pandemonium. Such was the court of France when Masillon preached and the vices of that court ended in bloody revolution.'[64]

Scandal in high places was a leitmotiv also of the revived 'bon ton' and 'crim. con.' periodicals of the early Victorian years, most of them modelled on Benbow's earlier *Rambler's Magazine*. Some typical examples included: John Duncombe's *Quizzical Gazette* (1831–2) and *New London Rambler's Magazine* [1828–30], both edited for a time by Jack Mitford; George Huckle-bridge's *Crim. Con. Gazette*, later *Bon Ton Gazette* (1838–40); Charles Brown's (pseud.) *Paul Pry* (1830–3); Renton Nicholson's *Town* (1837–42); and William Dugdale's *Exquisite* (1842–4) which was more lavish and pornographic than the others.[65] These periodicals were frequently prurient, often obscene and always sensationalist, but they were also populist and sometimes explicitly radical in their professed concern to expose and reform upper- and middle-class corruption and vice. Several of them supported radical franchise reform and opposed the New Poor Law, the Police Bill and of course everything relating to the SSV. Nicholson's *Town* described itself as 'like unto a popular representative of the people, returned to serve them weekly, and elected upon the glorious system of universal suffrage'.[66]

The old roués Melbourne, Palmerston and Wellington, and the hated royal dukes, Clarence and Cumberland, were favourite targets. Prince Albert and his Germanic countrymen were also abused with a xenophobic gusto reminiscent of Queen Caroline's day. The *Crim. Con. Gazette* of 5 October 1839 called them 'scheming foreigners', 'mealy mouthed Goths' and 'Hunnish irruptions upon Pimlico Palace'. Mitford composed bawdy anti-clerical litanies in 1831 that were creditable descendants of Hone's famous 1817 parodies, and his lurid particulars of clerical rapes, sodomies and frauds easily rivalled those published by Benbow in 1820–1. He even produced a new version of the favourite Regency radical ballad 'Pig of Pall Mall': this one began 'O thou delicious tythe pig'.[67] Such sentiments went hand in hand with accessible prices. *Bon ton* periodicals usually sold in 2d, 4d or 6d parts – cheap enough to reach artisans as well as the raffish middle classes. According to Mitford, the first issue of the *New London Rambler's Magazine* was planned, written, printed and published in five days, and sold all 1500 copies within a week.[68]

As in Regency days such exposés sometimes shaded into actual black-mail or extortion. Henry Vizetelly knew several exponents of this form of populist journalism during the 1830s. One of the most notorious was Barnard Gregory whose career had followed a typical hack's trajectory. A grocer's son, he had tried his luck as schoolmaster, itinerant preacher and druggist before founding the *Satirist* in the late thirties. This ferocious anti-Tory scandal rag supposedly earned him lucrative blackmailing fees, as well as numerous challenges, assaults and law-suits. Its chief rival was the *Age*, founded a few years earlier by a shady hack, Charles Molloy Westma-cott. It was more Tory in ambience but equally scurrilous, and is supposed

27 *Anti-clerical obscenity from Jack Mitford.*

to have netted its editor as much as £5000 from one blackmailing trans-
action alone. Westmacott employed another, more familiar, blackmailing
figure, the pro-Caroline hack Thomas Ashe, who operated in the mid-
twenties under the pseudonym of Bernard Blackmantle. Ashe produced a
smutty gossip miscellany which Westmacott published as the *English Spy*,
and a libertinist romance called *Fitzalleyne of Berkeley* which centred on
the Berkeley Peerage scandal.[69]

Whether these last two works had any explicit blackmailing intent is
hard to know, but there is no such doubt about another Ashe tract called
Osphia, or The Victim of Unlawful Oppression (1829) which, among other
things, revived the accusation that Cumberland had murdered his valet,
Sellis. Though *Osphia* had been commissioned by J.J. Stockdale, Ashe decided to by-pass the publisher and make a direct extortion approach to
Cumberland. His letter admitted with engaging candour that he had become a 'monster of iniquities' because he was 'steeped to the lips in poverty'.
Government law officers favoured paying up, but they and Cumberland
were saved from this or from Ashe's embarrassing revelations by an intemperate phrase in one of his letters which enabled them to convict him of the
separate charge of threatening to murder the Duke.[70]

The revival by gutter pressmen of the bygone Sellis scandal was prompted
by several other events around this time that brought Cumberland renewed
public attention and odium. The Duke's energetic prosecution of his position
as Grand Master of the Orange Lodge movement (publicised in a parlia-

mentary inquiry of 1835), combined with his earlier opposition to Catholic Emancipation and to political reform, infuriated both radicals and O'Connellites (whom law officers suspected of being behind Ashe's blackmail attempt). A scurrilous radical pamphlet (possibly written by Barnard Gregory) summed up the longstanding popular belief that Cumberland, even more than his dubious brothers and sisters, was a gross parasite on the public purse, 'a cats-paw of illiberalism' and 'an utter stranger to the principles upon which the constitution is based'. The Duke's flagrant affair with Lady Graves which in 1830 supposedly drove her husband to suicide – like Sellis, by cutting his throat – also revived old suspicions of Cumberland's 'propensity to the most fiend-like crimes'.[71] Pressmen such as Fairburn had a field day raising the ghost of Sellis (see Ill.3, p. 35) and punning on the morbid associations of the name Graves (see Ill.29). Claims that the Duke had murdered Sellis and instigated a coronial cover-up resurfaced in the press and parliament. The most detailed and damaging account of the affair, and of royal debauchery in general, was published in 1832 by another of Gregory's printer-publishers, Josiah Phillips. Entitled *Authentic Records of the Court of England for the last 70 years*, it was eventually prosecuted by the government despite Place's contrary advice. Evidently Place shared Phillips's opinion of 1838 that prosecution would 'not stop the tongues and ears of Englishmen' but only provoke a popular furore similar to Queen Caroline's trial.[72]

In the same year Cumberland's name was linked with yet another gothic-like sexual crime. In May 1838 newspapers carried a report that a prostitute named Eliza Grimwood had been brutally murdered at Wellington Terrace, Lambeth. Although her pimp was arrested, he somehow escaped conviction and fled the country, adding to widespread rumours that the real culprit had been an eminent foreign-born aristocrat with whom Eliza had long consorted. Cumberland was the immediate and unanimous popular choice as murderer, though radical pressmen dared only hint at the connection. Even Barnard Gregory allowed a few years to lapse before publishing an explicit accusation in the *Satirist*; in the event he was lucky to get away with a six months' prison sentence for libel.[73] However the Grimwood incident generated one publication of major interest, the anonymous novel *Eliza Grimwood* [c. 1839][74] which both encapsulates and reflects the Grub Street populist tradition pioneered by Dugdale and company.

Like most works of popular serial fiction in the early nineteenth century, *Eliza Grimwood* has a maze of plots, sub-plots and digressions. Grub Street, however, is a prominent theme. With earthy humour and vivid realistic detail, the author sketches the histories, mentalities, habitats and methods of London's penny-a-liner hacks and publishers, including two explicitly identified pornographers, J. (George?) Hucklebridge and John Benjamin

28 Pornographic blackmailers defied, 1826.

Brookes (who died in 1839). Two central characters, Gabriel Augustus Crowe (Sala?) and Percy Davidson, might almost have been modelled on George Cannon. After receiving a superficial classical education, Crowe migrates to London intending to become a clergyman, lawyer or man of letters, but is forced by poverty into taking up a career as a hack journalist. He becomes a specialist in writing both fictitious and real stories of dreadful horrors and accidents, which he intersperses with radical critiques of the Police Bill, the Bank of England and the currency system (pp. 82–3). Whilst working in this milieu he encounters Percy Davidson, a villain, who at one point successfully disguises his seedy background by posing as an enthusiastic preacher named Warden (possibly a dig at Benjamin Warden, radical pressman and ex-Freethinking Christian). Interestingly, Davidson also boasts: 'I am a patron of literary men and have been the means of elevating some ... to a high rank in society' (p. 91).

We follow these two into typical Grub Street habitats: dingy attic lodgings in Drury Lane; Eliza's Methodist-backed Waterloo Road brothel known as 'The New Jerusalem Joint Stock Company of Love and Liberty' (p. 142); a low coffee-shop near Wych Street frequented by radical hacks (p. 83); and the Harp tavern at Covent Garden. Here Hucklebridge presides over a convivial and benefit club which burlesques City government in a hubbub of 'songs, and glasses, and sentiments, and pipe lights, and

29 'Fiend-like crimes': Cumberland haunted by Lord Graves.

wit and philosophy, and chaff and slang' (pp. 64–8). The details of this portrayal of the Lushington Club, as it was called, tally with a description in Renton Nicholson's *Town* of 1837.[75] Thanks to Davidson's patronage, Crowe eventually becomes a successful pressman of 'red-hot republican' stamp. Davidson himself ends up as 'a popular writer in a weekly paper, professing to be a friend of the people, but in reality the promoter of vice ... by pandering to the vulgar taste of those who love to read of robberies, rapes, suicides and murders' (pp. 299–300).

Evoking London's Grub Street underworld serves also as a compelling device for addressing the novel's bold opening promise – to reveal who killed Eliza Grimwood. At one point the author includes a series of sensational excerpts from actual newspaper reports of the crime, a pointer to the fact that *Eliza Grimwood* is as much a product as a satire of Grub Street populism. The main plot depends heavily on the techniques and motifs of the *chroniques scandaleuses*; Eliza is situated in a tradition of populist courtesan heroines from Mary Anne Clarke to Harriette Wilson. She is given an exotic but humble background as a soldier's daughter born of a Spanish mother, then orphaned in France and raised in an English country house. Predictably, Lord Rakemore, a libertine and playmate of the Prince Regent, mounts a plot against this 'gentle-minded' girl which deprives her of her fortune, her true love and her virtue. Drugged, seduced and abandoned, Eliza gravitates inevitably to London and prostitution. At one point

30 *The Duke at bay: a French courtesan and the Duke of Wellington.*

she encounters a copy of Harriette Wilson's *Memoirs* which actually expose Eliza's own seducer, along with many other such libertines. Eliza feels an immediate bond of sympathy with the famous courtesan: 'the snares that had been laid by noble, rich middle-aged men, was the same in both cases' (p. 246).

The last portion of the book describes how Eliza is murdered by Davidson, the one-time agent of Lord Rakemore. It is deliberately vague, however, as to whether Davidson was acting on his own account or at the instigation of some noble who feared a Harriette Wilson style of exposure. The book terminates abruptly whilst quoting a number of contemporary press reports and hinting darkly at forthcoming revelations. All this sounds as if the publisher was fishing for suppression bribes. If so, this too was part of long Grub Street radical tradition. We do not know who wrote *Eliza Grimwood* but the publisher was Benjamin Cousins, one of the leading new ultra-radical pressmen of the 1830s and a lineal descendant of Dugdale and company. For all its commercial pragmatism and moral ambiguity, *Eliza Grimwood* is a powerful anti-establishment tract in the romantic-realist vein of Eugene Sue and the French *feuilleton* writers whose novels Dugdale, Cannon and Duncombe were also to popularise in mid-Victorian years. It represents the most positive legacy of these Grub Street Jacks.

The darker side of their legacy is perhaps symbolised in the fact that Cousins and many other young unstamped pressmen served their political apprenticeships at the Blackfriars Rotunda, one of the great theatres of popular radicalism in the early 1830s – where Hetherington and Watson organised the NUWC, Carlile and Taylor preached infidel sermons and Sharples and Macaulay lectured on feminism. By mid-Victorian years it had become a theatre for popular pornography.

Conclusion

On 22 November 1835 the spy Abel Hall delivered his epitaph on the old ultra-radical underworld: 'I have seen us fall from Pretension to Nothing and as is the usual course of Nature we have failed by the hand of death, as well as other political events.'[1] The hand of death had severed the heads of five of Abel Hall's close political companions in 1820, and by the time he wrote this poignant report it had accounted less dramatically for many more. Thomas Evans, the father of their ultra-radical underworld, probably died some time in the late twenties, possibly around 1826 like Thomas Davison whose health never really recovered from his two-year gaol sentence. Hall's immediate reflections on mortality were prompted by the recent death of Henry Medlar who, the spy noted, had been sufficiently well-off as a master carpenter to do much 'good' for the cause of ultra-radicalism since the days of his interrogation as a suspected Cato Street conspirator. Robert Wedderburn must have died around the same time, aged seventy, since he was alive in 1834 and does not appear in the death registers after 1836. If so his poverty and obscurity ensured that the occasion passed unnoticed. Three years later the former ultra political leader 'Dr' James Watson met the same fate; he was buried as a pauper in New York where he had migrated in the late twenties, perhaps to join his fugitive son. On the other side of the Atlantic in Somers Town another veteran radical and surgeon also received a pauper's funeral in 1838: Gale Jones's dubious medical skills had been unavailing against a succession of lung haemorrhages from 1834. Most former ultra colleagues who survived him were beginning to show similar signs of ill-health and infirmity as they entered their seventies. A month before Hall filed his report of 27 November 1835, veteran ultras had launched an appeal to pay the medical costs of a gravely ill Allen Davenport.

Political events – as Hall noted – had also taken their toll. He himself had been a victim of the ruling-class repression of 1819–25, during which time he had seen many colleagues driven out of radical politics and a few out of the country as well. By the 1830s some – like young Evans – had been detached from the old ultra underworld through their acquisition of social respectability and political moderation, others – like Dugdale and Cannon – by their adoption of unrespectable and politically unacceptable ways of making a living. In 1834 the NUWC, which expressed much of the old ultra militancy in new and invigorated form, had dissolved after seeing its radical suffrage goals defeated by a Reform Act which probably disenfranchised more members than it enfranchised. During the same year Hall's own trade, the tailors, were defeated in a major strike, and hopes of attaining wider artisan union ideals also collapsed with the Grand National Consolidated Trades' Union. Displaying schizophrenic loyalties as a spy and a radical, Hall had joined with political colleagues in vain protests against the gaoling or transportation of radicals, pressmen and trade unionists, and against the enactment of punitive centralist legislation like the New Poor Law of 1834. The Whigs seemed if anything to have added new venom to the fangs of 'Old Corruption'. Even so, Hall's epitaph of November 1835 was slightly premature; some of his colleagues were to pin their hopes on the ELDA a few years later, and to a lesser extent the LWMA as well. It was really the failure of the former organisation to win wider acceptance for its militant Jacobin ideals and tactics in 1839 and 1840 which saw the end of the old ultra underworld as a political force. When men like Waddington and Neesom could not persuade Londoners to stage a Newport-style uprising, and Benbow failed to bring about his 'National Holiday', the influence of the old ultras declined in favour of a new generation of O'Connorite Chartists.

Yet even after their collective demise, individuals, ideals and practices showed great resilience. Hall's pessimistic report of 1835 had nevertheless concluded with a list of ultras whom he still regarded as dangerous. One was the tailor-newsvendor, Charles Neesom, then living at 5 Moor Lane near the Mulberry Tree tavern. In the same year, he and his politically active wife, Elizabeth, expressed the old mutualist spirit of the Finsbury ultras by taking Allen Davenport to live in their house, where they nursed him back to health. Thereafter, until Davenport's death in 1846, he, Neesom and another longtime friend, Charles Jennison, threw themselves into radical education by joining local mutual instruction societies, mechanics' institutes and coffee-houses, as well as Lovett's National Association of 1844. Their forceful advocacy of Spencean ideas helped to convert younger radical leaders like G.J. Harney and to ensure that opposition to land monopoly became a key element of Chartist theory and practice.

Another tireless Spencean propagandist also listed as a dangerous character in Hall's 1835 report was Tommy Preston. No one better illustrates the tenacity of the old ultra-radical underworld. Here he was in 1835 – as in post-war years – scraping a bare living from a cobbler's stall near the Eagle Court, City Road. Nearly seventy years old, he was poor, lame, half-educated, a 'dishonourable' tradesman and a man whom spies had regularly described as a drunken buffoon; yet the trajectory of his political career runs through the Jacobin era, the post-war agitations, the 'hiatus' of the 1820s, the revival of the 1830s and Chartism – until his death in 1850.

London's explosion in population and growth of mercantile and financial capitalism helped to turn Preston from a master shoemaker with two shops employing more than forty men, into a jobbing-cobbler competing frantically with the rising tide of sweated and unskilled. He and his companions in the old declining handicraft trades and in the 'uneasy' demi-monde of shopkeepers, sub-professionals and literati constituted some of the most desperate and marginal men of early nineteenth-century England. To survive they sometimes begged, borrowed, stole, blackmailed, pimped, informed and peddled smut; yet most retained an aspiration for economic independence and social respectability. They wanted and needed to transform English society – both in backward and forward looking ways – because the world they lived in was so often intolerable. The effort cost most of them dear. Few English men and women experienced so directly the repressive force that England's ruling classes could muster when threatened. Over the years Preston and his companions were variously press-ganged, flogged, fined, imprisoned without trial, spied upon, harassed, transported and executed. Preston narrowly evaded the last fate himself in the wake of both the Spa Fields and Cato Street 'uprisings'. Yet he and his associates persisted with their plots, agitations and propaganda, apparently indifferent to their vulnerability, powerlessness and obscurity.

We have followed these men – and occasionally their spouses – into seedy alehouses, back-room chapels, low coffee-houses and Grub Street bookshops. We have heard them utter bloody toasts, sing rousing hymns, preach and debate a mélange of blasphemy, radical politics and millenarian Christianity. We have watched them perform drunken rituals and irreverent burlesques, organise mass meetings, contrive outlandish plots and publish literature which ranged from gutter scurrility to sceptical philosophy. We have traced some of the brave, comical, clever and unsavoury tactics which they used to evade detection, promote their cause and stay alive. We have argued that humour, escapism, sex, profit, conviviality, entertainment and saturnalia should be admitted to the popular radical tradition, along with the sober, strenuous and heroic aspects which are more customarily described. It was partly because Tommy Preston was so poor and poorly educated, so garrulous and convivial; because he loved to drink, sing, carouse and debate in pubs; because he used the ancient exhortary language of the scriptures and the populist rhetoric of the London mob that his brand of radical politics survived for so long. His was a radicalism which drew on an old but fluid culture fashioned in London's small-scale workshops, businesses and recreational centres. It perhaps survived longer in the metropolis than in the increasingly factory-based North, because old forms of capital, labour and finance, old institutions, neighbourhoods and traditions persisted there deep into the nineteenth century. One of the last expressions of this old artisan radical culture re-surfaced a full twenty years after Preston's death when the respectable middle-class intentions of Henry Solly's workingmen's club movement were subverted from below with demands for beer, tobacco, free-and-easy conviviality, republican and infidel debate, and irreverent songs and theat-ricals.

The specifically literary strand of this old radical underworld showed itself to be equally resilient, if rather more protean. Typically, during the same year that 'Little Waddy' involved himself in the abortive armed 'Shipyard conspiracy' (1839), he also took out a printer's licence (wit-nessed by his former patron William Mason) so as to complement the struggle at an ideological level. We have noted, too, that the publishing careers of William Dugdale, Edward and John Duncombe and George Cannon continued well into the mid-Victorian period. Much of this literary legacy obviously belongs outside the scope of the present book, and within the wider provenance of Victorian popular culture (where I hope to pursue it in a future work). Nevertheless, by 1840 some general patterns can be noted.

The least edifying but most portentous achievement of Dugdale and company was to pioneer the development in nineteenth-century England of a new profession and a new commercial branch of literature – that of pornography. These former ultra pressmen were to be the chief targets of Lord Campbell's Obscene Publications Act of 1857 and of the SSV's long moral crusade through the nineteenth century. They hatched a rank literary sub-culture which grew around Holywell Street for nearly half a century. Their publications dominated the smut market until the 1870s, when they began to be reproduced and extended by a new generation of professionals like Edward Avery, Leonard Smithers and John Camden Hotten. This long tradition of pornography was no 'counter-culture' as some students of this branch of Victorian literature would have us believe. True, it often did attack or parody the sexual values and taboos of respect-able society, but at bottom it was too hollow and fantastic, too parasitic on the genres it tried to burlesque, too commercially expedient, to be a sub-versive cultural force. At best it peddled masturbatory fantasies for frus-trated upper-class males; at worst it popularised debased versions of the cruelty, violence and perversion of the Marquis de Sade.

The significance of their wider, non-pornographic output is harder to assess. On the one hand these Grub Street entrepreneurs pioneered some trends in popular literature and culture that many modern analysts would regret. During the first half of Victoria's reign, Dugdale and company played an important part in commercialising, and perhaps domesticating, several traditional plebeian genres. John Duncombe's *Dramatic Tales* (1836–44) and *New British Theatre* (532 numbers published 1825–65) helped make him the leading entrepreneur of early Victorian script production, and especially of the burgeoning new form of melodrama whose sentimentality and sensationalism is so frequently decried. The brothers' Dugdale and Duncombe also helped to commercialise popular songwriting by wresting its production from the control of traditional street bards and blurring its political and class sentiments, then marketing it as songsters for the new music-hall entrepreneurs of the East and West End. Arguably, too, their 'bon ton' and 'crim. con.' scandal sheets of the late twenties were prototypes of the mid-century 'Sundays' which peddled escapism and prurience in exchange for profit.

In each instance Dugdale and his cronies had moved beyond the old restricted radical audience towards an emerging 'mass' reading public which cut across middle- and working-class boundaries. It included the hordes of not always respectable artisans, clerks, army and navy officers, students, journalists, professionals, businessmen, government officials and tourists who inhabited London and visited its seamy underworld. Many Grub Street publications were designed not only to sell within this metropolitan underworld but also, like the works of Pierce Egan, Dickens, Reynolds and Mayhew, to sell its exotic culture to a wider, more respectable middle-class audience. The overwhelming metropolitan slant of these Grub Street radicals probably gave them more in common with Parisian than with English provincial counterparts. They figured centrally in the 're-making' of English working-class culture from its political and class-conscious phase of the 1820s and 1830s to its more escapist, apolitical 'cockney' form of the 1870s and after. Dugdale and his cronies were active at both historical moments; their role helps explain how the new culture was born out of the old.

Some of their Grub Street publications displayed a boisterous, if ambiguous, strain of political populism. We have traced it through the *chroniques scandaleuses* pirated or ghosted in the names of Mary Anne Clarke, Queen Caroline and Harriette Wilson, and through the virulent anti-establishment squibs levelled against clerics like Church and Clogher, ministers like Castlereagh and Melbourne, princes like George, Cumberland and Albert. Two other similar genres were to reach full flower only during the mid-Victorian period. One was a tradition of popular romantic–realist fiction which runs from Ashe's *Spirit of the Book* (1811) and *Osphia* (1829) to the huge-selling mid-Victorian works of Reynolds and Sue – *Mysteries of London* and *Mysteries of Paris*; the other, a line of sensationalist periodicals which runs from Benbow's *Rambler's Magazine* to Reynolds's *London*

Journal, Political Instructor, and eventually to the mass-circulation *Reynolds's Weekly.* If nothing else, this 'populist' corpus encouraged elements of the nihilist libertinism of the eighteenth century. The ripples were to reach libertarian pressmen like Henry Vizetelly – Zola's English publisher – and bohemian middle-class literati like Wilde, Swinburne and Beardsley. All this might seem far removed from the ultra-radical journalism of Regency years; it was a significant radical tradition nonetheless, and one through which Grub Street pressmen echoed their lost political past.

Overall then, perhaps the most significant legacy of this tiny metropolitan underworld was to keep alive a tradition of plebeian unrespectability and irreverence in the face of powerful countervailing forces. These obscure artisan ultra-radicals and Grub Street hacks carried into Victorian society a ribald, saturnalian anti-establishment culture which we might call populist in both its positive and negative senses, and which found expression in coffee-houses, chapels, pubs and music halls, as well as in squibs, songsters and the Sunday press. Through this, if nothing else, they helped to influence the shape of modern England, less perhaps than they hoped, but more than they knew.

Notes

INTRODUCTION

1. S & S, handbill, fo. 14.
2. For Reid's capture in a raid on the Angel tavern, see *Gentleman's Magazine*, lxviii (1798), p. 166, cited in Michael J. Williams, 'The 1790s: The Impact of Infidelity', *Bulletin of the Thomas Paine Society*, 5 (1976), p. 21. For details of his informing to the government and of his publishing disputes with Hatchard, see PC 1/3490, correspondence between Reid, Canning and law officials, May 1800. For some translations of Barruel as well as pamphlets inspired by his thesis, see J. Robison, *Proofs of a conspiracy against all the religions and governments of Europe* (1798); Anti-Jacobin (pseud.), *New Lights on Jacobinism* (1798); R. Clifford, *Application of Barruel's 'Memoirs of Jacobinism' to the Secret Societies of Ireland and Great Britain* (1798); W. Cobbett, *Bloody Buoy ... Thrown out as a Warning to the Political Pilots of All Nations ...* (1797); S. Payson, *Proofs of the Real Existence and Dangers of Illuminism* (1802). Reid later apparently resumed his radical and freethinking loyalties; see his biographies of Colonel Wardle (1809) and John Horne Tooke (1812) and the printed catalogue of the contents of his bookshop (1806).
3. W.H. Reid, *The Rise and Dissolution of the Infidel Societies in this Metropolis* (1800), passim.
4. E.P. Thompson, *The Making of the English Working Class* (Harmondsworth, 1968), pp. 178, 672–4, 923–4.
5. *Chambers Twentieth Century Dictionary*, quoted in Donald A. Low, *Thieves' Kitchen: The Regency Underworld* (1982), p. 2.

I JACOBIN–SPENCEANS: THOMAS EVANS AND THE REVOLUTIONARY UNDERGROUND

1. PRO HO 42/160, John Castle, Feb. 1817; TS 11/199/868 (ii), Susannah Harrison [1816]; TS 11/197/859, fo. 33.
2. HO 42/136, disturbances, 1813, contains correspondence between a Mr James Smith and Under-Secretary of State John Beckett, reporting on information provided by Arthur Kidder.
3. *BDMBR*, pp. 164–6; Thompson, *Making*, pp. 177–8, 190; Gwyn A. Williams, *Artisans and Sans-Culottes: Popular Movements in France and Britain during the*

French Revolution (1968), pp. 103, 107, 109. I have been privileged to see a draft version of Dr Malcolm Chase's much fuller biographical entry on Evans for a forthcoming volume of the *Dictionary of Labour History*, ed. John Saville and Joyce Bellamy.

4 For assessments of Place as historian, see W.E.S. Thomas, 'Francis Place and Working-Class History', *HJ*, 5 (1962), pp. 61–70; D.J. Rowe, 'Francis Place and the Historian', *HJ*, 16 (1973), pp. 45–63.

5 BL Add. MS 27808, esp. fos. 91–3, 105–8; Add. MS 35143, fos. 62–3; *The Autobiography of Francis Place*, ed. Mary Thale, (Cambridge, 1972), pp. 176–81, 196–7.

6 Add. MS 27812, fo. 33; HO 42/30, fos. 88–9; Add. MS 27813, fos. 113, 121; PC 1/23/A38, Report of the General Committee, 8 Dec. 1796.

7 Add. MS 27808, fo. 30.

8 I am indebted to Dr Malcolm Chase of Leeds University for this last piece of information. See also *Autobiography of Francis Place*, p. 179.

9 *Autobiography of Francis Place*, pp. 179–80; J. Ann Hone, *For the Cause of Truth: Radicalism in London, 1796–1821* (Oxford, 1982), pp. 113, 171–3, 182–6, 192–3.

10 Add. MS. 27813, fos. 128, 136; *The Correspondence of the London Corresponding Society* (1795), esp. pp. 23–4; Add. MS 27815, fos. 51–4; Hone, *Cause of Truth*, p. 37.

11 *LCS Correspondence*, pp. 4, 19, 40; John Baxter, *Resistance to Oppression* (1795), pp. 4–8; Williams, *Artisans and Sans-Culottes*, p. 98; P.A. Brown, *The French Revolution in English History* (1965), pp. 142–3. Albert Goodwin, *The Friends of Liberty: The English Democratic Movement in the Age of the French Revolution* (1979), pp. 369–71, disputes that Baxter was an advocate of physical force.

12 Add. MS 27808, fo. 81; PC 1/40/A132, reports of T. Milner, 17, 24 June; 2, 8, 10 July 1797.

13 Add. MS 27808, fo. 106; *Recollections of the Life of John Binns; twenty nine years in Europe and fifty three in the United States* (Philadelphia, 1854), p. 45.

14 Add. MS 27808, fos. 105–6; *Autobiography of Francis Place*, pp. 143, 154, 187–8.

15 Binns, *Recollections*, p. 46.

16 Marianne Elliott, *Partners in Revolution: The United Irishmen and France* (New Haven and London, 1982) pp. 59, 130, 141; Roger Wells, *Insurrection: The British Experience* (Gloucester, 1983), pp. 80–98; Binns, *Recollections*, pp. 64–6; W.J. Fitzpatrick, *Secret Service Under Pitt* (1892), pp. 105–15.

17 Elliott, *Partners*, p. 178.

18 *Ibid.*, pp. 144–50, 173–297; see also, Hone, *Cause of Truth*, pp. 41–117; Wells, *Insurrection*, esp. pp. 70–1, 121–7, 151–72.

19 For descriptions of activity at Furnival's Inn cellar, see Binns, *Recollections*, pp. 81–2; W.J. Fitzpatrick, *The Life, Times and Contemporaries of Lord Cloncurry* (Dublin, 1855), p. 165; PC 1/40/A123, Milner, 24 June–10 July 1797; Wells, *Insurrection*, pp. 123–4.

20 PC 1/42/A143, Powell, 4 May 1798, and Wright, 7 May 1798; *Report from the Committee of Secrecy ... relating to Seditious Societies, 15 March 1799* (1799),

Appendix 10, p. 35. See also, examinations of Evans, March 1798, in TS 11/689/2187 and HO 42/42; and 'Secret information respecting Quigley ... preserved in the Secretary of State's office', TS 11/122/333.

[21] HO 42/42 and PC 1/41/A136 contain Powell's reports March–April 1798. See also, Bodleian Lib., MS Eng. hist. C 296, Burdett Papers, affidavit of Thomas Evans, March 1801, fos. 63–6. Elliot, *Partners*, p. 149, believes Powell to be unreliable.

[22] TS 11/122/333, 'Secret information respecting Quigley'.

[23] *Ibid.*

[24] Elliott, *Partners*, pp. 178–9.

[25] *Report from the Committee of Secrecy* (1799), Appendix 9–14, pp. 29–37; PC 1/42/A143 and PC 1/43/A153 (enclosures).

[26] Eric Evans, *DMBR*, p. 65; even Thompson, *Making*, p. 188, appears to take Thomas Evans's stand at face value.

[27] PC 1/3526, examination of R. Hodgson, contains also his letter on this subject to the *Morning Chronicle* found among Joseph Bacon's papers, 30 April 1798. This was later printed separately.

[28] *Autobiography of Francis Place*, Appendix iii, pp. 236–7; for more on Jonathan King, see below, pp. 36–9. On the Loyal Lambeth Society, see PC 1/23/A38; Goodwin, *Friends of Liberty*, pp. 351–2.

[29] See reports, mainly of John Tunbridge and Wm Gent, 1798–9, in PC 1/42/A144; PC 1/43/A150; PC 1/3117 (ii); *Report from the Committee of Secrecy ... relative to the State of Ireland and certain disaffected Persons in both parts of the United Kingdom, 15 May 1801* (1801), p. 821; Hone, *Cause of Truth*, pp. 87–8; Wells, *Insurrection*, pp. 151–5, 213–14.

[30] PC 1/3526, Joseph Thomas, 4 April 1801.

[31] PC 1/3535, Powell to Ford, 25 Dec. 1801; PC 1/3526 and 3528, depositions of Burks, Bacon, Oliphant, etc., April–June 1801.

[32] For two excellent and complementary accounts of the 'Despard conspiracy', see Hone, *Cause of Truth*, pp. 86–121; Elliott, *Partners*, pp. 282–322, and 'The "Despard Conspiracy" Reconsidered', *P & P*, 75 (1977), pp. 46–61. Wells, *Insurrection*, pp. 220–52, presents a picture of a more extensive and organised insurrectionary attempt. For conflicting accounts of the role and extent of the revolutionary underground in the provinces, see J.R. Dinwiddy, '"The Black Lamp" in Yorkshire in 1801–2', and J.L. Baxter and F.K. Donnelly, 'The Revolutionary "Underground" in the West Riding: Myth or Reality', *P & P*, 64 (1974), pp. 113–32.

[33] See, for example, PC 1/3117 (i–ii); TS 11/122/333, 'Secret papers – Despard'; Hone, *Cause of Truth*, pp. 102–3, 105; Goodwin, *Friends of Liberty*, p. 468.

[34] PC 1/3117 (i), n–y, 21 Sept. 1802.

[35] The initiative may have come from him. There is an unsigned and undated letter of around June 1798 from Duffin which outlines the elements of the subsequent campaign: PC 1/44/A158. He had campaigned similarly against the administrations of the Fleet and New Compter prisons during an earlier imprisonment in 1793. For Duffin, see below, pp. 36–9.

[36] Bodleian Lib., MS Eng. hist. C 295, Evans, Webb, Roberts, Keir, Bone to Burdett, 19 Dec. 1798, p. 162, and C 296, 'Papers relating to Her Majesty's Prison in

Cold-bath Fields'. For an excellent secondary account of the affair, see Hone, *Cause of Truth*, pp. 121–33.

37 Bodleian Lib., MS Eng. hist. C 296, deposition of Thomas Aris, 31 Dec. 1798, fos. 44–51; PC 1/43/A153, deposition of Aris, 11 March 1799, and William Webb's account of his imprisonment; HO 42/50, R. Baker to the Duke of Portland, 15 Aug. 1800.

38 *Report of the Proceedings during the late contested election for the County of Middlesex* (J.S. Jordan, 1802), p. 34; see also *CPR*, 24 July 1802, col. 90.

39 *The Scum Uppermost when the Pot Boils Over* (1802), esp. pp. 9–10; John Bowles, *Thoughts on the late General Election as demonstrative of the progress of Jacobinism* (1802), pp. 9, 19; *Considerations on the late Elections for Westminster and Middlesex* (1802), pp. 48, 54. I am grateful to Dr Ann Hone for providing me with xerox copies of these pamphlets. For her own excellent account of the Middlesex election, see Hone, *Cause of Truth*, pp. 128–46.

40 See, for example, *CPR*, 31 July 1802, cols. 117–18.

41 PC 1/3535, Galloway to Richard Hodgson, 24 Dec. 1801.

42 Hone, *Cause of Truth*, pp. 134–7.

43 HO 42/73, J. King to the Lord Advocate, 7 Sept. 1803, fo. 10; PC 1/3117, Ford to Moody, 29 Sept. 1803.

44 G.D.H. Cole's phrase, quoted in A.W. Smith, 'Irish Rebels and English Radicals, 1798–1820', *P & P*, 7 (1955), p. 81.

45 Add. MS 27808, esp. fos. 201–8.

46 The pioneering work on Spence is by Olive D. Rudkin, *Thomas Spence and his Connections* (1927, repr. New York, 1966). E.P. Thompson seems to have been the first to advance the case for Spence as father of the revolutionary underground: *Making*, pp. 176–9, 543–4, 672–3. Both arguments have been elaborated by T.M. Parsinnen, 'Thomas Spence and the Origins of English Land Nationalization', *Journal of the History of Ideas*, 34 (1973), pp. 135–41, and 'The Revolutionary Party in London, 1816–20', *Bulletin of the Institute of Historical Research*, 45 (1972), pp. 266–82. T.R. Knox, 'Thomas Spence: The Trumpet of Jubilee', *P & P*, 76 (1977), pp. 75–98, criticises Parsinnen, arguing that Spence was neither a land nationaliser nor a physical force revolutionary but admits that Spence attracted a following of such revolutionaries. The largest claims for Spence as a socialist thinker are made by P.M. Kemp-Ashraf, 'An Introduction to the Selected Writings of Thomas Spence', supplement to *Life and Literacy of the Working Classes: Essays in Honour of Willie Gallacher*, eds. P.M. Kemp-Ashraf and J. Mitchell (Berlin, 1966), pp. 271–91. Two excellent recent analyses of Spence and his ideas are: Malcolm Chase, 'The Land and the Working Classes, English Agrarianism, circa 1775–1851', University of Sussex DPhil., 1985, esp. pp. 33–90; G.I. Gallop, 'Introduction', *Pig's Meat: The Selected Writings of Thomas Spence, Radical and Pioneer Land Reformer* (Nottingham, 1982), pp. 11–53.

47 HO 42/142, Conant to Beckett, 21 Feb. 1815.

48 In TS 11/199/868 (i) (enclosure). Snow's involvement in writing it is mentioned by the spy James Hanley, fo. 147.

49 *The Life and Opinions of Thomas Preston, Patriot and Shoemaker* (1817), pp. 20–1.

50 Thomas Wooler was by 1812–13 a radical journalist and renowned debater

both at Gale Jones's British Forum and in taverns like the Mermaid. Wright had been a member of the LCS who had founded a debating club in conjunction with John Binns and Gale Jones in 1795. He became as famous an orator as Gale Jones, and continued to associate and debate with the Spenceans at least until 1817. There is an excellent detailed memoir of him, probably written by William Benbow, in *RM*, i [1822], pp. 536–44.

51   Patten: see, for example, PC 1/3528, examination of Robert Oliphant c. June 1801; Constable: Add. MS 27808, T. Constable to T. Spence, 22 July 1808; Callender: see Hone, *Cause of Truth*, p. 242; Baxter: it has been suggested to me that this man, described in one report, HO 42/162, 9 March 1817, as a local surgeon is not the early Baxter who was a silversmith. However, William Clark, the Spencean, indentified him to Major Cartwright as the earlier Baxter in December 1816, see TS 11/199/868 (ii), 9 Dec. 1816. He is also listed in Add. MS 27816, fo. 89, as attending M. Margarot's funeral along with other veterans in 1815; Edwards, W? and G.: PC 1/44/A161, prisoners taken at the George, April 1798; TS 11/202/872, report to Conant [1817]; HO 40/8 (4), w–r, 31 Jan. 1818, fo. 167; R.C. Fair: Add. MS 27808, R.C. Fair to Place, 9 March 1831, fos. 319–20; Snow: TS 11/199/868 (i) and HO 42/168, Thomas Evans to T.J. Evans, 18 Sept. 1814; Maxwell and Lewis: PC 1/44/A161, United Englishmen taken at the Nag's Head, 9 April 1798; Clark: HO 42/170, 29 Oct. 1817; HO 42/162, police report, alehouses, 1 March 1817; Blythe: PC 1/42/A144, reports of Tunbridge and Gent, June–Sept. 1798; Preston: *Life*, esp. pp. 12–21; Pemberton: PC 1/3117 (i), Ford to Moody, 14 Oct. 1802; Johnson: PC 1/42/A144, list of persons apprehended for treason, 7 Aug. 1798; Add MS 27808, fo. 139.

52   Pendrill: see Smith, 'Irish Rebels and English Radicals', p. 83; Moggridge, Carr and Pendrill: HO 40/10(2), Moggridge's examination, 30 April 1817; Carr: HO 40/7 (4), w–r, [Jan.–Feb. 1818]; Curry: PC 1/42/A144, Wm Gent, 10 Sept. 1798; HO 42/189, w–r, 14 July 1819, meeting to commemorate Thomas Spence's birthday; George: HO 42/181, Stafford to Clive, 19 Oct. 1818; HO 42/182, w–r, 11 Nov. 1818; Bacon: PC 1/3526, examination of Joseph Bacon, 24 April 1801; subscription list for J. Watson, HO 42/168, [1817]; HO 42/163, G. Sangster, 13 April 1817.

53   Add. MS 27808, fo. 139.

54   S & S, handbill, 18 March 1801, and W. Hone to F. Place, 6 Nov. 1830, fo. 2; Add. MS 27808, Hone to Place, 23 Sept. 1830, fo. 314; HO 42/172, handwritten comments attached to *Humorous Catalogue of Spence's Songs, Pts I–III* [1811?]. Chase, 'Land and the Working Classes' (thesis), pp. 85–6, points out that Tilly composed Spence's best-known song 'The Spencean Jubilee'.

55   Dr Malcolm Chase has made the later, more plausible dating of *Spence's Songs* on the basis of a watermark: Chase, 'Land and the Working Classes', p. 87.

56   For Smith, see TS 11/122/333, 'Secret information respecting Quigley'; Hone, *Cause of Truth* pp. 25, 56–8; for Seale, see TS 11/939/3362, King vs. Seale; PC 1/3117, correspondence between Ford and Moody, Oct.–Nov. 1803; for Panther, see TS 11/939/3361, King vs. Panther; Add. MS 27808, Spence to Panther, 20 Nov. 1801, fo. 226; PC 1/3117 (i), [Sept. 1802]; for Cullen, see signed MS notes on BL copy of *The Important Trial of Thomas Spence* (1803), p. 10, and his notes on Spence's *The Restorer of Society to its Natural State*

(1801) bound with *A Letter from the author to a friend*; for discussion of Cullen's involvement with Evans in 1812–13, see below, p. 34.

[57] Thompson, *Making*, p. 178.

[58] Add. MS 27812, fo. 41; Add. MS 27813, fos. 14, 72; HO 119/1, Spence's deposition fo. 41; *Report from the Committee of Secrecy* (1799), Appendix 2, p. 3; Add. MS 27808, cutting, 16 Feb. 1793; S & S, *The Case of Thomas Spence, Bookseller* (1793); Chase, 'Land and the Working Classes', pp. 73–4.

[59] T. Spence, *The End of Oppression, being a dialogue between an old mechanic and a young one* (1795), pp. 6–7; see also *A Fragment of an Ancient Prophecy* (1796) and *Restorer of Society*. For two careful analyses of Spence's views on violence, see Gallop, *Pig's Meat*, pp. 41–9; Chase, 'Land and the Working Classes', pp. 75–82.

[60] Section xiv of the Seditious Meetings Act required a magistrate's licence for lecturing and debating halls where admission was charged and politics discussed, and also outlawed public meetings exceeding fifty persons, but was persistently ineffective against small, informal tavern free-and-easies.

[61] 'Address to All Mankind' in *Spence's Songs* (no pagination).

[62] I cannot therefore agree with Knox, 'Trumpet of Jubilee', 93–8, who sees Spence's support for rational diffusion as separating him from other Jacobin revolutionaries. Cf. Iorwerth Prothero's excellent analysis of ultra-radical ideas on this subject, 'William Benbow and the Concept of the "General Strike"', *P & P*, 63 (1974), pp. 132–71.

[63] PC 1/43/A150, J.T., 2 Nov. 1798; PC 1/42/A144, enclosure W. Gent, 26 July 1798; PC 1/3117 (ii), J.T., 22 Jan. 1799; PC 1/40/A132, June 1797.

[64] Add. MS 27823, esp. fos. 101–3, Add. MS 35144, fos. 35–60. For a general account of this radical educational experiment, see Hone, *Cause of Truth*, pp. 237–45.

[65] 'Spence and the Barber', *Spence's Songs, Pt II*, fo. 18.

[66] Gallop. *Pig's Meat*, p. 44.

[67] HO 42/136, disturbances, 1813, Smith to Beckett, Jan.–Feb. 1813. On Margarot at this time, see Add. MS 27818, Hardy to Cobbett, 6 April 1811, fo. 114, and HO 42/110, Margarot to Ryder, 7 and 23 Feb. 1811.

[68] For the Thistlewood–T.J. Evans trip, see HO 42/172, 'A statement of the grounds on which the several persons apprehended under Lord Sidmouth's Warrants and detained under the Acts of 57 Geo. 3 Cap. 3 and 55 were so arrested and detained'; HO 44/5 (19), information, Mr Daniel of Beaumont St; HO 42/168, Thomas Evans to T.J. Evans, 18 Sept. 1814; Add. MS 27818, Hardy to O'Connor, 24 Dec. 1814, fo. 184.

[69] Parsinnen, 'Spence and Land Nationalization', 137–8; Kemp-Ashraf, 'An Introduction to … Spence', 271–91.

[70] T. Spence, *The Rights of Man* (4th edn, 1803), pp. 23–5. The fifteen original queries also drew heavily on the laws of nature, pp. 36–7. For his further use of Locke, see *Important Trial*, pp. 59–60; *One Pennyworth of Pig's Meat* (1793–5), vii, p. 69; x, pp. 112–14, 137–8, 142–3; xvii, pp. 200–1; see also, *The Meridian Sun of Liberty* (1796), p. 12.

[71] Some Volney-influenced works of Spence include: *A Letter from Ralph Hodge to his cousin, Thomas Bull* (1795), pp. 8–12; 'Ode to Burke', attached to *Fragment*

of an Ancient Prophecy, p. 11; 'Propagation of Spensonianism ...' and 'A Dream' in *Spence's Songs*, and *A Suitable Companian to Spence's Songs. A fable* (n.d.). Such traces of Volney's influence belie the claim of Knox, 'Trumpet of Jubilee', p. 79, fn. 8, that Enlightenment material was never integrated into Spence's thinking. On Volney in the 1790s, see Thompson, *Making*, pp. 107–8.

[72] *Important Trial*, p. 9: *The Reign of Felicity, being a plan for civilizing the Indians of North America* (1796), p. 11; *Restorer of Society* pp. 24–5; Add. MS 27808, *Giant Killer, or Anti-Landlord*, i, 6 Aug. 1814, pp. 7–8; Gallop, *Pig's Meat*, pp. 20–4.

[73] Spence had earlier produced *The Constitution of a Perfect Commonwealth: being the French Constitution of 1793, amended and rendered entirely conformable to the whole rights of man* (1798); for the other two constitutions, see PC 1/42/A144, enclosure from Wm Gent, 26 July 1798; PC 1/43/A153 [1798].

[74] Chase, 'Land and the Working Classes', *passim*.

[75] Baxter, *Resistance to Oppression*, pp. 5–8; Knox, 'Trumpet of Jubilee', p. 91; Thompson, *Making*, p. 155; Michael Roe, 'Maurice Margarot: A Radical in Two Hemispheres, 1792–1815', *Bulletin of the Institute of Historical Research*, 31 (1958), pp. 68–78.

[76] PC 1/43/A153, esp. clauses 2 and 10.

[77] Gallop, *Pig's Meat*, p. 24, see also pp. 32–9 where he criticises Kemp-Ashraf's analysis of Spence as a socialist thinker and substitutes his own version of Spencean socialism. For another critique of Kemp-Ashraf, see Noel W. Thompson, *The People's Science: The Popular Political Economy of Exploitation and Crisis 1816–34* (Cambridge, 1984), pp. 38–52.

[78] Gareth Stedman Jones, *Languages of Class: Studies in English Working Class History 1832–1982* (Cambridge, 1983), esp. pp. 18–20, 153–8.

2 OLD BLACKGUARD SPENCEANS: EVANS AND UNRESPECTABLE RADICALISM

[1] *Autobiography of Francis Place*, esp. pp. 20–34, 41–59, 72–90; Add. MS 27829, fo. 119; see also, M. Dorothy George, *London Life in the Eighteenth Century* (Harmondsworth, 1966), pp. 271–6.

[2] E.P. Thompson, 'Eighteenth-Century English Society: Class Struggle without Class', *Journal of Social History*, 3 (1978), p. 151.

[3] *Autobiography of Francis Place*, esp. pp. 14–15, 46–135, 176, 198–9; see also Add. MS 27825 (ii); 27827, vols. 3–4; 27828 (ii); 27829, vol. 5 (i–ii); George, *London Life*, pp. 208–9.

[4] *Autobiography of Francis Place*, esp. pp. 198–9; see also Add. MS 27838, 27839 and 27850 for material on the involvement of Place, Galloway and Richter in Westminster radicalism during these years (1802–17), and Add. MS 27791, 'Historical Account of the NPU, 8 Oct.–31 Dec. 1831', for their later involvement in supposedly moderate radical politics. On the material improvement of these Jacobins, see also Samuel Bamford, *The Autobiography of Samuel Bamford: Vol. II: Passages in the Life of a Radical*, ed. W.H. Chaloner (1893, repr. 1967), pp. 49, 51; Binns, *Recollections*, p. 42; Hone, *Cause of Truth*, p. 246; Rowe, 'Francis Place', pp. 48, 52–8.

[5] Add. MS 35152, fos. 60–3; Add MS 27851, fos. 6–7.

[6] TS 11/41/148, anonymous letter [F. Place], 14 March 1813. For further details on King and his gang, see below, pp. 34–9.

[7] Add. MS 27809, fo. 72; Add. MS. 35152, fo. 60; Add. MS 27797, vol. ix, fo. 15.

[8] I.J. Prothero, *Artisans and Politics in Early Nineteenth-Century London: John Gast and his Times* (Folkestone, 1979). It must be said that a recent critique (which I believe goes too far) has claimed Gast as typical of those artisan leaders who collaborated in capitalistic changes in the labour processes of their trades, especially those favouring a wage economy, and whose absorption of respectability made them 'proctors' to artisan 'Gradgrinds' like Place: Peter Linebaugh, 'Labour History without the Labour Process: A Note on John Gast and his Times', *Social History*, 7 (1982), 319–27.

[9] See, for example, E.P. Thompson, 'Time, Work-Discipline and Industrial Capitalism', *Essays in Social History*, eds. M.W. Flinn and T.C. Smout (Oxford, 1974), pp. 39–77; Jeffrey Weeks, *Sex, Politics and Society: The Regulation of Sexuality since 1800* (1981), pp. 57–80.

[10] For example, Eric Trudgill, *Madonnas and Magdalens: The Origins and Development of Victorian Sexual Attitudes* (1976), pp. 159–87; Ford K. Brown, *Fathers of the Victorians* (Cambridge, 1961).

[11] Trygve Tholfsen, *Working-Class Radicalism in Mid-Victorian England* (1976), pp. 25–123; Brian Harrison, *Peaceable Kingdom: Stability and Change in Modern Britain* (Oxford, 1982), pp. 157–8.

[12] Stedman Jones, *Languages of Class*, p. 185.

[13] *Autobiography of Francis Place*, pp. 57, 78, 229; Add. MS 27825, fos. 144, 151; 27827, fos. 53–4; 36625, fo. 8.

[14] Bodleian Lib., MS Eng. hist. C296, Burdett Papers, affadavit of Thomas Evans, March 1801, fos. 63–6; PC 1/42/A144, Janet Evans to Duke of Portland, 12 July 1798.

[15] PC 1/3535, Galloway to Hodgson, 24 Dec. 1801; see also, PC 1/3582, examination of Wm St John, 30 Oct. 1803.

[16] PC 1/44/A161, Janet Evans to J. Binns, 8 Oct. 1799. Galloway might have received a similar portion of the legacy. He had originally set up his business in High Holborn through the assistance of his uncle, but claimed to be struggling in December 1801.

[17] *Reformists' Register*, 25 Oct. 1817, pp. 424–6.

[18] For Janet's connection with underground politics, see TS 11/122/333, 'Secret information respecting Quigley'; for a typical example of a letter from Thomas to Janet, see PC 1/44/A161, enclosed with letter from gaoler, John White, 1 Sept. 1799, and for an example of Janet's letters on behalf of Thomas, see PC 1/44/A158, 13 June 1799.

[19] Galloway to Ford, 6 Aug. 1799, PC 1/44/A161.

[20] See, HO 42/115, Galloway to Hodgson, 20 Feb. 1811; HO 42/168, Thomas Evans to T.J. Evans, 18 Sept. 1814; Add. MS. 27818, T. Hardy to R. O'Connor, 24 Dec. 1814, fo. 184; HO 42/141, T.J. Evans to Julian Thistlewood, 4 Nov. 1814.

[21] Add. MS 27840, cutting, Crown and Anchor Tavern, 28 Sept. 1812; Hone, *Cause of Truth*, p. 217.

22 Add. MS 27823, fos. 24–33, 94–105; Add. MS 35144, fos. 35–60; Add. MS 35152, fos. 58–72.

23 I am indebted to Dr Iorwerth Prothero of Manchester University for first alerting me to these connections. Most of the details, including copies of pamphlets on the subject, are contained in Add. MS 27851, esp. fos. 5–7, 52–70, 85–107; Add. MS 27852, fos. 77, 140, 204; Add. MS 35152, fo. 60. TS 11/41/148, contains copies of libels from the *IW* and the anonymous letter in Place's handwriting, 14 March 1813. For similar earlier charges against White in 1810–11, see KB 28/433/34 and 28/436/31. On the Sellis affair in general, see *A minute detail of the attempt to assassinate His Royal Highness, the Duke of Cumberland* (Stockdale, 2nd edn, 1810), pp. 31, 55–7, 94–7.

24 TS 11/1071/5075, 'Schedule of Papers taken from Mr Sedley', TS 11/594/1950 also contains numerous blackmailing letters, as well as negotiations between Sedley and government officials and dignitaries.

25 [Thomas Ashe], *Memoirs and Confessions*, 3 vols. (1815), iii, p. 148.

26 HO 42/131, fos. 220–2; TS 11/1071/5075; TS 11/594/1950. Sedley made repeated and unsuccessful attempts to retrieve his papers from the government on the rather disingenuous grounds that they were essential to his livelihood, see HO 42/127–8, 137, 140. He was back to his old tricks in August–September 1814 with an attempted blackmail of Lady Douglas, see DCRO, Addington Papers, Corr, Sedley to Lady Douglas, 4 Aug., 6 Sept. 1814.

27 On King, see *CPPS*, ix, p. 2; John Taylor, *Records of My Life*, 2 vols. (1832), ii, pp. 341–4; *Scourge*, i (Jan. 1811), pp. 1–26; PC 1/3535, Galloway to Hodgson, 24 Dec. 1801; Place, *Autobiography*, appendix iii, pp. 263–9; *Monthly Repository*, 18 (1823), p. 672 (obituary). I am indebted to Dr Ann Hone for this last reference.

28 On Duffin and King, see PC 1/44/A158, Rex vs. Patrick William Duffin; Add. MS 27851, fos. 6–7; *Scum Uppermost*, fn., p. 10; Mary Anne Clarke (pseud.), *The Rival Princes*, 2 vols. (Chubb edn, 1810), i, p. 163; ii, pp. 31–2, 246–7; C.H. Timperley, *A Dictionary of Printers and Printing* (1849), p. 835.

29 *Scourge*, i (Jan. 1811), p. 1.

30 *Monthly Repository*, 18 (1823), p. 672.

31 Taylor, *Records*, ii, pp. 341–4; *Memoirs of the late Thomas Holcroft …*, ed. William Hazlitt, 3 vols. (1816), iii, p. 75.

32 *Dissertations on the Prophecies of the Old Testament, containing all such prophecies as are applicable to the Coming of the Messiah, the Restoration of the Jews and the Resurrection of the Dead*, 2 vols. (1817), i, p. xxiii; see also *Autobiography of Francis Place*, p. 236; Add. MS 27851, fos. 5–6.

33 TS 11/594/1950, John Davis to Spencer Perceval, 13 Nov. 1810.

34 Clarke, (pseud.), *Rival Princes*, i, pp. 163–4; ii, pp. 31–2, 246–7; cf. Robert Darnton, *The Literary Underground of the Old Regime* (Cambridge, Mass., and London, 1982), esp. pp. 1–121.

35 See TS 11/40/144 (ii); TS 11/41/147 (i); TS 11/41/148 (ii); TS 11/603/1974; KB 28/436/31; Timperley, *A Dictionary of Printers and Printing*, pp. 832–3, 835, 839.

36 M. Dorothy George, *English Political Caricature. A Study of Opinion and Propaganda* (Oxford, 1959), ii, pp. 116–18.

37 See Clarke (pseud.), *Rival Princes*, i–ii; W. Clarke (pseud.?), *The Authentic and Impartial Life of Mrs Mary Anne Clarke* (1809), esp. pp. 84–91; William Hamilton Reid, *Memoirs of the Life of Colonel Wardle, including thoughts on the state of the nation* (1809), pp. 44–9, 66–77, 101; Mary Anne Clarke (pseud.?), *The Rival Dukes* (M. Jones edn, 1810), p. 133; Hone, *Cause of Truth*, pp. 169–70, 177, 182; A.D. Harvey, *Britain in the Early Nineteenth Century* (1978) pp. 220–50.

38 TS 11/41/148 (ii), [F. Place] to Litchfield, 14 March 1813, see also enclosed transcript of *IW* articles, 30 Aug., 27 Sept. 1812; Add. MS 27851, fo. 70, report in *Weekly Dispatch*, 7 April 1850, and fo. 76, Hunt's speech to the House of Commons, 21 June 1832; *Memoirs of Henry Hunt*, 3 vols. (1820), ii, p. 424; TS 11/120/329, Mary Anne Clarke, *Recollections: exhibiting the Secret History of the Court of St James's and of the Cabinet of Great Britain … communicated to her by the Duke of York* (printer, publisher, date and *dramatis personae* have been cut out), i, pp. 96–7. For typical examples of caricatures implying Cumberland's guilt, see *CPPS*, ix, nos. 11914, 12063, 12067, 12591.

39 E.P. Thompson, 'The Crime of Anonymity', in *Albion's Fatal Tree: Crime and Society in Eighteenth-Century England*, eds. Douglas Hay *et al.* (New York, 1975), pp. 255–308.

40 *CPPS*, viii, pp. xi–xiii, xxxviii.

41 TS 11/120/329, Clarke, *Recollections*, pp. vi–xxxii.

42 Correspondence and negotiations between Perceval and his officials on the one hand, and various printers and blackmailers on the other, is contained in TS 11/594/1950; see also [Ashe], *Memoirs and Confessions*, iii, pp. 42–59, 74–6; (J.M. Richardson, pub.), *Chancery Injunction - Letters to H.R.H. Caroline, Princess of Wales: comprising the only true history of the celebrated Book* (1813), esp. pp. 16–34, 50–99; TS 11/120/330, (Richard Edwards, pub.), *Edwards's genuine edition of 'The Book', or the Proceedings and Correspondence upon the Subject of the Inquiry into the Conduct of Her Royal Highness, the Princess of Wales* (1813), esp. pp. x–xxxii, 68–117; *Remarks on the Suppressed 'Book', as connected with the impending Bill of Pains and Penalties, To Divorce and Degrade Queen Caroline* [1820], pp. 5–19; Chancery injunctions issued against Edward Harris Blagdon's *Phoenix*, Feb.–March 1808, are contained in TS 11/462/1565.

43 Prothero, *Artisans and Politics*, esp. pp. 4–70; Thompson, *Making*, pp. 259–384, 894–6.

44 Preston, *Life*, pp. 5–12; *The Life and Literary Pursuits of Allen Davenport* (1845), pp. 29–30, 41–2. I am indebted to Dr Malcolm Chase of Leeds University for providing me with a photocopy of this long-lost autobiography; for more detail about Wedderburn's life, see below, pp. 51–72. For an excellent analysis of the shoemaker's trade in its European context, see E.J. Hobsbawm and Joan Wallach Scott, 'Political Shoemakers', *P & P*, 89 (1980), pp. 86–114.

45 Bodleian Lib., MS Eng. hist. C296, Burdett Papers, affidavit of Thomas Evans, March 1801, fo. 63.

46 Preston, *Life*, pp. 16, 25.

47 Add. MS 27809, fo. 72.

48 Davenport, *Life*, pp. 53–76.

49 Prothero, *Artisans and Politics*, pp. 26–7.

50 On Porter, see HO 40/8 (1), C, 30 Sept. 1817, fos. 45–8; HO 42/172, comments appended to *Spence's Songs*; HO 44/1, anon., April 1820.

51 A full, but often inaccurate account of Thistlewood's life is contained in G.T. Wilkinson, *Authentic history of the Cato Street Conspiracy* (1820), esp. Appendix; see also Clive Emsley's entry in *BDMBR*, pp. 471–5; HO 42/136, James Smith to John Beckett, 8 Feb. 1813; Ad. MS 27797, vol. ix, fo. 15; Add. MS 27818, Hardy to O'Connor, 13 Oct. 1813, fos. 163–4; Add. MS 27823 and Add. MS 35152, fo. 60.

52 The entry on Watson by T.M. Parsinnen, *BDMBR*, pp. 512–14, supplies no details of his background. The best source of these is in an undated (and seemingly misfiled) report by a friend of his named Whitfield in HO 42/143 [c. 1815–16]. The names, birthplaces and dates of Watson, his wife and children are in TS 11/201/870 (i); see also the record of his examination in Coldbath Fields prison, Dec. 1816, in TS 11/200/869.

53 Preston, *Life*, pp. 16–19, 33–5; and TS 11/203/873, examination before the Lord Mayor, 4 Dec. 1816.

54 Preston, *Life*, p. 22; see also Add. MS 27808, 'Memoir of Spence', written by Place, drawing on Eneas Mackenzie's memoir in the *Newcastle Magazine* (1821) and his *History of Newcastle* (1820), esp. fos. 151–226, 307; letter from T.J. Evans, fos. 229–30; letter from Wm Hone, 23 Sept. 1830, fos. 314–15; correspondence between Spence and Charles Hall, June–Aug. 1807, fos. 280–4; *A Memoir of Thomas Bewick, written by himself*, ed. Iain Bain, (Oxford, 1979); Chase, 'Land and the Working Classes', pp. 39–42, 59–62.

55 Spence, 'Resignation', attached to *Fragment of an Ancient Prophecy*, pp. 6–8.

56 Allen Davenport, *The Life, Writings and Principles of Thomas Spence* (1836), p. 1.

57 Spence, 'A Dream', *Spence's Songs*, Pt III, no pagination.

58 Spence to Charles Hall, 28 June 1807, Add. MS 27808, fos. 280–4.

59 S & S, *Receipt to make a Millennium or Happy Worker* (n.d.), pp. 5–6; Spence, *The Rights of Infants; or, The imprescriptable right of mothers to such a share of the elements as is sufficient to enable them to suckle and bring up their young* (1797); Add. MS 27808, *Giant Killer*, ii (Aug. 1814), pp. 14–15.

60 Olivia Smith, *The Politics of Language, 1791–1819* (Oxford, 1984), pp. 97–109.

61 Spence, *Restorer of Society*, pp. 8–9.

62 For Porter's ballad, see paper appended to Goldsmith Lib. edn of *Important Trial of Thomas Spence* (2nd edn, 1807).

63 S & S, *Spence's Songs*, fo. 17.

64 HO 42/177, A. Thistlewood to Julian, 11 June 1818; see also Thistlewood's letter to John Hunt, 21 June 1818 and Hunt's to Susan Thistlewood, 19 June 1818.

65 Jacques Rancière, 'The Myth of the Artisan: Critical Reflections on a Category of Social History', *International Labor and Working-Class History*, 24 (1983), pp. 1–16; see also the responses by William H. Sewell and Christopher H. Johnson, pp. 17–25; Donald Reid, 'The Night of the Proletarians: Deconstruction and Social History', *Radical History Review*, 28–30 (1984), pp. 445–63. I am indebted to Dr J. Epstein of Duke University for providing me with these references.

66 Davenport, *Life of Spence*, p. 8; Thomas Evans, *Christian Policy, the Salvation of the Empire* (1816), p. 20.

3 MILLENARIAN SPENCEANS: ROBERT WEDDERBURN AND METHODIST PROPHECY

[1] See, however, Harold Perkin, *The Origins of Modern English Society, 1780–1880* (1969) for a persuasive version of this 'stepping stone' thesis.

[2] For a summary of the bibliography of the long-standing debate over Elie Halévy's thesis see E.S. Itzkin, 'Working Hypothesis: English Revivalism: Antidote for Revolution and Radicalism, 1798–1815', *Church History*, 44 (1975), pp. 47–66. Two recent interesting supporters of the thesis from revisionist perspectives are: Bernard Semmel, *The Methodist Revolution* (1973), and A.D. Gilbert, 'Methodism, Dissent and Political Stability in Early Industrial England', *Journal of Religious History*, 10 (1979), 381–99.

[3] Thompson, *Making*, p. 428.

[4] DCRO, Addington MS, Corr. 1811, 'Dissenting Ministers', 'An old man' to Lord Sidmouth, 8 June 1811; for an example of Sidmouth's similar view see *Morning Post*, 10 May 1811, p. 2.

[5] On the affinities between Puritanism and Methodism, see J.F.C. Harrison, *The Second Coming: Popular Millenarianism, 1780–1850* (1979), esp. pp. 13–18, 223; J.D. Walsh, 'Elie Halévy and the Birth of Methodism', *Transactions of the Royal Historical Society*, 25 (1975), pp. 16–19.

[6] Reid, *Infidel Societies*, pp. 41, 46.

[7] Lady Stephens MS, 'The Smiths of "the Cannon by London Stone"', ch. xi, p. 16, in Cambridge University Library, William Smith Family Papers, Add. MS 7621, Box 1.

[8] *Morning Post*, 22 May 1811, pp. 2–3; see also J.D. Walsh, 'Methodism and the Mob in the Eighteenth Century', in *Popular Belief and Practice*, eds. G.J. Cuming and D. Baker (Cambridge, 1972), p. 218.

[9] R. Wedderburn, *The Horrors of Slavery exemplified in the life and history of the Rev. R. Wedderburn, V.D.M.*, (1824), pp. 4–15.

[10] *Ibid.* p. 24; on the anxieties and deprivations of free mulattos in Jamaica at this time, see Edward Brathwaite, *The Development of Creole Society in Jamaica, 1770–1820* (Oxford, 1971), pp. 172–4. A similar insecurity, coupled with ambition, also encouraged his future ultra-radical associate, William 'Black' Davidson, to migrate to England around 1800, even though he was in the relatively secure position of having the island's Attorney-General as his father.

[11] *Axe to the Root*, v [1817], pp. 71–2; HO 42/196, BC, 6 Oct. 1819.

[12] HO 42/198, 3 Nov. 1819; *Axe to the Root*, v [1817], p. 71; on the connections between radicalism and the mutinies, see esp. Wells, *Insurrection*, pp. 80–98.

[13] James Dugan, *The Great Mutiny* (1965), pp. 62–3, illustration centrepiece.

[14] On Davidson, see G.T. Wilkinson, *Authentic history of the Cato Street Conspiracy* (1820), pp. 406–9; *Trials of A. Thistlewood, J. Ings, J. Brunt, R. Tidd, W. Davidson and others* (1820), pp. 172–95; TS 11/202/872, MS transcript of Davidson's speech on receiving sentence [1820].

[15] HO 42/141, 9 Oct. 1814; for other similar complaints, see HO 42/142, Samuel Birch, 3 Feb. 1815, and James Knask, March 1815; HO 42/169, G. Prinsep, 7 Aug. 1817.

[16] George, *London Life*, p. 139; James Walvin, *The Black Presence: A Documentary*

History of the Negro in England, 1555–1860 (1971), pp. 12–28; Peter Fryer, *Staying Power: The History of Black People in Britain* (1984), pp. 191–202, 227–36; Low, *Thieves' Kitchen*, p. 119.

17 *Axe to the Root*, iii [1817], p. 49; HO 42/198, 9 Nov. 1819; HO 42/164, list of persons mentioned by Mr Caldecott, April 1817; CLRO, 'Index to Persons Indicted', Oct. 1813.

18 HO 42/19, 24 Nov. 1819; George Rudé, *Paris and London in the 18th Century: Studies in Popular Protest* (Fontana, 1970), p. 289.

19 Ian Duffield, 'London's Black Transportees to Australia', unpublished paper, Conference on the History of Black People in London, University of London, 27–9 Nov. 1984.

20 *Axe to the Root*, v [1817], pp. 76–7.

21 HO 42/181, Stafford, 22 Oct. 1818; TS 11/45/167, handbill; cf. Prothero, *Artisans and Politics*, pp. 22–50.

22 Rev. Robert Wedderburn, *Truth Self-Supported; A Refutation of certain doctrinal errors generally adopted in the Christian Church* [c. 1802], p. 4. The British Library estimates the date at 1790 but a watermark on one of the pages suggests 1802.

23 Arnold Rattenbury, 'Methodism and the Tatterdemalions', in *Popular Culture and Class Conflict, 1590–1914: Explorations in the History of Labour and Leisure*, eds. Eileen and Stephen Yeo (Sussex and New Jersey, 1981), p. 28.

24 *Truth Self-Supported*, pp. 8, 10, 14–19; Roger Anstey, 'Slavery and the Protestant Ethic', in *Roots and Branches: Current Directions in Slave Studies*, ed. Michael Craton (Oxford, 1979), pp. 157–65.

25 *Axe to the Root*, vi [1817], p. 85.

26 *Horrors of Slavery*, p. 12; *Axe to the Root*, iv [1817], pp. 50–1; *Forlorn Hope, or Call to the Supine*, ii [1817], p. 36; *Address of the Rev. Robert Wedderburn to the Court of King's Bench ... 9 May 1820* (1820), p. 4; *Trial of the Rev. Robert Wedderburn ... for Blasphemy* (1820), pp. 4–5.

27 Rattenbury, 'Methodism and the Tatterdemalions', in Yeo, *Popular Culture*, pp. 28–61; John Rule, 'Methodism, Popular Beliefs and Village Culture in Cornwall, 1800–50', in *Popular Culture and Custom in Nineteenth-Century England*, ed. Robert D. Storch (1982), pp. 61–7; J. Obelkevich, *Religion and Rural Society: South Lindsey, 1825–75* (Oxford, 1976); Harrison, *Second Coming*, pp. 39–41, 130–1; Alan Smith, *The Established Church and Popular Religion, 1750–1850* (1971), pp. 19–24.

28 Michael Craton, 'Slave Culture, Resistance and Achievement', *Slavery and British Society, 1776–1846*, ed. James Walvin (1982), pp. 112–13.

29 Rattenbury, in Yeo, *Popular Culture*, esp. pp. 45–6.

30 Davenport, *Life*, pp. 12–14. For an interesting evaluation of Wesley's hymnody, see Rachel Trickett, 'To Instruct and Inflame', *Times Literary Supplement*, 21 Dec. 1984, p. 1467.

31 *Truth Self-Supported*, pp. 19–24; I am grateful for the helpful comments on Wedderburn's textual references which Dr E. Royle of the University of York supplied for an earlier draft of this chapter.

32 *Truth Self-Supported*, p. 24; cf. *The Works of John Wesley: Volume 7, A Collection of Hymns for the use of the People called Methodists*, eds. Franz Hilderbrandt, Oliver A. Beckerlegge and James Dale (Oxford, 1983), pp. 500–1.

33 *Truth Self-Supported*, p. 4.
34 Reid, *Infidel Societies*, pp. 42, 47; cf. Walsh, 'Methodism and the Mob', in Cuming and Baker, *Popular Belief*, pp. 218–19.
35 *Truth Self-Supported*, pp. 3–6.
36 Rattenbury, in Yeo, *Popular Culture*, p. 30.
37 Reid, *Infidel Societies*, pp. 20, 47.
38 See, for example, Christopher Hill, *The World Turned Upside Down. Radical Ideas during the English Revolution* (Harmondsworth, 1975), p. 336.
39 Harrison, *Second Coming*, pp. 15–17.
40 Semmel, *Methodist Revolution*, pp. 23–80.
41 *Truth Self-Supported*, p. 9.
42 John Church,*The Thirteen Names of the First Patriarchs, considered as figurative of the progressive influences of the Spirit* (1811), pp. 36–9. For the accusations against Church, see [R. Bell], *Religion and Morality Vindicated against Hypocrisy and Pollution; or, an Account of the Life and Character of John Church, the Obelisk Preacher, who was formerly a frequenter of Vere St., and who has been charged with unnatural practices in various places* (1813), esp. p. 27; anon., *The Devil and Parson Church* [c. 1817], pp. 2–5; for Wedderburn's knowledge of him, see HO 42/199, 24 Nov. 1819; and other ultras, HO 42/172, Glasville, 10 Dec. 1817. I am grateful to Professor J.D. Walsh of Jesus College, Oxford, for drawing my attention to Church.
43 *Truth Self-Supported*, p. 6.
44 Semmel, *Methodist Revolution*, esp. pp. 93–104.
45 R. Wedderburn, *High Heel'd Shoes for Dwarfs in Holiness* [1821]; *Truth Self-Supported*, p. 12.
46 *Truth Self-Supported*, pp. 5–6.
47 *Ibid.*, pp. 6, 12–13.
48 Reid, *Infidel Societies*, p. 2, see also, pp. 14, 91–2.
49 Cf. W.H. Oliver, *Prophets and Millennialists: The Uses of Biblical Prophecy in England from the 1790s to the 1840s* (Auckland and Oxford, 1978), pp. 11–24, 34–5, 45–7, 50–6; Harrison, *Second Coming*, pp. 57–83, 120, 208.
50 J.F.C. Harrison, 'Thomas Paine and Millenarian Radicalism', unpublished paper, History Workshop Religion and Society Conference, London, 7–9 July 1983, p. 10. I am grateful to Professor Harrison for providing me with a copy.
51 Binns, *Recollections*, pp. 47–51.
52 PC 1/3490, W.H. Reid, 19, 21 May 1800, depositions, 15, 20, 23, 25 May 1800; TS 11/223/937 (i–ii).
53 Hone, *Cause of Truth*, p. 97.
54 HO 42/123, 11–30 May 1812. There were more than forty of them; postmasters were notified and £1000 reward offered for information revealing the author or authors: HO 42/124, Freeling, 25 June 1812.
55 Rev. Robert Wedderburn, *A Letter addressed to the Rev. Solomon Herschell, the High Priest of Israel … concerning the origin of the Jewish prophecies and their expected Messiah* (1819), p. 6; HO 42/199, John Eshelby, 29 Nov. 1819.
56 See frontispiece, Nathaniel Brassey Halhed, *Two Letters to Lord Loughborough* (Riebau, 1795): on Riebau, see Harrison, *Second Coming*, p.67.
57 Walsh, 'Halévy and the Birth of Methodism', pp. 16–17.

[58] John Ward, *Zion's Works: New Lights on the Bible from the coming of Shiloh*, 16 vols. (1899–1904), x, pp. 75–89; [C.B. Holinsworth], *Memoir of John Ward named Zion by the Call of God in the year 1818* (Birmingham, 1881), pp. 3–12.

[59] Reid, *Infidel Societies*, p. 117.

[60] *Axe to the Root*, ii [1817], pp. 21–2.

[61] For good analyses of the influence of James Murray on Spence, see Chase, 'Land and the Working Classes', pp. 39, 50–3; Knox, 'Trumpet of Jubilee', pp. 79–85.

[62] *Memoir of Bewick, passim*; see also Spence, *Fragment of an Ancient Prophecy*, one of the many examples amongst his writings and songs where his debt to this tradition may be seen. On the connections of this tradition with popular millenarianism, see Harrison, *Second Coming*, pp. 39–41, 44–5, 51–3; and with popular protest, Thompson, 'The Crime of Anonymity', in Hay *et al.*, *Albion's Fatal Tree*, pp. 287–8; and with Puritanism, Reginald Nettel, 'Folk Elements in Nineteenth-Century Puritanism', *Folklore*, 80 (1969), 272–85. For general discussions of the tradition and its transmission, see Keith Thomas, *Religion and the Decline of Magic: Studies in Popular Beliefs in Sixteenth and Seventeenth Century England* (Harmondsworth, 1973), esp. chs. 8, 13; Bernard Capp, *Astrology and the Popular Press: English Almanacs, 1500–1800* (1979), pp. 255–67; Hill, *World Turned Upside Down*, pp. 87–98; Deborah Valenze, 'Prophecy and Popular Literature in Eighteenth-Century England', *Journal of Ecclesiastical History*, 29 (1978), pp. 75–92.

[63] Spence, *Rights of Man*, p. 33.

[64] Chase, 'Land and the Working Classes', pp. 59–63.

[65] Spence, *Rights of Man*, p. 22; see also Add. MS 27808, E. Mackenzie, *Memoir of Thomas Spence of Newcastle-upon-Tyne* (1826), p. 8, for a description of his tokens carrying the theme of 'the Millennium' and 'The World Turned Upside Down'. Spence also published a ballad under the last name in 1805: Hill, *World Turned Upside Down*, p. 380.

[66] HO 42/172, *Spence's Songs*: see also Spence, *End of Oppression*, p. 11; *Rights of Man*, pp. 21–3; *Restorer of Society*, pp. 12–23; Add. MS 27808, *Giant Killer*, ii (1814), p. 3; *Meridian Sun of Liberty*, p. 8.

[67] *Universalist's Miscellany*, i (1797), pp. 502–3, 534–9; ii (1798), pp. 8–10, 112–15; v (1801), pp. 139–43.

[68] Spence, *Fragment of an Ancient Prophecy*, pp. 2–3.

[69] S & S, *Spence's Songs*, fo. 18.

[70] 'Address to All Mankind', *Spence's Songs*; Add. MS 27808, Spence to Hall, 28 June 1807, fo. 284.

[71] Chase, 'Land and the Working Classes', pp. 66–8.

[72] Spence, *Fragment of an Ancient Prophecy*, p. 3; see also *Meridian Sun of Liberty*, p. 8.

[73] Add. MS 27808, *Giant Killer*, i (1814), p. 3.

[74] Thomas Evans, *A Brief Sketch of the Life of Mr Thomas Spence, author of the Spencean system of agrarian fellowship ... with a selection of the songs* (Manchester, 1821).

[75] Hill, *World Turned Upside Down*, pp. 139–50, 174–5.

[76] Spence, *Important Trial*, pp. 57–9; *Restorer of Society*, p. 20.

[77] Quoted in Rudkin, *Spence and his Connections*, p. 115.

[78] Add. MS 27808, Constable to Spence, 22 July 1808. Perhaps this was an oblique reference to the passage from Isaiah 29 with which Spence had begun his *Important Trial*: 'But in that day shall the Deaf hear the words of the Book, and the Eyes of the Blind shall see out of Obscurity, and out of Darkness'.

[79] Levi, *Dissertations on the Prophecies*, i, introduction, pp. xxvii–lxxvi.

[80] Hone, *Cause of Truth*, p. 96; Harrison, *Second Coming*, pp. 223–4. Seale remained active in Evans's Spencean circle during post-war years.

[81] HO 42/173, W. Benbow to Jane Benbow, 14 Dec. 1817.

[82] Preston, *Life*, pp. 24, 32.

[83] Davenport, *Life*, pp. 35–6, 41–2; HO 42/202, Davenport, *The Kings, or Legitimacy Unmasked* (1819), p. 8; Davenport, *Life of Spence*, p. 11.

[84] Add. MS 27809, fos. 33, 99–100.

[85] Evans, *Life of Spence*, p. 6.

[86] [Thomas Evans], *Address and regulations of the Society of Spencean Philanthropists* ... (1815), pp. 4–5.

[87] Evans, *Christian Policy*, esp. pp. 8–11, 37; *IW*, 22 Oct. 1815, p. 340; 14 April 1816, p. 117.

[88] *Christian Policy*, pp. 11, 15, 17, 20–1; cf. Hill, *World Turned Upside Down*, pp. 139–41, and 'The Religion of Gerrard Winstanley', *P & P Supplement*, 5 (Oxford, 1978), pp. 18–20, 46–9.

[89] P.G. Rogers, *Battle in Bossenden Wood: The Strange Story of Sir William Courtenay* (1962), pp. 4–5. If so, he was probably influenced by the Spenceans during the post-war years when Evans was leader.

[90] Guildhall Lib., Register of Dissenters' Meeting Houses, John Shegog, 6 Sept. 1816, 3 North Audley Street, 'Methodists'; HO 42/172, Glasville to Day, 10 Dec. 1817; HO 42/170, draft of an address by J. Shegog, 5 Sept. 1817, and 29 Sept. 1817 (preaching under licence at 1 Spital/Spicer Street, Stepney).

[91] Add. MS 27808, fos. 159–60, 176, 218, 287.

[92] *Axe to the Root*, i [1817], pp. 5–11. See also the fervent Spencean pamphlet, S & S, [Rev. Robert Wedderburn], *Christian Policy; or Spence's Plan, in Prose and Verse, by a Spencean Philanthropist* (1818), pp. 3–5. On the phenomenon of prophetic 'madmen' or 'holy fools' in the seventeenth century, see Hill, *World Turned Upside Down*, pp. 279–83.

[93] *Axe to the Root*, i [1817], pp. 5, 10. He also claimed that Spenceanism would not withhold an equal share of the rents 'even from a criminal'.

[94] *Ibid.*, pp. 3–15; ii, pp. 22–31.

[95] *Ibid.*, i, pp. 11–13; vi, pp. 84–91, 95–6.

[96] *Ibid.*, ii, pp. 17–18.

4 INFIDEL SPENCEANS: GEORGE CANNON AND RATIONALIST PHILOSOPHY

[1] These facts can be deduced from his death certificate: General Register Office, London, 11 April 1854 (Clerkenwell House of Correction), col. 167, which gives his age as sixty-five, and from his reply to the 1841 Census, when he was living at No. 2 Great Mays' Buildings, St Martins Lane; see also PRO, MS

216/4, Chancery Solicitors Records, 'Index: Admission Registers', G. Cannon, Staple Inn, 1812.

2 The Union was a shortlived and more democratic rival of the Hampden Club: *The Life and Correspondence of Major Cartwright*, ed. F.D. Cartwright, 2 vols. (1826), ii, pp. 10–11, 24, 377–80. I am indebted to Dr Ann Hone for this reference. See also her discussion of the Union: Hone, *Cause of Truth*, pp. 209–11.

3 *The Life and Letters of Sydney Dobell*, ed. E.J. [E. Jolly], 2 vols. (1878), i, appendix, pp. 64–76; see also *FCM*, ii (1812), pp. 50–1; iii (1813), p. 555; *FCQR*, i (1823), 'preface'; John Evans, *Sketches of the Different Denominations of the Christians* (1814), pp. 311–21; 'Samuel Thompson', *DNB*, pp. 701–2; the society is discussed briefly in Geoffrey Powell, 'The Origins and History of Universalist Societies in Britain, 1750–1850', *Journal of Ecclesiastical History*, xxii (1971), pp. 43–4.

4 Guildhall Lib., MS 9580/3, 'Registers of Dissenters' Meeting Houses', 16 Feb. 1801 and 8 March 1810; *FCM*, ii (1812), pp. 55–61.

5 Add. MS 35152, Place to Thompson and Fearon [1810], fo. 3; *FCM*, i (1811), preface, pp. iv–vii.

6 For example, *FCM*, i (1811), pp. 179–86; ii (1812), pp. 52–5. On their use of the philosophes, see *ibid.*, i (1811), pp. 474–5; ii (1812), pp. 161, 193, 512–14; iii (1813), pp. 152–65, 224–6.

7 *FCM*, iii (1813), p. 32, and retrospective report in *FCQR*, i (1823), p. 230.

8 The dispute is mainly between 'A Deist' and 'Christophilius', the latter subsequently reproduced his ideas in a separate tract: *FCM*, ii (1812), pp. 54–7, 62–3, 123–4, 162–8, 209–14. 'A Deist' also admitted to having written under the pseudonym of 'AB'. There is no certainty that it was Cannon, but the style and contents resemble other of his writings, particularly his use of distinctive anecdotes which became key-notes of his later work. See, for example, the anecdotes of Charles V, *FCM*, ii (1812), pp. 62–3; cf. *CPR*, 4 Feb. 1815, cols. 152–8, Erasmus Perkins, Letter VI, 'On Religious Persecution'. He also wrote similarly under the pseudonym of 'Eunomus Wilkins, Pentonville', in his *Theological Inquirer* of 1815.

9 Burdon had been a Fellow of Emmanuel College, Cambridge, from 1788–96, when he resigned rather than take holy orders. He then alternated between his coal mines at Hertford, Morpeth, and a house in Cavendish Square, living the life of a scholar and controversialist. The book which most influenced Cannon was *Materials for Thinking*, first written in 1806 and reissued in revised edition in 1810 when Cannon probably encountered it. The *DNB*, p. 299, describes Burdon as a moderate reformer but his private correspondence conveys a far more extreme impression, both politically and theologically. See, for example, Emmanuel College, Cambridge, MS 269, Burdon Papers, p. 254, Wm Burdon to Major Le Marchant, Cambridge, 1796. He also admitted to being an atheist in *FCM*, iii (1813), pp. 405–7.

10 Erasmus Perkins (Cannon), 'Letter to Mr Justice Best', *DM* [1820], pp. 201–2; for Ellenborough's conduct of the trial, see *Trial of Mr Daniel Isaac Eaton, for publishing the third and last part of Paine's 'Age of Reason' ... 6 March 1812 ...* (1812).

11 Cannon seems to have written both under 'A Friend to True Christianity' and 'A Friend to Truth': *FCM*, ii (1812), pp. 185–92; iii (1813), pp. 55–7. Again they can be identified by comparison with his articles in *CPR*, 1813–15 (Erasmus Perkins). For Burdon's estrangement from the Freethinking Christians, see *FCM*, iii (1813), pp. 130, 188–90; and the retrospective discussion in Carlile's *Republican*, 17 Oct. 1823.

12 *FCM*, iii (1813), 188–90, 313.

13 For information on this Rev. Thomas Cannon, see Walter Wilson, *The History and Antiquities of Dissenting Churches and Meeting Houses in London, Westminster and Southwark, including the lives of their Ministers, from the rise of Nonconformity to the present time*, 4 vols. (1810), iii, p. 386, and *Triennial Directory of London* (1808), 'Thomas Cannon'.

14 Reid was also part-owner and controller of the *European Magazine*. His circle included Romney, Hayley and Kemble: T. Cato Worsfeld, *The Staple Inn and its Story* (1903), pp. 105–7.

15 For an excellent discussion of the *Ecce Homo* controversy and its context, see John Dinwiddy, 'William Cobbett, George Houston and Freethought', *Notes and Queries*, ccxxii (1977), pp. 355–9. I am indebted to Dr Dinwiddy for providing me with an expanded version of this article and with much helpful material from the Privy Council and Treasury Solicitor's files.

16 On the Wimbledon Common circle, see William Hamilton Reid, *Memoirs of the Public Life of John Horne Tooke, esq.* (1812), esp. pp. 178–82; Hone, *Cause of Truth*, pp. 22–3, 63–4, 114–19, 220–2.

17 Their involvement can be pieced together mainly from information supplied by George Houston to the authorities when in prison in 1816: PC 1/4032, Notes respecting the work entitled *Ecce Homo*, and Additional Notes respecting *Ecce Homo*, 5 March 1816; TS 11/47/183, Rex vs. Houston. For details of Baverstock's life and background, see James Baverstock, *Treatises on Brewing, with an introduction containing a biographical sketch of the author* (1824), introduction, pp. xv–xxiii; on Joseph Webb, see TS 11/47/183, testimony of Joseph Webb, (not to be confused with Evans's LCS associate, William Webb). Joseph later became a disciple of Richard Carlile. There is a good deal of information on Cobbett's friendship with Brown in the above files.

18 See the copies of *Ecce Homo! or, A critical enquiry into the history of Jesus Christ ...* (1813), contained in TS 11/47/183 and TS 11/978/3560, Rex vs. D.I. Eaton, copy of the libel. These have the most offensive passages marked up for prosecution, esp. pp. 7, 42–5, 67–8, 71, 83–8, 141, 155–6.

19 PC 1/4032, Notes, Brown to Houston, 14 Sept. 1813.

20 *CPR*, 15 May 1813, cols. 709–13; 3 July 1813, cols. 6–7; 14 Aug. 1813, col. 200.

21 *FCM*, iii (1813), pp. 337–47, 367–8, and earlier articles, pp. 261–75, 291–314; *CPR*, 12 June 1813, cols. 846–8; 3 July 1813, cols. 9–10.

22 See Dinwiddy, 'William Cobbett, George Houston and Freethought', *passim*; George Spater, *William Cobbett: The Poor Man's Friend*, 2 vols. (Cambridge, 1982), ii, Appendix I, pp. 544–9.

23 *CPR*, 4 Sept. 1813, cols. 298–302; 27 Nov. 1813, cols. 680–3; 8 Jan. 1814, cols. 43–5. Again these can be identified as Cannon's by close comparison

with his earlier letters in the *FCM*, and by his later letters as Erasmus Perkins in *CPR*. The persona and style resembles that of Perkins; he uses common citations, including those from Burdon's *Materials for Thinking*, and he shows an early familiarity with Shelley, see below, pp. 80–1.

24 PC 1/4032, Additional Notes, 5 March 1816, p. 2; TS 11/47/183, 9 Nov. 1814.

25 *CPR*, 8 Jan. 1814, cols. 43–5; cf. *FCM*, iii (1813), pp. 55–7.

26 Houston identified himself as 'Observator', in PC 1/4032, Notes, 22 Nov. 1813, p. 10.

27 I think 'Varro' was Brown, first, because the articles show that he knew Cannon and was influenced by him – they cited similar authorities, and some articles under this name later appeared in Cannon's *Theological Inquirer*. Houston claimed that Brown 'encouraged and flattered' Cannon at this time and 'exercised his pen on the same topics': PC 1/4032, Additional Notes, p. 2. The list of authorities cited by 'Varro' also corresponds with books which Brown was reading at that time: PC 1/4032, Notes, Brown to Houston, 13 Aug. 1813. Finally, 'Varro' admitted knowing both Houston and Eaton, as did Brown: *CPR*, 17 Dec. 1814, cols. 793–4. A pencilled note beside one of Varro's contributions in the British Library copy of the *Theological Inquirer*, i (1815), pp. 96–102, identifies him as Leigh Hunt but after careful checking I doubt this.

28 Burdon had used the nom-de-plume of 'Veritas' earlier in his life, see Emmanuel Coll., MS 269, Burdon Papers, Burdon to *Morning Post*, 1790, pp. 135–7. He was also presenting similar arguments under his own name in *FCM*, iii (1813), pp. 357–9, 405–7. But it was a common pseudonym and Burdon seems generally to have used his own name at this time. It might equally have been Baverstock; he was deeply embroiled in the controversy and had written to Cobbett's newspaper on earlier occasions: Baverstock, *Treatises on Brewing*, pp. xxi–xxii.

29 PC 1/4032, Notes, pp. 10–12.

30 Brown furnished him with various sceptical texts though he was already familiar in 1813 with the major sceptical works of Voltaire, Volney and Paine. He admitted that *Ecce Homo* was inclined towards 'jocularity' but denied its having any lewd implications: *CPR*, 16 Oct. 1813, col. 488; 30 Oct. 1813, cols. 545–52; 13 Nov. 1813, cols. 617–18; he admitted his doubts on 4 Dec. 1813, cols. 716–17. Houston was requested to prepare a letter outlining these 'doubts and difficulties' for Cobbett 'to put his name to': PC 1/4032, Notes, Brown to Houston, 1 Jan. 1814, p. 13.

31 Confirmation of Perkin's real identity was made by Houston in PC 1/4032, Notes, p. 2, and some years later by Richard Carlile, *Republican*, 12 May 1826.

32 J.M. Robertson, *A History of Freethought in the Nineteenth Century*, 2 vols. (1929), i, p. 61.

33 See the essay on Perkins in Christopher Hill, *Puritanism and Revolution: Studies in Interpretation of the English Revolution of the Seventeenth Century* (1968), pp. 212–33, and *The Century of Revolution, 1603–1714* (1961), p. 81, where he points out that Perkins had been particularly influential amongst those who 'received some legal education at one of the Inns of Court'. Cannon might have picked up the tail-end of this tradition at Staple Inn.

[34] Rev. Erasmus Perkins, 'On Religious Persecution', Letters I–VIII, *CPR*, 3 Dec. 1814, cols. 730–6; 17 Dec. 1814, cols, 797–800; 31 Dec. 1814, cols. 853–8; 7 Jan. 1815, cols. 19–24; 21 Jan. 1815, cols. 92–6; 4 Feb. 1815, cols. 152–8; 18 Feb. 1815, cols. 214–17, 250–6; 8 April 1815, cols. 433–7; cf. Caroline Robbins, *The Eighteenth-Century Commonwealthman* (Cambridge, Mass., 1959), pp. 5–18, 223–31, 291.

[35] *CPR*, 25 March 1815, col. 378.

[36] *Ibid.*, 25 Feb. 1815, col. 251; see also 21 Jan. 1815, cols. 92–6.

[37] *Ibid.*, 3 Dec. 1814, cols. 732–3; 17 Dec. 1814, cols. 798–800; 31 Dec. 1814, cols. 853–8; 7 Jan. 1815, cols. 20–3; 4 Feb. 1815, col. 155; 25 Feb. 1815, col. 251.

[38] *Ibid.*, 7 Jan. 1815, col. 23.

[39] *Ibid.*, 21 Jan, 1815, col. 96.

[40] *TI*, i (1815), pp. 60, 242–7.

[41] *Ibid.*, pp. 352–3.

[42] See, for example, the exchange between 'Varro' and 'Justus' in *CPR*, 24 Dec. 1814, cols. 819–21; 7 Jan. 1815, cols. 24–6; 21 Jan. 1815, cols. 87–91; Drummond was himself a noted pseudonymous controversialist who published lengthy defences of *Oedipus Judaicus* under the names of 'Vindex', 'Biblicus' and 'Candidus'. On Drummond, see Robertson, *Freethought*, i, pp. 82–3; also *TI*, i (1815), pp. 350–3.

[43] *Mary Shelley's Journal*, ed. F.L. Jones (Norman, 1947), pp. 36–7.

[44] See, for example, the fragment of correspondence between Shelley and someone unknown, dated 12 Aug. 1812, found floating in a bottle near the entrance of Milford House on 12 Sept.: HO 42/127. News of his typically flamboyant action of dropping bottles containing his radical writings into the sea was getting back to the authorities. See Kenneth Neill Cameron, *The Young Shelley: Genesis of a Radical* (1951), p. 174. Especially interesting is his strongly infidel 'Declaration of Rights', including the poem 'The Devil's Walk', sent to the Home Office by Samuel Bembridge of Barnstaple, 19 Aug. 1812: HO 42/127.

[45] Cameron, *Young Shelley*, pp. 259, 397.

[46] This is in the letter signed 'Guilelmus', *CPR*, 4 Sept. 1813, col. 301.

[47] Cameron, *Young Shelley*, pp. 219–20.

[48] *Mary Shelley's Journal*, pp. 413–14.

[49] *Ibid.*, pp. 25–47.

[50] Their appearance in the *Theological Inquirer* has intrigued and puzzled Shelley scholars for decades. The discovery was first made by Bertram Dobell in 1885 and published in the *Athenaeum*, 7 March 1885. He also correctly identified 'F', the commentator on 'Queen Mab', as R.C. Fair. A few further details on Fair were added in Newman Ivey White, *Shelley*, 2 vols. (New York, 1940), ii, pp. 696–7. Erasmus Perkins was correctly identified as a radical named George Cannon by Louise S. Boas in 'Erasmus Perkins and Shelley', *Modern Language Notes*, lxx (1955), pp. 408–13. Unfortunately, this article, whilst throwing some light on the affair, is full of errors, including the suggestion that Cannon migrated to America c. 1820 and was dead by 1826. Later writings by Shelley scholars have added little to this article. See Richard

Holmes, *Shelley: The Pursuit* (1974), pp. 279–80; Newman Ivey White, *The Unextinguished Hearth, Shelley and his Contemporary Critics* (New York, 1966), pp. 45–52.

51 *TI*, i (1815), pp. 6–24, 121–31.

52 *Ibid.*, pp. 242–5.

53 *Ibid.*, pp. 34–9, 105–10, 205–9, 358–62, 446–8. The identification of 'F' as Fair is revealed in a rhyming riddle, *ibid.*, pp. 417–18. Information about Fair can be pieced together from his letter to Francis Place of 9 March 1831, Add. MS 27808, and a note which describes him as a shoemaker, fo. 129; he was included in the *Polemic Fleet of 1816* and there are various references to him in the spy reports of 1816–17, esp. HO 42/162.

54 For more detailed discussion of the relationship between these two works, see Gerald McNiece, *Shelley and the Revolutionary Idea* (Cambridge, Mass., 1969), pp. 123–4, and I. McCalman, 'Popular Radicalism and Freethought in Early Nineteenth-Century England: A Study of Richard Carlile and his followers, 1815–32', MA thesis, Australian National University, 1975, pp. 145–9.

55 *TI*, i (1815), pp. 209, 362.

56 *Ibid.*, preface, signed E.P., 30 Aug. 1815.

57 *Ibid.*, pp. 49–59, 87–93, 182–5; for an example of an anti-infidel extract from the *Arminian Magazine*, see pp. 112–13.

58 *Ibid.*, pp. 44–9, 201–5, 233–40, 297–300, 385–8, 392–400, 458–60, 461–80.

59 CLRO, Sessions Records: Oaths and Declarations of Dissenting Ministers, 1813–43, George Cannon, 9 Nov. 1815.

60 Add. MS 27808, fo. 322. Cannon was in Tothill Fields prison at the time, and, unlike Fair and Wedderburn, did not reply to Place's letter of inquiry. For his prominence in the society by 1816, see TS 11/199/868 (i), *Polemic Fleet of 1816*.

61 M.E. Ogborn, *Staple Inn* (1964), pp. 15–16; 'Account of the Staple Inn taken from Mr Archibald Day's Presidential Address', *Institute of Actuaries Year Book 1928–9* (1929), pp.7–8.

62 Pisanus Fraxi (pseud.) [Henry Spencer Ashbee], *Index librorum prohibitorum: Being Notes Bio-Biblio-Icono-graphical and Critical, on Curious and Uncommon Books* (1877), p.114.

63 See Robert Robson, *The Attorney in Eighteenth-Century England* (Cambridge, 1959), pp. 134ff; G. Millerson, *The Qualifying Associations* (1964), pp. 47ff, 121ff.

64 *Autobiography of Francis Place*, p. 27.

65 *Town*, 3 June, 19 Aug., 26 Aug., 4 Nov. 1837.

66 *Ibid.*, 26 Aug. 1837.

67 PC 1/44/A161, Barlow, c. Aug. 1799.

68 PC 1/40/A132, Milner, 2 July 1797.

69 For earlier instances of this phenomenon, see Pat Rogers, *Grub Street: Studies in a Subculture* (1972), esp. pp. 207–11; Darnton, *Literary Underground*, esp. pp. 1–40.

70 PC 1/4032, Notes, p. 2.

71 *Republican*, 12 May 1826.

72 PC 1/4032, Notes, and Additional Notes, *passim*; also TS 11/47/183, memorial of George Houston, 25 May 1814, and minutes of information given by Charles Mitcham, 13 May 1814.

73 Clarke (pseud.), *Rival Princes*, ii, p. 265.

74 PC 1/4032, Additional Notes, p. 2.

75 See PC 1/4032, Notes, pp. 14–15, and Additional Notes, p. 1.

76 *Mary Shelley's Journal*, p. 37.

77 He denied seeking a remission of sentence which was anyway nearly over, but hinted that it might be necessary to put him out of reach of Cobbett and his friends. For his successful infidel career in America, see Albert Post, *Popular Freethought in America, 1825–50* (New York, 1943), pp. 45ff. For an account of a Grub Street informer who similarly retained a revolutionary animus, see Darnton, 'A Spy in Grub Street', *Literary Underground*, pp. 41–70.

78 See Perkin, *Origins of Modern English Society*, pp. 255–6; John Gross, *The Rise and Fall of the Man of Letters: English Literary Life since 1800* (Harmondsworth, 1969), esp. pp. 12–28; J.W. Saunders, *The Profession of English Letters* (1964), pp. 116–45.

79 *Scourge*, 2 Nov. 1812, pp. 379–80.

80 *CPR*, 3 Dec. 1814, col. 731.

81 *The Times*, 11 June 1831, p. 3. It was probably a false claim; at the time of the 1841 Census he only had three children living with him.

82 TS 11/199/868 (i), *Polemic Fleet*.

83 *FCM*, i (1811), p. 112; see also Gwyn A. Williams, *Rowland Detrosier: A Working Class Infidel, 1800–34* (York, 1965), pp. 20–1, on the appeal of 'clerisy' to infidels.

84 Rogers, *Grub Street*, pp. 206, 226, 299; Philip Pinkus, *Grub Street Stripp'd Bare* (1968), pp. 81–2.

85 Fraxi (pseud.) [Ashbee], *Index librorum prohibitorum*, p. 114.

86 See the extensive dossier in TS 11/978/3560, Rex vs. D.I. Eaton, and the retrospective report in HO 42/183, C. Bourchier to H. Hobhouse, 8 Jan. 1817.

87 *Scourge*, 1 Dec. 1814, p. 457.

88 Guildhall Lib., Register of Dissenters' Meeting Houses, 8 March 1810, Cateaton Street. For a brief description of Hodgson, see *DNB*, pp. 966–7. I am also indebted to Dr Daniel McCue of Boston College for information about Eaton's associates at this time.

89 HO 42/124, Gifford, 29 June 1812 (includes confiscated handbills); HO 42/125, 7 July 1812; HO 48/15, Law Officers – Cases and Reports; HO 65/2, Police Letter Book, 1811–20, letters between Beckett and Gifford, 11 June and 8 July 1812.

90 *CPR*, 31 Dec. 1814, col. 855; 7 Jan. 1815, cols. 20–2; 8 April 1815, col. 433.

91 TS 11/47/183, Houston memorial, and affidavit, 9 Nov. 1814.

92 See, Address of Daniel Isaac Eaton, attached to *The Moseiade* and *A Preservative Against Religious Prejudices* (1812), p. 2; Hone, *Cause of Truth*, p. 228.

93 Quoted in Theophilia C. Campbell, *The Battle of the Press, as Told in the Story of the Life of Richard Carlile* (1899), p. 75.

94 HO 42/136, disturbances, 1813, particulars as stated by Kidder relative to Margarot.

⁹⁵ See, John Gale Jones, *Original Oration, November 29, 1796, in the Great Room in Brewer Street, on the resignation of General Washington* (1796); HO 42/30, handbill, Westminster Forum, 23 Feb. 1797; HO 42/40, poster, 6 April 1797, extract of speeches, 27 Feb., 2 March 1797, Gale Jones, farewell oration, 16 March 1797. On the Seditious Meetings Bill, see Henry Jephson, *The Platform*, 2 vols. (1892), i, pp. 254–8.

⁹⁶ *Satirist*, ii (May 1808), pp. 237–8; for further details of their activities, see *Satirist*, iv (Jan. 1809), p. 11; vii (Aug. 1810), p. 128; (Sept. 1810), pp. 273–87.

⁹⁷ *RM*, i (1822), pp. 536–66.

⁹⁸ Bodleian Lib., MS Eng. hist., Burdett Papers, b 199, fos. 7ff (debate on Gale Jones's committal); *A Warning to Frequenters of Debating Clubs; being a short history of the rise and progress of those clubs; with a report on the trial and conviction of John Gale Jones, the manager of one of them called the British Forum* (1810), esp. pp. 1–27; see also the retrospective comments in HO 42/143, *Rules and Regulations of the British Forum* (1815), pp. 11–31.

⁹⁹ Preston, *Life*, pp. 20–1.

¹⁰⁰ For two excellent examples of this stance on enthusiasm, see *TI*, i (1815), pp. 3–4, preface by E.P., 30 Aug. 1815; and 'Varro' on 'Liberty of the Press and Free Inquiry', *CPR*, 24 Dec. 1814, cols. 816–23.

¹⁰¹ *Axe to the Root*, iii [1817], pp. 36–42.

¹⁰² Reid, *Infidel Societies*, p. 19.

¹⁰³ *CPR*, 18 Feb. 1815, cols. 215–16, 250–6.

¹⁰⁴ See, for example, *CPR*, 17 Dec. 1814, cols. 797–8; 18 Feb. 1815, cols. 252–6; *TI*, i (1815), p. 84, article by 'Eunomus Wilkins' [Cannon], and pp. 261–2, 268–9, for others possibly also by him.

¹⁰⁵ Wedderburn, *Letter to the Archbishop of Canterbury* [1820], p. 19. For discussion of Cannon's authorship, see below pp. 153–4.

¹⁰⁶ *Newcastle Magazine*, iii (1821), pp. 316–17.

¹⁰⁷ Smith, *Politics of Language*, pp. 99–101.

¹⁰⁸ Spence, *Pig's Meat*; see also, Chase, 'Land and the Working Classes', p. 75; Gallop, *Pig's Meat*, p. 16.

¹⁰⁹ Add. MS 27808, Hone to Place, 23 Sept. 1830, fo. 315.

¹¹⁰ *Important Trial* (1803 edn), p. 9.

¹¹¹ Add. MS 27808, fo. 287.

¹¹² Boulanger (pseud.) [Holbach], *Christianity Unveiled* (New York, 1795), pp. 236–7 (annotations), 95, 102–3, p. 238 (reverse of end title page).

¹¹³ *A Letter from the author to a friend*, annotation p. 9, bound with Spence, *Important Trial*, (1803 edn), annotation p. 10, BL 900.h. 24 (i).

¹¹⁴ See Harrison, *Second Coming*, p. 222.

5 SPENCE'S SUCCESSOR, 1814–17

¹ *Report from the Committee of Secrecy, 19 Feb. 1817* (1817); *CPR*, 1 March 1817, col. 268, 8 March 1817, cols. 301–10.

² Add. MS 27809, fos. 45, 59–66.

³ See, for example, Parsinnen, 'Revolutionary Party', p. 274.

[4] Hone, *Cause of Truth*, p. 270.
[5] Evans, *Life of Spence*, p. 24.
[6] See John Wilson, *Introduction to Social Movements* (New York, 1973), pp. 192–223; Clifford Geertz, 'Centers, Kings and Charisma: Reflections on the Symbolics of Power', *Culture and its Creators*, eds. J. Ben David and T.N. Clark (Chicago, 1977), pp. 150–71.
[7] [Thomas Evans], *Address of the Society of Spencean Philanthropists, To all Mankind, On the means of promoting Liberty and Happiness* [1819]; see also TS 11/204/875 (ii), G.R., 17 Dec. 1816.
[8] Evans, *Life of Spence*, pp. 3–4; HO 42/168, Thomas Evans to T.J. Evans, 18 Sept. 1814.
[9] Davenport, *Life of Spence*, p. 5; Add. MS 27808, R.C. Fair to Place, 9 March 1831, fos. 319–20.
[10] See for example, TS 11/201/876 (i), 1 July 1816, fo. 355; Evans, *Life of Spence*, pp. 14–15.
[11] Thompson, *Making*, esp. pp. 674–6. He observes that 'the step from informal tavern group to the avowed Radical club … was a long one'.
[12] See [Evans] *Address and Regulations* (1815), esp. pp. 8–10; TS 11/202/871 (ii), G.R., 14 Jan. 1817. Details of the Spencean organisation can be gauged from reports in TS 11/204/875 (ii), Dec. 1816–Jan. 1817; also HO 42/155–8; cf. *A New Edition of the Rules and Regulations etc. of the British Forum* (1808), and West, *Tavern Anecdotes* (1825), pp. 126–7.
[13] Parsinnen, 'Revolutionary Party', p. 275.
[14] See TS 11/199/868 (i) [Evans], *Address and Regulations* (1815); *IW*, 27 Aug. 1815, p. 277; 17 Sept. 1815, pp. 301–2; 22 Oct. 1815, p. 340; 14 April 1816, p. 117; 30 June 1816, p. 212; *Christian Policy*, pp. iii–viii, 1–48. He claimed to have produced articles in the same vein in the *Day* and *Traveller* at around this time, but I have been unable to trace them.
[15] Williams, *Artisans and Sans-Culottes*, p. 109.
[16] *Quarterly Review*, xvi (Oct. 1816), p. 271.
[17] Gertrude Himmelfarb, *The Idea of Poverty: England in the Industrial Age* (New York, 1984), pp. 207–29; Craig Calhoun, *The Question of Class Struggle: Social Foundations of Popular Radicalism during the Industrial Revolution* (Oxford, 1982), esp. pp. 75–105; G. Ionescu and E. Gellner (eds.), *Populism* (1969), pp. 158–61; Michael Roe, *Kenealy and the Tichborne Cause: A Study in mid-Victorian Populism* (Melbourne, 1974), esp. pp. 173–7; W.D. Rubinstein, 'British Radicalism and the "Dark Side" of Populism', unpublished paper, 1985, pp. 1–58. I am grateful to Dr Rubinstein for furnishing me with a copy and permitting me to quote from it. The paper will appear in a book of his essays to be published by the 'Past and Present' Society.
[18] For discussion of the tract's ideas and influence, see Noel Thompson, *The People's Science*, pp. 192–4; Himmelfarb, *Idea of Poverty*, pp. 209–10; McCalman, 'Popular Radicalism and Freethought', pp. 17–19. For Evans's discussion of Paine's tract, see *Christian Policy*, pp. 12–16.
[19] Rubinstein, '"Dark Side" of Populism', p. 4.
[20] His critique of Russia is developed even more fully in *IW*, 27 Aug. 1815, p. 227; G. Claeys, 'Documents: Thomas Evans and the Development of

Spenceanism, 1815–16: Some Neglected Correspondence', *Bulletin of the Society for the Study of Labour History*, 48 (1984), p. 24, argues that Evans was unusual in his Russophobia. He certainly developed his ideas more fully than most radicals, but the attitude was common in the post-war radical press.

21 On the idea of the 'Norman Yoke', see Hill, *Puritanism and Revolution*, pp. 58–125.

22 Cf. Rubinstein, '"Dark Side" of English Populism', pp. 6, 18.

23 Cf. Roe, *Kenealy*, pp. 165, 185; Karel D. Bicha, 'Prairie Radicals: A Common Pietism', *Journal of Church and State*, 18 (1976), pp. 79–94.

24 See Rubinstein, '"Dark Side" of English Populism', pp. 5, 8–9.

25 *Quarterly Review*, xvi (Oct. 1816), p. 271.

26 Rubinstein, '"Dark Side" of English Populism', p. 4.

27 See Prothero, *Artisans and Politics*, esp. pp. 22–70.

28 Rubinstein, '"Dark Side" of English Populism', p. 19.

29 Cf. Smith, *Politics of Language*, esp. pp. 69–109.

30 See, for example, TS 11/204/875 (ii), G.R., 27 Jan. 1817, fo. 903; HO 42/159, C.H., [1817], reporting on 22 Dec. 1816.

31 *CPR*, 14 Dec. 1816, col. 748; *Reformists' Register*, Oct. 1817, p. 426; Add. MS 36623, 'Memoranda', 6 Oct. 1816; *Quarterly Review*, xvi (Oct. 1816), pp. 270–1.

32 I am grateful to Malcolm Chase for this information.

33 Preston, *Life*, pp. 24–5, 32.

34 See *Forlorn Hope*, i [1817], pp. 15–16; ii, pp. 36–8; *Axe to the Root*, i [1817], pp. 6–7; ii, pp. 17–20; iii, p. 46; S & S [Wedderburn], *Christian Policy*, pp. 3–5, 11–12; *Essay on Printing* [1818], pp. 1–7.

35 Davenport, *Life of Spence*, pp. 15–16, 20, 22.

36 *High Treason! Fairburn's Edition of the Whole Proceedings on the Trial of James Watson, Senior, for High Treason ...*, 2 vols. (1817), ii, p. 53; Add. MS 27809, fos. 59, 65–6.

37 HO 42/168, Boswell to Sidmouth, 4 July 1818.

38 *Christian Policy*, pp. iv–viii.

39 HO 42/168, Account of subscriptions to defray the legal expenses occurred in the defence of Watson *et al.*, [1817].

40 Noel Annan, 'The Intellectual Aristocracy', *Studies in Social History. A Tribute to G.M. Trevelyan*, ed. J.H. Plumb (1955), p. 243; for some interesting attempts at such radical genealogical work, see Deborah Gorham, 'Victorian Reform as a Family Business: The Hill Family', in *The Victorian Family: Structure and Stresses*, ed. A.S. Wohl (1978), pp. 119–47; Paul Pickering, 'The Social Culture of Chartism, 1837–42', unpublished BA Hons. thesis, Latrobe University, 1982, pp. 17–26, 33–8.

41 TS 11/199/868 (i), *Polemic Fleet*; HO 40/8 (4), 31 Jan. 1818, fo. 167.

42 HO 40/7 (2), C, 9 Oct. 1817.

43 These included John, James, Charles and Thomas Savage, most of whom were expelled from the Freethinking Christians for political extremism in 1819, see William Stevens, *An Antidote to Intolerance and Assumption; or, a Peep into Mr Coate's view of the only true Church of God, denominated Freethinking Christians ...* (1821).

44 See reports of 1816–17 in TS 11/204/875 (ii) and HO 42/158.

45 HO 40/8 (4), w–r [Edwards], 31 Jan. 1818, fo. 167.

46 HO 42/143, Whitfield, [1815–16]; cf. Thompson, *Making*, p. 673, who suggests that Watson had been in 'underground political work for a number of years'.

47 Ellen Corbold, Maria and Margaret Foulkes, TS 11/203/873, [1816], fo. 756; and *The Trials at large of Arthur Thistlewood, gent, James Watson, the elder, surgeon, Thomas Preston, cordwainer and John Hooper, labourer, for high treason ... June 9, 1817* (W. Lewis, 1817), p. 244.

48 HO 42/143, Whitfield; TS 11/200/869, first secret report of conversations with older Watson in Coldbath Fields, Vincent Dowling.

49 HO 42/177, A. Thistlewood to Julian, 11 June 1818.

50 See TS 11/197/859; TS 11/200/869; HO 40/10 (3); HO 44/4, fos. 360ff, testimony of John Castle; HO 42/168; *Trials ... of Thistlewood, Watson, Preston and Hooper*, esp. pp. 135–43; Add. MS 27809, fos. 11–45. For good secondary accounts, see J.C. Belchem, 'Henry Hunt and the Evolution of the Mass Platform', *EHR*, xciii (1978), esp. pp. 742–7, and 'Republicanism, Popular Constitutionalism and the Radical Platform in Early Nineteenth-Century England', *Social History*, 6 (1981), pp. 5–6; T.M. Parsinnen, 'Association, Convention and Anti-Parliament in British Radical Politics, 1771–1848', *EHR*, lxxxviii (1973), pp. 504–33; Prothero, *Artisans and Politics*, pp. 74–91.

51 *Memoirs of Hunt*, iii, pp. 327–36; TS 11/200/869 (i), Hunt to Preston, 10 Nov. 1816; TS 11/202/871 (ii), Report of Proceedings at third public meeting held at Merlin's Cave, Spa Fields, 10 Jan. 1817, p. 3.

52 HO 40/3, C.H., 29 Jan. 1817, fo. 38; HO 40/8 (4), w–r, Jan.–Feb. 1818, fo. 167; HO 40/9 (5), James Hanley to Litchfield, [1816]; TS 11/199/868 (i), interviews T. and T.J. Evans, 9 Feb. 1817; TS 11/199/868 (ii), James Hanley, 9 Dec. 1816; TS 11/204/875 (ii), interviews T. and T.J. Evans, 9 Feb.–10 March 1817.

53 TS 11/199/868 (i), *Polemic Fleet*.

54 HO 42/155, Spa Fields petition, 15 Nov. 1816.

55 *Christian Policy*, pp. 14, 29, 31.

56 TS 11/199/868 (i), J.E., 12, 22 Dec. 1816; TS 11/204/875 (ii), G.R., 11 Dec. 1816–30 Jan. 1817; HO 40/3, Barclay, Feb. 1817, fo. 39; HO 42/158, Mulberry Tree, 9 Jan. 1817; Cock, 15 Jan. 1817; Mulberry Tree, 16 Jan. 1817; 19 Counter Street, 28 Jan. 1817; Mulberry Tree, 30 Jan. 1817.

57 HO 40/4 (6), Hanley, 15 Nov. 1816.

58 See, for example, HO 40/8 (4), w–r, Jan.–Feb. 1818, fo. 167; HO 40/4 (6), Hanley, 15 Nov. 1816; HO 40/9 (5), Hanley to Litchfield (n.d.); HO 40/10 (2), examinations of Moggridge, 2, 3 May [1817]; HO 42/159, statement of A.B., [1816]; TS 11/200/869, Dowling, first secret report of conversations with Watson in Coldbath Fields.

59 HO 42/172, 'A Statement of the grounds on which the several persons apprehended ...', [1817].

60 HO 40/3, C.H., 29 Jan. 1817, fo. 38; HO 40/9 (2), narrative of Oliver; HO 40/9 (5), Hanley to Litchfield, (n.d.); HO 42/158, G.R., 29 Jan. 1817.

61 For details of the conspirators' preoccupation with these talismanic artifacts,

see TS 11/199/868 (ii), John Stafford, 30 Nov. 1816; HO 40/3, proceedings of the Spa Fields meeting, fos. 14, 16, 24, 41; HO 42/160, testimony of Castle, Feb. 1817. This is not to deny that such symbols could have a significant effect in mobilising the London crowd to riot, as young Watson proved when he ran off towards the tower carrying the tri-colour and invoking the example of Wat Tyler.

[62] TS 11/200/869, Dowling, first secret report.

[63] TS 11/203/873, Preston's examination, 4 Dec. 1816; TS 11/200/869, Dowling, first secret report.

[64] See, for example, HO 44/5, questions to Bowdens, fo. 476; HO 42/158, Mulberry Tree, 6 Feb. 1817; HO 42/168, NN, 17, 22 Feb. 1817.

[65] *Trials ... of Thistlewood, Watson, Preston and Hooper*, p. 135; TS 11/197/859, brief for the Crown.

[66] In addition to Castle there was Spitalfields tailor James Hanley [A]; John Shegog [JS, B], an artisan-preacher from Lambeth; John Emblin [J.E.] who was employed by Stafford in December 1816 to watch the Spenceans at the Cock; John Williamson [C], a trimming-weaver from Spitalfields; Vincent Dowling, a shorthand writer and ex-Jacobin; T. Thomas who may have been a disguised policeman; George Ruthvens [G.R.] who certainly was one, as well as a series of unidentified police officers E. F. H. N.; the infamous Oliver also put in a brief appearance early in 1817 before heading North; and bust-modeller George Edwards [w–r] joined the government payroll early in 1818. This information is derived from sifting numerous reports. The best single source is a spy key contained in HO 40/9 (4); for Hanley's recruitment, see TS 11/199/868 (i); for an early report from Shegog, TS 11/204/875 (ii), 23 Jan. 1817; for Emblin's recruitment, TS 11/201/870 (i), Stafford, 12 Dec. 1816, fo. 388; on Williamson, see depositions and reports, Sept.–Oct. 1817 in TS 11/197/859, fos. 3–7; Dowling's secret reports are in TS 11/200/869; for an early report from Thomas, see HO 40/3, 14 Dec. 1816, fo. 34; on Oliver, see HO 40/9 (2), narrative of Oliver, and depositions of Charles Pendrill in *CPR*, 16 May 1818, cols. 552–64; on Edward's recruitment, see HO 42/158, 29 Jan. 1817; HO 40/8 (4), 31 Jan. 1818, fo. 167. So many overlapping reports enable considerable cross checking for accuracy; the most reliable seem to be those of Ruthvens, Hanley, then Williamson; the least reliable are undoubtedly those of Shegog who was sensationalist, obsessively anti-infidel and was suspected by the conspirators by winter 1817.

[67] HO 40/3, Thomas, 14 Dec. 1816, fo. 34.

[68] HO 42/168, NN, 22 Feb. 1817.

[69] Add. MS 27818, T. Hardy to O'Connor, 6 Oct. 1817, fos. 262–3.

[70] TS 11/197/859, brief for the Crown.

[71] On Miles, see *Satirist*, 1 June 1808, p. 427; correspondence between Hardy and Miles, 1808–15, in Add. MS 27818, fos. 85, 154, 206. A son W.A. Miles also had radical leanings. He bore a strong resemblance to the Regent and was possibly a bastard son: see Place's comments, Add. MS 35146, Diaries, 20 May 1827.

[72] TS 11/200/869, Dowling, second secret report as a result of private conversations with Watson in Coldbath Fields. Watson might have been referring to the

merchant and Freethinking Christian patriarch, Samuel Thompson, who gave Preston and Hooper a covert contribution just before the uprising; TS 11/197/860, brief against Thistlewood; HO 40/7 (1), A, Sept. 1817; HO 42/156, 3, 6 Dec. 1816.

73 *CPR*, 14 Dec. 1816, cols. 746–50.

74 TS 11/200/869 (i), Dowling, fourth public examination of Preston; TS 11/203/874, Newman to Litchfield, 27 Jan. 1817; HO 40/3, Thomas, 14 Dec. 1816, and the retrospective report by Banks, HO 42/200, BC, 12 Dec. 1819.

75 See, for example, HO 42/182, intercepted letter from Moggridge, 26 Dec. 1818.

76 HO 42/168, account of subscriptions occurred (*sic*) in the defence of Watson *et al.*; TS 11/197/859, payment for Hooper.

77 See the detailed account and republished letters in *Sherwin's Political Register*, 26 Sept. 1818.

78 Prothero, *Artisans and Politics*, pp. 73–6; Belchem, 'Hunt and the Mass Platform', pp. 742–7, and 'Republicanism, Constitutionalism and the Radical Platform', pp. 5–6; Parsinnen, 'Revolutionary Party', p. 271 and 'Association, Convention and Anti-Parliament', pp. 515–16.

6 TAVERN DEBATING CLUBS: SPENCEAN STRATEGY AND CULTURE, 1815–17

1 See Peter Clark, *The English Alehouse: A Social History, 1200–1830* (1983), esp. pp. 145–65, 250–72, 306–32; Hill, *World Turned Upside Down*, pp. 201–2; Steven R. Smith, 'The London Apprentices as Seventeenth-Century Adolescents', *P & P*, 61 (1973), pp. 71–82; J. Redwood, *Reason, Ridicule and Religion: The Age of Enlightenment in England, 1660–1750* (1976), pp. 14–15, 35–9, 175–90; Hans Medicks, 'Plebeian Culture in the Transition to Capitalism', in *Culture, Ideology and Politics*, eds. Raphael Samuel and Gareth Stedman Jones (1982), pp. 84–113; *Autobiography of Francis Place*, esp. pp. 71–82.

2 Reid, *Infidel Societies*, p. 87; Robert J. Allen, *Clubs of Augustan London* (Cambridge, Mass., 1933), pp. 129–33; John Brewer, *Party Ideology and Popular Politics at the Accession of George III* (Cambridge, 1976), esp. pp. 149ff; John Money, 'Taverns, Coffee Houses and Clubs: Local Politics and Popular Articulacy in the Birmingham Area in the Age of the American Revolution', *HJ*, xiv (1971), pp. 15–47; Brown, *French Revolution*, esp. pp. 59, 83–5.

3 TS 11/204/875 (ii), report of G.R., 19 Dec. 1816.

4 HO 42/158, Cock, 29 Jan. 1817; HO 40/9 (4), reports of Manchester prisoners' utterances, [1817].

5 Quoted in Thompson, *Making*, p. 676.

6 Clark, *English Alehouse*, pp. 324–5.

7 Reid, *Infidel Societies*, p. 10.

8 Add. MS 27813, 'London Corresponding Society, Minute and Letter Book, 30 May–2 July 1795', fos. 77, 88, 102, 111, 117–18, 122.

9 David Goodway, *London Chartism, 1838–1848* (Cambridge, 1982), p. 172.

10 See the long description of a conversation between Evans and Johnson on the subject of private property: Evans, *Life of Spence*, p. 8.

11 HO 40/3, [1817], fo. 20.

[12] DCRO, Addington Papers, Law and Order, Sir Henry Hawley to Lord Sidmouth, 5 Jan. 1817; R. Wissell to Sidmouth, [1817]; H. Pounslett to Sidmouth, April 1817.

[13] HO 42/163, petition of Thomas Evans, 10 April 1817.

[14] Add. MS 27809, fo. 59.

[15] For example, HO 40/8 (1), A, Sept. 1817, fos. 31–2; C, 24 Sept. 1817, fos. 33–4; B, 28 Sept. 1817, fos. 39–42; C, 30 Sept. 1817, fos. 45–8. On pub 'male republics' and popular radicalism, see Brian Harrison, 'Pubs', in *The Victorian City; Images and Realities*, eds. H.J. Dyos and Michael Wolff, 2 vols. (1976), i, pp. 172–81.

[16] HO 40/3, fo. 20, and Feb. 1817, Barclay, fo. 39; HO 40/8 (2), J.S., 18 Oct. 1817, fo. 80; HO 42/158, NN, [Feb. 1817], and Mulberry Tree, 9 Jan. 1817; HO 42/172, list of publications transmitted to the Home Department by magistrates, 1817 (63 items); TS 11/200/869, fo. 143.

[17] Stan Shipley, *Club Life and Socialism and Mid-Victorian London* (1983), pp. 23–4; Hugh McLeod, *Class and Religion in the Late Victorian City* (1974), pp. 48–9, 55.

[18] HO 42/158, 13 Jan. 1817.

[19] HO 42/158, 28 Jan. 1817.

[20] HO 42/158, 15 Jan. 1817; TS 11/200/869, Dowling, 18 Dec. 1816; HO 42/160, Feb. 1817.

[21] Add. MS 27809, fos. 65–6; Thomas Frost, *Paul, the Poacher* (1848), pp. 130–1.

[22] *Satirist*, 1 May 1808, pp. 239–45.

[23] HO 42/172, *Spence's Songs*, Pts I–III.

[24] A small part of this sung by Edwards is transcribed in HO 42/158, Mulberry Tree, 16 Jan. 1817, and there is a full printed version in HO 44/3, 16 Aug. 1820, fo. 192.

[25] Transcribed from a meeting at the Bull's Head in 1820, HO 44/1, anon., April 1820.

[26] HO 42/155, n.d. [c. Nov.–Dec. 1816].

[27] HO 42/156, Gifford to Sidmouth, 8 Dec. 1816; HO 44/5, questions to Bowdens, fo. 476.

[28] See William Rose, *A Letter to the Rev. W.M. Douglas ... containing a review of the Spencean philosophy* (1817), in HO 42/165, Cookman, 15 May 1817.

[29] T. Williams, *Constitutional Politics* (1817), pp. 5–9, in HO 42/172.

[30] TS 11/202/872, *Report of the Secret Committee of the House of Lords, 23 June 1817* (1817), fo. 6.

[31] HO 40/8 (1), C, 30 Sept. 1817, fos. 45–8.

[32] See, for example, HO 42/162, Mulberry Tree, 2, 12, 13 March 1817.

[33] Cf. West, *Tavern Anecdotes*, pp. 126–7; Douglas A. Reid, 'Popular Theatre in Victorian Birmingham', in David Bradby, Louis James and Bernard Sharrat, eds., *Performance and Politics in Popular Drama: Aspects of Popular Entertainment in Theatre, Film and Television, 1800–1976* (New York, 1980), pp. 72–4. Brewer, *Party Ideology and Popular Politics*, pp. 190–1, has noted the same atmosphere of deliberate festivity and licence at many Wilkite political meetings. For an interesting if jargonistic analysis of sociability and play behaviour patterns in a modern setting, see Julian B. Rosebuck and Wolfgang Frese, *The Rendez-Vous: A Case Study of an After-Hours Club* (New York and London, 1976), pp. 48ff.

[34] For a discussion of this aspect of social movements, see Wilson, *Introduction to Social Movements*, pp. 17–20; Frank Parkin, *Middle Class Radicalism: The Social Bases of the British Campaign for Nuclear Disarmament* (Manchester and Melbourne, 1968).

[35] See E.P. Thompson's pioneering articles, 'Patrician Society, Plebeian Culture', *Journal of Social History*, 7 (1974), pp. 382–405; 'Class Struggle Without Class', pp. 133–65; Hay *et al.*, *Albion's Fatal Tree*, esp. chs. 1–2; Brewer, *Party Ideology and Popular Politics*, esp. pp. 174–84.

[36] Hill, *World Turned Upside Down*, pp. 200–2.

[37] HO 42/160, Castle's testimony, Feb. 1817.

[38] Clark, *English Alehouse*, pp. 145–65.

[39] TS 11/204/875 (ii), Mulberry Tree, 12 Dec. 1816.

[40] HO 42/158, Mulberry Tree, 16 Jan. 1817; cf. Smith, *Politics of Language*, pp. 79–109.

[41] Cf. Redwood, *Reason, Ridicule and Religion*, pp. 14–15, 35–9, 175–90; Brewer, *Party, Ideology and Popular Politics*, pp. 168–71; Richard Hendrix, 'Popular Humor and "The Black Dwarf"', *Journal of British Studies*, xvi (1976), pp. 108–28; Thompson, 'Class Struggle without Class', pp. 151–2; Robert W. Malcolmson, *Popular Recreations in English Society, 1700–1850* (Cambridge, 1973), chs. 2–4; V.V.R.G.C. Clinton-Baddeley, *The Burlesque Tradition in the English Theatre after 1660* (1952).

[42] Cf. Thompson, 'Patrician Society, Plebeian Culture', pp. 389–90.

[43] HO 42/172, Williams, *Constitutional Politics*, pp. 5, 9.

[44] HO 42/158, Mulberry Tree, 9 Jan. 1817, Nag's Head, Jan. 1817; Mulberry Tree, 30 Jan. 1817; TS 11/202/872, fo. 6.

[45] The huge national circulation of Hone's parodies can be traced through HO 42/158–70, also 175, Pilling's inventory, 3 April 1817; HO 40/9 (1); HO 49/7, Entry Book, Hobhouse to Litchfield, 13, 26 Aug. 1817, 3 Jan. 1818.

[46] Cf. Hendrix, 'Popular Humor', p. 118; Malcolmson, *Popular Recreations*, pp. 81–2; Alfred Violet, 'Rough Music or Charivari', *Folklore*, lxx (1959), p. 506; John Dunlop, *The Philosophy of Artificial and Compulsory Drinking Usage in Great Britain and Ireland* (1839), pp. 231, 242; *Rogue's Progress: An Autobiography of 'Lord Chief Baron' Nicholson*, ed. John L. Bradley (1966), pp. 245–53; Low, *Thieves' Kitchen*, p. 54; John Taylor, *From Self-Help to Glamour: The Working Man's Club, 1860–1972* (Oxford, 1972), pp. 34–5.

[47] HO 44/2, J. Brittain, 14 Feb. 1820, fo. 120; Preston, *Life*, p. 24; TS 11/199/868 (i), *Polemic Fleet*; HO 42/162, Northumberland Arms, 8 March 1817.

[48] *Spence's Songs*, Pts I–III; cf. Hobsbawm, *Primitive Rebels: Studies in Archaic Forms of Social Movement in the 19th and 20th Centuries* (New York, 1959), pp. 150–9, 171–3; Calhoun, *Class Struggle*, pp. 89, 175; Brewer, *Party Ideology and Popular Politics*, pp. 187–8.

[49] John Dunlop, *The Universal Tendency to Association in Mankind, Analysed and Illustrated* (1840), p. 197.

[50] TS 11/199/868, interview with Keenes, December 1816.

[51] *IW*, 14 April 1816, p. 117; *Christian Policy*, pp. 14, 34, 37–8, 40, 46; cf. Hill, *World Turned Upside Down*, pp. 198–9.

[52] Calhoun, *Class Struggle*, p. 101.

[53] HO 42/160, G.L., 17 Feb. 1817; HO 42/162, police report–alehouses, 17, 22, 24, 27 Feb., 1 March 1817.

[54] HO 40/7 (1), B, 26, 28 Sept. 1817; HO 40/8 (1), B, 18 July 1817, fo. 11; 8 Dec. 1817, fos. 138–9.

[55] HO 42/162, police report–alehouses, Mulberry Tree, 2, 9, 11, 16, 18 March 1817.

[56] TS 11/202/871 (ii), G.R., Cock, 12 Feb. 1817; Mulberry Tree, 13, 20, Feb. 1817.

[57] HO 42/158, anon., [Feb. 1817]; HO 42/159, T.J. Evans to Janet Evans, 16 Feb. 1817; HO 42/166, petition, 1 May 1817; HO 42/168, NN, 17 Feb. 1817; HO 42/172, J.S., 2 Dec. 1817; HO 44/5, questions to Bowdens, fo. 476; TS 11/469/1604, anon. 13 Feb. 1817; *Reformists' Register*, 25 Oct. 1817; *Forlorn Hope*, i [1817], pp. 4–6; *IW*, 18 Jan. 1818, pp. 36–7. For a general discussion of women and radicalism in this period, see I.D. McCalman, 'Females, Feminism and Freelove in an Early Nineteenth-Century Radical Movement', *Labour History*, 38 (1980), pp. 1–25.

[58] HO 42/172, Shegog, 2 Dec. 1817.

[59] See esp. reports of B, H and N, Nov.–Dec. 1817, in HO 40/8 (3–4); HO 42/172, John B., 16 Dec. 1817.

[60] HO 40/8 (3), B, 13 Nov. 1817, fos. 113–14; for other examples of attendance figures, see HO 40/7 (3), A, 13 Nov. 1817; HO 40/7 (4), H, 14 Dec. 1817; HO 40/8 (4), H, 6, 8, 13, 15 Dec. 1817.

[61] *Forlorn Hope*, i [1817], pp. 16, 51–6.

[62] *Ibid.*, p. 15.

[63] HO 40/7 (4), 14 Dec. 1817.

[64] HO 40/8 (4), 20 Jan. 1818; HO 42/173, 22 Jan. 1818.

7 BLASPHEMOUS CHAPELS: THE PREACHER AS INSURRECTIONARY, 1818–20

[1] T. Evans, *Address to the Society of Christian Philanthropists* (1818), in HO 42/191, w–r, 6 Aug. 1819; for details of the setting up of the chapel, see R. Wedderburn, 'A Few Plain Questions for an Apostate', handbill, in HO 42/190, A, 15 April 1819; see also, HO 42/180, handbill, [16 Sept. 1818], and Stafford to Clive, 28 Sept. 1818; HO 42/181, ticket 160, enclosure, Stafford to Clive, 8 Oct. 1818.

[2] HO 42/181, Stafford, 1 Oct. 1818; Glasville, 24 Oct. 1818; HO 42/182, anon., [1818]; HO 42/183, Arthur, 16 Jan. 1819.

[3] DCRO, Addington Papers, Unrest, draft bills, Francis Ludlow Holt to Lord Sidmouth, 1818.

[4] Evans, *Address to the Society of Christian Philanthropists*, pp. 18–21, and *Christian Policy in Full Practice Among the People of Harmony* (1818), in Add. MS 27808, fos. 295–303. On Shegog and Bone see Guildhall Lib., Register of Dissenters' Meeting Houses, 25 March 1817 and 22 Sept. 1817; HO 42/172, Glasville, 10 Dec. 1817; HO 42/170, J. Shegog, 5 Sept. 1817 and 5 Oct. 1817; HO 42/190, B, 29 Dec. 1818; HO 40/8(1), B, 5 Sept. 1817, fo. 15; *Axe to the Root*, v [1817], p. 78.

[5] HO 40/8(4), w–r, 31 Jan. 1818, fo. 167.

[6] HO 42/182, Stafford, 5, 9 Nov. and w–r, 11 Nov. 1818; on Watsonite radicalism in 1818, see reports of A and C, HO 42/177–182; Prothero, *Artisans and Politics*, pp. 92–107; Parsinnen, 'Association, Convention and Anti-Parliament', pp. 515–16.

[7] HO 42/158, Nag's Head, 13 Jan. 1817; TS 11/204/875 (ii), Nag's Head, 13 Jan. 1817, fo. 898.

[8] HO 40/8(4), H, 15 Dec. 1817, fo. 169; HO 42/172, N, 16 Dec. 1817.

[9] *Sherwin's Political Register*, 26 Sept. 1818; *Shamrock, Thistle and Rose*, 29 Aug. 1818; HO 42/177, H. Hunt to Thistlewood, 19 June 1818; HO 40/7(4), w–r, 31 Jan. 1818; HO 42/180, 26 Sept. 1818. Susan Thistlewood had applied to Galloway for money on 15 Feb. 1818, see enclosure, HO 42/174.

[10] Wedderburn, 'A Few Lines for a Double Faced Politician', enclosure, HO 42/202.

[11] HO 42/182, A, 2 Nov. 1818.

[12] *Ibid.*, and Wedderburn, 'A Few Plain Questions for an Apostate', enclosure, HO 42/190, A, 15 April 1819. For the numbers attending their lectures, see HO 42/181, Stafford, 19 Oct. 1818; HO 42/182, Stafford, 16 Nov. 1818, and for some transcriptions, HO 42/177, A, 26 June 1818; HO 42/181, Stafford, 8, 22 Oct. 1818; HO 42/182, Sir D. Williams to Hobhouse, 15 Dec. 1818.

[13] Guildhall Lib., Register of Dissenters' Meeting Houses, 23 April 1819; HO 42/191, Rev. Chetwode Eustace, 10 Aug. 1819; TS 11/45/167, Rex vs. Wedderburn, deposition of Joseph Wood, 13 Oct. 1819.

[14] HO 42/197, 27 Oct. 1819.

[15] Shaw: HO 42/189, Lord Mayor, 18 July 1819; HO 42/197, 18 Oct. 1819; Pinley: HO 42/198, 3 Nov. 1819; Davidson: TS 11/203/874, deposition of T. Dwyer; TS 11/205/876, depositions T. Carr and R. Woods; HO 44/4, fo. 322 (application for relief from Society for Suppression of Mendacity); Hartley: HO 44/6, 12 April 1820, fo. 38; HO 42/191, w–r, 6 Aug. 1819; Harrison: HO 44/5, fo. 483; Hill: HO 42/191, w–r, 6 Aug. 1819; HO 42/199, BC, 12 April 1820.

[16] This was Samuel Waddington, a young unmarried shoemaker, whose radical career commenced around this time (see *The Times*, 26 Aug. 1819, p. 3, and HO 42/181, Stafford, 19 Oct.; C, 26 Oct. 1819). He was not, as some historians assume, the same man as Samuel Ferrand Waddington, a well-connected former hop-merchant with a large family, who was a veteran radical and still occasionally wrote for the radical press in post-war years. (For example, HO 42/116, petition of Samuel Ferrand Waddington, 4 July 1811.)

[17] For more on these figures, see below pp. 153–62.

[18] See Prothero, *Artisans and Politics*, esp. pp. 109–25; Belchem, 'Hunt and the Mass Platform', esp. p. 751.

[19] HO 42/191, BC, 1, 2, 5 Aug. 1819; A, 2 Aug. 1819; HO 42/192, 16 Aug. 1819; on Wedderburn and the Smithfield meeting, see also HO 42/190, C, 29 June 1819; Mayor Atkins, 21 July 1819; HO 44/5, examination of B, [8 July 1819].

[20] HO 42/191, BC, 5, 8 Aug. 1819.

[21] DCRO, Addington Papers, Unrest, Lord Sidmouth to H.R.H., the Prince

Regent, 12 Aug. 1819. For details of the government's concern about and subsequent arrest of Wedderburn, see HO 49/7, 'Law Officers Entry Book, 1817–31', H. Hobhouse to G. Maule, 12 Aug. 1819; HO 42/191, Dyer and Baker's reports, 12 Aug. 1819; HO 41/25, 'Entry Book, London Disturbances, 1815–20', H. Hobhouse to Rev. Chetwode Eustace, 11 Aug. 1819, fo. 190/147, and Hobhouse to magistrates, Great Marlborough Street, 12 Aug. 1819; TS 11/45/167, Hobhouse to Treasury Solicitor, 12 Aug. 1819, and deposition, J. O'Brien, manifold writer.

22 HO 44/2, JB [John Brittain], n.d. [1820], fo. 120. This is retrospective information given to Brittain by three sailors who were Hopkins Street regulars; see also, HO 42/192, handbill, enclosure, Stafford, 16 Aug. 1819.

23 HO 42/192, C, and W. Allen, 18 Aug. 1819.

24 HO 42/192, BC, 22 Aug. 1819; HO 42/193, A and w–r, 23 Aug. 1819; BC, 24 Aug. 1819.

25 HO 42/193, BC, 23 Aug. 1819; Mayor Atkins, 25 Aug. 1819; Watson to Atkins, 26 Aug. 1819.

26 HO 42/194, anon., White Lion, 8 Sept. 1819; A, 8 Sept. 1819; JS, 9 Sept. 1819; Mayor Atkins, 13 Sept. 1819; *Black Dwarf*, 25 Aug. and 15 Sept. 1819; *Cap of Liberty*, 15 Sept. 1819; *London Alfred*, 25 Aug., 8, 15 Sept. 1819; *The Triumphal Entry of Henry Hunt, esq., into London on Monday Sept. 13, 1819* (1819).

27 See Hunt's letters in *Black Dwarf*, 27 Oct. 1819, and *Morning Chronicle*, 23 Oct. 1819. Watson and Thistlewood's replies are reprinted in *Radical Reformer*, 27 Oct. 1819. Preston's denunciation of Hunt is in HO 42/195, Preston to Hunt, 17 Sept. 1819. There are letters from Hunt, Thistlewood, Watson and Blandford in *The Times*, 25 and 26 Oct. 1819.

28 HO 42/194, BC, 15 Sept. 1819.

29 See Thistlewood's letter in *Radical Reformer*, 27 Oct. 1819, and reports of Watsonite speeches at the Finsbury meeting of 1 Nov. 1819 in *Cap of Liberty*, 3 Nov. 1819; *Black Dwarf*, 3 Nov. 1819; *London Alfred*, 10 Nov. 1819; also, Prothero, *Artisans and Politics*, pp. 118–21; Belchem, 'Hunt and the Mass Platform', pp. 763–5.

30 HO 42/194, BC, 1 Sept. 1819; HO 42/199, Lloyd, 23 Nov. 1819.

31 HO 42/195, BC, 17, 20, 21, 26, 29 Sept., 4 Oct. 1819, and J. Hanley, 20 Sept. 1819.

32 HO 42/195, 29 Sept. 1819; HO 42/196, BC, 4, 6 Oct. 1819; HO 42/196, BC, 11, 18 Oct. 1819.

33 HO 44/6, 12 April 1820, fo. 38 (retrospective); HO 42/196, BC, 6, 7 Oct. 1819; HO 42/197, BC, 11, 14, 18 Oct. 1819.

34 HO 42/196, BC, 7, 8 Oct. 1819; HO 42/197, BC, 10, 18 Oct. 1819; 'Precis of secret information furnished by C, July 1819–23 Feb. 1820', 3, 12, 14, 15 Oct. 1819; James Bryant, 21 Oct. 1819.

35 HO 42/197, BC, 22, 24 Oct. 1819; Hanley, 25 Oct. 1819; Mr Barber, Nottingham, 26 Oct. 1819; HO 42/198, Norris, Manchester, 7 Nov. 1819 (retrospective).

36 HO 42/197, précis, C, 1 Nov. 1819; HO 42/198, BC, 1 Nov. 1819; Place Coll., 40, i, *The Times*, 1 Nov. 1819 and *Democratic Recorder*, 2 Nov. 1819; for

reports of the meeting and aftermath, see also *Cap of Liberty*, 3 Nov. 1819; *Black Dwarf*, 3 Nov. 1819; *London Alfred*, 10 Nov. 1819; HO 42/197, précis, C, 5 Nov. 1819; HO 42/198, Birnie, 1 Nov. 1819; BC, 1 Nov. 1819.

[37] HO 42/197, BC, 24, 29, 31 Oct. 1819; HO 42/198, W. Plush, 3 Nov. 1819; Alex. B. Richmond, *Narrative of the Conditions of the Manufacturing Population* (1824), pp. 185–6.

[38] HO 42/199, J. Hanley, 22 Nov. 1819; see also HO 42/199, handbill, Hopkins Street chapel, 15 Nov. 1819; HO 42/197, précis, C, 5 Nov. 1819.

[39] HO 42/199, Lloyd, 23 Nov. 1819, w–r, 20 Dec. 1819, 23 Jan. 1820; HO 42/201, BC, 20 Dec. 1819; HO 79/4, 'Entry Books', H. Hobhouse to Holland Watson Congleton, 7 Jan. 1820; Prothero, *Artisans and Politics*, p. 138.

[40] HO 44/2, J. Brittain, 14 Feb. 1820, fo. 120; see also, 42/199, handbill, Hopkins Street, 29 Nov. 1819, and enclosure, J. Eshelby, 29 Nov. 1819; BC, 30 Nov. 1819, w–r, 12 Dec. 1819; HO 42/200, BC, 1 Dec. 1819, 12 Dec. 1819.

[41] HO 44/4, miscellaneous letters and papers, Feb. 1820, fo. 70. Most of those named in this section had been regular attendants and speakers at Hopkins Street. They were: Banks, Medlar, Hamer, Hayward, Hall, Shaw, Cox, Moody, Smith, Bowyer and [Parde?].

[42] HO 42/197, BC, 11 Oct. 1819 (Wedderburn's speech); see also, HO 42/199, w–r, 24 Dec. 1819.

[43] *Trial of Wedderburn*, pp. 3–5, 19–20; *Address of Wedderburn*, pp. 13–15.

[44] Wilberforce to Lord Milton, quoted in Ursula Henriques, *Religious Toleration in England, 1787–1833*, (1961), p. 206.

[45] HO 44/5, 'Examination by David Ruell, Chaplain of the House of Correction, Clerkenwell, of the religious tenets of the Cato Street prisoners', fos. 424–8, enclosure, 27 March 1820.

[46] HO 42/197, anon., Hopkins Street chapel, 18 Oct. 1819.

[47] *Address of Wedderburn*, pp. 3, 10–11; also, HO 42/198, 9 Nov. 1819, Rev. Chetwode Eustace, 11 Nov. 1819.

[48] For a discussion of the character and significance of parochialism amongst the London poor later in the century, see McLeod, *Class and Religion*, pp. 42, 44–8. Cf. O.H. Hufton, *The Poor of Eighteenth Century France, 1750–89* (Oxford, 1974), pp. 355–67.

[49] J.F. Maclear, 'Popular Anti-Clericalism in the Puritan Revolution', *Journal of the History of Ideas*, xvii (1956), p. 443.

[50] George, *English Political Caricature*, i, pp. 16–30, 84; see also, Rudé, *Paris and London in the 18th Century*, pp. 259–316.

[51] Eric J. Evans, 'Some Reasons for the Growth of English Rural Anti-Clericalism c.1750–c.1830', *P & P*, 66 (1975), pp. 84–109, has emphasised the increasing use of clerical magistrates because of administrative convenience, as well as the intensified burden of tithes, as reasons for an upsurge in rural anti-clericalism during this period. Speeches at Hopkins Street lend support to these claims, see HO 42/198, 9 Nov. 1819; Plush and Matthewson, 24 Nov. 1819.

[52] HO 42/199, Plush and Matthewson, 24 Nov. 1819. For an excellent analysis of folk anxieties and beliefs associated with death and burial, see Peter Linebaugh, 'The Tyburn Riot against the Surgeons', in Hay *et al.*, *Albion's Fatal*

Tree, pp. 65–117. Wedderburn exploited these feelings on another occasion when he claimed that agents of the government had attempted to open up the grave and to steal and burn the body of John Lees (killed at Peterloo) so as to prevent the inquest jury from seeing his 'mangled carcase': HO 42/198, Hopkins St, 8 Nov. 1819.

53 TS 11/45/167, 'Rex vs. Wedderburn', speeches of 13 Oct. 1819, reported by Plush and Matthewson.

54 HO 42/197, 18 Oct. 1819 (speeches of W. Carr and D. Shaw).

55 Wedderburn, *Horrors of Slavery*, p. 6; HO 42/193, H.P. Hocombe, 28 Aug. 1819.

56 HO 42/196, BC, 4 Oct. 1819; see also his speech of 15 Nov. 1819, HO 42/198.

57 HO 44/2, J. Brittain, 14 Feb. 1820, fo. 120.

58 Reid, *Infidel Societies*, p. 14; Rudkin, *Spence and his Connections*, pp. 17–18; cf. Rosario Villari, 'Masaniello: Contemporary and Recent Interpretations', *P & P*, 108 (1985), pp. 117–32.

59 TS 11/45/167, Rex vs. Wedderburn (transcripts of speeches).

60 *Ibid.*

61 See, for example, HO 42/195, BC, 27 Sept. 1819 (all speeches); HO 42/197, 27 Oct. 1819 (Wedderburn); HO 42/198, 15 Nov. 1819 (Davenport and others); TS 11/45/167, Rex vs. Wedderburn (transcripts of Wedderburn's speeches). One debater did make the claim that Paine had said he was entitled to one tenth of land. HO 42/196, 6 Oct. 1819.

62 *The Times*, 22 Sept. 1819, p. 3 (Wedderburn); for some examples of Waddington's biblical defences, see *The Times*, 1 Sept. 1819, p. 2; 6 Oct. 1819, p. 3; 22 Sept. 1820, p. 3; TS 11/91/290, Rex vs. Waddington, Sept. 1820; *Examination and Trial of Samuel Waddington ... Aug. 31, 1819* (1819).

63 See Smith, *Politics and Language*, pp. 154–201.

64 HO 47/177, [J?] D.E. Smith, 25 June 1818.

65 HO 42/195, 27, 29 Sept. 1819.

66 HO 42/199, Plush and Matthewson, 24 Nov. 1819; see also, HO 42/195, handbill, enclosure J. Hanley, 20 Sept. 1819; HO 42/197, 16, 26, 27 Oct. 1819; HO 42/198, 10, 15 Nov. 1819.

67 TS 11/45/167, Rex vs. Wedderburn, transcript of speech of 13 Oct. 1819; Davenport made the same point, HO 42/198, 15 Nov. 1819.

68 HO 42/196, reports of Plush and Matthewson, and BC, 6 Oct. 1819; HO 42/198, Plush, 3 Nov. 1819; for Thistlewood, see HO 44/5, testimony of Robert Adams, fo. 132.

69 HO 42/198, 8, 9 Nov. 1819; HO 42/199, Plush and Matthewson, 24 Nov. 1819.

70 Darnton, *Literary Underground*, p. 204.

71 Eileen Yeo, 'Christianity in Chartist Struggle, 1838–42', *P & P*, 91 (1981), pp. 110–11.

72 Cf. Harrison, *Second Coming*, pp. 78–9, 225–6; Valenze, 'Prophecy and Popular Literature', pp. 87–8.

73 HO 42/177, Preston to Sidmouth, 18 June 1818; HO 44/5, Preston to Sidmouth, March 1820, fo. 460. See also William Carr's similar letter to Sidmouth, HO 42/175, 9 March 1818.

[74] TS 11/199/868(i), J. Watson to R. Watson, 29 Aug. 1818; HO 42/182, *Shamrock, Thistle and Rose*, i (Aug., 1818), pp. 12–16.

[75] HO 42/195, 9 Aug. 1819.

[76] HO 42/197, 18 Oct. 1819 (Shaw's speech); HO 42/193, D. Shaw to H. Hunt, 23 Aug. 1819 (letters found on E.J. Blandford). On oaths, see HO 44/5, Edwards, fos. 271, 312; Robert Chambers, fo. 507; HO 42/193 [Aug. 1819] contains copies of the oaths. Thistlewood and Preston had also sworn oaths on the Bible in 1817, and Preston had kissed it as well: HO 40/7(2), C, 15 Oct. 1817.

[77] HO 44/5, W. Sutch, 3 March 1820; Emmanuel Francis, fo. 34; W. Simmons, 26 Feb. 1820, fo. 243; G. Edwards, March 1820, fos. 286–8; anon., 17 March 1820; T. Hazard, 3, 25 March 1820, fos. 64, 405. See also the printed poem, T. Hazard, *A True Picture of Society as displayed by certain Rich Characters towards their poor neighbours* (1819), in HO 44/5, fos. 376–8. Hazard's premises had been the suggested headquarters for the conspiracy until a last minute switch was made to Firth's Cato Street stable.

[78] HO 42/199, 24 Nov. 1819 (Walker was criticising Carlile for mixing irreligion and politics); see also HO 44/5, Ruell's examination ..., fo. 429.

[79] Cf. Harrison, *Second Coming*, pp. 39–54; Valenze, 'Prophecy and Popular Literature', pp. 87–93; Obelkevich, *Religion and Rural Society*, esp. pp. 258–62; John Rule, 'Methodism, Popular Beliefs and Village Culture in Cornwall, 1800–50', in *Popular Culture and Custom in Nineteenth Century England*, ed. Robert D. Storch (1982), pp. 48–70.

[80] Preston, *Life*, p. 36.

[81] TS 11/197/859, Williamson, 15 Oct. 1817, fo. 6.

[82] HO 44/5, Edwards, fo. 212; HO 42/200, Stafford, 8 Dec. 1819; HO 42/199, w–r, 19 Dec. 1819; HO 42/197, Hanley, 25 Oct. 1819.

[83] *Axe to the Root*, iv [1817], pp. 50–1; HO 40/7(3), C, 10 Nov. 1817. When Thistlewood announced this to a group of Spitalfields workers at the Knave of Clubs, one suggested that they stage an uprising at her funeral since 'the Almighty had ordained a day very fitting for them to do it'.

[84] HO 42/199, w–r, 22 Feb. 1820.

[85] HO 44/2, fo. 120.

[86] HO 42/192, Hocombe, 21 Aug. 1819.

[87] HO 42/195, 9 Aug. 1819; BC, 24 Sept. 1819; HO 42/199, handbill, 22 Nov. 1819; H. Eshelby, 29 Nov. 1819; TS 11/45/167, Rex vs. Wedderburn (transcripts of speeches).

[88] HO 42/179, A, 31 Aug. 1818.

[89] HO 44/4, 27–8 Jan. 1820, fo. 7; HO 44/15, B, fo. 14.

[90] HO 42/158, 15 Jan. 1817; see also, HO 42/198, 9 Nov. 1819.

[91] HO 42/191, W. Porden, 10 Aug. 1819; HO 42/194, handbill, 13 Sept. 1819.

[92] Cf. Spence, *Letter from Ralph Hodge*, p. 5; John Church, *A Few Remarks on the Scripture History of Saul and the Witch of Endor* (1816), pp. 15–17; HO 42/198, W. Plush, 1 Nov. 1819.

[93] Speech of 25 Oct. 1819, cited in *Trial of Wedderburn*, pp. 4–5.

[94] HO 44/5, Ruell, fo. 428.

[95] MS annotations, Boulanger (pseud.) [Holbach], *Christianity Unveiled* (BL copy),

pp. 232–3; cf. Thomas, *Religion and the Decline of Magic*, p. 202; McLeod, *Class and Religion*, pp. 52–3.

[96] HO 42/191, BC, 4 Aug. 1819.

[97] HO 44/5, Ruell, fos. 426–8.

[98] HO 42/198, 10 Nov. 1819.

[99] *Republican*, 3 March (*sic*) [May] 1822; see also HO 42/197, 18 Oct. 1819.

[100] Roe, *Kenealy*, pp. 170–3.

[101] Cf., for example, Louis James, 'Taking Melodrama Seriously', *History Workshop*, 3 (Spring, 1977), pp. 153–6; Bradby *et al.*, *Performance and Politics in Popular Drama*, pp. 4–14 (James), 77 (Reid), 150 (Green); Lucian W. Minor, *The Militant Hackwriter: French Popular Literature, 1800–48; its Influence Artistic and Political* (Bowling Green, Ohio, 1975), pp. 1, 23–6, 65. It is conceivable that Wedderburn acquired an early familiarity with the kindred theatrical tradition of mumming which was very strong amongst West Indian blacks. See Roger D. Abrahams, 'Pull out your Purse and Pay: A St George Mumming from the British West Indies', *Folklore*, 79 (1968), pp. 176–203, and 'British West Indies: Folk Drama and the "Life Cycle" Problem', *Folklore*, 81 (1971), pp. 241–5.

[102] HO 42/200, J.K., 19 Nov. 1819.

[103] HO 42/198, 3 Nov. (Pinley), 8 Nov. (Wedderburn), 15 Nov. 1819 [Davenport?].

[104] Cf. Raymond Mander and Joe Mitchenson, *Pantomime* (1973), esp. pp. 8–16; for Waddington's 'Black Dwarf' nickname, see HO 46/16, 'Secret Service, Miscellaneous, 1830', C.R. Edwards, 7 Jan. 1831.

[105] On Fisher, see Hill, *World Turned Upside Down*, pp. 259–68; on Dunstan and House, John Brewer, 'Theatre and Counter-Theatre in Georgian Politics: The Mock Elections at Garrat', *History Today*, 33 (1983), pp. 15–23.

[106] See HO 42/185, Capt. Littlewood, 27 March 1819; HO 42/190, C, 13 April 1819; HO 42/200, R. Bevill, 1 Dec. 1819; BC, 1 Dec. 1819; Place Coll., 40, i, *Morning Advertiser*, 2 March 1820; HO 42/197, précis of secret information, 1, 5 Nov. 1819; *The Times*, 26 Aug. 1819, p. 3; 6 Oct. 1819, p. 3; 31 Aug. 1820, p. 3; 22 Sept. 1820, p. 3; 19 Sept. 1821, p. 3; 29 June 1822, p. 4.

[107] Parsinnen, 'Revolutionary Party', pp. 275–6. When Waddington threatened to carry the murdered ministers on his back and hang them from a lamp-post, the likely response – given his size and personality – was mirth (see, for example, the crowd response to his speech at Finsbury, Place Coll., 40, i, *The Times*, 2 Nov. 1819).

[108] Quoted in John McManners, *The French Revolution and the Church* (1969), pp. 92–3.

[109] See, for example, HO 42/199, J. Eshelby, 29 Nov. 1819; HO 42/200, J.K., 19 Nov. 1819. Cf. Hill, *World Turned Upside Down*, pp. 246–8, 254.

[110] HO 44/5, J.S., 1 March 1820, fo. 23.

[111] HO 44/2, J. Brittain, 14 Feb. 1820, fo. 120.

[112] HO 42/200, BC, 12 Dec. 1819; HO 44/2, Brittain, 14 Feb. 1820, fo. 120. Followers would not reveal the whereabouts of the new venue to Brittain, but it was probably in Lambeth, see HO 41/25, 'Entry Books: London Disturbances, 1815–20', Hobhouse to Union Hall magistrates, fos. 180/213; also, HO 40/15, J.S., 8 Jan. 1820, fo. 1.

[113] HO 40/12, W. Plush, 8 April 1820, fo. 77; HO 44/1, anon., Spotted Dog, [April 1820]; Spotted Dog, 19 April 1820.

8 THE ULTRA-RADICAL PRESS: PHILOSOPHES AND POPULISTS, 1819–21

[1] Thompson, *Making*, pp. 781–843.

[2] Patricia Hollis, *The Pauper Press. A Study in Working-Class Radicalism of the 1830s* (Oxford, 1970), pp. 99–100.

[3] Joel H. Wiener, 'Thomas Davison', *BDMBR*, p. 114.

[4] This estimate is based on Dr Hollis's excellent analysis, *Pauper Press*, pp. 124–36.

[5] Rancière, 'Myth of the Artisan', p. 11.

[6] *Letter to the Archbishop; Letter to Solomon Herschell.*

[7] *High Heel'd Shoes.*

[8] *Letter to the Archbishop*, pp. 6–8; Rev. Erasmus Perkins, *A Few Hints Relative to the Texture of Mind and the Manufacture of Conscience* [1820], p. 22; cf. *Letter to Solomon Herschell*, pp. 2, 7; *CPR*, 3 Dec. 1814, col. 736.

[9] Both tracts were addressed to the Archbishop of Canterbury and both were written when the supposed authors were in gaol and being assisted by Cannon, see below pp. 159–60.

[10] See, for example, *BDMBR*, pp. 114–16; Wiener, *Radicalism and Freethought*, p. 29n; Prothero, *Artisans and Politics*, pp. 110, 113–14; 122–3; Thompson, *Making*, pp. 742, 777, 793; Hollis, *Pauper Press*, pp. 96–9.

[11] For example: *Medusa*, 17 April 1819, p. 66; 15 May 1819, pp. 100–1; 22 May 1819, pp. 105–7, 141–2. There were also several contributions under pseudonyms that he often used such as 'Friend to Reason' and 'E.P.'; see also, *Theological Comet*, 31 July 1819, p. 24; 28 Aug. 1819, p. 45; 11 Sept. 1819, p. 24; 18 Sept. 1819, pp. 65–71; 25 Sept. 1819, pp. 74–80.

[12] For example, *DM* [1820], pp. 2–16, 43–8, 78–80, 88, 101. When Davison was tried for a blasphemous libel in the *DM* (pp. 3–12) he admitted that the article had come from Erasmus Perkins's *Theological Inquirer*, being an extract from Shelley's *Refutation of Deism*: *Trial of Thomas Davison … Oct. 23, 1820* (1820), pp. 27–8.

[13] The editor and publisher are distinguished, *DM* [1820], pp. 24, 208.

[14] HO 42/189, Mayor Atkins, 17 July 1819; HO 42/191, Mayor Atkins, 3 Aug. 1819; also HO 44/4, Birnie, 28 Feb. 1820, fo. 291.

[15] HO 42/191, w–r, 6 Aug. 1819; HO 42/199, w–r, 31 Jan. 1820; HO 44/5, 30–1 Jan. 1820, fo. 255; TS 11/45/172, Rex vs. Davison; TS 11/205/876, Wm Mason, fo. 659; *The Times*, 29 Oct. 1819, p. 3; 11 April 1820, p. 2; HO 44/4, testimony of Davison, 26 Feb. 1820, fo. 241.

[16] James Griffin was a young, unemployed journeyman apothecary before being set up, probably by Mason, as editor of *Cap of Liberty*: Place Coll. I, *The Times*, 2 Nov. 1819. For an example of his acting as front-man for Cannon, see the edition (which appeared under the name of Erasmus Perkins, translator) of Chemin's *Manual of the Theophilanthropists* published by Griffin in 1822 and printed by Mason.

[17] The writer of the preface and translator of the notes signed himself 'A Pantheist, New York', but can be identified as Cannon, first, because he admitted having obtained a copy of the work from Shelley in 1815 (cf. *High Heel'd Shoes*), second, because he incorporated material written by Fair in the *Theological Inquirer* and, finally, because he used a characteristic insignia which Boas, 'Erasmus Perkins and Shelley', p. 411, thinks is a contraction of the Greek letters, 'επ'. I have made a close comparison of the notes in this edition with those in William Clarke's pirated edition of the same year (1821), and there is no doubt that Cannon's notes are more trenchantly atheistic. For useful discussions of the Benbow/Cannon edition, see White, *Shelley*, i, p. 62, and F. Buxton Forman, *The Vicissitudes of Queen Mab* (privately printed, 1887).

[18] *Biographie Universelle, Ancienne et Moderne* (Paris, 1826), v. 44, pp. 262–3.

[19] [F.-X. Swediauer], *The Philosophical Dictionary: being a judicious compilation of the opinions of all modern philosophers, in theology, legislation, political economy, metaphysics and normal philosophy* (1822); see also advertisements, 'W. Benbow's catalogue of cheap books', appended to his edition of Lord Byron, *English Bards, and Scotch Reviewers* (1823).

[20] J.B. Louvet de Couvray, *The Amours of the Chevalier de Faublas*, 4 vols. (1822). The lengthy preface and biographical memoir of the author is signed 'G.C.' (accompanied by the usual insignia). He claimed to have translated it from Didot's Paris edition of 1821. Benbow asserted in a court deposition of 1823 that he did not himself own the plates: *The Times*, 12 May 1823, p. 3; see also *The Times*, 25 Feb. 1823, p. 3; 2 May 1823, p. 3.

[21] S & S, *Essay on Printing, by a Spencean Philanthropists* (sic) [1818], p. 4.

[22] Davenport, *Life*, p. 39; see also, *Address of Wedderburn*, pp. 10–11; McCalman, 'Popular Radicalism and Freethought', pp. 116–17; cf. Williams, *Rowland Detrosier*, pp. 3–23.

[23] Saunders, *Profession of English Letters*, pp. 116–73; Gross, *Rise and Fall of the Man of Letters*, pp. 11–36; R.K. Webb, *The British Working Class Reader, 1790–1848: Literacy and Social Tension* (1955), chs. 1–2; R.D. Altick, *The English Common Reader* (Chicago, 1957), esp. chs. 4, 7.

[24] [Benbow], 'Memoir of an orator', *RM*, i [1822], p. 537; on Carlile, see McCalman, 'Popular Radicalism and Freethought', pp. 114–17; Davenport, *Life*, pp. 8–15; *Memoirs of Thomas Dolby ... late printer and publisher of Catherine Street, Strand* (1827), pp. 6–23; on Dugdale, see HO 42/172, W. Lloyd to Sidmouth, 19 May 1818.

[25] J.A. St John, 'Memoir [sic] d'un philosophe, ecrites par lui même' (unpublished MS journal, 1821–2), p. 15. This is in the private possession of Dr Sarah Spilsbury, to whom I am indebted for permission to read and quote the document. For a brief life of St John, see *DNB*. St John's friendship with Cannon is revealed in the 'Memoir', p. 14, and *High Heel'd Shoes*. For Carlile's connection with him, see Huntingdon Lib., Carlile MS, Carlile to T. Turton, 9 July 1840.

[26] HO 42/193, Waddington's examination, 23 Aug. 1819; HO 42/197, BC, 16 Oct. 1819; HO 42/198, Donald Thomas, 9 Nov. 1819; HO 44/4, 27–8 Jan. 1820, fo. 7; HO 48/185, Waddington, declaration of Press, 15 March 1819.

[27] Rhoda Helder took out a printer's licence at 10, Duke St, Smithfield, in 1820: William B. Todd, *A Directory of Printers and Others in Allied Trades, London and*

Vicinity 1800–40 (1972), p. 95. Some catalogues cite her as co-publisher of Davison's works and, after he was imprisoned in 1820, she took over sole publishing responsibility. She also published some of Cannon and Wedderburn's material. Davison's wife, Lois, became a printer and publisher from the same address in 1823, Todd, *Directory of Printers*, p. 55.

28 Dolby, *Memoirs*, p. 114. Sherwin had at the age of fourteen replaced his father as keeper of the Southwell Bridewell, a sinecure which he held for several years before being dismissed for his Paineite sympathies, see *Republican*, 3 March 1820, 30 May 1823. On Clarke and Hodgson's connections with him, see Add. MS 27818, T. Hardy to [Mrs Fletcher], 10 Feb. 1819, fo. 331. Both men have brief entries in the *DNB*.

29 Dolby, *Memoirs*, pp. 87–94; see also, Huntingdon Lib., Carlile MS, Carlile to Turton, 9 July 1840; Davenport, *Life*, p. 9; for Benbow and Dugdale, see Add. MS. 36350, Broughton Corr., J. Hunt to J. Hobhouse, fo. 169; Todd, *Directory of Printers*, pp. 61, 207.

30 *Essay on Printing*, pp. 1–4; cf. J.A. St John, 'Philosophical Essays on Government and Religion', *Republican*, 5 Oct. 1819.

31 *Radical Magazine*, i (Feb. 1821), pp. 1–16.

32 (W. Dugdale), 'Memoir', F.M.A. de Voltaire, *The Philosophical Dictionary*, 2 vols. (1843), i, p. 1.

33 Cannon's authorship of Wedderburn's defence pleas can be seen by comparing the *Trial of Wedderburn* with Cannon's articles in *CPR*, Dec. 1814–April 1815. Wedderburn admitted that he had had someone else write down his defence for him because he could not write, *Address*, p. 13, and he feigned eye trouble and had a member of the court read out the defence. HO 44/2, J. Brittain, fo. 120, confirms that the author was Cannon. Davison's defence was almost identical to Wedderburn's, as Cannon himself pointed out: Rev. Erasmus Perkins, 'Prefatory Letter to Justice Best', in *Trial of Thomas Davison* (1820), p. iii, and in *DM*, [1820], p. 203.

34 *DM* [1820], p. 211; *Annual Register*, 28 Nov. 1820, p. 489; TS 11/45/172, Rex vs. Davison.

35 See, for example, *Radical Magazine*, i (Feb. 1821), pp. 103–4; *DM* [1820], pp. 24, 39, 71–2, 89–90, 115, 126, 171–2, 201, 208–9, 222–3, 249.

36 *Address of Wedderburn*, p. 13; *Trial of Davison*, p. 17.

37 Reliable circulation figures are difficult to come by but a likely estimate for *Medusa, Cap of Liberty, Theological Comet* and *Deists' Magazine* is between 2000–6000 copies per week. A seemingly reliable report of circulation figures is contained in HO 42/197, L. Gordon, 19 Oct. 1819; see also, *Republican*, 31 Dec. 1824; Hollis, *Pauper Press*, p. 119; McCalman, 'Popular Radicalism and Freethought', p. 6. All these periodicals were effectively closed down by the Six Acts, and so lasted on average for around six months.

38 *DM* [1820], pp. 71–2.

39 Wedderburn, *High Heel'd Shoes*; *Republican*, 4 Jan. 1822; *Medusa*, 6 Nov. 1819.

40 *Radical Magazine*, i (Feb. 1821), pp. 9–14.

41 Wedderburn, *Letter to the Archbishop*, p. 19.

42 Wedderburn, *Cast-Iron Parsons, or Hints to the Public and the Legislature on Political Economy* [1820], pp. 3–11.

43   *DM* [1820], p. 172; *Cast-Iron Parsons*, p. 4.
44   John Stevenson, 'The Queen Caroline Affair', *London in the Age of Reform*, ed. John Stevenson (Oxford, 1977), pp. 117–48; Prothero, *Artisans and Politics*, pp. 132–55; Calhoun, *Class Struggle*, pp. 105–15; Thomas W. Laqueur, 'The Queen Caroline Affair: Politics as Art in the Reign of George IV', *Journal of Modern History*, 54 (1982), 417–66; Spater, *Cobbett*, ii, pp. 398–408.
45   Laqueur, 'The Queen Caroline Affair', pp. 417–66.
46   See, for example, *Republican*, 8 Dec. 1820; McCalman, 'Popular Radicalism and Freethought', pp. 61–3.
47   Spater, *Cobbett*, ii, pp. 398–400.
48   George, *English Political Caricature*, ii, pp. 130–4, 170–1.
49   [Thomas Ashe], *The Spirit of 'The Book'; or, memoirs of Caroline, Princess of Hasburgh; A Political and Amatory Romance*, 3 vols. (1811).
50   (Richardson, pub.), *Chancery Injunction*, pp. 49–51.
51   [Thomas Ashe], *A Concise Abridgement of … the Spirit of 'the Book', or Memoirs of Caroline, Princess of Hasburgh, A Political and Amatory Romance* (1812), pp. 4–85.
52   See *The Book Itself, or Secret Memoirs of an Illustrous Princess, interspersed with singular anecdotes of those persons connected with the Court of Albion: A Political, Amatory and Fashionable Work* (E. Thomas, pub., 1813); TS 11/120/329, Mary Anne Clarke, *Recollections*, pp. 66–93; [Ashe], *Memoirs and Confessions*, ii, pp. 149–243.
53   William Hone, *Napoleon and the Spots in the Sun* (1816), p. 24.
54   See MS note on BL edition, (E. Wilson, pub.), *R-y-l Stripes; or a kick from Yar-h to W-s …* (1812).
55   See, for example, *Republican*, 16 June 1820; cf. (W.P. Chubb, pub.), *The Amatory Life of the Marchioness of C-n-g-h-m …* (1820), pp. 3–7; (W. Lowe, pub.), *Secrets of the Castle! The Life of the Marchioness of Co-y-n-h-m* (n.d. [c.1820]), pp. 5–7; (J. Turner, pub.), *The Depraved Husband – a Dream* [1820], fo. 649.
56   Leslie Shephard, *John Pitts, Ballad Printer of Seven Dials, London, 1765–1844* (1969), pp. 60–1; C. Hindley, *The Life and Times of James Catnach, Ballad-Monger* (1878, repr. 1970), pp. 103–4.
57   BL, 'Satirical Songs and Miscellaneous Papers on the Return of Queen Caroline to England', A.D. [Allen Davenport], *Queen of the Isles* [1820]; Allen Davenport, *Claremont; or the Sorrows of a Prince: an elegaic poem* [1820?], pp. 6–7.
58   See *Quizzical Gazette*, xx (6 Jan. 1832), 'Obituary', pp. 158–60; *Sketches of Obscure Poets with Specimens of their Writings* (1823), pp. 91–5; [J. Mitford and W. Benbow], *Description of the Crimes and Horrors … in Warburton's private mad-house of Hoxton … called Whitmore House* (1825), pp. iii–iv, 15–21; *Scourge*, vii (April, May, June 1814), pp. 303–15, 361–7, 454–69; John Mitford, *The Important Trial of J. Mitford, Esq. on the prosecution of … Viscountess Perceval for perjury …*, ed. T.A. Phipps (1814), pp. vi–xxi, 3–57, 112.
59   *Quizzical Gazette*, xx (6 Jan. 1832), p. 160.
60   *CPPS*, x, p. xliv.
61   BL, *Pindaric Poems*, vol. xi, *A Peep into W-r Castle, after the Lost Mutton – with additions and notes by J. Mitford of Mitford Castle …* (Benbow, 1820); John

Wardroper, *Kings, Lords and Wicked Libellers: Satire and Protest 1760–1837* (1973), p. 211.

62 *A Peep into W-r Castle*, pp. 2, 17.

63 [Benbow], *RM* [1822], 'Memoirs of Mrs. Q', pp. 298–306.

64 Place Coll. 18, fos. 97–9; BL, *Pindaric Poems*, vol. xi, *A Peep at the Pxr–n, or Boiled Mutton with Caper Sauce* [1820].

65 *CPPS*, x, pp. xii, xliv–l.

66 Thompson, *Making*, p. 810.

67 TS 11/115/326, fos. 47, 78. These files contain what the Treasury Solicitor's office regarded as the most offensive pro-Caroline prints. Benbow is well represented.

68 See HO 40/15, JS, 7 July 1820, fo. 31; Place Coll. 18 (ii), *New Times*, 30 Sept. 1820; TS 11/115/326; KB 28/477/76–7.

69 Add. MS. 36541, Broughton Papers, 'Diary', July–Nov. 1820, pp. 54–5, 63, 90–3, 101, 113. For Benbow's posters, see Place Coll. 18, fos. 35, 49, 70, 72; HO 40/14, fo. 9; George, *English Political Caricature*, ii, pp. 193–4.

70 See Place Coll. 18, fos. 49, 137, 145; BL, 'Satirical Songs', fos. 23, 29, 30, 31; T. Dolby, *A Letter to the People of England upon Passing Events* [1820?], pp. 10–13.

71 HO 40/14, July–Aug. 1820, fos. 44, 95, 194–5; HO 40/15, JS, 7 July 1820, fo. 31; 10 July 1820, fo. 33.

72 W. Benbow, *Fair Play, or, Who are the Adulterers, Slanderers and Demoralizers?* (1820), pp. 6–7; *Horrida Bella; Pains and Penalties vs. Truth and Justice* (1820); *Sultan Sham and his Seven Wives, by Hudibras the Younger* (1820); *Khouli Khan; or, the Progress of Error* (1820).

73 Rubinstein, '"Dark Side" of English Populism', pp. 29–30.

74 Benbow, *Fair Play*, pp. 23–31; W. Benbow, *A Peep at the Peers: An Alphabetical List of All Peers who sit in the House … showing the offices, pensions, grants, church preferments and other things attached to the Peers and their families* (1820), pp. 1–16 (contained in Place Coll. 18, fo. 135); *Letter to the King; shewing by incontestable facts, the fundamental causes of our unexampled national distress* (1820) (Benbow's authorship of this is confirmed in Place Coll. 18 (ii), 'Books published by W. Benbow'); A.J.C. Rüter, 'William Benbow as Publisher', *Bulletin of the International Institute of Social History*, 1 (1940), pp. 3–4, argues that Benbow might have been responsible for *A Peep at the Commons* published by Dolby in 1820. In 1821 Benbow also started publishing his monumental *Crimes of the Clergy* in instalments.

75 *RM* [1822], p. 538. Hone and Cobbett might also have been associated with editions of this work. Cobbett gave the estimate of its sales: Laqueur, 'Queen Caroline Affair', p. 429.

76 HO 40/15, reports of JS, May–June 1820, fos. 16–26; HO 40/16, 17 Feb. 1821, fo. 22, 17 March 1821, fo. 23.

77 HO 40/14, Bennett to Sidmouth, 31 Aug. 1820, fos. 239–41.

78 Place Coll. 18, resolutions of meeting, 31 July 1820, fo. 82; *Morning Herald*, 1 Aug. 1820, fo. 83; meeting of mechanics, Holborn Hill, fo. 97; see also, Roger Sales, *English Literature in History – 1780–1830; Pastoral and Politics* (1983), p. 182.

[79] Place Coll. 18, Mansion House, fo. 101; *The Times*, 31 Aug. 1820, p. 3; 22 Sept. 1820, p. 3; *Republican*, 29 Sept. 1820; TS 11/91/290, King vs. Waddington, Sept. 1820.

[80] *The Times*, 9 Sept. 1821; see also, Place Coll. 18 (iii), fos. 18, 173; 40 (ii), *Morning Chronicle*, 16 Oct. 1820; 71, placard, 24 Aug. 1821; *The Times*, 27 Aug. 1821; Prothero, *Artisans and Politics*, esp. pp. 138–52.

[81] *Republican*, 29 Dec. 1820.

[82] Darnton, *Literary Underground*, esp. pp. 1–40, 199–208.

[83] Laqueur, 'Queen Caroline Affair', p. 465.

[84] HO 40/3, correspondence between Hobhouse and Mr Browne, Dec. 1820, fos. 181–2.

[85] *CPPS*, ix, pp. xxii; x, p. xvii; Wardroper, *Kings, Lords and Wicked Libellers*, p. 213.

[86] F.B. Smith, 'Sexuality in Britain, 1800–1900: Some Suggested Revisions', in *A Widening Sphere: Changing Roles of Victorian Women*, ed. Martha Vicinus (Bloomington, Indiana, 1973), p. 184.

[87] HO 44/2, I.N., 17 June 1820.

[88] Henry Mayhew, *London Labour and the London Poor*, 4 vols. (1861, repr. 1986), i, p. 200, ii, p. 468.

[89] Louis James, *Fiction for the Working Man, 1830–50* (Harmondsworth, 1974), esp. pp. 89–134, and 'Taking Melodrama Seriously'.

9 THE ULTRA-RADICAL MARCH OF MIND: POLITICS, RELIGION AND RESPECTABILITY

[1] HO 64/11, Hall to Stafford, 13 Aug. 1827, fo. 5; 10 June 1878, fo. 53; 25 Sept. 1830, fo. 165. For confirmation of the reliability of Hall's reports, see T.M. Parsinnen and I.J. Prothero, 'The London Tailors' Strike of 1834 and the Collapse of the Grand National Consolidated Trades' Union: A Police Spy's Report', *International Review of Social History*, xxii (1977), p. 66.

[2] See, for example, R.J. White, *Waterloo to Peterloo* (Harmondsworth, 1968), pp. 198–9; G.D.H. Cole, *The Common People, 1746–1946* (1956), pp. 226–36, 244–7; Hendrix, 'Popular Humor'.

[3] *Autobiography of Francis Place*, pp. 14–15, 46–135, 176, 198–9; see also his copious material in Add. MS 27825 (ii), 27827, vols. 3–4; 27828 (ii); 27829, vol. 5 (i–ii).

[4] Add. MS 27828, March 1829, 'Coffee Shops' (quoting Mr Merle).

[5] Thompson, *Making*, pp. 781–915; see also Prothero, *Artisans and Politics*, chs. 9–13; Edward Royle and James Walvin, *English Radicals and Reformers, 1760–1848* (Brighton, 1982), pp. 124–41.

[6] See, for example, John Foster, *Class Struggle and the Industrial Revolution: Early Industrial Capitalism in Three English Towns* (1974); Richard Johnson, 'Really Useful Knowledge – Radical Education and Working Class Culture, 1790–1848', in *Working-class Culture: Studies in history and theory*, eds. John Clarke, Charles Crichter and Richard Johnson (1979), pp. 75–102; R.S. Neale, *Class and Ideology in the Nineteenth Century* (London and Boston, 1972), esp. pp. 1–15; *Class in English History, 1680–1850* (Oxford, 1981), esp. ch. 4;

Alexander Tyrrell, 'Class Consciousness in Early Victorian Britain: Samuel Smiles, Leeds Politics and the Self-Help Creed', *Journal of British Studies*, ix (1970), pp. 102–25; Patricia Hollis and Brian Harrison, 'Chartism, Liberalism and the Life of Robert Lowery', *EHR*, lxxxii (1967), pp. 503–35; Tholfsen, *Working-Class Radicalism*.

7 Hollis, *Pauper Press*, pp. 220–58; Thompson, *People's Science*, chs. 5–8; Himmelfarb, *Idea of Poverty*, pp. 230–52.

8 Add. MS 36457, Place to Hobhouse [1818], fo. 93.

9 HO 42/182, CHY to Sidmouth, 3 Nov. 1818; Conant, 10 Nov. 1818 (enclosing inscription in window); HO 42/190, B, 29 Dec. 1818.

10 Hone, *Cause of Truth*, p. 345.

11 HO 40/14, Sharp, Manchester, 13 Aug. 1820, fo. 126; Norris, 25 Sept. 1820, fo. 293; HO 40/15, Norris, 20 Nov. 1820; placard, 29 Nov. 1820, fo. 62; Norris, 30 Nov. 1820, fo. 142; report of delegate meeting, 30 Nov. 1820, fo. 239; *Manchester Observer*, 29 April 1820, 2 Sept. 1820, 28 Oct. 1820, 4 Nov. 1820; Place Coll. 18 (ii), report of meeting, union rooms of George, Leigh Street, fo. 57.

12 Bamford, *Autobiography*, ii, p. 104.

13 HO 40/14, Norris, 31 Oct. 1820, fo. 99; copy of libel, enclosed W.A. Milne, 12 Aug. 1820, fo. 120; HO 40/15, warrant against T.J. Evans, Dec. 1820, fo. 251; KB 28/476/76–77, indictments; TS 11/697/2210, Rex vs. T.J. Evans.

14 Add. MS 37950, Thomas J.B. Evans to F. Place, 17 July 1830; J.W. Hudson, *A History of Adult Education* (1851), p. 49. I am grateful to Dr Iorwerth Prothero for this last reference.

15 Quoted in Williams, *Rowland Detrosier*, p. 18.

16 See, for example, Tholfsen, *Working Class Radicalism*, pp. 16–23; Prothero, *Artisans and Politics*, pp. 183–231, 328–32; Geoffrey Crossick, *An Artisan Elite in Victorian Society* (1978), pp. 134–45; Robert Q. Gray, *The Labour Aristocracy in Victorian Edinburgh* (Oxford, 1976), pp. 136–43.

17 On the potentially radical social and political consciousness of the 'uneasy' middling strata in the early nineteenth century, see Neale, *Class and Ideology*, esp. pp. 32–40.

18 The best short summary of this argument is to be found in Trygve Tholfsen, 'The Intellectual Origins of Mid-Victorian Stability', *Political Science Quarterly*, lxxxvi (1971), pp. 57–91.

19 'Scientific Essays V., Mechanics', *Newgate Magazine*, 1 Feb. 1826, p. 255.

20 Prothero, *Artisans and Politics*, pp. 195–7.

21 Add. MS 27817, Galloway, 6 Nov. 1829, fo. 151; Add. MS 27827, Galloway, 'Minutes of Evidence', *Select Committee of the House of Commons on Artisans and Machinery* (1825), fos. 70–1; see also, Add. MS 27823, 'Early History of the London Mechanics' Institution', Aug. 1825, fos. 241ff.

22 Add. MS 37950, Thomas J.B. Evans to F. Place, 17 July 1830; Davenport, *Life of Spence*, p. 22.

23 McCalman, 'Popular Radicalism and Freethought'; W.H. Wickwar, *The Struggle for the Freedom of the Press, 1819–32* (1928); Wiener, *Radicalism and Freethought*, chs. 3–7; Edward Royle, *Victorian Infidels: The Origins of the British Secularist Movement, 1791–1866* (Manchester, 1974).

[24] See B.B. Jones's description in Edward Royle, *Radical Politics 1790–1900, Religion and Unbelief* (1971), p. 105.

[25] TS 11/424/1345, Rex vs. Waddington, Trinity Term 1822; HO 49/7, 'Law Officers' Entry Book, 1817–31', fo. 191; *Black Dwarf*, 16 Jan. 1822; Todd, *Directory of Printers*, p. 201.

[26] TS 11/424/1345, Rex vs. Waddington (passages selected for prosecution) and John Ewen Poole to Peel, 16 April 1822; *The Times*, 6 May 1822, p. 3; 20 May 1822, p. 3; 24 Oct. 1822, p. 2; 15 Nov. 1822, p. 3.

[27] *Republican*, 3 March (*sic*) [May] 1822.

[28] McCalman, 'Popular Radicalism and Freethought', pp. 110–23.

[29] *Black Dwarf*, 30 Jan. 1822.

[30] *The Times*, 15 Nov. 1822, p. 3; see also, 24 Oct. 1822, p. 2.

[31] Samuel Waddington, *The People's Universal Prayer for the Destruction of Tyrants and the Liberty of Nations* (1822), pp. 7–8; see also *Letter to the Editor of the 'Traveller' upon his committal to the New Bastile, Clerkenwell...* (1822). Both are contained in TS 11/424/1345.

[32] *The Times*, 29 June 1822, p. 4.

[33] HO 64/11, [Hall], 16 Sept. 1831, fo. 417; see also *The Times*, 25 Feb. 1823, p. 4; TS 11/424/1345, Waddington to the Attorney General, 7 March 1823; LCRO, 'Middlesex Calendar of Indictments, 1812–Feb. 1824', Samuel Waddington, April 1823, 'Rape'.

[34] HO 64/11, [Hall], Feb. 1828, fos. 41, 43–6; 20 April 1828, enclosure, fo. 73; n.d., fos. 74–5; n.d. [April–May 1828], fos. 86–9, 94; on Taylor, see *BDMBR*, entry by E. Royle, pp. 467–70; McCalman, 'Popular Radicalism and Freethought', pp. 129–32.

[35] Rev. Robert Taylor, *The Holy Liturgy, or Divine Service on the Principles of Pure Deism as performed every Sunday in the Chapel of the Society of Universal Benevolence ...* (1827), p. 30.

[36] *Radical Magazine*, i (Feb. 1821), pp. 125–6; see also HO 44/7, Blandford to Sidmouth, 8 Jan. 1821, fo. 28; 'Creed of the Anglo-Carbonarian Union', 9 March 1821, fo. 66.

[37] Taylor, *Holy Liturgy*, pp. 3, 21, letter to the *Republican*, 9 July 1824.

[38] *Prompter*, 20 Nov. 1830.

[39] HO 40/25, papers found on William Knight, 8 Nov. 1830, fo. 150.

[40] H. Hetherington, *Cheap Salvation, or an Antidote to Priestcraft* [1822?]; *Principles and Practice Contrasted, or, a peep into 'The only true Church of God upon earth', commonly called Freethinking Christians* (1828); *Scourge* (Carlile), 18 Oct. 1834; see also, W. Daye, *Republican*, 15 Oct. 1819; R. Morris, *DM* [1820], pp. 76–8.

[41] [Cannon] Rev. Erasmus Perkins (pseud.), *Manual of the Theophilanthropists*, pp. 3–4.

[42] Taylor, *Moral Catechism*, in *Holy Liturgy*, pp. 32–9; *First to Thirteenth Moral Discourses* (1833–4); Williams, *Rowland Detrosier*, p. 14. For Rev. Jos. Fitch's moral concerns, see *Lion*, 29 Feb. 1828, 14 Nov. 1828, 20 Feb. 1829.

[43] See, Taylor, *Third Moral Discourse*, pp. 44–5; *Second Moral Discourse*, p. 18; his *Manifesto of the Christian Evidence Society* (1825) is in TS 24/3, fo. 104; for Fitch, see *Republican*, 3 Sept. 1819; HO 44/4, Birnie, 26 Feb. 1820; HO 64/11,

[Hall], n.d. [1828], fos. 77–8, 83–6, 89, and *Prompter*, 18 June 1831 (obituary); for Detrosier, see Williams, *Rowland Detrosier*, pp. 12–15 and *Prompter*, 25 June 1831.

44 See *Newgate Magazine*, 1 Sept. 1825; *Republican*, 1 Dec. 1826; *Lion*, 18 Jan. 1828; HO 64/11, [Hall], 23 Feb. 1828, fo. 43; n.d., fo. 46; 7 Aug. 1829, fo. 167. On W.D. Saull, see HO 64/11, 22 Nov. 1830, fo. 167. He, Freeman, Pummell and Brushfield also put up £400 for the lease on Fitch's Grub Street chapel after Taylor was imprisoned; HO 64/11, n.d., fo. 78.

45 Huntingdon Lib., Carlile MS, Carlile to W. Holmes, 14 June 1825.

46 On Eliza Sharples, see McCalman, 'Females, Feminism and Freelove', pp. 13–25; Neale, *Class in English History*, pp. 205–14; on Macaulay, Barbara Taylor, *Eve and the New Jerusalem: Socialism and Feminism in the Nineteenth Century* (1983), pp. 71–3.

47 *Lion*, 21 March 1828; HO 64/11, [Hall], n.d. [1828], fo. 86.

48 *Lion*, 28 March 1828; see also, *Republican*, 19 May, 8 Sept., 20 Oct. 1820; for evidence of Wedderburn's bare literacy, see his handwritten letter to Place, Add. MS 27808, 22 March 1831, fo. 322.

49 HO 64/11, [Hall], 3 May 1828, fo. 48; fos. 73–4; n.d. [c.June 1828], fos. 83, 86–9, 94.

50 R.P. Ward, *Tremaine; A Man of Refinement*, 3 vols. (1825), i, p. 291.

51 HO 64/11, [Hall], n.d., fos. 86–9, 94.

52 HO 40/25 (ii) [Hall], 15 Aug. 1829, fo. 488.

53 CLRO, 'Index to Persons Indicted, Jan. 1821–Dec. 1834', R. Wedderburn, Sept. 1830, bawdy house; Add. MS 27808, Wedderburn to Place, 22 March 1831, fo. 322.

54 See below, ch. 10.

55 *Autobiography of Francis Place*, pp. 51–2, 72–8, 88–91. For a discussion of working-class sexual values in the late eighteenth and early nineteenth centuries, see Weeks, *Sex, Politics and Society*, pp. 59ff.

56 Davenport, *Life*, pp. 53.

57 For examples of Davenport's writings on this subject, see his letters to the *Republican*, 9 Jan. 1824, 25 Aug. 1826, 15 Dec. 1826; *Cosmopolite*, 22 Sept. 1832; 'Hornsey Wood', 'Matter', 'Cooperation', in *The Muse's Wreath* (1827), pp. 7–12, 66–8; *Life*, pp. 56–7, 68–9. For the similar ideas of Carlile and his Zetetic followers, see McCalman, 'Popular Radicalism and Freethought', pp. 135–71 and 'Females, Feminism and Freelove', pp. 1–25.

58 Davenport, *Life*, 57–67; *Life of Spence*, p. 22; *Prompter*, 19 March 1831; Prothero, *Artisans and Politics*, esp. pp. 257–8.

59 Davenport, *Life*, p. 63.

60 *Ibid.*, pp. 63–75; Add. MS 27797, vol. ix, fo. 305. For an excellent discussion of this aspect of the Owenite involvement generally, see articles by J.F.C. Harrison and Eileen Yeo, in *Robert Owen: Prophet of the Poor*, eds. S. Pollard and T. Salt (1971).

61 Neville Kirk, *The Growth of Working-Class Reformism in Mid-Victorian England* (1985), pp. 174–240.

62 Peter Bailey, '"Will the Real Bill Banks Please Stand Up?" Towards a Role Analysis of Mid-Victorian Working-Class Respectability', *Journal of Social*

History, 12 (1979), pp. 336–53; see also Harrison, *Peaceable Kingdom*, pp. 157–216.

[63] HO 64/11, [Hall], 13 Nov. 1830, fo. 119.

[64] Clark, *English Alehouse*, pp. 294–323; James, *Fiction for the Working Man*, pp. 8–9.

[65] HO 40/15, J.S., 6 May 1820, fo. 12; HO 40/16, J.S., 17 March 1821, fo. 23; 7 June 1821, fo. 31; see also HO 40/8 (i), B, 18 July 1817, fo. 11; HO 44/4, Edwards, fo. 227; HO 44/2, J. Brittain, 10 May 1820, fo. 120; HO 42/157, n.d. (report on radical coffee-houses).

[66] See, for example, HO 64/11, [Hall], fo. 90, [c.21 June 1828], 7 Aug.–25 Sept. [1829 or 30], fos. 161–5; 13 Nov. 1830, fo. 119; HO 64/16, Samuel Tryford (based on reports of Isaacson), 19 Nov. 1830.

[67] HO 40/25(2), Charles Brophy, [c.Dec. 1830], fos. 342–3, 411–16; Rev. J. Phillot, 24 Dec. 1830, fo. 434.

[68] Hudson, *History of Adult Education*, pp. 49; *Black Dwarf*, 13 Nov. 1822; 18 June 1823; *Republican*, 28 June 1822; 6 Feb. 1824; for a satirical but interesting account of British Forum proceedings, see Jack Mitford's *Hoxton Sausage*, 4 [1829?], pp. 30–1; see also, John Gale Jones, *An Oration on the late General Washington* (1825), esp. list of subscribers.

[69] HO 64/11, [Hall], n.d. [c.June 1828], fo. 86.

[70] See I.D. McCalman, 'Anti-Slavery and Ultra-Radicalism in Early Nineteenth-Century England: The Case of Robert Wedderburn', *Slavery and Abolition*, 7 (September 1986), pp. 101–17.

[71] *The Life and Struggles of William Lovett in his pursuit of bread, knowledge and freedom* (1876, repr. 1920), p. 29; HO 64/16, report to Stafford, 20 Oct. 1830 (contains versions of several of Baume's British Forum speeches); Prothero, *Artisans and Politics*, p. 275.

[72] *Republican*, 20 Feb. 1824; for details of the Liberals, see letters, reports and subscription lists: 7 Feb. 1823; 23 Jan., 6 Feb., 20 Feb., 5 Aug., 10 Sept., 3 Dec. 1824; 11 Feb., 27 May 1825; and esp. letter from W. Millard, 29 Dec. 1826.

[73] HO 64/11, [Hall], Feb. 1828, fo. 41; 11 Sept. [1829/30], fo. 163; 25 Sept. [1829/30], fo. 165; HO 79/4, 'Entry Books', Peel to Postmaster General, 2 Aug. 1825.

[74] *Age*, 9 Oct. 1831.

[75] See Add. MS 27791, esp. fos. 242–57, 349; Add. MS 27797, esp. fos. 4–6; for regular reports of the NUWC, and of the Finsbury division, see *PMG*, esp. i, Oct.–Nov. 1831. For secondary accounts of these organisations, see D.J. Rowe, 'Class and Political Radicalism in London, 1831–2', *HJ*, 13 (1970), pp. 31–47; I.J. Prothero, 'Chartism in London, *P & P*, 44 (1969), esp. pp. 78–9, 89; Prothero, *Artisans and Politics*, pp. 313–25; Jennifer Bennett, 'The London Democratic Association 1837–41: A Study in London Radicalism', in *The Chartist Experience*, eds. James Epstein and Dorothy Thompson (1982), pp. 87–119.

[76] See, for example, HO 44/52, J. Towler, 16 Jan. 1839, fos. 217–18; N. Pearce, 22 Jan. 1839, fo. 220; Sam Hughes, 23 Jan. 1839, fo. 231; Bennett, 'The London Democratic Association', pp. 91, 100.

77 HO 64/12, 7 June 1832, fo. 102; see also HO 44/52, G.L. Archbold, 29–30 July 1839, fo. 134; HO 64/16, report to Stafford on history of the Optimist chapel, 20 Oct. 1830; HO 64/11, [Hall], 7 Aug. [1829], fo. 161; HO 64/12, 22 May 1832, fo. 96; 9 Nov. 1832, fo. 168; *Prompter*, 10 Sept. 1831; *PMG*, 13, 20 April 1833; *Cosmopolite*, 20 Feb. 1833, 9, 30 March 1833.

78 Add. MS 27791, 'Historical Account of the NPU', fos. 22, 48–53; 'Historical Sketch of the NUWC', fos. 247–8; Add. MS 27797, 'Proceedings of … the NUWC', fo. 12, p. 15; Add. MS 27789, 'Proceedings of the NUWC', 1 May 1833, fo. 60. On Benbow's 'Grand National Holiday' scheme, see Add. MS 27791, fos. 334–40; Add. MS 27796, fo. 304, and Prothero's excellent analysis 'Benbow and the "General Strike"', esp. pp. 169–70. On NUWC tactics generally, see Prothero, *Artisans and Politics*, pp. 292–8; D.J. Rowe, 'London Radicalism in the Era of the Great Reform Bill', in Stevenson, *London in the Age of Reform*, esp. pp. 165–70.

79 HO 64/15, Feb. 1834, fo. 146.

80 Goodway, *London Chartism*, pp. 32–4; Bennett, 'The London Democratic Association', pp. 95–101. For the 'Shipyard' conspiracy, see also MEPO 1/32, 'Outgoing Correspondence', 11 May 1839; HO 61/22, G, 11 May 1839; for the Clerkenwell meeting, see HO 44/52, Archbold, 16 Aug. 1839, fo. 164.

81 Stedman Jones, 'Rethinking Chartism', in *Languages of Class*, pp. 90–178; see also Hollis, *Pauper Press*, pp. 203–58.

82 Thompson, The *People's Science*, esp. pp. 219–28.

83 Stedman Jones, 'Rethinking Chartism', in *Languages of Class*, esp. pp. 158–61.

84 Davenport, *Life*, pp. 58–61; *Reformists' Register*, 23 Aug. 1817; Prothero, *Artisans and Politics*, esp. pp. 245–57; Prothero, 'William Benbow and the "General Strike"', pp. 155–8.

85 HO 64/19, G. Ball, 20 March 1834.

86 Stedman Jones, 'Rethinking Chartism', in *Languages of Class*, p. 155.

87 HO 40/44, G. Archbold, 21 May 1839, fo. 683; see also, for George, *PMG*, 5 May 1832; HO 44/52, Underhill, 28 Feb. 1839, fo. 242; for Preston, *PMG*, 19 Nov. 1831; HO 40/32(4), handbill, *Thomas Preston's Address to his Fellow-Countrymen* (1834), fo. 326; for Davenport, *Cosmopolite*, 30 March 1833; Davenport, *Life of Spence*, esp. pp. 13–21.

88 Add. MS 27797, pp. 8–15, fos. 5–12.

89 HO 44/52, *Address … of the LDA*, pp. 3–4, fo. 221.

90 Bennett, 'The London Democratic Association', pp. 104–14; for an excellent analysis of these and other trades, see Goodway, *London Chartism*, pp. 153–218.

91 HO 44/52, *Address … of the LDA*, pp. 3–4, fo. 221.

92 HO 40/25(i), report to Stafford, 6 Nov. 1830, fo. 71; (ii), [Hall], 15 Nov. 1830; HO 64/11, 'Secret Service, 1829–31', n.d., fos. 195, 212–14, 235; 'Police/Secret Service, 1831', n.d., fos. 380–1, 412; 7 Oct. 1831, fo. 423; 19 Oct. 1831, fo. 475; HO 64/14, Benbow's speech at Theobald's Road, 3 March 1833, fos. 166ff; *PMG*, 21 April, 12 May, 25 Aug. 1832, 14 Sept. 1833.

93 Ward, *Zion's Works*, xiv, p. 181.

94 HO 64/12, 8 Oct. 1832, fo. 150; 9 Nov. 1832, fo. 168; 12 Nov. 1832, fo. 170;

Isis, 20 Sept., 20 Oct., 13 Nov. 1832. On 'Shepherd' Smith, see Harrison, *Second Coming*, pp. 142–57; Oliver, *Prophets and Millennialists*, pp. 196–216.

95 Taylor, *Eve and the New Jerusalem*, pp. 159–60.
96 Davenport, *Life*, p. 75.
97 *Ibid.*, p. 72.
98 HO 40/44, 17 Aug. 1839; HO 44/52, Archbold, 16 Aug. 1839, fo. 164; see also, HO 40/32 (iv), G. Ball, 22 Dec. 1834, fo. 332; HO 64/16, C.R. Edwards, 7 Jan. 1831; *PMG*, 18 July 1835.
99 HO 64/12, 25 Oct. 1832, fo. 158.
100 HO 64/19, Ball, 17 March 1834; see also Ball's reports of Taylor's services Feb.–May 1834 in HO 64/15. For Taylor's earlier praise of Wedderburn, see *Lion*, 28 March 1828.

10 GRUB STREET JACKS: OBSCENE POPULISM AND PORNOGRAPHY

1 KB 28/515/13, 21 Oct. 1830; *The Times*, 11 Dec. 1830, p. 6; 1 Jan. 1831, p. 4; 11 Feb. 1831, p. 3; Fraxi (pseud.) [Ashbee], *Index librorum prohibitorum*, pp. xliii–xlv, 397–401; Pisanus Fraxi (pseud.) [Henry Spencer Ashbee], *Catena librorum tacendorum* (1885), pp. 298–300.
2 I have used the generic term 'obscene publications' or 'erotica' to cover the whole corpus of printed material regarded as liable for prosecution as obscene libel under the common law definition laid down in the Edmund Curll case of 1727: Alec Craig, *The Banned Books of England and Other Countries* (1962), p. 32; Norman St John-Stevas, *Obscenity and the Law* (1956), esp. pp. 22–5. The concept of pornography (the word came into use after 1864) is still hotly debated, though – as Brian Harrison has rightly pointed out – what matters most to historians is pornography in particular societies: 'Underneath the Victorians', *Victorian Studies*, x (1967), pp. 247–8. I have followed general usage in reserving 'pornography' to describe literary material which was intended primarily to arouse sexual desire and fantasies. This differed from 'bawdy' literature, which generally used sexuality as a source of amusement or ridicule and was not necessarily illegal, and 'obscene' literature, which usually aimed to shock and often possessed a political dimension. See David Foxon, *Libertine Literature in England, 1660–1745* (New York, 1965), pp. 46–8; Roger Thompson, *Unfit for Modest Ears* (1979), pp. ix–x; Peter Gay, *The Bourgeois Experience, Victoria to Freud: Volume I: Education of the Senses* (New York and Oxford, 1984), p. 495; Steven Marcus, *The Other Victorians: A Study of Sexuality and Pornography in Mid-Nineteenth Century England* (1969), pp. xx–xxi.
3 For Brookes, see KB 28/512/19, July–Aug. 1830; *CPPS*, x, p. l; for J. Duncombe, see TS 11/43/56, Sept. 1819; KB 28/473/13 and KB 28/509/21, Dec. 1829; for E. Duncombe, see KB 28/509/22, Dec. 1829–Jan. 1830; KB 28/534/14, Jan.–Feb. 1835, April–May 1835; KB 28/543/4, April 1837; for W. Dugdale, see HO 44/3, anon., [1818], fo. 154; KB 28/512/4, Nov. 1830; KB 28/535/45, Feb. 1835; *The Times*, 28 May 1830, p. 6. For further information on these pressmen and their milieu, see I.D. McCalman, 'Unrespectable Radicalism: Infidels and Pornography in Early Nineteenth-Century London',

P&P, 104 (1984), pp. 75–84; Donald Thomas, *A Long Time Burning: The History of Literary Censorship in England* (1969), pp. 279–81.

4 McCalman, 'Infidels and Pornography', p. 77; see also, (R. Fores), KB 28/479/28; *CPPS*, x, pp. xlviii–xlix; Fraxi (pseud.) [Ashbee], *Index librorum prohibitorum*, p. 140; Todd, *Directory of Printers*, pp. 15, 61, 109, 133, 207; *Quizzical Gazette*, 6 Jan. 1832, pp. 158–9 (obituary of John Mitford).

5 *CPPS*, x, p. xvii. For an excellent general account of this type of material throughout the 1820s, see Henry Vizetelly, *Glances Back Through Seventy Years*, 2 vols. (1893), i, pp. 5–6, 31–2, 47; for some examples, see Lady Elizabeth Conyngham, *The Memoirs of the Celebrated Lady C – m* (H. Price edn [1825]) (contains portrait from Marks); (J.L. Marks, pub.), *A Curious and Interesting Narrative of Poll House and the Marquis of C xxxx, late Lord T –* (n.d. [1822/3?]); Edward Eglantine (pseud.) [William Benbow], *Memoirs of the Life of the Celebrated Mrs Q –* (1822); *Fairburn's Genuine Edition of the Death-bed Confessions of the late Countess of Guernsey* [1822?]; (John Fairburn, pub.) *The Northern Excursion of Geordie, Emperor of Gotham …* [1822]; (J.L. Marks, pub.), *A Voyage to the North in search of a new Mistress, By an amorous old dandy* [1822].

6 [Mitford and Benbow], *Description of the Crimes and Horrors*, i, esp. pp. 6–13, 24–5; ii, pp. 17–18.

7 'Lion in Tears', anonymous balladsheet bound with (J.L. Marks, pub.), *A Correct Account of the Horrible Occurrence … in which … the … Bishop of Clogher was a principal actor with a common soldier* [1822], in BL, *Pindaric Tracts*, vol. v; see also (John Fairburn, pub.), *The Bishop* [1822]; Thomas Dolby, *Sketch of the Life and Sufferings of James Byrne* (1822); *Subscription for James Byrne* (1822); *Black Dwarf*, 7 Aug., 9 Oct. 1822; *Republican*, 2, 9, 16 Aug., 27 Sept. 1822. For government concern, see HO 49/7, 'Law Officers' Entry Book', Peel to King's Advocate, 24 July 1822.

8 See, for example, his two 6d works, *Atrocious Acts of Catholic Priests, who have lately committed the most Horrid and Diabolical Rape and Murders in Ireland and France* [1824]; *Rape and Assassination … of Marie Gerin … by Mingrat, a French Catholic Priest* (1824).

9 Pisanus Fraxi (pseud.) [Henry Spencer Ashbee], *Centuria librorum absconditorum* (1879) dedicates over 300 pages to discussion of such material, most of it French. See also, Darnton, *Literary Underground*, pp. 1–40, 122–47. On the English side, see Thompson, *Unfit for Modest Ears*, pp. 133–57, and, though of slightly later provenance, Geoffrey Best, 'Popular Protestantism in Victorian Britain', in *Ideas and Institutions of Victorian Britain*, ed. Robert Robson, (1967), pp. 115–42.

10 I have not seen Benbow's 1s 6d edition of d'Emilliane entitled, *The Frauds of the Roman Catholic Clergy*, but it is cited in a catalogue of his works attached to *The Confessions of Julia Johnston* [1826], p. 6. I have seen another English translation put out at much the same time: [W. Curry], *The Frauds of Romish Monks and Priests* (Dublin, 1827). On the works of Fairburn, Brookes and Dugdale, see Fraxi (pseud.) [Ashbee], *Index librorum prohibitorum*, pp. 99, 184; *Catena librorum tacendorum*, pp. 129–30; Ivan Bloch, *Sexual Life in England* (1965), pp. 463–5; C.R. Dawes, 'A Study of Erotic Literature in England, Considered with Especial Reference to Social Life' (Cheltenham, 1943), pp. 108–10, un-

published typescript contained in BL, Cup. 364, d. 15; [William Dugdale, pub.], *Nunnery Tales, or Cruising under False Colours: A Tale of Love and Lust*, 3 vols. (n.d.).

11 See, for example, Foxon, *Libertine Literature*, esp. pp. 47–51; Patrick J. Kearney, *A History of Erotic Literature* (1982), pp. 53–100; Henry L. Marchand, *The Erotic History of France: Including a History of its Erotic Literature* (New York, 1933); Dale Underwood, *Etherage and the Seventeenth-Century Comedy of Manners* (New Haven and London, 1957), pp. 10–36.

12 Redwood, *Reason, Ridicule and Religion, passim*; Roy Porter, 'Mixed Feelings: The Enlightenment and Sexuality in Eighteenth-Century Britain', *Sexuality in Eighteenth-Century Britain*, ed. Paul-Gabriel Boucé, (Manchester, 1982), pp. 1–27.

13 [W. Dugdale], 'Preface', Lord George Byron, *Don Juan* (1823), p. iv; 'Memoir', Voltaire, *The Philosophical Dictionary* (1843), pp. 14–47.

14 'On Love', *RM*, i [1822], pp. 1–3; see also the 'Preface', pp. iii–iv, probably written by Benbow and expressing similar sentiments.

15 *Ibid.*, p. 487. The work is serialised, pp. 293–8, 343–7, 389–92, 485–7, 528–31, under a characteristic Cannon insignia, p. 298.

16 [Cannon], 'preface', *Amours of Faublas*, i, pp. iii, viii.

17 *RM*, i [1822], pp. 17–23, 69–74, 136–7, 181–9, 217–18, 363–7, 381. For Benbow's prosecutions, see *The Times*, 11 July 1822, p. 3; 27 May 1822, p. 3; 21 Feb. 1823, p. 3; 2 May 1823, p. 3; 12 May 1823, p. 3.

18 This publishing information has been pieced together from diverse sources. Extant works can often be traced using Patrick J. Kearney, *The Private Case. An Annotated Bibliography of the Private Case Erotica Collection in the British (Museum) Library* (1981). However, the best single source is James Campbell Reddie, 'Bibliographic Notes on Illustrated Works' (with pencil notes by H.S. Ashbee), 3 vols., BL, Add. MS 38828–30.

19 Benbow's 1s edition of this work is cited in the catalogue attached to *The Confessions of Julia Johnston*, p. 9. It is probably the edition I have seen, supposedly translated by W. Brown and published by H. Bostock, 1838. Another edition, translated by 'T. Tooly' and published by 'Bickerton, 1719', was also circulating. Dugdale, Duncombe and McCreery all produced editions of Ovid's *Art of Love*. On Cannon's Latin publications, see *The Times*, 11 Feb. 1831, p. 3.

20 See, McCalman, 'Infidels and Pornography', p. 97.

21 There is an extant edition in the BL published by Dugdale under the pseudonym of H. Smith, *Memoirs of Fanny Hill* [c.1841]. For the long and complex history of the book, see William H. Epstein, *John Cleland: Images of a Life* (New York and London, 1976), and Foxon, *Libertine Literature*, appendix.

22 See *DNB* entry for Thomas Cannon's father, Rev. Robert Cannon, *Notes and Queries*, 2nd ser., viii (1959), pp. 65–6; *The Life of Thomas Holcroft*, ed. William Hazlitt, 2 vols. (repr. 1975), i, pp. 208–11.

23 Wickwar, *Freedom of the Press*, pp. 259–64.

24 Thomas Frost, *Forty Years Recollections, Literary and Political* (1880), pp. 45, 49, 52, 102; see also, [W. Dugdale], 'preface', Byron, *Don Juan*, p. iv; [Benbow], *RM*, i [1822], p. 431. Between 1819 and 1826 the following radical pressmen issued editions of *Don Juan* (often illustrated), as well as many others of Byron's works: Hone, Hodgson, W. Wright, W. Clarke, Griffin, Benbow, Dugdale and

Duncombe. I have also seen the following obscene memoirs, most based on Mitford's works: [John Mitford], *A Narrative of the Circumstances which attended the separation of Lord and Lady Byron* (R. Edwards, 1816); [Mitford], *The Private Life of Lord Byron: comprising his voluptuous amours* (H. Smith, pseud., [W. Dugdale], 1836). Duncombe produced an earlier edition of this work and there was a Paris edition in French in 1837; *RM*, i [1822], pp. 16–21; i (1824), pp. 99–102; [Mitford], *New London Rambler's Magazine*, i (n.d. [c. 1828–30?], pp. 16–21, 57–60, 66, 91–4, 123–7, 162–6, 195–9.

[25] See, however, Edward J. Bristow, *Vice and Vigilance: Purity Movements in Britain since 1700* (Dublin, 1977), pp. 32–47; Weeks, *Sex, Politics and Society*, pp. 84–5; M.J.D. Roberts, 'Making Victorian morals? The Society for the Suppression of Vice and its Critics, 1802–1886', *Historical Studies*, xxi (1984), pp. 157–73.

[26] See, for example, Dugdale's successful acquittal: *The Times*, 28 May 1830, p. 6.

[27] *Republican*, 1 July 1825. He might have felt some sympathy for men like Dugdale if only because they advertised the cause of contraception – and sometimes sold the wares as well. See Dugdale's 1s pamphlet: *On the Use of Night-Caps, or Seven Years Experience on the Practicability of limiting the number of a family by the best known methods* (n.d.). He offers a contraceptive mail order service from his premises on p. 22.'

[28] See *The Times*, 11 Dec. 1830, p. 6; 1 Jan. 1831, p. 4; 11 Feb. 1831, p. 4; 11 Dec. 1845, p. 7.

[29] Anthony Smith, 'Technology and Control: The Interactive Dimensions of Journalism', *Mass Communication and Society*, eds. James Curran *et al.* (1977), pp. 188–9. Paper also cheapened in the 1820s following the implementation of John Gamble's new paper-making machine (1801); James, *Fiction for the Working Man*, p. 12.

[30] Dolby, *Memoirs*, esp. pp. 164–70.

[31] Hollis, *Pauper Press*, pp. 124–36.

[32] St John, 'Memoir [*sic*] d'un philosophe', p. 11.

[33] Post, *Freethought in America*, pp. 32–3, 47–50, 76–7.

[34] Hendrix, 'Popular Humour', p. 111.

[35] F.W. Hackwood, *William Hone: His Life and Times* (1912), pp. 22–63 (reprint of Hone's brief autobiography).

[36] Dolby, *Memoirs*, pp. 164–70.

[37] *RM*, i [1822], pp. 105–8, 271, 350–4.

[38] For discussions of the social origins of pornography see Foxon, *Libertine Literature*, pp. 47–51; Marcus, *Other Victorians*, pp. xx–xxi, 65–6, 269–89; Thompson, *Unfit for Modest Ears*, pp. 213–14.

[39] For the growing efficiency of the SSV, see Society for the Suppression of Vice, *Address, Objects, Members* (1825); *The Constable's Assistant; being a compendium of the duties and powers of constables and other peace officers* (1831), pp. 22–3; Thomas, *Long Time Burning*, pp. 197, 284–8; Bristow, *Vice and Vigilance*, pp. 32–47.

[40] The British Library has Avery's 1881 reprint of Cannon's edition, c.1830, entitled *Birchen Bouquet; or, Curious and Original Anecdotes of Ladies fond of administering the Birch Discipline*; Dugdale's reprint, c.1860 (Theresa Berkeley,

pseud.), of Cannon's edition c.1830 of *The Exhibition of Female Flagellants*, pts I–II; and Avery's reprint, c.1880 of Cannon's original edition, c.1830 (repr. by Dugdale c.1860) of *The Elements of Tuition and Modes of Punishment*. For discussion of this flagellation genre, see Marcus, *Other Victorians*, pp. 126–7, 255–8; Ian Gibson, *The English Vice: Beating, Sex and Shame in Victorian England and After* (1978), esp. pp. 233–9.

41 [Dugdale, pub.], *Nunnery Tales*, i, p. 27.

42 For some evidence and comments by Cannon on his readership, see *The Times*, 11 Dec. 1830, p. 6; 11 Feb. 1831, pp. 3–4; Fraxi (pseud.) [Ashbee], *Index librorum prohibitorum*, pp. 399–400; see also (Carlile), *Republican*, 1 July 1825; Thomas Frost, *Reminiscences of a Country Journalist* (1886), pp. 53–4.

43 (Cannon), *The Times*, 8 Dec. 1853, p. 8. On W. Dugdale, see *Bookseller*, 1 July 1868, pp. 448–9.

44 See McCalman, 'Females, Feminism and Freelove', esp. pp. 20–5.

45 See *Republican*, 11, 19 July 1822, 12 May 1826; Huntingdon Lib., Carlile MS, Carlile to T. Turton, 2, 11 April 1842. For J.W. Trust's involvement in pornography, see KB 28/512/2, 22 Aug. 1830; and for Alfred Carlile, *The Times*, 16 Sept. 1845, p. 8.

46 See Brian Harrison, 'Underneath the Victorians', pp. 259–61.

47 *RM*, i [1822], p. 240.

48 Frost, *Reminiscences*, pp. 52–3. Michael Sadleir's racy fictional evocation of a pornographer and his milieu in *Forlorn Sunset* (1947), pp. 410–22, is supposedly based on Dugdale. Cannon's circumstances can be pieced together from the 1841 Census when he was living at 2 Great Mays Building. He was in no.11 of the same building in 1851 but evaded the census.

49 [William Dugdale, pub.], *Yokel's Preceptor: or, More Sprees in London! Being a Regular and Curious Show-Up of all the Rigs and Doings of the Flash Cribs in this Great Metropolis* (n.d. H. Smith, pseud.).

50 London General Register Office, 'Certificate of Death', George Cannon, Middlesex House of Correction, 7 June 1854. For Dugdale's death in the Clerkenwell House of Correction, 11 Nov. 1868, see Fraxi (pseud.) [Ashbee], *Index librorum prohibitorum*, p. 127.

51 Frost, *Reminiscences*, p. 53.

52 Hollis, *Pauper Press*, p. 22.

53 *PMG*, 5 April 1834; Vizetelly, *Glances Back*, i, p. 218; see also Hollis's comprehensive list of unstamped periodicals, 1830–6, *Pauper Press*, pp. 319–27.

54 On Vickers, see James, *Fiction for the Working Man*, esp. pp. 34, 47, 215. For Frost, see *Reminiscences*, esp. pp. 39–40, 57–76; *Penny Punch, a chip off the Old Block*, i–vii (1849) (W. Dugdale, pub.); *Paul, the Poacher* (1848); *Emma Mayfield* (1857 edn); *Alice Leighton; or the Murders at Druid's Stones* (1857). On Grieves, see *The Times*, 29 Jan., 17 Feb. 1870.

55 W.B. Jerrold, *The Life and Remains of Douglas Jerrold* (1859), pp. 57, 65, 126–35, 141.

56 Nigel Cross, *The Common Writer: Life in Nineteenth-Century Grub Street* (Cambridge, 1985), esp. pp. 93–117; Vizetelly, *Glances Back*, i, pp. 14–17 (on W. Clarke, see also *DNB* entry).

57 *The Times*, 11 May 1857, p. 11; Thomas, *Long Time Burning*, pp. 261–4. On

Berger and Strange, see Hollis, *Pauper Press*, pp. 307–8, 14; James, *Fiction for the Working Man*, appendix II, pp. 212–15. For some of the later history of the *Confessional Unmasked*, see Best, 'Popular Protestantism', pp. 133–4. I am grateful to Dr L.L. Robson of the University of Melbourne for the Van Diemen's Land reference.

[58] Hendrix, 'Popular Humor', pp. 109, 128.

[59] On Harriette Wilson, see [William Dugdale, pub.], *Memoirs of Hariette [sic] Wilson by herself* [c.1825, reissued c.1838]; Eglantine (pseud.), [Benbow], *Memoirs of the Life of the Celebrated Mrs Q – ; [W. Benbow], *Harriette Wilson: memoirs of this too famous courtesan* (n.d.), 4s edn in 6d parts, cited in catalogue attached to *Confessions of Julia Johnston*; (E. Duncombe, pub.), *Memoirs of Harriette Wilson – including her Amatory adventures with most of the Nobility of the Present Day* [c.1826], 2s 6d edn; (W.P. Chubb, pub.), *Memoirs and Amorous Adventures of Harriette Wilson* (n.d.), chap-book edn printed by W. Mason; [Mitford], *New London Rambler's Magazine*, ii [c.1829], pp. 259–61; for a secondary account, see Lesley Blanch, *The Game of Hearts, Harriette Wilson and Her Memoirs* (1957). On Madame Vestris, see [Avery], New Villon Society (pseud.), *Confessions of Madame Vestris* (1891, a re-issue of Dugdale's edition, c.1826); A. Griffinhoofe (pseud.) (J. Duncombe, pub., J. Mitford, author), *Memoirs of the Life, Public and Private Adventures of Madame Vestris* (1839, 1845).

[60] *Town*, 28 Oct. 1837.

[61] (W. Emans, pub.), *The Murdered Queen, or Caroline of Brunswick. A diary of the court of George IV. By a lady of rank* (1838). (Emans employed Thomas Frost as a hack writer at one time.)

[62] See, for example (J. Duncombe, pub.), *The Swell! or Slap-up Chaunter* [c.1833], his numerous editions of *Labern's Original Comic Songs* (1842–52), Metford (pseud.) (J. Duncombe, pub.), *The Flash Olio* [c.1833]; [W. West, pub.], *The Nobby Songster ... now singing at Offley's Cider Cellar, Coal Hole* (1842); *The Randy Songster* (1834); *The Cockchafer* (1865); *The Rambler's Flash Songster* [1838?].

[63] Laurence Senelick, 'Politics as Entertainment: Victorian Music-Hall Songs', *Victorian Studies*, xix (1975), p. 159.

[64] [William Dugdale, pub.], *The Lady Flora Hastings: Her Life and Death. With Questions for the Queen and Criticisms of her Court* (n.d. [c.1839]), p. 5.

[65] Others of the same genre which I have not been able to locate are cited in Dawes, 'Erotic Literature', p. 121, BL, Cup. 364, d. 15.

[66] *Town*, 3 June 1837; see also *Crim. Con. Gazette*, i, 25 Aug. 1838; ii, 30 March 1839; *Quizzical Gazette*, i, 27 Aug. 1831; x, 29 Oct. 1831; *Exquisite*, i (1842), p. 8; *Paul Pry*, 28 Feb., 14 March 1830.

[67] *Quizzical Gazette*, ix, 22 Oct. 1831; see also, ii, 3 Sept. 1831; i, 14 Jan. 1832; *Crim. Con. Gazette*, i, 25 Aug., 8, 22 Sept., 10 Nov. 1838; 24 Aug., 5 Oct. 1839; *New London Rambler's Magazine*, i [1829–30], pp. 105–6, 143–4, 174, 155–6, 240–1; ii, 42–3, 45–61, 115.

[68] *New London Rambler's Magazine*, i [c.1829], preface to no. 2.

[69] Vizetelly, *Glances Back*, i, pp. 168–9, 172–6; Bernard Blackmantle (pseud.), [Thomas Ashe], *Fitzalleyne of Berkeley: a romance of the present times* (1825).

[70] The full correspondence is contained in TS 11/469/1604, July 1829–July 1830.

71 (J. Thompson, pub.), *Secret Life and Extraordinary Amours of Ernest, King of Hanover, with all the particulars of the seduction of Lady Graves and mysterious death of Sellis exposed* [1839?], pp. 4–8. J. Thompson was also the first printer and publisher of Gregory's *Satirist*.

72 *Trial of Josiah Phillips for a libel on the Duke of Cumberland* (1833), p. 32; see also Add. MS 27851, fos. 52–70, for Place's correspondence and records of this incident.

73 KB 28/567/24 (1843).

74 (B. Cousins, pub.), *Eliza Grimwood, A Domestic Legend of Waterloo Road* [c.1839].

75 James, *Fiction for the Working Man*, p. 188. I am grateful to Louis James for his helpful comments on the subject of *Eliza Grimwood* and related literature.

CONCLUSION

1 HO 40/33(3), Hall, 27 Nov. 1835, fo. 194.

Select bibliography

Unless otherwise stated all works are published in London.

PRIMARY SOURCES

Manuscripts

PUBLIC RECORD OFFICE

Home Office Papers
HO 16/1–5, Old Bailey Sessions, 1815–34; HO 26/35–7, Criminal Registers, Middlesex, 1829–31; HO 27/38–42, Criminal Registers, M-Y, 1829–31; HO 40/3–44, Correspondence, military and other reports, riots and disturbances, 1817–39; HO 41/1–12, 24–7, Disturbances, Entry Books, 1815–35; HO 42/5, 20, 30, 40–207, Correspondence and Papers, Domestic and General, 1790–1820; HO 43/11–21, Domestic Letter Books (out-letters), 1798–1813; HO 44/1–8, 15, 32–7, 46, 52, Original Correspondence, 1820–39; HO 45/102, Domestic Disturbances, 1839–41; HO 48/15–17, Law Officers, Cases and Reports, 1808–18; HO 49/4, 7, Entry Books, Home Office to Law Officers; Law Officers' Entry Book, 1817–31; HO 52/3–19, 24, in-letters from magistrates, officers and other county authorities; HO 59/1–2, in-letters, Metropolitan Police Courts and Magistrates, 1820–31; HO 60/1–2, Police Entry Books, 1821–36; HO 61/21–5, Metropolitan Police Correspondence, 1838–40; HO 62/4–7, Metropolitan Police, Printed Daily Reports, July 1829–June 1831; HO 64/1–3, 11–19, Police Correspondence, 1820–33; Rewards, Pardons and Secret Service, 1827–33; Seditious Publications, 1830–4; HO 65/2, Police Letter Book, 1811–20; HO 79/4, Entry Books, Private and Secret, 14 Sept. 1819–14 June 1844; HO 119/1, 8–9, 11–16, Private and Secret Correspondence, 1792–9; Reports of Civil Cases, 1827–33; Criminal Reports, 1821–35.

Privy Council Papers
Series PC 1/ unbound papers, corresponding societies, treason, spies: 22/ A 35–7, LCS, treason, corresponding societies, 1794; 23/ A 38, Powell's reports, 1795–6; 34/ A 90, treason, 1796; 38/ A 123, Barlow's reports, 1797; 40/ A

129–33, corresponding societies; reports of Milner and others; 41/ A 136, United Englishmen; reports of Powell, 1798; 41/ A 138, LCS papers, 1798; 42/ A 143–44, O'Connor papers, 1798; United Englishmen, 1798–9; 42/ A 150, 152, treason, United Irish and English and LCS, 1798–9 (reports of Tunbridge and Gent); 43/ A 153, United Irishmen, depositions and papers; 44/ A 158, 161, 164, prisoners' depositions, letters and petitions, 1799; 3117, Despard's followers, reports of Tunbridge and Gent, 1798–9; 3490 (2), James Hadfield, depositions and papers, May 1800; 3526, 3528, 3535, 3536A, 3582, treason: examination of prisoners, reports of Moody and Powell, 1800–2; 3670, report on R. Brothers and followers; 4032, George Houston, Notes respecting *Ecce Homo*, 20 Feb. 1816; Additional Notes respecting *Ecce Homo*, 14 March 1816.

Treasury Solicitor's Papers
Series TS 11/ cases for the prosecution:

T. Ashe	469/1604
J.G. and E.H. Blagdon	462/1565
J. Brooks	1076/5315
J. Cahuac	762/2393
M.A. Clarke, *Recollections*, 3 vols. (n.d.)	120/329
T. Davison	45/172
E. Despard, Trial and Secret Papers	121–2/332–3
J. Duncombe	43/156
D.I. Eaton	978/3560
T.J. Evans	697/2210
J. Hadfield	223/937
W. Hodgson	459/1539
W. Hone	44/164
J. Hooper	1031/4431
G. Houston	7/183
J. Gale Jones	541/1755
R. Moggridge	839/2847
J. O'Coigley	689/2187
J. Panther	939/3361
T. Preston	197/859
Queen Caroline, prints and libels	94/304, 115/326, 120/330, 462/1565, 594/1950
T. 'Clio' Rickman	157/612
W.D. Saull	146/393
A. Seale	939/3362
D. Sedley	594/1950, 1071/5075
R. Shorter	42/155
Spenceans and Cato Street Conspirators 1816–20	197–206/859–79, 208 [pikeheads, 1820]
R. Taylor	1072/5112
C. Trust	47/182
S. Waddington	91/290, 424/1345

W. Watling   155/468
R. Wedderburn   45/167
H. White and the *Independent Whig*,   40/144, 41/147–8,
1808–14   603/1974, 978/3561
T. Williams   978/3561
Series TS 24/ Sedition Cases and Pamphlets, Confiscated Pamphlets, Leaflets and
Letters: 3/104, R. Taylor, *Manifesto of the Christian Evidence Society* (1825); 5/
27–71, *Independent Whig*, 1817–21; 7/ 44–51, *Democratic Recorder and Reformer's Guide*, 1819; 11/ 6–11, Correspondence, 1795–7 (includes Thelwall
and White); 99, *Address and Regulations of the Society of Spencean Philanthropists* (1815); 157, T. Evans, *Christian Policy* (1816); 175, 'Triumph of Liberty'
[Spencean song, n.d.].

King's Bench Records
Series KB 28: Crown Roll Indictments for Conspiracies and Misdemeanours (sedi-
tious and obscene libels):
W. Benbow   477/76–7 (1821)
J.B. Brookes   512/19 (1830), 511/30
                                                                   (1830)
G. Cannon   515/13 (1830), 604/2 (1853)
W. Clarke   483/52 (1822)
T. Davison   475/58 (1820)
T. Dolby   477/94 (1821)
J. Dugdale   602/2 (1853)
W. Dugdale   512/4 (1830), 535/45 (1835),
                                                            600/3 (1853)
E. Duncombe   509/22 (1829), 534/14
                                             (1835), 543/4 (1837), 602/1
                                                                   (1853)
J. Duncombe   473/13 (1820), 509/21
                                                                   (1829)
E. Dyer   504/13 (1828), 602/3 (1853)
T.J. Evans   476/76–7 (1820)
J. Ferguson   512/3 (1830)
R. Fores   479/28 (1821)
B. Gregory   567/24 (1843)
J. Mawbey   504/34 (1828)
T. Preston   460/13 (1817)
J.W. Trust   512/2 (1830)
R. Wedderburn   472/19 (1820), 473/55
                                                                   (1820)
H. White   433/34 (1810), 436/31
                                                                   (1811)

Records of the Metropolitan Police Office
Series MEPO 1/ Office of the Commissioner: Letter Books: 32, March-July 1839;
33, July-Oct. 1839; 34, Oct.-Dec. 1839.

Chancery Solicitor's Papers
MS, C. 216/4, Index: Admission Registers, Staple Hall.

BODLEIAN LIBRARY, OXFORD

Burdett Papers, MS Eng. hist b 199; c 295–6.

BRITISH LIBRARY

Additional Manuscripts:

Broughton Papers	Corr. 36350, 36457; Diary, 1820–1, 36541
William Cobbett, Letters and Transcripts, 1806–19	31125–7, 31857
William Drummond, Letters to Lord Grenville, 1800–12	59023
William Hone, Correspondence, 1780–1842	40120, 40856, 41071, 50746
James Leigh Hunt, Correspondence	38108, 38523
Francis Place Papers	27789–97, 27808–9, 27811–18, 27823, 27825–31, 27838–9, 27850–2, 35146, 35152–3, 36623–5, 37949–50
James Campbell [Reddie], 'Bibliographic Notes on Illustrated Works' (pencil notes by H.S. Ashbee)	38828–30

BRITISH LIBRARY, SCRAPBOOKS, UNPUBLISHED WORKS AND NEWSPAPER COLLECTIONS

Place Newspaper Collection, Sets 18, 39–40, 59–61, 71.
'Satirical Songs and Miscellaneous Papers on the Return of Queen Caroline to England'.
C.R. Dawes, 'A Study of Erotic Literature in England, Considered with Especial Reference to Social Life', Cheltenham, 1943, typed manuscript, Cup. 364, d. 15.

CAMBRIDGE UNIVERSITY LIBRARY

William Smith, Correspondence and Family Papers, 1756–1835, Add. MS 7621.

CORPORATION OF LONDON RECORD OFFICE

London Session Books, Index to Persons Indicted, 1756–1820, 1821–34.
Sessions Records, Oaths and Declarations of Dissenting Ministers – Signatures to Oaths under 52 G III, c.155, 1813–43.
Certificates of Dissenting Meeting Houses, 1792–1841.
Sessions Papers, Printers' Notices, 1799–1808, 1808–24, 1821–8, 1829–39.

CORPORATION OF LONDON RECORD OFFICE, GUILDHALL LIBRARY

Isaac Reid's Copy of the Rolls of the Young Men of Staple Inn, 1716–1807.
Mormon Index to Baptisms and Marriages (select names).
Letter Book of John Atkins, Lord Mayor, 1818–19.
Register of Dissenters' Meeting Houses, 1791–1852.
Norman Collection: London Taverns ... Public Houses ... and other places of amusement ... Introduction and vols. 1–5.

LONDON COUNTY HALL RECORD OFFICE

Register of Dissenting Ministers under 1 W+M, C.18 (1688), Middlesex, 1755–1829.
Register of Printing Presses: Middlesex, 1799–1819, 1821–67; Westminster, 1799–1814, 1821–5.
Register of Quaker and Dissenter's Meeting Places, Certs. 1789, 1829, 1832.
Newgate Calendars, 1820–2, 1830–53.
Calendars of Indictments, 1754–1832.
Printing Press Licences, 1799–1825.
Westminster Sessions Records, Sessions Papers, 1689–1844 (selected papers).
Middlesex June Sessions, 1829, Return of Persons Tried for Felonies and Misdemeanours.

DEVON COUNTY RECORD OFFICE, EXETER

Addington Papers: Corr. 1811. (Dissenting Ministers); Corr. 1812, Ecclesiastical; Corr. 1813–19, Law and Order, Unrest, Home Affairs; Corr. 1820, Law and Order, Unrest, Social Unions.

EMMANUEL COLLEGE LIBRARY, CAMBRIDGE

William Burdon Papers: Correspondence, 1781–1813.

GENERAL REGISTER OFFICE, LONDON

Certificate of Death, George Cannon, 7 June 1854, Middlesex House of Correction, Clerkenwell.

HUNTINGDON LIBRARY, CALIFORNIA

Richard Carlile Papers, 1790–1843.

LONDON SCHOOL OF ECONOMICS LIBRARY

Correspondence of William Hone, 1830, Pamphlet Collection P/194418–39; R(SR) 422h, 'Spence and the Spenceans'.

MANCHESTER COLLEGE LIBRARY, OXFORD

Correspondence of Rev. William Shepherd, 1768–1847, vols. ix–x.

MANCHESTER PUBLIC LIBRARY
Diary of Henry Hunt, 1820–1, 13262.

PRUDENTIAL ASSURANCE COMPANY LIBRARY, LONDON
Admissions to Chambers, Staple Inn, 17 June 1767–1813.

UNIVERSITY COLLEGE, LONDON
Ogden Papers, MS 74, Correspondence of William Hone, 4 vols.

UNIVERSITY OF NOTTINGHAM LIBRARY
Portland Papers, Correspondence of 3rd Duke of Portland, Home Secretary, July
    1794–1801, Pwf. 3928–44, 9845, 10511–16.

DR WILLIAMS LIBRARY, LONDON
Diary of Henry Crabb Robinson.

PRIVATE POSSESSION
Dr S. Spilsbury, Bristol: journal of J.A. St John, 'Memoir [*sic*] d'un philosophe,
    ecrites par lui même', 1821–2.

Printed Sources

REPORTS FROM PARLIAMENTARY COMMITTEES:

   1799, 1801, x: *Report from the Committee of Secrecy ... relating to Seditious
      Societies, 15 March 1799; Report from the Committee of Secrecy ... relative to the
      State of Ireland and certain disaffected Persons in both parts of the United Kingdom,
      13 April, 15 May 1801.*
   1817, iv: *Report from the Committee of Secrecy, 19 Feb. 1817; Second Report of the
      Committee of Secrecy, 20 June 1817; Report of the Secret Committee of the House
      of Lords, 23 June 1817.*
   1818, iii: *Report from the Committee of Secrecy, 27 Feb. 1818.*

NEWSPAPERS AND PERIODICALS

(Published in London unless otherwise stated. Editor's name, where known, ap-
    pears in brackets.)
Annual Register, selected dates, esp. 1802, 1812–14, 1816–21.
Axe Laid to the Root, or Fatal Blow to the Oppressors, [1817], i–viii (R. Wedderburn).
Black Dwarf, Jan. 1817–Jan. 1824, 5 vols. (T.J. Wooler).
Bookseller, 1868, pp. 448–9, 'Mischievous Literature'.

Cap of Liberty, 8 Sept. 1819–4 Jan. 1820, i–xiii (James Griffin).

Champion, Jan.–Dec. 1821 (J. Thelwall).

Christian Corrector, April 1831–June 1832 (W. Parkin).

Cigar, 1825, 2 vols. (W. Clarke).

Cobbett's Weekly Political Register, 1802–35, intensively 1812–13, 1816–21 (W. Cobbett, G. Houston, W. Benbow).

Correspondent, New York, 20 Jan. 1827–18 July 1829, i–v (G. Houston).

Cosmopolite, 10 March 1832–23 Nov. 1833 (A. Somerville?).

Crim. Con. Gazette, later *Bon Ton Gazette*, 25 Aug. 1838–4 Jan. 1840 (G. Hucklebridge).

Deist, 1819–20, 2 vols. (R. Carlile).

Deists' Magazine, or Theological Inquirer, published by T. Davison, alternatively entitled *Polemical Magazine and Theological Inquirer*, [1820] (G. Cannon).

Democratic Recorder and Reformer's Guide, later *Democratical Recorder*, Sept.–Oct. 1819, in TS 24/4/7 (G. Edmonds).

Devil's Pulpit, 1832, 2 vols. (R. Taylor, R. Carlile).

Examiner: A Sunday Paper, 1808–21 (J. Leigh Hunt and John Hunt).

Exquisite, 1842–4 (W. Dugdale).

Flowers' Political Review and Monthly Miscellany, 1811, ix (B. Flower).

Forlorn Hope, or Call to the Supine, [1817] i–ii (R. Wedderburn, Chas. Jennison).

Freethinking Christians' Magazine, Feb. 1811–Dec. 1814, 4 vols. (S. Thompson, W. Coates?).

Freethinking Christians' Quarterly Register, 1823–5, 2 vols.

Gauntlet, 10 Feb. 1833–30 March 1834 (R. Carlile).

Giant Killer, or Anti-Landlord, Aug. 1814, i–ii (T. Spence), in BL, Add. MS 27808.

Gorgon, May 1818–April 1819 (J. Wade).

Hogs' Wash, or A Salmagundy for Swine, later *Politics for the People*, 1794–5, 2 vols. (D.I. Eaton).

Hoxton Sausage [1829?] (J. Mitford).

Illustrated London Life, 1843 (R. Nicholson).

Independent Whig, selected dates especially 1812–17 (H. White).

Isis, 11 Feb. 1832–15 Dec. 1832 (R. Carlile, E. Sharples).

Liberal, 1822–3, (J. Leigh Hunt *et al.*).

Lion, 4 Jan. 1828–25 Dec. 1829 (R. Carlile).

London Alfred, or People's Recorder, 25 Aug. 1819–10 Nov. 1819 (T. Davison).

Man: Rational Advocate for Universal Liberty, 1833, i (R. Lee).

Manchester Observer, 1820–1, Manchester (T.J. Evans).

Mechanics' Magazine, 1823–4 (J. Robertson).

Medusa, or Penny Politician, 20 Feb. 1819–1 Jan. 1820 (T. Davison?).

Minerva, or Literary, Entertaining and Scientific Journal, New York, 6 April 1822–2 Sept. 1825 (G. Houston).

Mirror of Literature, Amusement and Instruction, 1822–3 (J. Limbird).

Monthly Repository of Theology and General Literature, select numbers 1811–12, 1823.

Morning Chronicle, 1816–33, selected dates (J. Black).

Newgate Monthly Magazine, or Calendar of Men, Things and Opinions, Sept. 1824–Aug. 1826 (W. Campion, R. Hassell, T.R. Perry).

New London Rambler's Magazine, n.d. [c.1828–30?] ([J. Mitford]; publisher J. Duncombe).

One Pennyworth of Pig's Meat; or Lessons for the Swinish Multitude, 1793–5, 3 vols. (T. Spence).

Paul Pry, 1826, nos. 2–4, 7–11, 13–17.

Paul Pry, later *Intelligence*, then *Alfred*, 28 Feb. 1830–28 April 1833.

Penny Punch, 1849 (T. Frost; publisher W. Dugdale).

Philanthropist, 1795–6, 2 vols. (D.I. Eaton).

Philanthropist: or Repository for Hints and Suggestions calculated to promote the comfort and happiness of Man, 1811–14 (W. Allen).

Philomathic Journal and Literary Review, 1825, ii.

Picture of the Times, in a letter addressed to the people of England, 1795, i–xxxi (H.D. Symonds).

Pocket Magazine of Classic and Polite Literature, 1820, v (J. Arliss).

Political Letters and Pamphlets, 1830–1 (W. Carpenter).

Poor Man's Guardian, 9 July 1831–26 Dec. 1835 (H. Hetherington, T. Mayhew, B. O'Brien).

Prompter, 13 Nov. 1830–12 Nov. 1831 (R. Carlile).

Quizzical Gazette, 1831–2 (J. Mitford; publisher J. Duncombe).

Radical Magazine, or Reformer's Guide, i, Feb. 1821 (W. Benbow).

Radical Reformer, or People's Advocate, Sept.–Dec. 1819, i–x (Wm Mason).

Rambler's Magazine, [Jan. 1822–Dec. 1823, April 1824–July 1825] (W. Benbow).

Ranger's Magazine, or man of fashion's companion, 1795, i (J. Sudbury), in BL. Add. MS 27825.

Reasoner, 1808, i (J. Bone).

Reformists' Register, 28 Sept. 1811–25 Jan. 1812 (J. Hunt).

Reformists' Register and Weekly Commentary, 1 Feb.–25 Oct. 1817 (W. Hone).

Republican, A Weekly Historical Magazine, Jan.–May 1813 (T.J. Wooler).

Republican, 1 March–29 March 1817 (W. Sherwin).

Republican, 27 Aug. 1819–29 Dec. 1826 (R. Carlile).

Satirist, or Monthly Meteor, 1808–14, (publisher M. Jones).

Satirist, or Censor of the Times, 10 April 1831–Dec. 1835, selected nos. 1838–9 (B. Gregory).

Scourge for the Littleness of Great Men, 4 Oct. 1834–21 Jan. 1835 (R. Carlile).

Shadgett's Weekly Review, 1 Feb. 1818.

Shamrock, Thistle and Rose, Aug.–Sept. 1819 (J. Watson), in PRO, HO 42/182.

Shepherd, A London weekly Periodical illustrating the Principles of Universal Science, 1834–8, 3 vols. (J.E. Smith).

Sherwin's Weekly Political Register, March 1817–Aug. 1819 (W. Sherwin, R. Carlile).

Slap at the Church, 1832 (W. Carpenter, J. Cleave).

Theological Comet, or Freethinking Englishman, 24 July–13 Nov. 1819 (R. Shorter).

Theological Inquirer; or, Polemical Magazine, March–Sept. 1815, I vol. (G. Cannon).

Thief, 21 April–1 Sept. 1832.

The Times, 1800–67, selected dates.

Town, 3 June 1837–26 Jan. 1842 (R. Nicholson).

Universalist's Miscellany, or Philanthropist's Museum, 1797–1801, 5 vols. (W. Vidler).

Wag, 1837.
White Hat, Oct.–Nov. 1819 (C. Teulon).
Yellow Dwarf, 1818 (J. Hunt).

CONTEMPORARY BOOKS, PAMPHLETS, AUTOBIOGRAPHIES,
CORRESPONDENCE ETC.

Lengthy titles have been shortened. Where appropriate anonymous works have
been filed under publisher in brackets followed by 'pub.'. It is not certain in such
cases that the publisher is also the author.

Adventures of Thomas Eustace, by a Clergyman (1820).
Anti-Jacobin (pseud.), *New Lights on Jacobinism, abstracted from Professor Robison's
'History of Freemasonry'* (1798).
[Ashbee, Henry Spencer], Fraxi, Pisanus (pseud.), *Index librorum prohibitorum; Being
Notes Bio-Biblio-Icono-graphical and Critical, on Curious and Uncommon Books*
(1877).
 *Centuria librorum absconditorum: Being Notes Bio-Biblio-Icono-graphical and Criti-
cal, on Curious and Uncommon Books* (1879).
 *Catena librorum tacendorum; Being Notes Bio-Biblio-Icono-graphical and Critical, on
Curious and Uncommon Books* (1885).
[Ashe, Thomas], *The Spirit of 'The Book'; or, memoirs of Caroline, Princess of Has-
burgh*, 3 vols. (1811).
 *A Concise Abridgement of ... the Spirit of 'The Book', or Memoirs of Caroline, Princess
of Hasburgh, A Political and Amatory Romance*, published by W. Mason.
 Memoirs and Confessions, 3 vols. (1815).
 Algernon and Caroline, or the Spirit of the Spirit (1820).
 Blackmantle, Bernard (pseud.), *Fitzalleyne of Berkeley: a romance of the present
times* (1825).
Bamford, Samuel, *The Autobiography of Samuel Bamford*, ed. W.H. Chaloner, 2 vols.
(1893, repr. 1967).
Barlow, Joel, *Advice to the Privileged Orders* (1795).
Baverstock, James, *Treatises on Brewing ... containing a biographical sketch of the
author ... by J.H. Baverstock* (1824).
Baxter, John, *Resistance to Oppression: The Constitutional Right of Britons Asserted ...*
(1795).
[Bell, R.], *Religion and Morality Vindicated ... or, An Account of the Life and Character
of John Church, the Obelisk Preacher ...* (1813).
Benbow, William, *Censorship Exposed* (Manchester, 1818).
 Fair Play, or, Who are the Adulterers, Slanderers and Demoralizers? (1820).
 Horrida Bella; Pains and Penalties vs Truth and Justice (1820).
 Khouli Khan; or, the Progress of Error (1820).
 *Letter to the King; shewing by incontestable facts, the fundamental causes of our
unexampled national distress ...* (1820).
 Letters from the Queen to the King (1820).
 A Peep at the Peers ... (1820), in Place Coll. 18, fo. 135.
 Sultan Sham and his Seven Wives ... (1820).
 The Whigs Exposed: or Truth by Daylight (1820).

Woolwich Law! Placards in Defence of the Queen (1820).

Eglantine, Edward (pseud.), *Memoirs of the Life of the Celebrated Mrs Q –* (1822).

The Crimes of the Clergy, or the Pillars of priest-craft shaken, 2 vols. (1823).

A Scourge for the Laureate, in reply to his infamous letter of 13 Dec. 1824 ... [1825].

Confessions of Julia Johnston [1826].

The Trial of William Benbow and others at the Middlesex Sessions, 16 May 1832, for leading the procession on Fast day, March 1821 (1832).

Grand National Holiday, and Congress of the Productive Classes (1832).

Brown, W.J. (pseud.), *Basia: The Kisses of Joannes Secundus* (1838), published by Benbow.

Bewick, Thomas, *A Memoir of Thomas Bewick written by himself,* ed. Iain Bain (Oxford, 1979).

Binns, John, *The Trial of John Binns, Deputy of the London Corresponding Society, for sedition ... Aug. 12, 1797 ...* (Birmingham, 1797).

Recollections of the Life of John Binns ... (Philadelphia, 1854).

Bone, John, *The Age of Civilization, a work designed to indicate and promote the progress to human perfection* (1816).

Bowles, John, *Thoughts on the late General Election as demonstrative of the progress of Jacobinism* (1802).

Brandreth, Jeremiah, *Trials of J. Brandreth, Wm Turner, I. Ludlum, G. Weightman and others for High Treason* (1817).

British Forum, *A New Edition of the Rules, Regulations etc. of the British Forum* (1808), in HO 42/143.

Brock, I., *A Letter to the Inhabitants of Spitalfields on the character and views of our modern reformers ...* (1817).

[Brookes, J.B., pub.], *The Inutility of Vice* (Avery's reprint, pseud., Paris, 1880; original edn c.1830).

Burdett, Sir Francis, *A Complete Account of the Proceedings and Disturbances relative to Sir Francis Burdett, containing his committal to the Tower ...* (1810).

Fairbairn's edition of the Trial of Sir Francis Burdett on a charge of seditious libel against His Majesty's Government ... 22 March 1820 (1820).

Burdon, William, *Three Letters Addressed to the Bishop of Llandaff* (Cambridge, 1795).

A Reply to two pamphlets, in answer to the question, 'Why do we Go to War?' ... (1803).

Materials for Thinking (1810).

Burke, Edmund, *Thoughts on a Regicide Peace* (1796).

Reflections on the Revolution in France (Harmondsworth, 1968).

Byron, G.G.N., Baron, *Don Juan* (Thomas Davison, 1819) (Benbow, 1822) (Hodgson, 1822 (with preface)) (Dugdale, 1823 (with preface)) (P. Griffin, 1823 (with notes)) (Benbow, 1824) (For the Booksellers, pseud., J. Duncombe, n.d.).

The Two Visions or Byron vs. Southey, containing 'The Vision of Judgement' (Dugdale, 1822).

English Bards, and Scotch Reviewers (Benbow, 1823).

Cain: A Mystery (Benbow, 1824) (Dugdale, 1826) (W. Croft, 1830) (J. Watson, 1832).

Manfred, A Dramatic Poem (Dugdale, 1824).

Childe Harold's Pilgrimage (Dugdale, 1825).

The Giaour; A Fragment of a Turkish Tale (Dugdale, 1825).

Miscellaneous Poems (Benbow, 1825).

Prophecy of Dante (Dugdale, 1825).

Cahuac, J., *Her Majesty's Protest against the decision of the Privy Council* (1821).

[Cannon, George], Perkins, Rev. Erasmus (pseud.), *Collectanea Sceptica-Prospectus* (Davison, n.d. [1819]).

A *Few Hints Relative to the Texture of Mind and the Manufacture of Conscience ...* [1820].

(translator, editor), Louvet de Couvray, J.B., *The Amours of the Chevalier de Faublas*, 4 vols. (Benbow, 1822).

(translator, editor), *Manual of the Theophilanthropists: or, Address of God and Lovers of Mankind* (Griffin, 1822).

(editor) [Swediauer, F.-X.], *The Philosophical Dictionary* (Benbow, 1822).

The Bagnio Miscellany, containing The Adventures of Lois Lovecock (Carrington edn, 1892; orig. c.1828–30).

Birchen Bouquet; or, Curious and Original Anecdotes of Ladies fond of administering the Birch Discipline (Avery edn, 1881; orig. c.1830).

The Elements of Tuition and Modes of Punishment ... (Avery edn, Booksellers, pseud., 1880; orig. c.1830, G. Peacock 1794, pseud.).

The Exhibition of Female Flagellants, pts I–II (Dugdale edn, Theresa Berkeley, pseud., c.1860; orig. c.1830).

Mustapha, Abdul (pseud.), *Festival of Passions; or, Voluptuous Miscellany, by an Amateur* (Dugdale edn, Andrew White, pseud., 1863, vol. 2; orig. c.1830).

(translator, editor), Wilson, Mary (pseud.), *The Voluptuous Night: or, Ne Plus Ultra of Pleasure*, with *The Whore's Catechism* (Sarah Brown, pseud., 1830).

Carlile, Richard, *An Address to the Men of Science ...* (1821).

A New Year's Address to the Reformers of Great Britain (1821).

Everyman's Book, or, What is God? (1826).

The Gospel According to Richard Carlile ... (1827).

A View and Review of Robert Owen's Projects; or, the manspel according to Robert Owen (n.d. [1838]).

[Carlile, Richard], Philanthropos (pseud.), *The Character of the Jew Books* (1821).

The Character of a King (1821).

The Character of a Peer (1821).

The Character of a Priest (1821).

Cartwright, John, *The Life and Correspondence of Major Cartwright*, ed. F.D. Cartwright, 2 vols. (1826).

(Chubb, W.P., pub.), *Memoirs and Amorous Adventures of Harriette Wilson* (n.d., chap-book edn printed by W. Mason).

Memoirs of the Public and Private Life ... of Madam Vestris ... (n.d.)

The Amatory Life of the Marchioness of C-u-n-g-h-m ... (1820).

Church, John, *The Thirteen Names of the First Patriarchs ...* (1811).

A Feast for Serpents, being the substance of a Sermon preached at the Obelisk Chapel, 31 March 1813 [1813].

The Living Letter written with the Pen of Truth ... (1814).

A Few Remarks on the Scripture History of Saul and the Witch of Endor (1816).

The Believer's Confidence in a Faithful God ... (1817).

The Gracious Designs of God accomplished by the malice of his enemies ... (1819).

Is this Your Likeness? A Scriptural Definition of Hypocrisy (1826).

Clarke, Mary Anne (pseud.), *A Plain Statement of Facts, wherein the character and conduct of G. Lloyd Wardle is rescued from the malignancy of party* ... (n.d.).

(pseud.), *Biographical Memoirs and Anecdotes* ... (W. Wilson edn, 1809).

Memoirs (C. Chapple edn, 1809).

(pseud.), *The Rival Princes; or, a faithful narrative of facts*, 2 vols. (Chubb edn, 1810).

(pseud.?), *The Rival Dukes* ... (M. Jones edn, 1810).

Clarke, W. (pseud.?), *The Authentic and Impartial Life of Mrs Mary Anne Clarke* (1809).

Clarke, William, *Reply to the anti-matrimonial hypothesis and supposed atheism of P.B. Shelley, as laid down in 'Queen Mab'* (1821).

Every Night Book; or Life After Dark (1827).

Three Courses and a Dessert ... (1830).

Clifford, Robert, *Memoirs Illustrating the History of Jacobinism*, 4 vols. (1797).

Application of Barruel's 'Memoirs of Jacobinism' to the Secret Societies of Ireland and Great Britain (1798).

Coates, William, *A Plea for the Unity of the Christian Church* ... (1821).

Cobbett, William, *Bloody Buoy* ... *Thrown Out as a Warning to the Political Pilots of All Nations* ... (1797).

Cobbett's Paper Against Gold; the history and mystery of the Bank of England (1821).

Cobbett's Sermons (1822).

The Autobiography of William Cobbett, ed. William Reitzel (1967).

Coldbath Fields, *An Impartial Statement of the Inhuman Cruelties Discovered in the Coldbath Fields Prison, by the Grand and Traverse Juries for the County of Middlesex* ... (1800).

A Further Account ... *of the Cruelties discovered in the Coldbath Fields Prison, as reported in the House of Commons on* ... *22 July 1800* ... (1800).

Considerations on the late Elections for Westminster and Middlesex (1802).

Conyngham, Lady Elizabeth, *The Memoirs of the Celebrated Lady C – m* (H. Price edn [1825]).

The Amatory Life of the Marchioness of C-ny-gh-m, first lady of the Royal Bedchamber ... [1835].

Cornelius (pseud.), *Extracts from Professor Robison's 'Proofs of a Conspiracy'* ... (1799).

(Cousins, B., pub.), *Eliza Grimwood, A Domestic Legend of Waterloo Road* [c.1839].

Davenport, Allen, *The Kings, or Legitimacy Unmasked* (1819), copy in HO 42/202.

Claremont; or the Sorrows of a Prince [1820?].

Queen of the Isles [1820].

The Muses' Wreath (1827).

The Life, Writings and Principles of Thomas Spence ... (1836).

The Life and Literary Pursuits of Allen Davenport ... (1845).

The Origin of Man and Progress of Society (1846).

Davison, Thomas, *The Trial of Thomas Davison for publishing a Blasphemous libel in the 'Deists' Magazine', in the Court of Kings Bench, Oct. 23, 1820, with a prefatory letter from Erasmus Perkins* (1820).

An Appeal to Public Feeling on Behalf of the Wife and three infants of Mr Davison, who is now confined in Okeham Gaol for two years, for a libel (1820).

The First Chapter of a New Book; or, The Complaints and Sufferings of a patient nation made manifest by the Goddess of Liberty (1820).

The Second Chapter of a New Book ... (1820).

A Short Way with the Deists; or Sound Reasons for being a Christian [1820?].

A Declaration of the Rights of the People, adapted to the present period (1821).

Plain Questions to Trinitarians Addressed to His Grace, the Archbishop of Canterbury (1821).

The Right Assumed by the Judges to fine a Defendant while making his defence in person denied ... (1821).

Despard, Edward Marcus, *The Trial of Edward Marcus Despard esq. for High Treason* (1803).

Detrosier, Rev. R., *An Address on the necessity of an extension of moral and political instruction among the working classes ...* (1832).

Dobell, Sydney, *The Life and Letters of Sydney Dobell*, ed. E.J. [E. Jolly], 2 vols. (1878).

Dolby, Thomas, *A Letter to the People of England upon Passing Events* [1820?].

Sketch of the Life and Suffering of James Byrne ... (1822).

Subscription for James Byrne (1822).

Memoirs of Thomas Dolby ... late printer and publisher of Catherine Street, Strand ... (1827).

Douglas, Lady Charlotte, *A Vindication of the conduct of Lady Douglas during her intercourse with the Princess of Wales* (1814).

Drummond, Sir William, *Oedipus Judaicus* (1811).

[Dugdale, William, pub.], *The Lady Flora Hastings: Her Life and Death. With Questions for the Queen and Criticisms of her Court* (n.d. [c.1839]).

An Essay on Women ... Suppressed by Authority (n.d., R. Smith, pseud. [c.1860]).

On the Use of Night-Caps, or Seven Years Experience on the Practicability of limiting the number of a family ... (n.d., J. Turner, pseud.).

Nunnery Tales, or Cruising under False Colours: A Tale of Love and Lust, 3 vols. (n.d.).

The Singular Life, Amatory Adventures and Extraordinary Intrigues of John Wilmot, the renowned Earl of Rochester ... (n.d., H. Smith, pseud. [c.1861]).

Yokel's Preceptor: or, More Sprees in London! ... (n.d., H. Smith, pseud.).

Memoirs of Hariette [sic] Wilson by herself [c.1825, reissued c.1838].

Memoirs of Fanny Hill (H. Smith, pseud. [c.1841]).

(preface and memoir), F.M.A. de Voltaire, *The Philosophical Dictionary* (1843).

Don Leon; a poem by the late Lord Byron ... and forming part of the private journal of his lordship ... [1866].

(Duncombe, E., pub.), *Abduction; une nouvelle maniere d'attraper une femme ...* (n.d.).

Memoirs of Harriet [sic] Wilson – including her Amatory adventures with most of the Nobility of the Present Day [c.1826].

Memoirs, Public and Private ... of Mrs Charles Mathews, late Madame Vestris [c.1830].

[Duncombe, E., pub.], *Memoirs of a Man of Pleasure* [c.1835].

(Duncombe, J., pub.), *Beppo in London, a metropolitan story* (1819).

   The Loyal Anthem of God Save the Queen (1820).

   Mathews in America (1820).

   Duncombe's edition of Mathews at Home ... (1821, 1826).

   Nell Gwynne (1825).

   New British Theatre, selected nos. 1–532 (1825–65).

   Mathews' Drolleries [c.1830].

   The Fal-Lal Songster ... [c.1833].

   Metford (pseud.), *The Flash Olio* ... [c.1833].

   Metford (pseud.), *The Funny Songster* ... [c.1833].

   The Rummy Cove's Delight ... [c.1833].

   The Swell! or Slap-up Chaunter ... [c.1833].

   Adventures of Famous Highwaymen [c.1834].

   Griffinhoofe, A. (pseud.), *Memoirs of the Life* ... *of Madam Vestris* (1839, 1845).

   Brigand Tales, 2 vols. [1840].

   J. Labern's Original Comic Songs ... (1842).

   Labern's new comic song book (1852).

Dunlop, John, *The Philosophy of Artificial and Compulsory Drinking Usage in Great Britain and Ireland* (1839).

   The Universal Tendency to Association in Mankind, Analysed and Illustrated (1840).

Eaton, D.I. *The Catechism of Man, pointing out from sound principles and acknowledged facts, the rights and duties of every rational being* (1793).

   Extermination; or, An Appeal to the people of England on the present war with France (1793).

   Behold the Man (handbill, 1812).

   Trial of Mr Daniel Isaac Eaton, for publishing the third and last part of Paine's 'Age of Reason' ... *6 March 1812* ... (1812).

   Extortions and Abuses of Newgate, exhibited in a memorial and explanation ... (1813).

[Eaton, D.I.], Verax, Ebenezer (pseud.), *Wonderful Sermon, or truth undisguised to be described on the Fast Day* (1796).

   Antitype (pseud.), *The Pernicious effects of the art of printing upon society, exposed* ... (1794).

[Edwards, G.K., pub.], *Fanny Hill's New Friskey Chanter and Amorous Toast Master* (1836).

(Edwards, Richard, pub.), *Edwards's genuine edition of 'The Book', or the Proceedings and Correspondence upon the Subject of the Inquiry into the Conduct of Her Royal Highness, the Princess of Wales, under a commission appointed by the King in the year 1806* ... (1813).

(Emans, W., pub.), *The Murdered Queen, or Caroline of Brunswick. A diary of the court of George IV. By a lady of rank* (1838).

Evans, John, *Sketches of the Different Denominations of the Christians* (1814).

Evans, Thomas, *Humorous Catalogue of Spence's Songs*, Pts I–III [1811?], contains songs by Evans.

   Christian Policy, the Salvation of the Empire. Being a clear ... *examination into the causes that have produced the impending* ... *national bankruptcy* (1816).

The petitition of Thomas Evans ... to the House of Commons, 28 Feb. 1817 (1817).
Address to the Society of Christian Philanthropists (1818), in HO 42/191.
Christian Policy in Full Practice Among the People of Harmony ... To which are subjoined a concise view of the Spencean system of agrarian fellowship (1818).
A Brief Sketch of the Life of Mr Thomas Spence, author of the Spencean system of agrarian fellowship ... with a selection of the songs (Manchester, 1821).
[Evans, Thomas], *Address and regulations of the Society of Spencean Philanthropists ... with an abstract of Spence's plan* (1815).
Address of the Society of Spencean Philanthropists to all mankind, on the means of promoting liberty and happiness (1817).
Address of the Society of Spencean Philanthropists, To all Mankind, On the Means of promoting Liberty and Happiness [1819].
(Fairburn, John, pub.), *The Life of Joanna Southcott, the Prophetess* (1814).
The British Seamen and their Beloved Queen (1820).
Comic Constellation, or songster's galam-an-frey for 1820 (1820).
Fairburn's Edition of the Life, Amours and Exploits of Nell Gwinn [1820].
Fairburn's Laughable Jester (1820).
Fairburn's Quizzical Valentine for the Present Year (1820).
A Frown from the Crown, or, The Hydra Destroyed (1820).
God Save the Queen (1820).
Italian Liars! Witnesses against our Queen (1820).
The Royal Runaway; or, C– ... and Coachee!! [1820?].
The Queen's Budget Opened: or correspondence extraordinary relative to the defence of Her Majesty (1820).
The Queen of Hearts (1820).
The Queen that Jack Found (1820).
Salve Regina (1820).
A Warning to Noble Lords! previous to the Trial of Queen Caroline (1820).
The Bishop!! particulars of the charge against the Hon. Percy Jocelyn, Bishop of Clogher, for an abominable offence with John Molvelly ... [1822].
Fairburn's Genuine Edition of the Death-Bed Confessions of the late Countess of Guernsey ... [1822?].
The Northern Excursion of Geordie, Emperor of Gotham ... [1822].
Fairburn's Everlasting Songster (1823).
Atrocious Acts of Catholic Priests, who have lately committed the most Horrid and Diabolical Rape and Murders in Ireland and France ... [1824].
Rape and Assassination ... of Marie Gerin ... by Mingrat, a French Catholic Priest ... [1824].
Fairburn's Edition of the Trial of Cox vs. Keen (1825).
The Chronicle of the Kings of England, from William the Norman to the Death of George III (1826).
Social Songster [c.1842].
Fairburn's Annual Budget of New Songs (1843).
Fearon, Henry Bradshaw, *Sketches of America; a narrative of a journey ... with remarks on Mr Birbeck's 'Notes and Letters'* (1818).
Fitzpatrick, W.J., *The Life, Times and Contemporaries of Lord Cloncurry* (Dublin, 1855).

(Fores, S.W., pub.), *The Magic Lantern, or Green Bag Plot laid open* ... [1820], with MS notes.

Freethinking Christians, *Declaration of certain Members of the Church of God, to the Church Meeting at St. John's Square, London, and to the Churches of God meeting at Battle, Sussex and Dewsbury, Yorkshire* (1835).

Frost, Thomas, *Paul, the Poacher* (1848).

　Emma Mayfield (Caffyn, 1857 edn; orig. 1848).

　Alice Leighton; or the Murders at Druid's Stone (1857).

　Forty Years Recollections, Literary and Political (1880).

　Reminiscences of a Country Journalist (1886).

Galloway, Richard Hodgson, *Refutation of Certain Calumnious Statements concerning the late Alexander Galloway* ... (1871).

George IV (anonymous tracts attributed to, or about, him), *A Horn-Book for the Prince* (1811).

　The Acts of Adonis the Great (1820).

　The Depraved Husband, A dream (1820).

　The Old Black Cock in Jeopardy (1820).

　The Pig of Pall Mall (1820).

　The Royal Progress; a canto with notes [1821].

　Royal Rumping (1821).

Halhed, Nathaniel Brassey, *Two Letters to the Right Honourable Lord Loughborough, Lord High Chancellor of England on the present confinement of Richard Brothers in a private madhouse* (Riebau, 1795).

　Testimony of the Authenticity of the prophecies of Richard Brothers and of his mission to recall the Jews (1795).

Hall, Charles, *The Effects of Civilization on the People in European States* (1805).

Hardy, Thomas, *Memoir of Thomas Hardy, founder of and secretary to the London Corresponding Society* ... (1832).

Hazard, T., *A True Picture of Society as displayed by certain Rich Characters towards their poor neighbours* (1819), in HO 44/5, fos. 376–8.

Hazlitt, William, *Political Essays, with Sketches of Public Characters* (1819).

Hetherington, Henry, *Cheap Salvation, or an Antidote to Priestcraft, being a succinct, practical and essential rational religion adduced from the New Testament* (n.d. [1822?]).

　Principles and Practice Contrasted, or, a peep into 'The only true Church of God upon earth', commonly called Freethinking Christians (1828).

　The Objects and Laws of the National Union of the Working Classes (1831).

Hibbert, Julian, *A Dictionary of Modern Anti-Superstitionists* ... (1826).

Hodgson, William, *The Commonwealth of Reason* (1795).

　The Case of W. Hodgson, now confined in Newgate for the payment of £200 ... *considered and compared with the laws of the country* (1796).

[Holbach, Baron], Mirabaud (pseud.), *The System of Nature; or the Laws of the Moral and Physical World* (4 vols., W. Hodgson, 1795) (2 vols., 1817) (3 vols., T. Davison, 1820).

　Boulanger (pseud.), *Christianity Unveiled* (New York, 1795, BL edn, 900.h.24(7), contains MS notes by George Cullen).

　Freret, Nicholas (pseud.), *The Moseiade* (Eaton, 1812).

Freret, Nicholas (pseud.), *A Preservative against Religious Prejudices* (Eaton, 1812).
Ecce Homo! or, A critical inquiry into the history of Jesus Christ ... (1813).
Helvetius (pseud.), *The True Sense and Meaning of the System of Nature* (Eaton, 1812) (Carlile, 1824).
Holcroft, Thomas, *Memoirs of the late Thomas Holcroft* ..., ed. William Hazlitt, 3 vols. (1816).
The Life of Thomas Holcroft, ed. William Hazlitt, 2 vols. (repr. 1975).
[Holinsworth, C.B.], *Memoir of John Ward named Zion by the Call of God in the year 1818* (Birmingham, 1881).
Holyoake, G.J., *The Life and Character of Henry Hetherington* (1849).
Hone, William, *The meeting in Spa Fields. Hone's authentic and correct account ... of all the proceedings on Monday, Dec. 2, with the resolutions and petition of Nov. 15, 1816* (1816).
Hone's Riots in London, Part II, With most important and full particulars ... including original memoirs and anecdotes of Preston, Dyall, the Watson family, Thomas Spence ... (1816).
Napoleon and the Spots in the Sun (1816).
Bartholomew Fair Insurrection; and the Pie-bald Pony Plot (1817).
Full Report on the Third Spa Fields Meeting (1817).
The Late John Wilkes's Catechism of a Ministerial Member (1817).
The Political Litany (1817).
The Three Trials of William Hone ... (1818).
The Political House that Jack Built (1819).
The Apocryphal New Testament (1820).
Non Mi Ricordo (1820).
The Queen's Matrimonial Ladder (1820).
Ancient Mysteries Described, especially the English Miracle Plays (1823).
[Houston, George], *Israel Vindicated; being a refutation of the calumnies propagated respecting the Jewish Nation* (New York, 1823).
Hudson, J.W., *A History of Adult Education* (1851).
Hunt, Henry, *The Green Bag Plot* (1819).
A Letter from Mr. Hunt to Mr. Giles (1819).
A Letter from Mr. Hunt to Mr. West (1819).
The Triumphal Entry of Henry Hunt, esq., into London on ... Sept. 13, 1819 (1819).
Memoirs of Henry Hunt esq. ..., 3 vols. (1820).
Trial of Henry Hunt, J. Knight, J. Johnson, J.T. Saxton, S. Bamford, J. Healey ... for an alleged conspiracy to overturn the government (1820).
To the Radical Reformers, male and female, of England, Ireland and Scotland ... (1820–2).
Hunt, J. Leigh and John, *The Prince of Wales vs. 'The Examiner': a full report of the trial of John and Leigh Hunt* (1812).
Iliff, E.H., *Summary of the Duties of Citizenship; Written expressly for the members of the London Corresponding Society* ... (1795).
Jephson, Henry, *The Platform*, 2 vols. (1892).
Jerrold, W.B., *The Life and Remains of Douglas Jerrold* (1859).
(Johnston, J., pub.), *Odes to the Pillory* ... (n.d.).
Royal Quarrels ... (n.d.).

Letter from the Queen in reply to one from the King (1821).

Jones, John Gale, *Sketch of a Speech delivered at the Westminster Forum ... Dec. 1794* ... (1795).

   Substance of a Speech delivered at the Ciceronian School, Globe Tavern, 2 March 1795 ... (1795).

   Original Oration, November 29, 1796, in the Great Room in Brewer Street, on the resignation of General Washington (1796).

   Sketch of a Political Tour through Rochester, Chatham, Maidstone, Gravesend ... (1796).

   The Abuse of Prisons, or an interesting and Impartial Account of the House of Correction in Cold Bath Fields and the treatment of Mr. Gale Jones (1811).

   Substance of the Speeches of John Gale Jones delivered at the British Forum, 11, 18, 22 Mar. 1819 (1819).

   An Oration on the late General Washington ... (1825).

[Kaygill], *The Devil and Parson Church; or Birds of a Feather ...* (n.d. [1817]).

(King, Jonathan, ed.), Levi, D., *Dissertations on the Prophecies of the Old Testament, containing all such prophecies as are applicable to the Coming of the Messiah, the Restoration of the Jews and the Resurrection of the Dead ...*, 2 vols. (1817).

(L., H.), *The Horns exalted over the People ...* (1809).

Lee, 'Citizen', *King Killing* (handbill, 1794).

Lee, R.E., *Victimization, or Benbowism Unmasked. Addressed to the National Union of the Working Classes* (1832).

Linton, W.J., *James Watson; Memoir of the days of the fight for a free press ...* (Manchester, n.d.).

London Corresponding Society, *The Correspondence of the London Corresponding Society revised and corrected with explanatory notes ...* (1795).

   A Narrative of the proceedings at the general meeting of the London Corresponding Society held on Monday, July 31, 1797, in a field, near the Veterinary College, St. Pancras ... (1797).

Lovett, William, *The Life and Struggles of William Lovett in his pursuit of bread, knowledge and freedom* (1876, repr. 1920).

(Lowe, W., pub.), *The Highly Interesting Life of Lady William Lennox ...* (n.d.).

   Secrets of the Castle! The Life of the Marchioness of Co-y-n-h-m, First Lady of the Royal Bedchamber ... (n.d. [c.1820]).

Margarot, Maurice, *Proposal for a grand national Jubilee, restoring to every man his own, and therefore extinguishing both want and war* (Sheffield, n.d. [1812]).

   Thoughts on Revolutions (Harlow, 1812).

(Marks, J.L., pub.), *A Curious and Interesting Narrative of Poll House and the Marquis of C xxxx, late Lord T –* (n.d. [1822/3?]).

   The Queen of Trumps; or the Cabinet in Consternation (1820).

   A Correct Account of the Horrible Occurrence ... in which ... the ... Bishop of Clogher was a principal actor with a common soldier ... [1822], BL, *Pindaric Tracts*, vol. v.

   A Voyage to the North in search of a new Mistress, By an amorous old dandy [1822].

Mason, William, *Life of the Renowned Patriot and Reformer, John Hampden* (1819).

Mitford, John, *The Important Trial of J. Mitford, Esq. on the prosecution of ... Viscountess Perceval for perjury ...*, ed. T.A. Phipps (1814).

[Mitford, John], *A Narrative of the Circumstances which attended the separation of Lord and Lady Byron* (R. Edwards, 1816).

Burton, Alfred (pseud.), *The Adventures of Johnny Newcome in the Navy* ... (1818).

The Poems of a British Sailor (1818).

Extract of a letter, containing an account of Lord Byron's residence in ... *Mitylene* (1819).

A Peep into W-r Castle, after the Lost Mutton – with additions and notes by J. Mitford of Mitford Castle ... (Benbow, 1820), BL *Pindaric Poems*, vol xi.

[and Benbow, W.], *Description of the Crimes and Horrors* ... *in Warburton's private mad-house at Hoxton* ... *called Whitmore House*, 2 pts (1825).

The Private Life of Lord Byron; comprising his voluptuous amours (H. Smith, pseud. [W. Dugdale], 1836).

Monk, Maria, *Awful Disclosures of Maria Monk* (1833).

More, Hannah, *Remarks on a Speech of M. Dupont, made in the National Convention of France* ... (1793).

A Country Carpenter's Confession of Faith, with a few plain remarks on the 'Age of Reason' (1794).

Nicholson, John Renton, *Cockney Adventures* (1838).

The Swell's night guide; or, A peep through the great metropolis under the dominion of Nox ... (1846).

Rogue's Progress: An Autobiography of 'Lord Chief Baron' Nicholson, ed. John L. Bradley (1966).

[Nicholson, William], *The Doubts of Infidels, or queries relative to scriptural inconsistencies and contradictions* ... (1819).

Nightingale, Joseph, *The Religions and Religious Ceremonies of all Nations* (1821).

Norton, T., *The Duke of Cumberland* ... (1822).

Owen, Robert, *The New Religion; or, Religion founded on the immutable Laws of the Universe* ... *as developed in a public lecture delivered by Mr. Owen, at the London Tavern, Oct. 20, 1830* (1830).

Second Lecture on the new religion ... *delivered by Mr. Owen* ... *Dec. 15, 1830* (1830).

A New View of Society (1813–14) and *Report to the County of Lanark* (1821), ed. V.A.C. Gatrell (Harmondsworth, 1970).

Paine, Thomas, *Rights of Man* (part II, Symonds, 1792) (parts I and II, Eaton, 1795).

The Age of Reason (part I, Symonds, 1795) (parts I and II, Carlile, 1819) (part III, Eaton, 1811).

Letter to Erskine on the Prosecution of Thomas Williams for publishing the 'Age of Reason' (Paris, 1796).

The Decline and Fall of the English System of Finance (Eaton, 1796) (Carlile, 1819).

Agrarian Justice opposed to Agrarian Law ... (Carlile, 1819).

Age of Reason and other Theological Writings (Benbow [1821]).

Palmer, Elihu, *Principles of Nature, or a development of the moral causes of happiness and misery among the human species* (1819).

Payson, S., *Proofs of the Real Existence and Dangers of Illuminism* ... (1802).

Phillips, Josiah, *The Trial of Josiah Phillips for a libel on the Duke of Cumberland* (1833).

(Pitts, J., pub.), *The Royal Songster* ... (n.d.).

Place, Francis, *The Autobiography of Francis Place*, ed. Mary Thale (Cambridge, 1972).
  Illustrations and Proofs of the principle of population ... (1822).
Playfair, William, *The History of Jacobinism, its crimes, cruelties and perfidies* ... (1795).
Plowden, Francis, *Crim. Con. Biography* (1830).
Polemic Fleet of 1816, in TS 11/198/868.
Preston, Thomas, *The Life and Opinions of Thomas Preston, Patriot and Shoemaker* ... (1817).
  A Letter to Lord Viscount Castlereagh; being a full development of all the circumstances relative to the diabolical Cato St. plot (1820).
Reid, William Hamilton, *The Rise and Dissolution of the Infidel Societies in this Metropolis* ... (1800).
  Memoirs of the Life of Colonel Wardle ... (1809).
  Memoirs of the Public Life of John Horne Tooke, esq ... (1812).
Remarks on the Suppressed 'Book', as connected with the impending Bill of Pains and Penalties, To Divorce and Degrade Queen Caroline [1820].
Report of a Committee appointed by a public meeting ... on 23 Aug. 1820 ... for the purpose of ... raising subscriptions to present to ... the Queen, A Service of Plate (1820).
Report of the Proceedings during the late contested election for the County of Middlesex (J.S. Jordon, 1802).
(Richardson, J.M., pub.), *Chancery Injunction – Letters to H.R.H. Caroline, Princess of Wales: comprising the only true history of the celebrated Book* ... (1813).
Richmond, Alex B., *Narrative of the Conditions of the Manufacturing Population and Proceedings of Government which Led to the State Trial in Scotland* ... (1824).
Rickman, Thomas Clio, *Poems* (1820).
Robison, Professor John, *Proofs of a conspiracy against all the religions and governments of Europe carried on in the secret meetings of Freemasons, illuminati and reading societies* (1798).
Rose, William, *A Letter to the Rev. W.M. Douglas, M.A., Chancellor of the Diocese of Salisbury containing a review of the Spencean philosophy and in which its opposition to Holy Scriptures and fact is pointed out* (1817), in HO 42/165.
The Scum Uppermost when the Pot Boils Over (1802).
[Sellon, Edward], *The New Epicurean; or the Delights of Sex, Facetiously and Philosophically Considered* ... (1740, pseud. [Dugdale, 1865]).
Shelley, Mary, *Mary Shelley's Journal*, ed. F.L. Jones (Norman, 1938).
Shelley, Percy Bysshe, *Queen Mab: a philosophical poem with notes* (privately printed, 1813) (W. Clarke, 1821) (W. Baldwin, New York, pseud. [Cannon/Benbow, London]) (Carlile, 1822) (Brooks, 1829) (S. Hunt, 1830) (J. Carlile, Watson, 1832) (Hetherington, Watson, 1839).
  A Refutation of Deism, in a Dialogue (privately printed, 1814).
  The Letters of Percy Bysshe Shelley, Vol. One: Shelley in England, ed. F.L. Jones (Oxford, 1964).
Sketches of Obscure Poets with Specimens of their Writings (1823).
Society for the Suppression of Vice, *Address, Objects, Members* (1825).
  The Constable's Assistant: being a compendium (1831).

Southey, Robert, *Letters from England* (1807, repr. 1851).

Wat Tyler, a dramatic poem (1817).

Spence, Thomas, *The Jubilee Hymn. To be sung a hundred years hence, or sooner* (n.d.).

A New and Infallible way to make trade (n.d.).

Spence's Miscellanies. A New and Infallible Way to Make Peace at Any Time (n.d.).

A Suitable Companion to Spence's Songs. A fable (n.d.).

The Rights of Man as exhibited in a lecture read at the Philosophical Society in Newcastle ... (1793, 4th edn 1803).

The Case of Thomas Spence, Bookseller, ... committed to Clerkenwell Prison ... 10 Dec. 1792 ... (1793).

Marine Republic, or a description of Spensonia (1794).

The End of Oppression, being a dialogue between an old mechanic and a young one, concerning the establishment of the rights of man (1795).

A Letter from Ralph Hodge to his cousin, Thomas Bull (1795).

Pig's Meat: The Selected Writings of Thomas Spence, Radical and Pioneer Land Reformer (1795–6), ed. G.I. Gallop, Nottingham, 1982.

A Fragment of an ancient prophecy. Relating, as some think, to the present revolutions (1796).

The Meridian Sun of Liberty; or, the whole rights of man displayed ... (1796).

The Reign of Felicity, being a plan for civilizing the Indians of North America ... (1796).

The Rights of Infants; or, The imprescriptable rights of mothers to such a share of the elements as is sufficient to enable them to suckle and bring up their young ... (1797).

The Constitution of a Perfect Commonwealth: being the French Constitution of 1793, amended and rendered entirely conformable to the whole rights of man ... (1798).

The Restorer of Society to its Natural State, in a series of letters to a fellow citizen ... (1801).

The Important Trial of Thomas Spence ... on May 22, 1801 ... (1803) (BL edn contains lengthy MS annotations by George Cullen).

Something to the purpose. A receipt to make a Millennium or happy world (1803).

Humorous Catalogue of Spence's Songs, Pts I–III [1811?].

Stevens, William, *An Antidote to Intolerance and Assumption; or, a Peep into Mr. Coate's view of the only true Church of God, denominated Freethinking Christians ...* (1821).

(Stockdale, J.J., pub.), *The Claims of Mr. Wardle to the Thanks of the Country ...* (1809).

Sonnets for the year 1809, consisting of Mrs Clarke's Garland, Miss Taylor's Wreath ... (1809).

A minute detail of the attempt to assassinate ... the Duke of Cumberland ... (1810).

Memoirs of Harriette Wilson, 4 vols. (1825), another edn, 8 vols. (1831).

Paris Lions and London Tigers ... (1825).

Taylor, John, *Records of My Life*, 2 vols. (1832).

Taylor, Rev. Robert, *Remonstrance addressed to H.E. the Lord Lieutenant and to the Lord Chief Justice of Ireland and also to his Grace the Lord Archbishop against the proceedings of a consistorial and metropolitical court holden in Dublin, Aug. 10, 1822 ...* (1823).

The Holy Liturgy, or Divine Service on the Principles of Pure Deism ... (1826, 1827).

Trial of Robert Taylor ... upon a charge of blasphemy, with his defence, as delivered by himself ... (1827).

Syntagma of the evidences of the Christian Religion ... (1828).

The Diegesis, being a discovery of the origin, evidences and early history of Christianity (1829).

First to Thirteenth Moral Discourses (delivered 1826) (Nov. 1833–April 1834).

Thistlewood, Arthur, *Trials of Arthur Thistlewood, gent, James Watson, surgeon, Thomas Preston, cordwainer, and John Hooper, labourer, for High Treason ... June 9, 1817* (W. Lewis, 1817) (J. Fairburn, 1817).

Trials of A. Thistlewood, J. Ings, J. Brunt, R. Tidd, W. Davidson and others (J. Fairburn, 1820).

(Thomas, E., pub.), *The Book Itself, or Secret Memoirs of an Illustrious Princess ... A Political, Amatory and Fashionable Work* (1813, repr. [1820]).

(Thompson, J., pub.), *Memoirs, Public and Private Life, Adventures and Secret Amours of Mrs C.M., late Madame Vestris* (n.d.).

Secret Life and Extraordinary Amours of Ernest, King of Hanover, with all the particulars of the seduction of Lady Graves and mysterious death of Sellis exposed [1839?].

Thompson, Samuel, *Evidences of Revealed Religion, on a new and original plan* (1842, orig. edn 1812).

Timperley, C.H., *A Dictionary of Printers and Printing* (1849).

The Trials at large of Arthur Thistlewood, gent, James Watson, the elder, surgeon, Thomas Preston, cordwainer, and John Hooper, labourer, for high treason ... June 9, 1817 (W. Lewis, 1817).

[Turner, J., pub.], *The Depraved Husband – a Dream* [1820].

Vizetelly, H., *Glances Back Through Seventy Years*, 2 vols. (1893).

Volney, Count C.F., *Lectures on History* (J. Watson, n.d.).

The Ruins, or Revolutions of Empires (J. Johnson, 1794) (Eaton, 1810) (T. Davison, 1819) (T. Tegg, 1820, 1822, 1835) (T. Allman, 1842) (Besant/Bradlaugh, 1881).

The Law of Nature, or Catechism of French Citizens (Eaton, 1796) (J. Watson, 1833).

Voltaire, F.M.A. de, *The Philosophical Dictionary* (1796) (Sherwood, Rickman, 1819) (Brooks, 1831).

Saul (Jane Carlile, 1820).

Waddington, Samuel, *The Examination and Trial of Samuel Waddington, charged with publishing a seditious libel ... Horsemonger Lane, Aug. 31, 1819* (1819).

Letter to the Editor of the 'Traveller' upon his [S. Waddington's] committal to the New Bastile, Clerkenwell; upon the prison discipline and the scandalous and infidel-like conduct of having neither Bible or Prayer Book or Word of God for poor criminals to fly to, in the agony of their soul, to cheer them in the Dungeon's Gloom (1822), TS 11/424/1345.

The People's Universal Prayer for the Destruction of Tyrants and the Liberty of Nations (1822), in TS 11/424/1345.

Wade, John, *The Black Book, or corruption unmasked* (1820).

Ward, John, *Zion's Works: New Lights on the Bible from the coming of Shiloh, the*

Spirit of Truth, 16 vols. and catalogue (1899–1904; vol. x contains the periodical *Judgement Seat of Christ*).

Ward, R.P., *Tremaine: or the Man of Refinement*, 3 vols. (1825).

A Warning to the Frequenters of Debating Clubs; being a short history of the rise and progress of those clubs; with a report on the trial and conviction of John Gale Jones, the manager of one of them called the British Forum (1810).

Watson, 'Dr.' James, *High Treason! Fairburn's Edition of the Whole Proceedings on the Trial of James Watson, Senior, for High Treason ...*, 2 vols. (1817).

The Trial of James Watson for High Treason ... 9–16 June, 1817, 2 vols. (1817).

Wedderburn, Rev. Robert, *Truth Self-Supported; A Refutation of certain doctrinal errors generally adopted in the Christian Church* [c.1802].

A Letter Addressed to the Rev. Solomon Herschell, the High Priest of Israel ... concerning the origin of the Jewish prophecies and their expected Messiah (1819).

Address of the Rev. Robert Wedderburn to the Court of the King's Bench on appearing to receive judgement for blasphemy ... 9 May 1820, ed. Erasmus Perkins (1820).

Cast-Iron Parsons, or Hints to the public and the legislature on political economy ... (1820).

A Critical, Historical and Admonitory letter to the Right Rev. Father in God, His Grace the Archbishop of Canterbury [1820].

Trial of the Rev. Robert Wedderburn ... for Blasphemy ... containing a verbatim report of the defence, ed. Erasmus Perkins (1820).

High Heel'd Shoes for Dwarfs in Holiness, being plain directions to weak Christians how they may escape the snares of the Devil and the dreadful gulphs of Scepticism and Infidelity [1821].

The Horrors of Slavery exemplified in the life and history of the Rev. R. Wedderburn, V.D.M. (1824).

[Wedderburn, Rev. Robert], *Essay on Printing, by a Spencean Philanthropists* [*sic*] [1818].

Christian Policy: or Spence's Plan, in Prose and Verse, by a Spencean Philanthropist (1818).

Wesley, John, *The Works of John Wesley: Volume 7, A Collection of Hymns for the use of the People called Methodists*, eds. Franz Hilderbrandt, Oliver A. Beckerlegge and James Dale (Oxford, 1983).

[West, W., pub.], *The Randy Songster ...* (1834).

The Rambler's Flash Songster ... [1838?].

The Nobby Songster ... (1842).

Cuckold's Nest [c.1860].

The Cockchafer ... (1865).

The Flash Chaunter ... (1865).

West, William, *Tavern Anecdotes and reminiscences of the origins of signs, clubs, coffee-houses ...* (1825).

White, H., *The Trials at large of the Editor and Printer of the Independent Whig ...* (1808).

[Whitworth, T.], *An Apology for Deism; or a candid review of the modern popular system of Christianity* (1820).

Wilkinson, G.T., *Authentic history of the Cato Street Conspiracy ...* (1820).

Williams, T., *Constitutional Politics; or, The British Constitution Vindicated* (1817), in HO 42/172.

(Wilson, E., pub.), *Suppressed Evidence; R-l Intriguing* ... (n.d.).

R-y-l Stripes; or a kick from Yar-h to W-s ... (1812).

Wilson, Harriette, *Clara Gazul; or, Honi Soit qui mal y pense* (n.d.).

Harriette Wilson's Memoirs, 3 vols. (T. Douglas, 1825).

The Memoirs of Harriet [sic] Wilson ... the whole forming the most astonishing Picture of Voluptuousness and Sensuality (1838).

Wilson, Walter, *The History and Antiquities of Dissenting Churches and Meeting Houses in London, Westminster and Southwark, including the lives of their Ministers, from the rise of Nonconformity to the present time* ..., 4 vols. (1810).

Wooler, Jonathan, *An Address to the Friends of Freedom* (1817).

A verbatim report of the two trials of Jonathan Wooler for alleged libels ... (1817).

(Wright, W., pub.), *Queen Consort, The Queen's Rights and the People's Wrongs* (1821).

SELECTED SECONDARY SOURCES

Altick, R.D., *The English Common Reader* (Chicago, 1957).

Bailey, Peter, *Leisure and Class in Victorian England, Rational Recreation and the Contest for Control, 1830–35* (1978).

'"Will the Real Bill Banks Please Stand Up?" Towards a Role Analysis of Mid-Victorian Working-Class Respectability', *Journal of Social History*, 12 (1979), 336–53.

Baxter, J.L., and Donnelly, F.K., 'The Revolutionary "Underground" in the West Riding: Myth or Reality', *Past and Present*, 64 (1974), 124–32.

Baylen, Joseph O., and Gossman, Norbert J., eds., *Biographical Dictionary of Modern British Radicals: Volume One, 1770–1830* (Brighton and New Jersey, 1979).

Belchem, J.C., 'Henry Hunt and the Evolution of the Mass Platform', *English Historical Review*, xciii (1978), 739–73.

'Republicanism, Popular Constitutionalism and the Radical Platform in Early Nineteenth-Century England', *Social History*, 6 (1981), 1–32.

Bellamy, J.M., and Saville, J., eds., *Dictionary of Labour Biography, Volume One* (1972).

Bennett, Jennifer, 'The London Democratic Association 1837–41: A Study in London Radicalism', in *The Chartist Experience: Studies in Working-Class Radicalism and Culture, 1830–60*, eds. James Epstein and Dorothy Thompson (1982), 87–119.

Best, Geoffrey, 'Popular Protestantism in Victorian Britain', in *Ideas and Institutions of Victorian Britain*, ed. Robert Robson (1967), 115–42.

Mid-Victorian England, 1851–75 (1971).

Bloch, Ivan, *Sexual Life in England* (1965).

Boas, Louise S., 'Erasmus Perkins and Shelley', *Modern Language Notes*, lxx (1955), 408–13.

Boucé, Paul-Gabriel, ed., *Sexuality in Eighteenth-Century Britain* (Manchester, 1982).

Bradby, David, James, Louis, and Sharrat, Bernard, eds., *Performance and Politics in*

Popular Drama: Aspects of Popular Entertainment in Theatre, Film and Television, 1800–1976 (New York, 1980).

Brathwaite, Edward, *The Development of Creole Society in Jamaica, 1770–1820* (Oxford, 1971).

Brewer, John, *Party Ideology and Popular Politics at the Accession of George III* (Cambridge, 1976).

'Theatre and Counter-Theatre in Georgian Politics: The Mock Elections at Garrat', *History Today*, 33 (1983), 15–23.

Bristow, Edward J., *Vice and Vigilance: Purity Movements in Britain since 1700* (Dublin, 1977).

Brown, P.A., *The French Revolution in English History* (1965).

London Publishers and Printers, c.1800–70 (1982).

Budd, Susan, *Varieties of Unbelief, Atheists and Agnostics in English Society, 1850–1960* (1977).

Butler, Marilyn, *Romantics, Rebels and Reactionaries: English Literature and its Background 1760–1830* (Oxford, 1981).

Calder-Marshall, A., 'The Spa-Fields Riots, 1816', *History Today*, xxi (1971), 407–15.

Calhoun, Craig, *The Question of Class Struggle: Social Foundations of Popular Radicalism during the Industrial Revolution* (Oxford, 1982).

Cameron, Kenneth Neill, *The Young Shelley: Genesis of a Radical* (1951).

Campbell, Colin, *Towards a Sociology of Irreligion* (1971).

Campbell, Theophilia C., *The Battle of the Press, as Told in the Story of the Life of R. Carlile* (1899).

Chesney, Kellow, *The Victorian Underworld* (Harmondsworth, 1974).

Claeys, G., 'Documents: Thomas Evans and the Development of Spenceanism, 1815–16: Some Neglected Correspondence', *Bulletin of the Society for the Study of Labour History*, 48 (1984), 24–30.

Clark, Peter, *The English Alehouse: A Social History 1200–1830* (1983).

Clarke, John, Crichter, Charles, and Johnson, Richard, eds., *Working-Class Culture: Studies in History and Theory* (1979).

Cobb, Richard, *The Police and the People: French Popular Protest 1789–1820* (Oxford, 1970).

Cole, G.D.H., *The Common People, 1746–1946* (1956).

Collins, H., 'The London Corresponding Society', in *Democracy and the Labour Movement*, ed. J. Saville (1954), 103–34.

Cone, C.B., *The English Jacobins: Reformers in Late Eighteenth-Century England* (New York, 1968).

Cornforth, Maurice, ed., *Rebels and their Causes: Essays in Honour of A.L. Morton* (1978).

Craig, Alec, *The Banned Books of England and Other Countries; A Study of the Conception of Literary Obscenity* (1962).

Craig, David, *The Real Foundations: Literature and Social Change* (Oxford, 1974).

Cross, Nigel, *The Common Writer: Life in Nineteenth-Century Grub Street* (Cambridge, 1985).

Crossick, Geoffrey, *An Artisan Elite in Victorian Society* (1978).

ed., *The Lower Middle Class in Britain, 1870–1914* (1977).

Darnton, Robert, *The Literary Underground of the Old Regime* (Cambridge, Mass. and London, 1982).

The Great Cat Massacre and Other Episodes in French Cultural History (1984).

Darvall, F.O., *Public Order and Popular Disturbance in Regency England, 1811–17* (1969).

Davis, R.W., *Dissent in Politics, 1780–1830: The Political Life of William Smith, M.P.* (1971).

Dickinson, H.T., *Liberty and Property: Political Ideology in Eighteenth-Century Britain* (1977).

Dinwiddy, J.R., 'The "Patriotic Linen-Draper": Robert Waithman and the Revival of Radicalism in the City of London, 1795–1818', *Bulletin of the Institute of Historical Studies*, xlvi (1973), 72–94.

'The "Black Lamp" in Yorkshire in 1801–2', *Past and Present*, 64 (1974), 113–23.

'William Cobbett, George Houston and Freethought', *Notes and Queries*, ccxxii (1977), 355–9.

'The Early Nineteenth Century Campaign against Flogging in the Army', *English Historical Review*, xcvii (1982), 308–31.

Dugan, James, *The Great Mutiny* (1965).

Elliott, Marianne, 'The "Despard Conspiracy" Reconsidered', *Past and Present*, 75 (1977), 46–61.

Partners in Revolution: The United Irishmen and France (New Haven and London, 1982).

Epstein, James, *The Lion of Freedom: Fergus O'Connor and the Chartist Movement, 1832–42* (1982).

Epstein, William H., *John Cleland: Images of a Life* (New York and London, 1976).

Evans, Eric J., 'Some Reasons for the Growth of English Rural Anti-Clericalism, c.1750–1830', *Past and Present*, 66 (1975), 84–109.

Fitzpatrick, W.J., *Secret Service under Pitt* (1892).

Forman, F. Buxton, *The Vicissitudes of Queen Mab* (privately printed, 1887).

Foster, John, *Class Struggle and the Industrial Revolution: Early Industrial Capitalism in Three English Towns* (1974).

Foxon, David, *Libertine Literature in England, 1660–1795* (New York, 1965).

Fryer, Peter, *Staying Power. The History of Black People in Britain* (1984).

Fulford, Roger, *The Trial of Queen Caroline* (1967).

Gay, Peter, *The Bourgeois Experience, Victoria to Freud: Volume I: Education of the Senses* (New York and Oxford, 1984).

George, M. Dorothy, *Catalogue of Political and Personal Satires Preserved in the Department of Prints and Drawings in the British Museum*, vols. v–xi (1935–54).

English Political Caricature. A Study of Opinion and Propaganda, 2 vols. (Oxford, 1959).

London Life in the Eighteenth Century (Harmondsworth, 1966).

Hogarth to Cruikshank. Social Change in Graphic Satire (1967).

Gibson, Ian, *The English Vice: Beating, Sex and Shame in Victorian England and after* (1978).

Gilbert, A.D., *Religion and Society in Industrial England: Church, Chapel and Social Change, 1740–1914* (1976).

'Methodism, Dissent and Political Stability in Early Industrial England', *Journal of Religious History*, 10 (1979), 381–99.

Goodway, David, *London Chartism, 1838–1848* (Cambridge, 1982).

Goodwin, Albert, *The Friends of Liberty: The English Democratic Movement in the Age of the French Revolution* (1979).

Gorham, Deborah, 'Victorian Reform as a Family Business: The Hill Family', in *The Victorian Family: Structure and Stresses*, ed. A.S. Wohl (1978), 119–47.

Gray, Robert Q., *The Labour Aristocracy in Victorian Edinburgh* (Oxford, 1976).

Gross, John, *The Rise and Fall of the Man of Letters: English Literary Life since 1800* (Harmondsworth, 1969).

Hackwood, F.M., *William Hone: His Life and Times* (1912).

Halévy, Elie, *A History of the English People in the Nineteenth Century*, 6 vols. (1961).

Harrison, Brian, 'Underneath the Victorians', *Victorian Studies*, x (1967), 239–62.

Drink and the Victorians: The Temperance Question in England, 1815–72 (1971).

'Pubs', in *The Victorian City: Images and Realities*, eds. H.J. Dyos and Michael Wolff, 2 vols. (1976), i, 161–190.

Peaceable Kingdom: Stability and Change in Modern Britain (Oxford, 1982).

Harrison, J.F.C., *Learning and Living 1790–1960: A Study in the History of the English Adult Education Movement* (1963).

'The Steam Engine of the New Moral World': Owenism and Education, 1817–29, *Journal of British Studies*, vi (1967), 76–98.

Quest for the New Moral World: Robert Owen and the Owenites in Britain and America (New York, 1968).

The Second Coming: Popular Millenarianism, 1780–1850 (1979).

Harvey, A.D., *Britain in the Early Nineteenth Century* (1978).

Hay, Douglas, *et al.*, *Albion's Fatal Tree: Crime and Society in Eighteenth-Century England* (New York, 1975).

Hendrix, Richard, 'Popular Humor and "The Black Dwarf"', *Journal of British Studies*, xvi (1976), 108–28.

Henriques, Ursula, *Religious Toleration in England, 1787–1833* (1961).

Hill, Christopher, *Puritanism and Revolution: Studies in Interpretation of the English Revolution of the Seventeenth Century* (1968).

The World Turned Upside Down. Radical Ideas during the English Revolution (Harmondsworth, 1975).

'The Religion of General Winstanley', *Past and Present Supplement*, 5 (Oxford, 1978), 1–57.

Himmelfarb, Gertrude, *The Idea of Poverty: England in the Industrial Age* (New York, 1984).

Hobsbawm, E.J., *Primitive Rebels: Studies in Archaic Forms of Social Movement in the 19th and 20th Centuries* (New York, 1959).

Labouring Men: Studies in the History of Labour (1968).

'Man and Woman in Socialist Iconography', *History Workshop*, 6 (1978), 121–38.

Hobsbawm, E.J., and Scott, Joan Wallach, 'Political Shoemakers', *Past and Present*, 89 (1980), 86–114.

Hollis, Patricia, *The Pauper Press. A Study in Working-Class Radicalism of the 1830s* (Oxford, 1970).

'Anti-Slavery and British Working Class Radicalism in the Years of Reform', in *Anti-Slavery, Religion and Reform: Essays in Memory of Roger Anstey*, eds. Christine Bolt and Seymour Drescher (Folkestone and Hamden, 1980), 294–315.

Hollis, Patricia, and Harrison, Brian, 'Chartism, Liberalism and the Life of Robert Lowery', *English Historical Review*, lxxxii (1967), 503–35.

Holmes, Richard, *Shelley: The Pursuit* (1974).

Hone, J. Ann, 'William Hone, Publisher and Bookseller: An Approach to Early Nineteenth Century London Radicalism', *Historical Studies*, xvi (1974), 55–70.

For the Cause of Truth: Radicalism in London, 1796–1821 (Oxford, 1982).

Humpherys, Anne, *Travels into the Poor Man's Country. The Work of Henry Mayhew* (Athens, Georgia, 1977).

James, Louis, *Fiction for the Working Man, 1830–50* (Harmondsworth, 1974).

'Taking Melodrama Seriously', *History Workshop*, 3 (Spring, 1977), 151–8.

'Cruikshank and Early Victorian Caricature', *History Workshop*, 6 (1978), 107–20.

Johnson, D., *Regency Revolution; The Case of Arthur Thistlewood* (Salisbury, 1974).

Kearney, Patrick J., *The Private Case. An Annotated Bibliography of the Private Case Erotica Collection in the British (Museum) Library* (1981).

A History of Erotic Literature (1982).

Kirk, Neville, *The Growth of Working-Class Reformism in Mid-Victorian England* (1985).

Kitson Clark, G.S.R., 'The Romantic Element – 1830–50', in *Studies in Social History*, ed. J.H. Plumb (1955), 209–37.

Knox, T.R., 'Thomas Spence: The Trumpet of Jubilee', *Past and Present*, 76 (1977), 75–98.

Laqueur, Thomas Walter, *Religion and Respectability: Sunday Schools and Working Class Culture, 1780–1850* (1976).

'The Queen Caroline Affair: Politics as Art in the Reign of George IV', *Journal of Modern History*, 54 (1982), 417–66.

Leventhal, F.M., *Respectable Radical: George Howell and Victorian Working Class Politics* (Cambridge, Mass., 1971).

Lillywhite, Bryant, *London Coffeehouses: A Reference Book of Coffeehouses of the Seventeenth, Eighteenth and Nineteenth Centuries* (1905).

Lincoln, A., *Some Social and Political Ideas of English Dissent, 1763–1800* (Cambridge, 1938).

Linebaugh, Peter, 'Labour History without the Labour Process; A Note on John Gast and his Time', *Social History*, 7 (1982), 319–27.

Low, Donald A., *Thieves' Kitchen: The Regency Underworld* (1982).

McCabe, Joseph, *A Biographical Dictionary of Modern Rationalists* (1920).

McCalman, I.D., 'Females, Feminism and Freelove in an Early Nineteenth-Century Radical Movement', *Labour History*, 38 (1980), 1–25.

'Unrespectable Radicalism: Infidels and Pornography in early Nineteenth-Century London', *Past and Present*, 104 (1984), 74–110.

'Anti-Slavery and Ultra-Radicalism in Early Nineteenth-Century England: The Case of Robert Wedderburn', *Slavery and Abolition*, 7 (September 1986), 99–117.

McLachlan, H., *The Unitarian Movement in the Religious Life of England* (1934).

McLaren, Angus, *Birth Control in Nineteenth-Century England* (1978).

Maclear, J.F., 'Popular Anti-Clericalism in the Puritan Revolution', *Journal of the History of Ideas*, xvii (1956), 443–70.

McLeod, Hugh, *Class and Religion in the Late Victorian City* (1974).

McNiece, Gerald, *Shelley and the Revolutionary Idea* (Cambridge, Mass., 1969).

Main, J.M. 'Radical Westminster, 1807–1820', *Historical Studies*, 12 (1966), 186–204.

Malcolmson, Robert W., *Popular Recreations in English Society, 1700–1850* (Cambridge, 1973).

Marcus, Steven, *The Other Victorians: A Study of Sexuality and Pornography in Mid-Nineteenth Century England* (1969).

Meacham, Standish, *A Life Apart. The English Working Class, 1890–1914* (1977).

Miller, N.C., 'John Cartwright and Radical Parliamentary Reform, 1809–19', *English Historical Review*, lxxxiii (1968), 705–28.

Minor, Lucian W., *The Militant Hackwriter: French Popular Literature 1800–48; Its Influence, Artistic and Political* (Bowling Green, Ohio, 1975).

Money, John, 'Taverns, Coffee Houses and Clubs: Local Politics and Popular Articulacy in the Birmingham Area in the Age of the American Revolution', *Historical Journal*, xiv (1971), 15–47.

Neale, R.S., *Class and Ideology in the Nineteenth Century* (London and Boston, 1972).

Class in English History, 1680–1850 (Oxford, 1981).

Nettel, Reginald, 'Folk Elements in Nineteenth-Century Puritanism', *Folklore*, 80 (1969), 272–85.

Obelkevich, James, *Religion and Rural Society: South Lindsey, 1825–75* (Oxford, 1976).

Oliver, W.H., *Prophets and Millennialists: The Uses of Biblical Prophecy in England from the 1790s to the 1840s* (Auckland and Oxford, 1978).

Oman, Sir Charles, *The Unfortunate Colonel Despard and Other Studies* (1922).

Osborne, John W., *John Cartwright* (Cambridge, 1972).

Parsinnen, T.M., 'The Revolutionary Party in London, 1816–20', *Bulletin of the Institute of Historical Research*, 45 (1972), 266–82.

'Association, Convention and Anti-Parliament in British Radical Politics, 1771–1848', *English Historical Review*, lxxxviii (1973), 504–33.

'Thomas Spence and the Origins of English Land Nationalization', *Journal of the History of Ideas*, 34 (1973), 135–41.

Parsinnen, T.M., and Prothero, I.J., 'The London Tailors' Strike of 1834 and the Collapse of the Grand National Consolidated Trades' Union: A Police Spy's Report', *International Review of Social History*, xxii (1977), 65–107.

Pearsall, Ronald, *The Worm in the Bud: The World of Victorian Sexuality* (Harmondsworth, 1971).

Perkin, Harold, *The Origins of Modern English Society, 1780–1880* (1969).

Pinkus, Philip, *Grub Street Stripp'd Bare* (1968).

Pollard, S., and Salt, T., eds., *Robert Owen: Prophet of the Poor* (1971).

Post, Albert, *Popular Freethought in America, 1825–50* (New York, 1943).

Price, Richard N., 'The Other Face of Respectability: Violence in the Manchester Brickmaking Trade, 1859–1870', *Past and Present*, 66 (1975), 110–32.

Prochaska, Franklyn K., 'Thomas Paine's "The Age of Reason" Revisited', *Journal of the History of Ideas*, 33 (1972), 561–76.

Prothero, I.J., 'Chartism in London', *Past and Present*, 44 (1969), 76–105.

'William Benbow and the Concept of the "General Strike"', *Past and Present*, 63 (1974), 132–71.

Artisans and Politics in Early Nineteenth-Century London: John Gast and his Times (Folkestone, 1979).

Quinault, R., and Stevenson. J., eds., *Popular Protest and Public Order: Six Studies in British History, 1790–1820* (1974).

Quinlan, M.J., *Victorian Prelude* (New York, 1941).

Rancière, Jacques, 'The Myth of the Artisan: Critical Reflections on a Category of Social History', *International Labor and Working-Class History*, 24 (1983), 1–16.

Rattenbury, Arnold, 'Methodism and the Tatterdemalions', in *Popular Culture and Class Conflict, 1590–1914: Explorations in the History of Labour and Leisure*, eds. Eileen and Stephen Yeo (Sussex and New Jersey, 1981), 28–61.

Redwood, J., *Reason, Ridicule and Religion: The Age of Enlightenment in England, 1660–1750* (1976).

Rickword, Edgell, *Radical Squibs and Loyal Ripostes* (Bath, 1971).

Robbins, Caroline, *The Eighteenth-Century Commonwealthman* (Cambridge, Mass., 1959).

Roberts, M.J.D., 'Making Victorian Morals? The Society for the Suppression of Vice and its Critics, 1802–1886', *Historical Studies*, xxi (1984), 157–73.

Robertson, J.M., *A History of Freethought in the Nineteenth Century*, 2 vols. (1929).

Roe, Michael, 'Maurice Margarot: A Radical in Two Hemispheres, 1792–1815', *Bulletin of the Institute of Historical Research*, 31 (1958), 68–78.

Kenealy and the Tichborne Cause: A Study in Mid-Victorian Populism (Melbourne, 1974).

Rogers, Pat, *Grub Street: Studies in a Subculture* (1972).

Rogers, P.G., *Battle in Bossenden Wood: The Strange Story of Sir William Courtenay* (1962).

Rowe, D.J., 'Class and Political Radicalism in London, 1831–2', *Historical Journal*, 13 (1970), 31–47.

'Francis Place and the Historian', *Historical Journal*, 16 (1973), 45–63.

Royle, Edward, *Radical Politics 1790–1900, Religion and Unbelief* (1971).

Victorian Infidels: The Origins of the British Secularist Movement, 1791–1866 (Manchester, 1974).

Radicals, Secularists and Republicans: Popular Freethought in Britain, 1866–1915 (Manchester, 1980).

Royle, Edward, and Walvin, James, *English Radicals and Reformers, 1760–1848* (Brighton, 1982).

Rubinstein, W.D., 'The End of "Old Corruption" in Britain 1780–1860', *Past and Present*, 101 (1983), 55–86.

Rudé, George, *Wilkes and Liberty: A Social Study of 1763 to 1774* (Oxford, 1962).

Paris and London in the 18th Century: Studies in Popular Protest (Fontana, 1970).

Rudkin, Olive D., *Thomas Spence and his Connections* (1927, repr. New York, 1966).

Rüter, A.J.C., 'William Benbow as Publisher', *Bulletin of the International Institute of Social History*, 1 (1940), 1–14.

St John Stevas, Norman, *Obscenity and the Law* (1956).

Sales, Roger, *English Literature in History – 1780–1830; Pastoral and Politics* (1983).

Samuel, Raphael, 'Quarry Roughs: Life in Headington Quarry, 1860–1920: An Essay in Oral History', in *Village Life and Labour*, ed. R. Samuel (1975), pp. 141–263.

'Art, Politics and Ideology', *History Workshop*, 6 (1978), 101–6.

Samuel, Raphael, and Stedman Jones, Gareth, eds., *Culture, Ideology and Politics* (1982).

Saunders, J.W., *The Profession of English Letters* (1964).

Sellers, I., 'Historians and Social Change, Part One: Varieties of Radicalism, 1795–1815', *Hibbert Journal*, 61 (1962), 16–22.

Semmel, Bernard, *The Methodist Revolution* (1973).

Senelick, Laurence, 'Politics as Entertainment: Victorian Music-Hall Songs', *Victorian Studies*, xix (1975), 149–80.

Sewell, William H., Jnr, *Work and Revolution in France, The Language of Labor from the Old Regime to 1848* (Cambridge, 1980).

Sheppard, Francis, *London, 1808–1870: The Infernal Wen* (1971).

Shipley, Stan, *Club Life and Socialism in Mid-Victorian London* (1983).

Smith, Alan, 'Arthur Thistlewood: A Regency Republican', *History Today*, 3 (1953), 846–52.

The Established Church and Popular Religion, 1750–1850 (1971).

Smith, A.W., 'Irish Rebels and English Radicals, 1798–1820', *Past and Present*, 7 (1955), 78–85.

Smith, F.B., 'The Atheist Mission, 1840–1900', in *Ideas and Institutions of Victorian Britain: Essays in Honour of George Kitson Clark*, ed. Robert Robson (1967), 205–35.

'Sexuality in Britain, 1800–1900: Some Suggested Revisions', in *A Widening Sphere: Changing Roles of Victorian Women*, ed. Martha Vicinus (Bloomington, Indiana, 1973), 182–305.

Smith, Olivia, *The Politics of Language, 1791–1819* (Oxford, 1984).

Spater, George, *William Cobbett: The Poor Man's Friend*, 2 vols. (Cambridge, 1982).

Stanhope, John, *The Cato Street Conspiracy* (1962).

Stedman Jones, Gareth, *Languages of Class: Studies in English Working Class History 1832–1982* (Cambridge, 1983).

Stevenson, John, ed., *London in the Age of Reform* (Oxford, 1977).

Storch, Robert D., ed., *Popular Culture and Custom in Nineteenth-Century England* (1982).

Taylor, Barbara, *Eve and the New Jerusalem: Socialism and Feminism in the Nineteenth Century* (1983).

Taylor, John, *From Self-Help to Glamour: The Working Man's Club, 1860–1972* (Oxford, 1972).

Tholfsen, Trygve, *Working-Class Radicalism in Mid-Victorian England* (1976).

Thomas, Donald, *A Long Time Burning: The History of Literary Censorship in England* (1969).

Thomas, Keith, *Religion and the Decline of Magic: Studies in Popular Beliefs in Sixteenth and Seventeenth Century England* (Harmondsworth, 1973).

Thomas, W.E.S., 'Francis Place and Working Class History', *Historical Journal*, 5 (1962), 61–70.

Thomas, William, *The Philosophic Radicals: Nine Studies in Theory and Practice, 1817–79* (Oxford, 1979).

Thomis, Malcolm I., and Holt, Peter, *Threats of Revolution in Britain, 1789–1848* (1977).

Thompson, Dorothy, *The Early Chartists* (1961).

Thompson, E.P., *The Making of the English Working Class* (Harmondsworth, 1968).
'Time, Work-Discipline, and Industrial Capitalism', in *Essays in Social History*, eds. M.W. Flinn and T.C. Smout (Oxford, 1974), 39–77.
'Patrician Society, Plebeian Culture', *Journal of Social History*, 7 (1974), 382–405.
'Eighteenth Century English Society: Class Struggle without Class?', *Journal of Social History*, 3 (1978), 133–65.

Thompson, Noel W., *The People's Science: The Popular Political Economy of Exploitation and Crisis 1816–34* (Cambridge, 1984).

Thompson, Roger, *Unfit for Modest Ears* (1979).

Todd, William B., *A Directory of Printers and Others in Allied Trades, London and Vicinity 1800–40* (1972).

Trudgill, Eric, *Madonnas and Magdalens: The Origins and Development of Victorian Sexual Attitudes* (1976).

Tyrrell, Alexander, 'Class Consciousness in Early Victorian Britain: Samuel Smiles, Leeds Politics and the Self-Help Creed', *Journal of British Studies*, ix (1970), 102–25.

Underwood, Dale, *Etherage and the Seventeenth-Century Comedy of Manners* (New Haven and London, 1957).

Valenze, Deborah, 'Prophecy and Popular Literature in Eighteenth-Century England', *Journal of Ecclesiastical History*, 29 (1978), 75–92.

Villari, Rosario, 'Masaniello: Contemporary and Recent Interpretations', *Past and Present*, 108 (1985), 117–32.

Walsh, J.D., 'Methodism and the Mob in the Eighteenth Century', in *Popular Belief and Practice*, eds. G.J. Cuming and D. Baker (Cambridge, 1972), 213–27.
'Elie Halévy and the Birth of Methodism', *Transactions of the Royal Historical Society*, 25 (1975), 1–20.

Walvin, James, *The Black Presence: A Documentary History of the Negro in England, 1555–1860* (1971).
ed., *Slavery and British Society, 1776–1846* (1982).

Wardroper, John, *Kings, Lords and Wicked Libellers: Satire and Protest, 1760–1837* (1973).

Webb, R.K., *The British Working Class Reader, 1780–1848: Literacy and Social Tension* (1955).

Weeks, Jeffrey, *Sex, Politics and Society: The Regulation of Sexuality since 1800* (1981).

Wells, Roger, *Insurrection: The British Experience* (Gloucester, 1983).

White, Newman Ivey, *Shelley*, 2 vols. (New York, 1940).

The Unextinguished Hearth, Shelley and his Contemporary Critics (New York, 1966).

White, R.J., *Waterloo to Peterloo* (Harmondsworth, 1968).

Wickwar, W.H., *The Struggle for the Freedom of the Press, 1819–32* (1928).

Wiener, Joel H., *Radicalism and Freethought in Nineteenth-Century Britain: The Life of Richard Carlile* (Westport, Connecticut, and London, 1983).

ed., *Innovators and Preachers. The Role of the Editor in Victorian England* (Westport, Conn., and London, 1985).

Williams, Gwyn A., *Rowland Detrosier: A Working Class Infidel, 1800–34* (York, 1965).

Artisans and Sans-Culottes: Popular Movements in France and Britain during the French Revolution (1968).

Williams, Michael, J., 'The 1790s: The Impact of Infidelity', *Bulletin of the Thomas Paine Society*, 5 (1976), 21–30.

Wilson, John, *Introduction to Social Movements* (New York, 1973).

Yeo, Eileen, 'Christianity in Chartist Struggle, 1838–42', *Past and Present*, 91 (1981), 109–39.

Yeo, Stephen, 'A New Life: The Religion of Socialism in Britain, 1883–1896', *History Workshop*, 4 (1977), 5–56.

Unpublished Theses and Conference Papers

Chase, Malcolm, 'The Land and the Working Classes, English Agrarianism, circa 1775–1851' (University of Sussex, DPhil. thesis, 1985).

McBriar, Marilyn, 'Burke, Paine and Fox as Interpreters of the French Revolution, with Some Reference to Other Contemporary British Views' (University of Melbourne, MA thesis, 1971).

McCalman, I.D., 'Popular Radicalism and Freethought in Early Nineteenth-Century England: A Study of Richard Carlile and his Followers, 1815–32' (Australian National University, MA thesis, 1975).

'A Radical Underworld in Early Nineteenth-Century London: Thomas Evans, Robert Wedderburn, George Cannon and their Circle, 1800–1835' (Monash University PhD thesis, 1984).

Pickering, Paul, 'The Social Culture of Chartism, 1837–1842' (Latrobe University, BA Hons. thesis, 1982).

Rubinstein, W., 'British Radicalism and the "Dark Side" of Populism', 1985.

Index

Winstanley, Gerrard, seventeenth-century sectary, 64, 68, 71
Wolseley, Sir Charles, reformer, 73
women, and ultra-radicalism, *see* Evans, Janet; Wilson, Mrs; Wright, Susannah
Woods, Matthew, city reformer, 174
Wooler, Thomas Jonathan, pressman, 19, 90, 117, 127, 135, 186, 214, 241–2 n.50

Wright, John, orator, debater, 19, 89, 125, 130, 241–2 n.50
Wright, Susannah, laceworker, female reformer, 193

York, Duke of, 35, 37, 39–41

Zetetic movement, 186–8, 216–17; *see also* Carlile, Richard